A History of Madagascar

Mervyn Brown

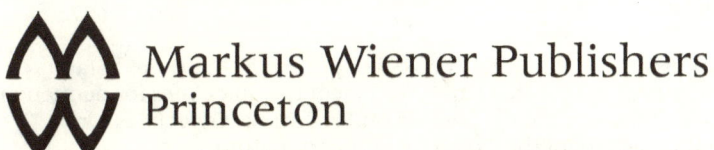
Markus Wiener Publishers
Princeton

Acknowledgements

I am grateful to Dr Césaire Rabenoro, the president of the Malagasy Academy, for writing the Foreword, as well as for his constructive comments and careful correction of numerous errors in the text. Dr Stephen Ellis and the late Jim Hardyman also drew my attention to errors and made helpful suggestions.

My thanks go also to the numerous Malagasy friends who have greatly helped my understanding of what has happened in Madagascar over the past half century or so. As always, the staffs of the British Library, the library of the School of Oriental and African Studies in London, the Bibliothèque Nationale in Paris and the National Archives in Antananarivo, have been unfailingly courteous and helpful.

I am also grateful to Jacques Tronchon for the photographs of the 1947 uprising.

Third printing, 2016.
© Mervyn Brown 1995 and 2000
Designed by the European Design Partnership

All rights reserved. No part of this book may be reproduced or transmitted in any form or by any means, whether electronic or mechanical—including photocopying or recording—or through any information storage or retrieval system, without permission of the copyright owners.

For information write to:
 Markus Wiener Publishers
 231 Nassau Street, Princeton, NJ 08542
 www.markuswiener.com

Library of Congress Cataloging-in-Publication Data

Brown, Mervyn.
 A History of Madagascar/Mervyn Brown.
 Includes bibliographical references and index.
   ISBN-13: 978-1-55876-292-3 (pbk)
   1. Madagascar—History.   I. Title.
 DT469.M285 B76 2001
 960—dc21   2001026978

Markus Wiener Publishers books are printed in the United States of America on acid-free paper, and meet the guidelines for permanence and durability of the Committee on Production Guidelines for Book Longevity of the Council on Library Resources.

Contents

List of maps   iv
Foreword   iv
Author's introduction   v
Malagasy pronunciation and place names   vii

PART 1. THE ISLAND AND THE PEOPLE   1
Chapter 1   A world apart   1
Chapter 2   The first Malagasy   10
Chapter 3   The occupation of the island   17

PART 2. EARLY EUROPEAN CONTACTS   30
Chapter 4   The arrival of the Europeans   30
Chapter 5   The dream of Madagascar   38
Chapter 6   The shipwrecked sailor   50
Chapter 7   The pirates of Madagascar   64
Chapter 8   The sons of the pirates   75
Chapter 9   The rise of the Merina   91

PART 3. TOWARDS A NEW CIVILISATION   111
Chapter 10   The king, the governor and the sergeant   111
Chapter 11   The missionaries   133
Chapter 12   The queen and the martyrs   147
Chapter 13   The tragedy of the prince and the playboys   170

PART 4. THE KINGDOM IN DANGER   182
Chapter 14   The prime minister and the Christian monarchy   182
Chapter 15   War and diplomacy   202
Chapter 16   The French conquest   217

PART 5. MADAGASCAR IN THE MODERN WORLD   241
Chapter 17   Colonial rule and nationalism   241
Chapter 18   The road to independence   269
Chapter 19   Independence and neo-colonialism   295
Chapter 20   The fall of the First Republic   310
Chapter 21   Revolutionary socialism   329
Chapter 22   Return to democracy   342

Sources   356
Notes   376
Index   396

List of Maps

Madagascar Physical	viii
Madagascar, the Comoros and the Mascarene Islands	9
Present distribution of the Malagasy ethnic groups	16
Drury among the Antandroy	57
The Sakalava kingdoms in the eighteenth century	60
The Betsimisaraka region	79
The raids of the Malagasy pirates, 1756–1820	88
The Merina kingdom under Andriamasinavalona	99
The expansion of the Merina kingdom 1787–1828	127

Foreword

What image does Madagascar conjure up to the average English-speaking person? Not very much, I expect, and yet, in the nineteenth century British influence was strong in this island off the east coast of Africa.

King Radama I opened Madagascar to the outside world by inviting missionaries who could teach useful trades, and in 1818 the London Missionary Society responded and sent the first missionaries who were from Wales.

Until the French occupation in 1895, English was used widely among educated people and in diplomacy. French replaced English during the French occupation and the Malagasy adapted to French ideas without rejecting the values of their own culture.

A History of Madagascar is the first modern history of Madagascar in English from its origins to the present day. This book is essential reading for all English-speakers interested in Madagascar.

—Dr Césaire Rabenoro, President of the Malagasy Academy

Introduction

The original work on which this history is based, entitled *Madagascar Rediscovered*, was published in 1978. The thought behind the title was that, whereas in the nineteenth century the English-speaking world was well informed about Madagascar through many books by missionaries and others, very little had been written in English since the French colonial occupation. The book therefore aimed to "rediscover" for English-speaking readers the history of a remote and fascinating island and to remind them of the important role played by the British in that history. The bulk of the book dealt with the history before the French conquest in 1895, and especially the nineteenth century when the British rôle was particularly important. The years of French rule were dealt with only briefly, partly because the British involvement was very much less but also because the period was still too recent for a serving diplomat to treat with complete frankness. Fifteen years later, retirement and the passage of time have removed the major constraint. Accordingly the section on the colonial period has been greatly expanded and almost completely rewritten.

I have also added four new chapters describing and endeavouring to interpret for the general reader the often turbulent years from independence right up to 1993, when the inauguration of the Third Republic provides a convenient cut-off point. Although initially reluctant, I was persuaded to cover this recent period because events in Madagascar receive virtually no coverage in the British or American press, and indeed very little in France, so that the general reader has very little idea of what has happened in Madagascar since independence.

This new section is put forward with all due reservations as to the imperfections and risks of "instant history". The justification is that the substantial new material comprising Part V of the book constitutes the only general survey of Madagascar in the twentieth century available at present, with the added advantage of being written by someone who, while passionately interested in the subject, can perhaps claim to be more objective than either a Malagasy or a French historian. The underlying aim has been to use the study of history to aid understanding of the present and to explain the antecedents of leading figures and parties who are prominent today. For example, the complex and often confusing evolution of

Introduction

political parties in the years just before independence is described in some detail since it helps to explain the equally complex and confusing multiplicity of parties that emerged in the run-up to the Third Republic in 1993.

The first four parts of *Madagascar Rediscovered* were based to a large extent on the study of original documents, mainly from the archives of the London Missionary Society, the Public Record Office and the manuscript collections of the British Library. They have stood the test of time, and have been incorporated into the new book with only minor changes and corrections. For the twentieth century the great mass of documentation available is beyond the capacity of a single general historian to master. The fifth part of the present book is therefore mainly a synthesis of the work of other researchers. What is original is my own personal experience of Madagascar during five years as ambassador during both the First and Second Republics and as a frequent visitor subsequently; and especially my personal acquaintance with many of the leading actors on the Malagasy political stage, from Ravoahangy to Ratsiraka. Much of the interpretation is based on conversations with some of these leading figures but, in order to encourage frankness, I undertook not to reveal the sources of particular information or opinions. Naturally I take full responsibility for the interpretations and opinions expressed in the book.

MB
London
September 1994

Malagasy Pronunciation and Place Names

Many Malagasy names are formidably long, but the spelling is phonetic and pronunciation is not too difficult once the rules are known.

The vowels are pronounced as in French, the "e" always as if with an acute accent. The important exception is that "o" is always pronounced "oo". Consonants are straightforward except that "j" is pronounced "dz" and "s" is often close to "sh" especially in some coastal dialects. The letter "h" is almost silent (but is not redundant since after certain prefixes it is transformed to "k").

The main problem is the placing of the tonic accent. Except in the case of "e", which is always accented, final vowels are almost, but not quite dropped. Thus "Hova" sounds like "óov". The main accent is then normally on the penultimate syllable, e.g. Morondáva (Mooroon-dav) or Mananjary (Man-an-dzar); except for nearly all words ending in "na", "ka" or "tra", when the accent is on the antepenultimate syllable, e.g. Mérina "Ranaválona", "Ratsíraka", "Betsimitátatra". Readers interested in the correct pronunciation should refer to the index, where accents have been placed on the stressed syllables of all the Malagasy names; but it should be noted that accents are not part of the normal written language.

In 1975 the names of five of the main towns of Madagascar were given Malagasy rather than European-style names. In two cases it was simply a matter of reverting to Malagasy spelling: Mahajanga (Majunga) and Toliara (Tulear). Diego Suarez took the name Antsiranana from a small town (previously known as Antsirane) located on the other side of a narrow strip of the bay; Tamatave reverted to its Malagasy name of Toamasina; and Fort Dauphin acquired the Malagasy name of Taolañaro (sometimes spelt Taolagnaro). However as the old names were generally used for several centuries before 1975 I have thought it less confusing to retain the old names in the last two chapters. Finally, the capital city, Antananarivo, is pronounced with the initial "a" and final "o" almost silent, hence the French spelling of "Tananarive".

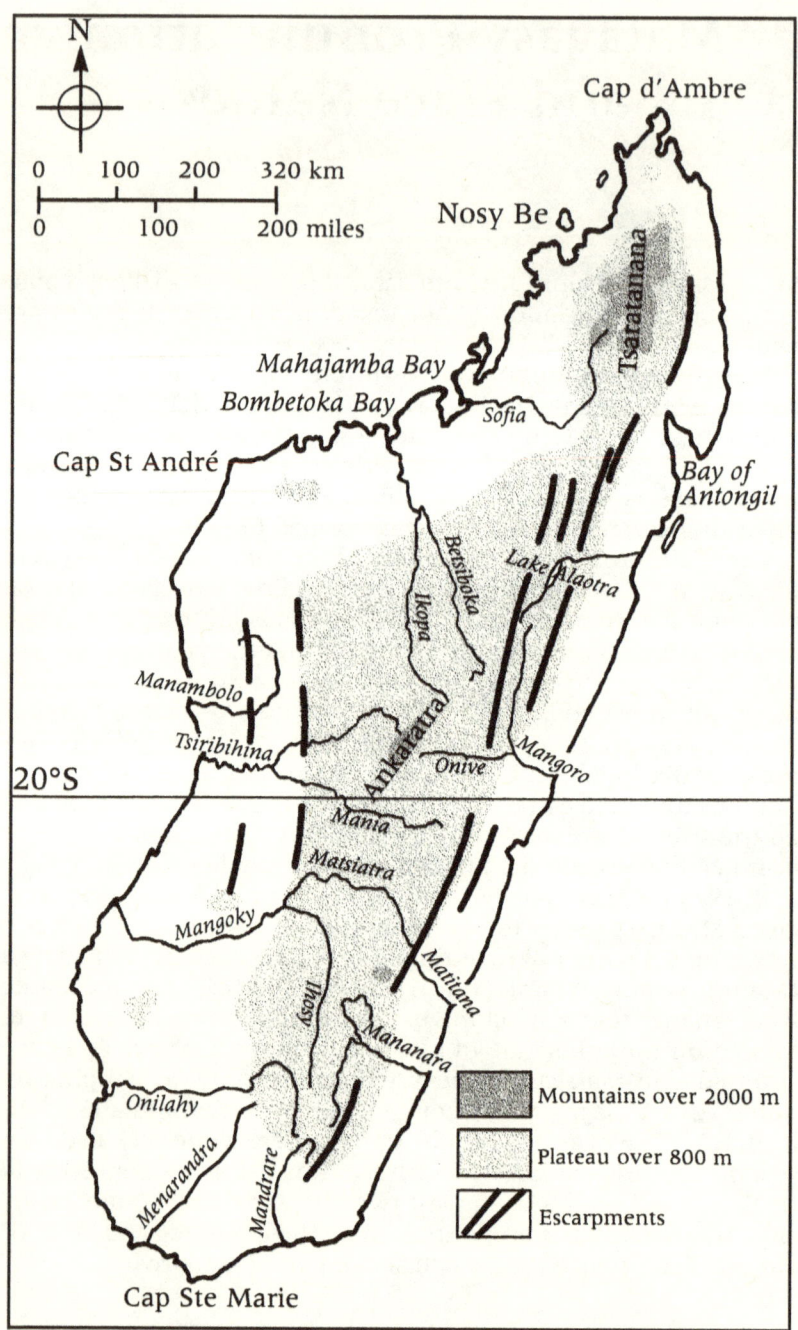

Madagascar physical

PART 1   THE ISLAND AND THE PEOPLE

Chapter 1
A world apart

When seen against the vast bulk of Africa, Madagascar appears to be of modest proportions. But it is one of the great islands of the world, the fourth largest after Greenland, New Guinea and Borneo. Nearly a thousand miles (1,600 km) long and 350 miles (560 km) across at its widest point, it is two and a half times the size of Great Britain. In shape it resembles the print of a gigantic left foot with an enlarged big toe pointing pigeon-toed slightly to the right of north. The east coast is for most of its length almost a straight line, where the endless westward swell of the Indian Ocean has built up a long line of sand dunes. The west coast is much more indented, and the bulges and hollows fit with remarkable precision into the hollows and bulges of the Mozambique coast, in the same way that the north and east coasts of South America fit snugly into the opposite coasts of Africa. The correspondence of these coastlines, together with biological and other evidence, lend strong support to the theory of "continental drift" which provides the most plausible explanation of the geological origin of Madagascar. According to this theory, South America, Africa, Madagascar, India, Australia and Antarctica originally formed one vast continent, to which the name of Gondwanaland has been given. At some remote period of pre-history a great fracture of the earth's crust opened up a gap between Antarctica and the rest of Gondwanaland; the two landmasses, resting on a base of viscous magma, drifted away from each other with the sea coming in between and helping to push them apart. The precise order of subsequent fractures is in dispute. But biological evidence suggests that the next fracture opened up between present day Africa and Madagascar, possibly as early as the end of the Palaeozoic era some two hundred million years ago. Land links may have been resumed during the upheavals of the Mesozoic era but separation was well established towards the end of the Cretaceous period, some seventy or eighty million years ago. Meanwhile Australia had broken off from Madagascar and drifted away at what must have been a substantial speed, geologically speaking, before reaching its present position some 4,000 miles (6,400 km) to the east. Next, the chunk of land which is now the Indian Deccan split off and drifted to the northeast until it collided with the main body of Asia, thrusting up the Himalayan mountain chain. Last to separate from Africa was South America.

If this version is correct, Madagascar has more recent geological links with India and Australia than with Africa. But there is no doubt that geographically Madagascar has much in common with Africa. Its physical structure and climatic zones make it a compressed version of southern Africa. The trade winds blowing without hindrance across the vast expanse of the Indian Ocean deposit their rain on the narrow coastal plain and the steep escarpment which hems it in. Except on the steeper slopes of the escarpment man has destroyed the original dense tropical forest, which has been replaced by a secondary vegetation known as *savoka*: the most characteristic plant is the fan-shaped traveller's tree (*ravenala*). The escarpment rises in two stages to the high plateau which has an average height of 4 to 5,000 feet (1300–1600 m) but rises to over 8,000 feet (2,600 m) in the Ankaratra. The plateau is not a high plain as in southern Africa but a disorderly jumble of gneissic hills with occasional majestic outcrops of granite and scattered volcanic cones. The climate is temperate but the original forest has been destroyed nearly everywhere and the general impression is of barren, eroded hills interspersed with terraced rice cultivation in the valleys. Here the thick crust of red laterite which covers much of the country, giving rise to the name "Great Red Island", is particularly evident. In most areas it has a covering of coarse grass (*bozaka*) but here and there recent accelerated erosion has laid it bare in great fan-shaped gashes (*lavaka*) on the hillside, looking from the air like wounds inflicted by some savage giant. Towards the west there is a more gradual decline to the sea with a drier tropical climate. In the southwest this becomes semi-desert with the main vegetation a thorny scrub punctuated with baobabs. In the far north the Tsaratanana mountain massif, rising to the highest peak in Madagascar at 9,468 ft (2,876 m), creates its own wet tropical climate. It also cuts off Diego Suarez, one of the greatest natural harbours in the world, from its potential hinterland and reduces it to a minor port serving mainly as a naval base.

Most of these geographical features have their counterpart in southern Africa: the tropical coastal plain of Mozambique and

Natal; the Drakensberg escarpment; the central plateau of the Transvaal; and the Kalahari desert in the southwest. The geological structure is also similar with the same westward tilt of the basic land mass to produce the eastern escarpment and the gentler slope to the west. Many of the valuable minerals of southern Africa – gold, uranium, coal, nickel, chromite – are found in Madagascar. But in most cases the quantities are too small, or the deposits too remote, for commercial exploitation. In the southwest there is a sizeable coalfield which, although of poor quality, might have been worth exploiting between the two World Wars; and along the southeast coast, north of Fort Dauphin, substantial deposits of bauxite and ilmenite have been discovered. But in both areas the lack of roads, railways and port facilities pose serious problems. Elsewhere, the minerals of Madagascar are little more than a collection of samples of those which contribute so much to the wealth of South Africa.

When we look at the forms of life in Madagascar, however, there is an almost total divorce from Africa. In this great island only 250 miles (400 km) off the coast of Africa there are no elephants, rhinoceros, giraffes or zebras, no lions, leopards or other great beasts of prey, no antelopes, gazelles or deer of any kind, not even any monkeys. The only zoological links with Africa are the crocodile, the river pig and the dwarf hippopotamus (now extinct); these are all swimmers and their ancestors could have crossed the Mozambique Channel relatively recently, probably at a time when it was shallower than at present and possibly with the aid of the Comoros as stepping-stones. Otherwise most of the animal life is unique to Madagascar, as a result of the island's long separation from other land masses. At the end of the Cretaceous period some 70 million years ago, when Madagascar's separation from Africa was complete, the highest forms of life were early marsupials and some small and primitive placental mammals. It is probable that at some stage during the next twenty or thirty million years a change in the ocean level created a land bridge, perhaps opposite the centre of the island where the Mozambique Channel is relatively shallow or further north at the level of the Comoros, which allowed later forms of life to cross over from Africa. But for at least forty million years the island has been cut off by the sea from the rest of the world, thus preserving until our own time Eocene forms of life which elsewhere were ousted or destroyed by more vigorous successors. Madagascar is thus a world apart, a living museum offering endless fascination to the zoologist and the botanist. And it is entirely appropriate that the deep waters surrounding this lost world are the home of the coelacanth, the "living fossil" fish which has survived with little change from the Palaeozoic era, hundreds of millions of years ago.

Unfortunately the most spectacular inhabitant of this lost world has not survived to our own time. This was the *aepyornis maximus*, a giant ostrich-like bird which probably became extinct about eight hundred years ago – the latest date furnished by carbon dating of bones and surviving eggs. Reconstructed skeletons show that it stood 8 to 10 ft (about 3 m) high with massive legs like tree trunks and only vestigial wings so that it was flightless and probably slow-moving. Its only rival to the title of the largest bird to have lived on earth was the giant moa of New Zealand, which may have survived until the eighteenth or even the early nineteenth century. The moa seems to have been taller but was probably less bulky; certainly it has to yield pride of place to the *aepyornis* for the size of its eggs. Complete *aepyornis* eggs have been found from time to time during the last century and a half and about ten still survive in museums and private collections. Each egg is over 12 inches (30 cm) long and over 9 inches (23 cm) in diameter, equivalent in size to eight or nine ostrich eggs or a hundred and fifty hen's eggs, so that one egg could produce an omelette for fifty people. The eggshell is a quarter of an inch (6 mm) thick and fragments could easily be mistaken for pieces of broken white pottery; large quantities of broken shell can still be found lying on beaches and other open spaces in the south of Madagascar.

The agents of the *aepyornis*'s destruction were of course the first human inhabitants of Madagascar. But it is likely that some of the birds survived long enough to be seen or heard about by Arab sailors and to give rise to the legend of the roc bird of Sinbad the Sailor and the gryphon or rukh mentioned in Marco Polo's brief description of the island which he was the first to name Madagascar. Basing himself on travellers' tales he heard while passing through Arabia in 1294 on his way home from China, Marco Polo wrote: "According to the report of those who have seen them ... they are just like eagles but of the most colossal size ... They are so huge and bulky that one of them can pounce on an elephant and carry it up to a great height in the air. Then it lets go, so that the elephant drops to earth and is smashed to pulp. Whereupon the gryphon bird perches on the carcass and feeds at its ease. They add that they have a wing-span of thirty paces and their wing-feathers are twelve paces long and of a thickness proportionate to their length ... I should explain that the islanders call them *rukhs* and know them by no other name."[1]

The accuracy is on a par with the rest of his account of the island which in fact he had confused with Mogadishu (of which Madagascar is an obvious corruption) and peopled with lions and camels as well as the elephants which provided the staple diet of the rukh. But his information could well have come from Arabs who, if they did not see the *aepyornis* itself may have seen the huge eggs and imagined a flying bird of corresponding size. It is a pity that the *aepyornis* did not survive until the arrival of the first Europeans, who might have brought home a sketch from life, or even a live or dead specimen; although, considering the ferocity with which Europeans slaughtered the harmless dodo in nearby Mauritius, they are more likely to have hastened than to have halted the extermination process.

Fortunately many other unique creatures survived the arrival of man along with various plants found nowhere else in the world. To mention only some of the more remarkable, there is the hedgehog-like *tenrec*, oldest of the insectivore mammals and a remote ancestor of man; numerous varieties of many-coloured chameleons; hordes of gorgeous butterflies and exotic beetles; more varieties of orchid than anywhere else in the world; the magnificent raphia palm; the travellers' tree, collecting fresh water in the centre of its fan-shaped leaves which can be tapped by the thirsty traveller; and in the south extraordinary varieties of thorny scrub and fantastically shaped cacti. Some of the vegetation, like certain animal species now extinct, has achieved gigantic proportions. There are giant varieties of cactus, reaching a height of 20 ft (6 m) or more. And in a remote part of the Mahafaly country in southern Madagascar there is a giant baobab, believed to be the largest in the world. It stands over 100 ft (30 m) high with a trunk of immense girth in the hollow inside of which twenty people can stand upright, if they don't mind the flock of bats fluttering and squeaking over their heads in the darkness.

For the zoologist, the great attraction of Madagascar lies in its population of lemurs, the most primitive of the primates and the earliest animals which can be said to look like ancestors of man. The lemur was once widely distributed in America and Europe as well as Asia and Africa. A few types survive in the forests of West Africa and of India, Malayasia and Indo-China. But their great stronghold is Madagascar. In the Eocene epoch, when the last landlinks between Africa and Madagascar were severed, a recognisable lemur, *Notharctus*, was already in existence. During the subsequent fifty million years or so, while lemurs elsewhere were being superseded by more aggressive animals, the lemurs in Madagascar were protected by their isolation. They proliferated and developed numerous species adapted to the different environments found in the island. At one end of the scale were the giant lemurs, as large as chimpanzees or gorillas. Like their fellow giants the *aepyornis* they failed to survive the coming of man; their disappearance was probably connected with the destruction by fire of the plateau forests where they lived. The largest living lemur is the three-foot long indri, *indris indris*, dark brown in colour with lighter patches and with only a vestigial tail. It is called in Malagasy *babakoto* or "father-son", presumably because of its anthropoid appearance which, as in the case of other species of lemur, has fostered the belief that it embodies the spirits of ancestors and is therefore regarded as *fady* or taboo. Competing with the indri in size is the vari, *varikandana* in Malagasy, with attractive black and white fur, a black face surrounded by a white ruff and a long black tail. At the other end of the scale is the tiny mouse lemur, which can be held in the palm of the hand. In between are many varieties of all sizes and colours and with different characteristics: most with tails but some without, some with the vestiges of a marsupial pouch, some nocturnal, some diurnal. But all are essentially tree-dwellers and all have the distinguishing features of the lemur – the large round eyes, the dog-like muzzle, the furry body and the well-developed hands and feet with long, prehensile fingers.

Zoologists classify the lemurs of Madagascar into three families – Lemuridae, Indridae and Daubentonidae – comprising altogether some thirty species. The Lemuridae include the vari and also the best- known and most widespread variety of lemur, which is represented in many zoos. This is the maki or ring-tailed lemur with its grey fur and long, bushy tail striped in black and white. Another relatively common member of the Lemuridae family is the macaco, of which the male is entirely black but the female is light brown with thick white side-whiskers framing the face. The Indridae take their name from the indri, and also include the beautiful, snow-white *sifaka* (so called because of its cry "see-fak" with the second syllable pitched on a higher note). Its long, prehensile tail, and speed at swinging through the trees have earned it the scientific name *propithecus* (pre-ape) *sifaka*. It is the most human-looking of the lemurs; and with its black face separated from a black crown by a white band across the forehead it reminds one irresistibly of a masked burglar.

The Daubentonidae family contains only one member, the Daubentonidae or *aye-aye*, the most archaic as well as one of the rarest and most curious of lemurs. It has rodent-like incisors and particularly long fingers, the middle finger longer still and very thin with the bones of the top two joints almost devoid of covering; this is used to scrape out grubs and beetles from under the bark of trees.

Most varieties of these attractive anthropomorphic creatures,

A world apart

with their bright, intelligent eyes and friendly, inquisitive natures, make admirable pets. They are so affectionate that they have been known to pine and die when their owners leave them. But they are now hard to come by. As a measure of protection the Malagasy government stringently controls their export and prohibits the keeping of them as pets. The danger of extinction is very real. Their numbers have declined with the progressive dwindling of the forest which is their natural habitat. A series of government orders forbidding their killing is largely ignored by the protein-hungry villagers, who find them an easy prey and a tasty addition to the stewpot. The *fady*, which is more effective protection than government decree, does not apply to all species or in all parts of the country: in the northwest, for example, the *sifaka* is *fady* on the east side of the Betsiboka river, but not on the west bank. The lemur's rate of reproduction is slow, with in general only one offspring a year. Numerous zoological expeditions from Europe and America have rallied international support for conservation measures and may have slowed down the process of extinction – indeed they have even discovered some new species of lemur. But the forest, which is the home of the lemurs and many other unique animals and plant species, continues to dwindle as the inexorably expanding human population clears the land for agriculture or chops down trees for fuel.

Soon the rarer species may only survive in zoos. Already it is not too easy to catch a sight of lemurs in their natural setting. First you must make a long journey by road to one of the remaining forested areas; then a walk into the forest with a local guide preferably at dawn or at sunset. If you are quiet and patient and lucky, you will suddenly become aware of one or more of these entrancing creatures gazing down at you; then, their curiosity satisfied, they will proceed with their business of plucking and eating fruit or simply gambolling from branch to branch with their companions. If you are somewhat less lucky you may hear only the cry of the lemur which startled and frightened the first Europeans to hear it. Certainly if you were not aware of the harmless, friendly nature of the source of the sound you might well be alarmed in the thick forest of the eastern escarpment by the cries of a troop of *babakoto*, rising and falling like high-pitched air-raid sirens out of phase. And it is an eerie and unforgettable experience to stand in the silence of the remote spiny forest by the tombs of the ancient Mahafaly kings and hear the eponymous, almost human, cry of the *sifaka* which, by local tradition, incarnate the spirits of the dead rulers and guard their tombs.

When one considers how the still rich flora and fauna of Madagascar have been depleted by the action of man, one cannot help envying the first humans who discovered the island. It must have then been an earthly paradise, almost completely covered with virgin forest, full of strange trees, plants and flowers and stocked with a marvellous variety of animals, insects and birds living in balanced harmony with little of the overt savagery characteristic of nature in other parts of the world. In the absence of large carnivores, apart from the crocodile, most species had no natural enemies and little need to develop defensive techniques. Thus the giant *aepyornis* had neither flight nor speed of foot to evade parties of hunters; and, what contributed perhaps even more to its extinction, it laid its eggs unprotected on the open ground where they could be easily found and eaten by man. Even today the only serious danger to man, apart from the dwindling number of crocodiles, is the malarial mosquito. There are not even any poisonous snakes; at least there is said to be one poisonous variety, but its fangs are placed well back in the throat so that the normal bite is not poisonous. There is only one great enemy, not only to other species, but to himself, and that is man. It is fortunate for the other forms of life on the island that man came to Madagascar very much later than to nearly all other habitable parts of the world.

A world apart

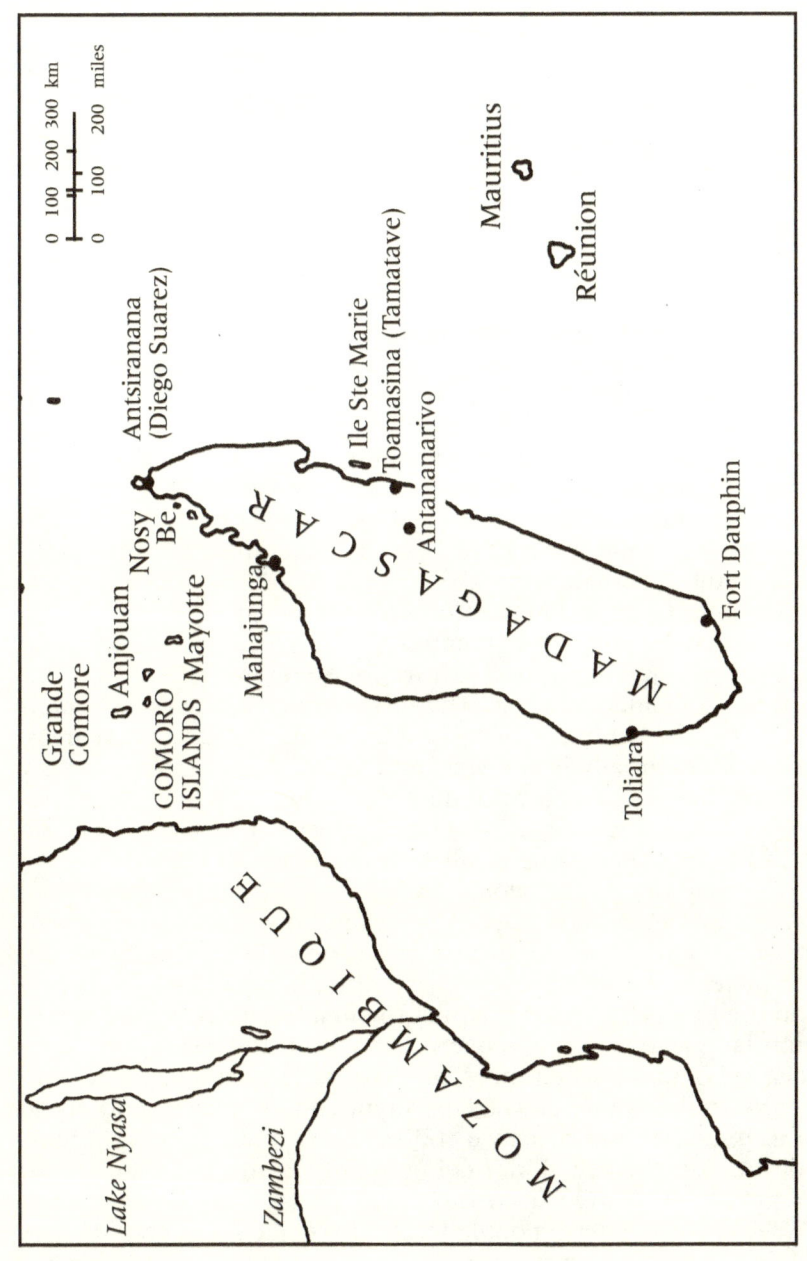

Madagascar, the Comoros and the Mascarene Islands

Chapter 2

The first Malagasy

The people of Madagascar are almost as unexpected as the fauna. Their origin has been the subject of much academic dispute, which is still only partially resolved. But two things can be stated with reasonable confidence. The first inhabitants of the island came originally from Indonesia: or to be more precise, the impulse which led eventually to the colonisation of Madagascar started in Indonesia. And, what is even more surprising, the first human occupation of Madagascar did not take place until some time after the beginning of the Christian era.

The idea of an Indonesian origin appears quite obvious in the central plateau area where many of the people have light skins and straight hair and in physical features often resemble Malayans, Indonesians or Indo-Chinese. The terraced ricefields are also reminiscent of the landscape of parts of Indonesia. In the coastal areas, however, especially in the west and south, Indonesia seems very distant. The people are much darker in colour and many have negroid features and short crinkly hair. The vast dusty plains scattered with herds of zebu cattle recall Africa rather than Asia.

The majority of the people are a mixture in varying degree of the extreme African and Asian types and this mixture is the dominant element in the population in all parts of the island, even on the plateau and on the west coast. The principal unifying factor, and the main clue to the origin of the first inhabitants, is the common language which is spoken throughout the island with only relatively minor differences of dialect. This language belongs clearly to the family of Malayo/Polynesian languages, entirely so in its grammar and structure and as to about eighty percent in its vocabulary (the remainder being mainly Bantu but also Arabic, French, English and Sanskrit).

The racially diverse population is also united to a considerable extent by a common culture, of which the main features are ancestor veneration, linked with the importance of the family tomb; the ritual importance of cattle, and to a less extent of rice cultivation; and the construction of rectangular houses aligned north-south with the door on the western side, and with different symbolic significance attached to the various sides and corners. The Malagasy attach special importance to the cardinal points of the compass and invariably give directions in terms of north, south, east and west rather than left or right. James Sibree, perhaps the best of the British missionary writers of the last century, recounts a delightful tale of one of his colleagues eating rice with a Malagasy family and getting a few grains caught in his moustache. When this was politely pointed out to him he wiped his moustache but on the wrong side, whereupon his host intervened: "No, no; on the south side of the moustache"!

The culture shows more regional variation than the language, often because of differing geographical conditions, sometimes because of the presence of certain ethnic influences in some areas. Thus all huts are rectangular but in the relatively treeless plateau areas they are built of mud or brick while on the coast they are made of wood, bamboo and palm thatch depending on what local materials are available. Similarly family tombs vary from the stone or brick "cold houses" of the Merina of the plateau through various wooden structures among different coastal peoples to the more substantial and impressive stone tombs of the Mahafaly and Antandroy herdsmen of the far south. The carving of statues on tombs is found only among some of the ethnic groups. It includes conventional figurative representation of the dead, for example, among the Bara; the *aloalo* of the Mahafaly – poles carved with symbolic representations of sun, moon and stars and surmounted either by cattle horns, a carving of a *zebu* or in more modern times carvings representing episodes in the dead person's life; and the notorious statuary of the Vezo tombs at Sakoambe near Morondava on the west coast, including traditional bird figures and more modern erotic couplings. Funeral rites also vary considerably. The well-known Merina custom, the "turning of the dead" or *famadihana*, under which the bodies of the dead wrapped in burial shrouds are removed from the family tomb at intervals of years and displayed at a joyous family gathering before being wrapped in a new shroud and returned to the tomb, is not found outside the plateau area.

Despite the regional differences one can still talk about a basic unity of Malagasy culture. It is more difficult to identify the sources of the different elements in that culture[2] One can say with reasonable certainty that the rectangular hut is of Indonesian origin; the round hut seen in many parts of Africa is not found here. Ancestor veneration is a feature of societies in many different parts of the world. Some funeral customs and types of tomb can be traced to

Asia, some seem to have developed uniquely in Madagascar and others can be traced to an African origin. There is, for example, a clear African origin for many of the funerary rites among the Sakalava, especially for royal funerals, for the cult of *dady* (i.e. great royal ancestors, represented by carefully preserved pieces of bone, fingernails and hair of former kings) and for the tradition of *tromba* or spirit possession by which a royally-appointed medium expresses the wishes of deceased Sakalava monarchs. The sacrificing of cattle and the use of cattle skulls and horns to decorate tombs is a link with Indonesia and Indo-China (among the aboriginal hill people[3] who are racially akin to the Indonesians); but the building up of herds of cattle as an end in itself to show the wealth of the cattle-owner is a well-known feature of some African societies, especially in East Africa. Slash-and-burn rice cultivation, practised in the forested areas of the eastern escarpment, is another link with parts of Indonesia and the mountain people of Indo-China; while knowledge of irrigated rice cultivation, as practised on the plateau, was probably brought at a later stage from India or Ceylon.

To summarise a vast amount of anthropological and ethnographic data one can conclude that the basic stock of the Malagasy people is a mixture of African and Indonesian, with the African element predominating, but speaking an essentially Indonesian language and possessing a culture which probably owes more to Indonesia than to Africa but which contains many elements common to both areas of origin. How and when did these people establish themselves in Madagascar?

It is now generally accepted, mainly because of the language, that the colonisation of Madagascar must have had its origin in Indonesia. Historical evidence exists of far-ranging Indonesian voyages into the western Indian Ocean in the early part of the Christian era, but there is no comparable record of any African voyages away from their own coastal waters. As for the route, there are still some partisans of the direct route across the southern Indian Ocean from Java to the east coast of Madagascar. This route is theoretically possible and is favoured by the trade winds and a strong east-west current south of the Equator.[4] But the distance from Indonesia to Madagascar is enormous, nearly 4,000 miles (6400 km), which is greater than any known Polynesian voyage. A conceivable, though extremely hazardous, route for an occasional accidental journey, when a canoe might be swept away by winds and currents; but highly improbable as a regular route for a substantial migration.[5] Moreover, if they had come this way it is unlikely that Mauritius and Reunion would have remained uninhabited until Europeans arrived in the sixteenth century. The alternative route around the northern and western shores of the Indian Ocean is more practicable and plausible and helps to explain, as the direct route does not, the presence of African racial and cultural elements in the basic stratum of the population throughout Madagascar. The present-day distribution of the Indonesian/Polynesian outrigger canoe in the Indian Ocean, and notably in Ceylon, the Maldives, the East African coast and, significantly, the west coast of Madagascar, is strong support for the northern route. There is plenty of evidence of an Indonesian presence on the East African coast during the first millenium, and one strong indication[6] that Indonesians probably reached this coast before the likely date of the first colonisation of Madagascar.

This leads us to the question of the timing of the migration. It is at first sight difficult to accept that this huge island so close to Africa (and to that part of Africa where it is probable that the earliest proto-humans developed) was completely uninhabited 2,000 years ago. But all the evidence points this way. The main objection comes from those who believe that there was an aboriginal population, possibly related to the Bushmen or Hottentots of southern Africa, on the island before the arrival of the proto-Malagasy from Indonesia via Africa. This belief is supported by oral traditions of a dark-skinned people of small stature known as the Vazimba who occupied the central plateau areas before being ousted by later immigrants (the Merina and the Betsileo); and by the continuing existence today of small pockets of such people, some of whom are still called Vazimba. But detailed studies[7] of these groups have shown that there is no essential difference in language or customs between them and other Malagasy peoples; and it is now generally accepted that the Vazimba were (and are) descendants of the earliest proto-Malagasy immigrants who were pushed into the interior by later arrivals. In any case archaeological and constructional digging has unearthed no remains of a pre-Malagasy population. Even more striking is the total absence of any stone implements, arrowheads or axe-heads, such as have been found in abundance in Africa. Such archeological diggings as have taken place have failed to unearth evidence of human occupation earlier than approximately 900 AD, apart from one isolated and unconfirmed carbon-dating of pottery from around 600 AD at a fishing settlement near St Augustine's Bay in the southwest.[8] The remarkable unity of language in this huge island points to a fairly recent human settlement. To a lesser degree, the cultural homogeneity and the similarity of racial composition of the Malagasy are an indication that there has not been much time for the widely separated groups of settlement to form separate cultures and racial identities. Another sign of recent arrival is the fact that the settlement of the island is still incomplete. Vast areas are still virtually uninhabited. Substantial internal migrations are known to have taken place within relatively recent times, and population movements are still continuing. A study[9] of the rate of deforestation resulting from human occupation suggests that the first inhabitants arrived not much more than a thousand years ago.

Other evidence points to a rather earlier date than a thousand years ago. In addition to destroying much of the primary forest, the early inhabitants were responsible, directly or indirectly, for the destruction of several important animal species, notably the giant lemur, the dwarf hippopotamus, the giant tortoise and the *aepyornis*.[10] Remains of these creatures indicate that they became extinct no later than 800 to 1,000 years ago. Given the size of the island and the smallness of the human population in the early days the process of extinction must have been spread over several hundreds of years, thus setting the arrival of man back at least several centuries before 1,000 AD. Pointing the same way is the fact that by 900 or 1,000 AD the original Malagasy settlers, with their special mixture of Indonesian and African race, language and culture were sufficiently well established, at least in the coastal areas, to absorb later immigrants from different and in some respects more advanced cultures with little effect on their basic identity.

Finally, a comparison between what we know of the level of culture of the proto-Malagasy and of the spread of various cultural features in Indonesia provides some clue to the time when the ancestors of the first Malagasy left Indonesia. For example there are no significant traces of Buddhism in early Malagasy culture, and the proto-Malagasy appear to have been ignorant of iron-working. As both Buddhism and knowledge of iron-working began to appear in Indonesia around the beginning of the Christian era, one might deduce very cautiously that the ancestors of the Malagasy left Indonesia about 2,000 years ago.[11]

In the light of all the evidence summarised above, and with a little aid from the imagination, we can now attempt to reconstruct the events leading to the first human arrival in Madagascar. The starting point is somewhere in Indonesia some centuries before the birth of Christ. A group of coastal Indonesians possibly related to the present-day Maanjan people of central Borneo (whose language most nearly resembles Malagasy)[12] became adept in navigation with the outrigger canoe and used it to trade with neighbouring islands. Over the centuries they may have traded throughout the Indonesian archipelago and even beyond, but at some stage the energies of one particular group at least became directed towards the west. They may have been pushed out of their

The first Malagasy

original home by waves of migration from Thailand or Indo-China; or the main impulse may have been the hope of rich trading opportunities in India and further west. By easy stages they extended their trading journeys, from Sumatra to the Andaman Islands and then on to Ceylon, southern India, the Maldives and the Laccadives and across the Arabian Sea to the island of Socotra and the coast of Africa. For the exploratory journeys they probably used the small double outrigger canoe which is still to be found at most points along this route. But for their main trading and migratory journeys it is likely that they sailed in much larger twin-hulled outriggers, such as were used for the main Polynesian migrations. Following the coast southward, they had reached the land known as Azania (present-day Kenya and Tanzania) by the first century AD.

In Azania the Indonesians found an unusually favourable combination of circumstances: a tolerable, even agreeable climate, abundant space and a small scattered population of less advanced civilisation on whom they could impose their culture and language. They set up trading posts to barter utensils, pottery and beads for the local ivory, rhinoceros horn and tortoise-shell. Later they established small settlements, reinforced by further migration from Indonesia over several centuries They introduced their techniques, some of which, like the outrigger canoe already mentioned, the rectangular wooden hut thatched with coconut palm, the equipentatonic xylophone and turtle-fishing, still survive on the East African coast. More important they brought with them their food plants – coconuts, breadfruit, yams, bananas, taro – thereby introducing the concept of food crops to tropical Africa where people had hitherto existed mainly by hunting and gathering fruit. Their settlements may have spread some distance inland; traces of Indonesian influence have been found as far west as the eastern Congo. In the course of time they inter-married to some extent with the local population, thus producing the special mixture of African and Indonesian which characterised the proto-Malagasy.

This enterprising people would certainly have engaged in further exploratory journeys to the south. Probably some time around the third century AD they arrived at the Comoros, from which it was but a short step in space and time to the shores of Madagascar, which they may have reached between 300 and 500 AD. Their arrival as the first colonists of this virgin island continent, more than four thousand miles (6,400 km) as the crow flies from their original homeland and much further by the route they followed in their outrigger canoes, completed one of the most remarkable migratory voyages in the history of mankind.

The island and the people

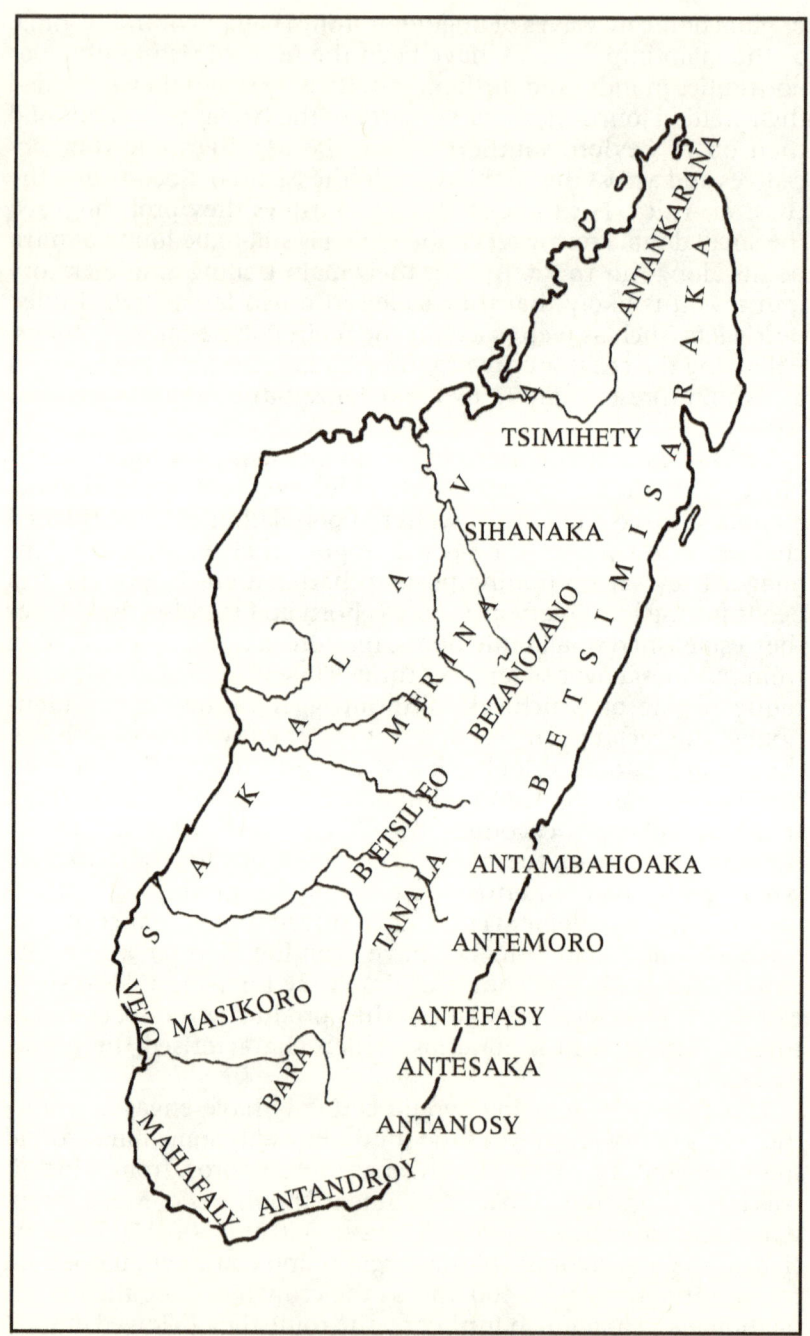

Present distribution of the Malagasy ethnic groups

Chapter 3
The occupation of the island

For some time, perhaps two centuries or so, the settlements in Madagascar were probably little more than outposts of larger Indonesian/proto-Malagasy settlement in East Africa, and confined to the northwest and west coasts of the island. But from about the middle of the first millennium external pressures on the settlers in Africa compelled more and more of them to seek refuge in Madagascar. First the expansion of Bantu-speaking negroes from their heartland in the Western Congo gradually pushed the inland settlements towards the coast. Ironically, it has been suggested1 that the Bantu population expansion, which led ultimately to their occupation of most of tropical and southern Africa, was made possible by the introduction of Indonesian yams, breadfruit and bananas, providing staple foods which were previously lacking in the African forest. Growing contact with the Bantu speakers during this expansion no doubt increased the African element in the racial make-up of this second wave of migration to Madagascar. The settlements on the coast of East Africa survived much longer, sustained by the continuing Indonesian trade in the Indian Ocean. But while the inland settlements were driven back or absorbed by the Bantu, the coastal settlements and the maritime trade on which they depended were threatened by the Arab expansion into the Indian Ocean. By the tenth century Arab sailors and merchants dominated the trade of the western half of the Indian Ocean. Some Indonesian trade continued for a while, but there is no historical reference to Indonesians in East Africa after the twelfth century. Long before then, the great majority of the Indonesian colony had taken refuge in Madagascar to assume the role of settlers rather than traders.

Thus, during the second half of the first millennium a second and more substantial migration of Indonesian-Africans to Madagascar took place. The African racial element in this second migration would be greater than in the first, but the way of life and especially the language reflected the continued dominance of the more advanced Indonesian culture. The second wave completed the occupation of the coasts by settling on the southern and especially the more hospitable eastern shores. But many of them no doubt chose to settle in the more accessible and already occupied areas of the northwest and west. The pressure of their numbers would cause some of the original colonists to look for new settlements inland; or in some cases it might have been the newcomers, finding the coastal areas firmly occupied, who moved inland. With thick forest still covering most of the country the obvious routes to the interior were up the valleys of the great rivers which run into the Mozambique Channel – the Betsiboka, the Tsiribihina and the Onilahy. Ascending these valleys over a period of many years, these descendants of the first Malagasy finally settled in the central plateau regions to become the Vazimba who were later ousted by the Merina in the north and the Betsileo in the south.

By the end of the first millennium the coasts and some inland areas of Madagascar were firmly settled by a remarkably homogeneous people. They were recognisably the ancestors of the Malagasy of today, racially a mixture of Indonesian and African (although at that stage the Indonesian element was probably still dominant) and speaking an essentially Indonesian language with the addition of some African vocabulary. With their rectangular wooden huts, on stilts in the wetter zones, and their slash-and-burn rice cultivation, supplemented by the cultivation of the other Indonesian crops which they brought with them and by fishing on the coasts and in the rivers, their way of life was close to that of their remote Indonesian forebears. But they had acquired new techniques in Africa notably in relation to domestic animals, and they had brought with them the forerunners of the great herds of hump-backed zebu cattle which are now an essential feature of the Malagasy landscape. Although the total population must still have been small, their occupation of the coastal areas at least was so effective and their civilisation and culture so well established that they were able to absorb new immigrants from different, and sometimes more advanced, civilisations with only relatively minor effects on their language and culture.

During the next five hundred years before the arrival of the Europeans, the original Malagasy – the *tompon-tany* or "lords of the land" – pushed further into the empty lands of the interior. The different geographical environments modified their way of life, producing some of the differences which distinguish the various ethnic groups[2] of Madagascar from each other. The fertile humid coastal belt of the east favoured the development of agriculture, while the vast arid plains of the south and west were more suited to the development of cattle herding as a way of life. During this period the early Malagasy completed the process, already well advanced, of extermination of various animal and bird species, notably the giant varieties – the *aepyornis*, the giant lemurs, the giant tortoise. This was achieved partly by hunting with primitive spears and in the case of the *aepyornis* by eating the unprotected eggs. But many species died out because of the destructive changes which man brought about in the environment, especially by the burning of the forest. In the tropical rain forest of the east the damage was limited by the extreme humidity, fortunately for the lemurs and other forest animals which still survive along the escarpment. But the drier deciduous forest of the plateau burned more easily and huge areas must have been devastated by forest fires which got out of control and of which folk memories survive to this day.

Meanwhile on the coasts, various contacts were taking place which were to produce the most important variations from the Indonesian-African norm of the Malagasy *tompon-tany*. The modern population is such a mixture that it is impossible to be dogmatic in this field. But one might conjecture that something like the original Indonesian-African mix might be found among ethnic groups like the Tsimihety who occupy the area between the northern plateau and the Tsaratanana mountain massif, and the Tanala who live in the forests of the south-eastern escarpment. Also close to the norm are the Betsileo of the southern plateau, with perhaps more than an average share of Indonesian blood, and the cattle-owning Mahafaly and the Antandroy of the south who lean rather more to the African side of the balance. But more significant differences are found in the southeast where several ethnic groups – the Antemoro, the Antambahoaka, the Antanosy – reveal substantial Arab/Islamic influence; among the Sakalava people of the west coast and the Bara of the inland areas of the south, where the African influence on race, language and culture is particularly strong; and among the Merina of the northern plateau around Antananarivo where there is an unusually high proportion of Indonesian types among the population. These variations can be explained by the arrival of further immigrants from various countries bordering on the Indian Ocean during the five centuries or so before the arrival of the Europeans.

The great variety of racial types in modern Madagascar and the existence of isolated culture and vocabulary links has led certain authors to suggest immigrations by Jews, Persians, Indians and even Chinese. One cannot exclude the possibility of coastal contacts with some of these people. In the early part of the fifteenth century a large Chinese fleet under a famous admiral Cheng Ho, also known as the "Three Jewel Eunuch", sailed the western Indian Ocean as far as the Red Sea and Mogadishu, and might possibly have visited Madagascar. But there is no evidence that any Chinese remained; the small present Chinese population, which has inter-married with the Malagasy to some extent, mostly arrived during the present century. On Ile Sainte Marie (which used to be called Nosy Ibrahim) and at Vohipeno on the southeast coast are small groups calling themselves Zafy-Ibrahim (descendants of Ibrahim or Abraham) who claim to be Jews; but the missionary author James Sibree who visited the group at Vohipeno a century ago could not detect any difference between them and the other peoples of the east coast[3], and it is perhaps more likely that they were descended from an Arab called Ibrahim. In the later Middle Ages Indian traders were active around the coasts of Madagascar, and small groups might have been left behind, more particularly the survivors of shipwrecks, such as the Voajiry whose name suggests an origin in Waziristan. But in general any small groups of this kind would be quickly absorbed into the local population, as happened with Portuguese sailors shipwrecked in the sixteenth century, whose descendants a hundred years later were found by the French to be indistinguishable from the other inhabitants apart from certain physical traits. And there is no evidence that any groups of Indians, Jews, Persians or Chinese who may have arrived in medieval times had any significant effect on the racial composition or customs of the Malagasy people or on the course of Malagasy history. The later immigrants who did make an appreciable impact on the culture and history of Madagascar had their origin in Arabia, in Africa or in Indonesia.

The first of the "new immigrants" were Arabs trading down the east coast of Africa. In this context "Arabs" is a convenient name covering various groups affected to a greater or less extent by Islam, originating in most cases in Arabia but having spent several generations on the way, in East Africa or elsewhere, before reaching Madagascar. They were known usually in Madagascar as the Antalaotra or "people from across the seas". By the time they arrived there both their Arab blood and their religious beliefs had been considerably diluted. The perhaps surprising failure of the Moslem religion to establish itself in Madagascar suggests a lack of proselytising zeal among the "Arab" newcomers; and is also an indication of the strength and coherence of the Malagasy culture at this early stage. At any rate, the present Moslem community in modern Madagascar consists largely of recent immigrants from the Comoros or Pakistan, mainly in the northwest, with only small

The occupation of the island

numbers of Malagasy converts in the same area. Elsewhere, and particularly along the east coast, there are numerous traces of Arab or Islamic cultural influence but no knowledge of some of the central features of the Moslem religion – the name Allah, the mosque, prayer, alms or the pilgrimage to Mecca; and where the name of Mohammed is distantly remembered it is as one prophet among others (including Ra-Issa or Jesus who was regarded as greater) rather than as *the* Prophet. This would seem to indicate that the Arabs who came to the east coast of Madagascar were either pre-Islamic or members of one of the sects who broke away from the orthodox Moslem faith during the turbulent times of the life of Mohammed and his immediate successors. Some of the later Islamised arrivals may well have had no direct connection with Arabia but have received their Islamic imprint elsewhere following the spread of the Moslem religion throughout the countries bordering the Indian Ocean.

Arabs are known to have traded far down the east coast of Africa well before the time of Mohammed. It is likely that the first Arabs to cross the Mozambique Channel were some of these pre-Islamic traders who had been pushed out of Africa by orthodox Sunnite Moslems expanding from the north. Racially they would already have a substantial mixture of African blood and their language would be a cross between Arabic and Bantu not unlike modern Swahili. Some time in the eighth or ninth centuries their dhows reached the Comoros where they would have had little difficulty in dominating the existing population of proto-Malagasy. Here in these small volcanic islands the prototype Antalaotra population was formed – a mixture of Arabs, Africans and Malagasy similar to that which inhabits the Comoros today, speaking a language derived from Swahili, with Arab clothes and customs and a small number of pure Arab leaders. From the Comoros they established trading links with Madagascar and in due course, probably by the tenth century, they set up a series of trading posts along the northwest coast.

Over the next five or six hundred years the Antalaotra traders, by now converted to Islam, thrived on the exchange of Malagasy products including beef, rice, tortoise-shell, beeswax and honey against imported tools, utensils, cloth, glass beads and porcelain. The slave trade played an important part in this traffic, at first mainly from Africa to Madagascar but later probably in both directions. At the beginning of the sixteenth century the Portuguese found Arab trading posts flourishing all along the northwest coast; and a fleet commanded by Tristan da Cunha attacked and burned a number of them. The Portuguese and other Europeans who followed them dealt a more serious blow to the Antalaotra in the longer term by ruining the Arab trade in the Indian Ocean. A century later a Jesuit missionary, Father Luis Mariano, found several Antalaotra settlements still surviving with forts and simple mosques. But another hundred years saw their final disappearance, driven out or absorbed by the northward expansion of the Sakalava empire at the end of the seventeenth century. Nothing now remains but the ruins of a few Arab-style houses and tombs, forts and mosques.

At a fairly early stage some of the Antalaotra rounded the northern tip of Cap d'Ambre and settled on the northeast coast. One of the few archaeological excavations that have taken place in Madagascar has revealed relics of a flourishing Moslem settlement at a site known as Iharana, near the modern town of Vohemar.[4] Tombs have been uncovered containing a remarkable variety of luxury articles – Chinese porcelain, fine Persian glassware, bead necklaces, bronze mirrors, silver jewellery, etc – some dating back to the twelfth century, others as recent as the seventeenth century. The Iharanian civilisation appears to have extended along the northeast coast as far south as Antalaha. By the eighteenth century all that remained of Iharana was the ruins of two buildings, and the bulk of the Iharanian people have been absorbed in the local Malagasy population. A small group known as the Onjatsy to the north of Vohemar, who claim an Arab origin and have a reputation as *ombiasy* (priest–doctors) and *mpisikidy* (diviners), are probably the last surviving relic of this intriguing civilisation.

With its extensive foreign trade, Iharana must have become well-known to sailors and traders in the western Indian Ocean, and it appears to have acted as a staging-post for other immigrants coming to Madagascar. One group was the Zafi-Raminia (descendants of Ramini) who probably arrived early in the fourteenth century. According to their traditions they came from Imaka (Mecca) and were descended from Mohammed's uncle. An alternative explanation is that they came from Ramni, which was the medieval name for Sumatra, some time after Islam had established itself in Indonesia in the thirteenth century. If so they would have spoken an Indonesian language which would have made it easier for them to be absorbed in the Malagasy population. Their traditions mention a stay in Mangalore on the west coast of India where the present-day population is largely Moslem and the use of outrigger canoes is a link with Indonesia. Whatever their origin or route to Madagascar they appear to have spent some time in Iharana before moving south to settle on the coast around Mananjary. Later arrivals, the Antemoro, caused some of them to move further south to the southeast corner around Fort Dauphin/Taolañaro. The remainder stayed in the Mananjary area and form the small present-day group known as the Antambahoaka. Those who moved to the Fort Dauphin area used the prestige of their "magical" knowledge to impose themselves as chiefs of the local people, the Antanosy ("people of the island"). Some of them provided the ruling families for the Antandroy ("people of the thorny bush") in the wild country to the west of Anosy. The long-standing belief that they also supplied the ruling dynasties for the main ethnic groups of the west and southwest is now disputed. But Zafi-Raminia *ombiasy* may have played a part in the formation of the ruling class of the Merina in the central plateau.

The ancestors of the Antemoro arrived some two centuries after the Zafi-Raminia, around the end of the fifteenth century. They are of special interest not only as the last significant group of pre-European immigrants but also as the possessors of important historical manuscripts, the *Sorabe* ("great writings"). Probably most of the Antalaotra had some knowledge of Arabic writing, but the Antemoro were unique in their scribal tradition and their ability to manufacture a special kind of paper from beaten bark. No doubt they wrote originally in Arabic but at an early stage they adapted the Arabic script to the Malagasy language. This is the language of the *Sorabe*, which are of two kinds. Some are concerned with subjects such as astrology, geomancy, divination and medicine, knowledge of which gave the possessors great prestige throughout Madagascar. Others are contemporary chronicles and historical works dealing with the mythical origins of the Antalaotra who came to settle in southeast Madagascar. Their reliability is uncertain: the two oldest are jealously guarded and cannot be seen by outsiders and many of the others appear to have been written relatively recently or to have been copied, with varying degrees of accuracy, from older documents. But they are nevertheless historical records of unusual interest.

Even the *Sorabe* do not enable us to be precise about the origin of the Antemoro. Like the Zafi-Raminia, with whom their traditions are sometimes confused, they claim noble descent from Mecca. On their way to Madagascar they passed through the Comoros, which creates a strong presumption that they came from Africa; and like the Zafi-Raminia they stopped a while at Iharana before moving south to settle in the coastal area around the modern town of Vohipeno, probably in the early years of the sixteenth century. Their name has previously been thought to derive from Namorona, a small river marking the northern limit of their territory, or *morona*, the Malagasy word for shore or coast. But it has recently been argued very plausibly[5] that the origin of both the name and the people is to be found in the Somali country of southeast Ethiopia, where there was a group called Temur which disappeared from the area in the fifteenth century – a time which is compatible with the date of arrival of the Antemoro in Madagascar. It is not impossible that the original ancestors came from Arabia to the Somali area of the Horn of Africa, which was traditionally a home for heretics and dissenters, and were subsequently driven out by internal religious strife and the expansion of the Galla people.

The Islamic faith of the original Antemoro seems to have declined rapidly and little trace now remains apart from a special respect for Fridays and a taboo on pork. Similarly the Arabic language disappeared quite quickly, from which one might deduce that the Antemoro immigrants, like the Antalaotra generally, were predominantly male and married local Malagasy women, from whom the children would learn to speak Malagasy rather than the language of their fathers. Nevertheless it was mainly through the Antemoro that Arabic loan-words were absorbed into the Malagasy language, notably the days of the week and words connected with astrology, arithmetic and divining. The prestige deriving from their "magical" arts enabled the Antemoro not only to provide the ruling clans in their own region but also to furnish *ombiasy* and *mpisikidy* to many other ethnic groups thereby spreading the vocabulary associated with their arts throughout the island. With better leadership the Antemoro might have used their priestly prestige to play a much more dominating role in the island's history, comparable perhaps to the Sakalava and the Merina. Instead they were weakened by constant strife between their component clans (they have no less than four clans of chiefs and four clans of priests), so that their direct influence never extended beyond the present limits of their territory.

The struggle for supremacy between the various Antemoro clans led directly to the "export" of unsuccessful Antemoro chiefs to other areas. One of these called Rambo was the ancestor of the Zafi-Rambo who founded the kingdom of Tanala ("people of the forest") in the forests of the southeast escarpment. Some traditions of the Betsileo ("the many unconquered"), the important people occupying the southern plateau around the modern town of Fianarantsoa, state that their chiefs came from the east, which strongly suggests an Antemoro, and possibly a Zafi-Rambo, origin. Even where they did not provide chiefs the Antemoro wielded great influence through their *ombiasy* who exercised their arts in most parts of the island and shared authority with local chieftains in a division of spiritual and temporal power such as is found in many societies.

The earliest French settlers at Fort Dauphin in the seventeenth century found the the local Antanosy were dominated by Antemoro *ombiasy*, who were employed by the Antonosy chiefs to weave spells against the French using their magic writing. Their method was to leave near the French fort baskets full of papers and various gifts such as eggs, earthen pots, small coffins, dugouts and oars, all covered with symbols and writing. As late as the end of the eighteenth century the great Merina king, Andrianampoinimerina, sent for Antemoro priests to act as his advisers on astrology and other magical arts. They accompanied the king on his military campaigns to advise him on the most propitious times to attack his enemies. They supplied the king with magical charms and also practised medicine, using the remedies described in the *Sorabe*. To this day Antemoro *ombiasy* are employed among the Merina and other groups as astrologers and fortune-tellers, especially to indicate favourable dates for family ceremonies.

The total numbers of the Antalaotra, and their contribution of Arab blood to the Malagasy racial mixture, were relatively small. But, especially on the west coast, they were responsible for greatly increasing the African element in the racial stock. Apart from the African blood already present in most of the Antalaotra themselves, they imported considerable numbers of African slaves, at first to act as their own servants and agricultural labourers, and later to sell to the Malagasy. In 1506 a Portuguese fleet led by Tristan da Cunha found at Sada on the northwest coast (modern Bay of Anorontsanga) a dense population of "Cafres" whom they believed to be escaped African slaves from the Arab trading settlements in East Africa. Along most of the coast, trade was in the hands of Arabs and consisted largely of the export of rice, with the beginnings of a reverse traffic in slaves from Madagascar to the mainland. A century later Father Mariano found that trade in the northwest was now largely in the hands of local Malagasy (or "Buques") and that slaves had replaced rice as the main export. He also found, further south along the west coast between Cap Saint André and the Tsiribihina river, substantial settlements of black people with frizzy hair, speaking a "Cafre" language, planting cassava and millet and keeping cattle. The large numbers mentioned by Mariano would appear to rule out the possibility that they were escaped slaves and it seems more likely that these African settlements were the result of voluntary migrations from Mozambique.[6]

A century after Mariano, by the beginning of the eighteenth century, these separate African settlements had ceased to exist. Perhaps some of the "Cafres" had become victims of the reverse slave trade to Africa, and others were driven out by the Sakalava expansion in the seventeenth century. Those who remained were assimilated into the general Malagasy culture and adopted the Malagasy language. Nevertheless a strong African element in the Sakalava people on the west coast and the Bara of the central south is evident from their physical appearance, the relatively high proportion of African words in their dialects and the retention of certain customs of clearly African origin such as the *tromba* (spirit possession) and the *dady* (cult of royal relics). Specific links with Africa include the name Masikoro, formerly applied to people in the southern interior and now to a subdivision of the Sakalava; there is no known Malagasy explanation of this name, but a possible origin is *mashokora*, a word used in parts of Tanzania for scrub forest of a kind similar to some of the vegetation in southwestern Madagascar.[7] More striking are the wooden carvings on the tombs at Sakoambe near Morondava. The name of the village suggests a link with the Sacumbe people, now extinct, who once occupied the Tete area of Mozambique. The notorious erotic carvings are modern and of local origin; but the traditional bird effigies carved alongside them, which are the only bird carvings on tombs in Madagascar, are very similar to soapstone carvings of birds found in the ancient African kingdom of Zimbabwe.

While some of the specific links with Africa could be questioned, the accumulation of evidence supporting such links is decisive. Less certain is the origin of the ruling dynasties which emerged somewhere around the sixteenth century among the Sakalava, the Bara and the other peoples of the south and southwest. Previously political organisation among the Malagasy had not risen above the level of village and clan. The development of wider political groupings under kings with semi-divine authority can be seen most clearly in the south and west. Numerous local traditions in these areas trace their dynasties back four or five centuries, but there is much confusion and overlapping. The main dynasty was the Maroserana which appeared among the Mahafaly in mid-sixteenth century. They were a Malagasy dynasty formed by the marriage of new immigrants, described as "white men" in several traditions, with the daughters of local chiefs. The Maroserana, or Volamena as their main branch was also called, later took over leadership of the Sakalava and were responsible for the rapid Sakalava expansion in the seventeenth century (it is interesting that the first Sakalava conqueror was called Andriandahifotsy, which means "Prince White Man"). One branch became the Zafimanely dynasty of the Bara, while the ruling chiefs of their neighbours the Masikoro were derived from another branch, the Zafindravola.

Hitherto it has been generally accepted that all these ruling dynasties were supplied by the Zafi-Raminia from Anosy, whose Arab or Indonesian origin might explain the legend of early white chiefs. But one scholar has argued[8] that the founders of the Maroserana came from black Africa, more specifically from the Zimbabwe empire around the upper Zambezi. Many of the practices and some of the vocabulary associated with kingship in Madagascar are clearly derived from Africa; and although the Zafi-Raminia or Antemoro could have absorbed some of this during a stay in Africa, the direct import of these ideas from Africa is perhaps more plausible. An African origin has also been suggested for the names of some of the early Maroserana kings, notably Andriamandazoala: this can be translated "crusher of trees" which was one of the titles of Mwena Mutapa, the great Zimbabwe king. The most interesting argument is based on the political and religious importance of gold in the Maroserana kingdoms. One Sakalava tradition is that the precursors of the Maroserana landed on the southwest coast with a shipload of gold which they used to gain supremacy over the local people. The alternative dynasty name of Volamena means in Malagasy "red silver" ie. gold, while Maroserana itself may be derived in part from *mari* which was the word for gold in Zimbabwe. Gold was not mined in Madagascar until the nineteenth century, and then only in the northern plateau area, whereas Zimbabwe was a major source of gold in the middle ages.

The main drawback to this interesting theory is the reference to white men in several traditions as being the origin of the Maroserana dynasty. The Malagasy *lahifotsy* (white man) does not necessarily imply European colouring; but it does imply that the person concerned, although he might be quite dark, is of lighter colouring than others in his group. It is therefore difficult to believe that Africans from Zimbabwe could be so described; and some contemporary descriptions of early kings in the southwest suggest that they were lighter-skinned than their subjects.[9] But there is a possible explanation which would reconcile a Zimbabwe origin of the dynasties with the "white men" tradition. In the later middle ages Zimbabwe gold played a major role in the trade of the western Indian Ocean, stimulated by the growing demand in Western Europe (the first gold coins struck at the London Mint in the thirteenth century have been found by assay to be African gold). In early days this trade may have been in the hands of Indonesians, but later it was taken over by the Arabs.[10] It is therefore possible that the ancestors of the Maroserana who landed on the southwest coast with a shipload of gold were Arabs who had decided to use the gold to set up kingdoms of their own on the model of the

Zimbabwe empire. A landing by such traders is at least more plausible than a sea journey by Zimbabweans from the interior of Africa.

We may never be certain about the origin of these southwestern dynasties. Even more problematical is the origin of the Merina, the most numerous of the Malagasy peoples, living in the northern plateau around Antananarivo. They have attracted the special attention of historians as the most advanced people of Madagascar who in the nineteenth century conquered and ruled most of the rest of the island; and of anthropologists as a group containing an unusually high proportion of pure Malayan or Indonesian types, with light-coloured skin and straight hair. Although Europeans did not penetrate their rocky domain until the end of the eighteenth century, their oral traditions, recorded in the nineteenth century, give a clear picture of their history back to the sixteenth century when their first small kingdoms were formed. These traditions and other evidence show that the region which is now called Imerina ("the land of the Merina") was formerly occupied by dark-skinned Vazimba, primitive descendants of early Malagasy immigrants. In the course of the sixteenth century a light-skinned people called Hova (pronounced 'oov(a)) arrived from somewhere to the east. They were able to overcome the Vazimba, partly by victory in battle and partly by marriage of their *andriana*, or chiefs, with Vazimba queens. Some of the Vazimba fled to the west, others remained in the area to become one of the components of the modern Merina people. The Merina have often, and especially in the nineteenth century, been called the Hova, but by current usage this name is usually limited to the middle-class of the Merina, descendants of the original Hova, as distinct from the other main classes, the nobles (*andriana*) and the slaves (*andevo*).

Thus far there is no problem. Where disagreement arises is over the origin of the Hova and their *andriana*, on which the oral traditions are surprisingly reticent. Because of the high proportion of pure Indonesian types, outside observers have tended to assume that they arrived late and came from Malaya or Java. Most of the Merina believe that their ancestors landed near Maroantsetra in the Bay of Antongil in the northeast in the thirteenth or fourteenth centuries and then made their way inland and south along the upper escarpment before turning west towards Antananarivo. But this belief seems to be based mainly on a vague tradition that the ancestors came from the northeast (possibly deriving from the traditional allocation of the northeast corner of the hut as the "corner of the ancestors"). Some historians believe that if they did come from the northeast their ancestors might have been Iharanians.

A third theory suggests an arrival on the northwest coast and an ascent up the Betsiboka and the Ikopa. Yet a fourth theory, supported by some traditions, is that they came from the south east, in which case they might have been a branch of the Zafi-Raminia.

A recent version of the southeast theory[11] suggests that the ancestral Hova were not late medieval arrivals like the Zafi-Raminia or the Antemoro, but a group of early Malagasy immigrants who had retained their Indonesian racial purity by a rigid endogamy. From an original homeland in the southeast at the end of the first millennium they gradually moved north, through the Ivohibe depression and the Betsileo country until, at the beginning of the sixteenth century, they came to Imerina where they found the Vazimba in possession. In order to overcome the Vazimba they accepted the leadership of the *andriana* who, according to this theory, were a small group of Zafi-Raminia "sages" or "astrologers" who had recently established themselves in the area, inter-married with the Vazimba and introduced iron-working, the Arabic calendar and the *sikidy* method of divination. A Zafi-Raminia role in the formation of the *andriana* seems quite likely, but for the Hova a late arrival is more plausible than the preservation of racial purity over nearly a thousand years.

The year 1500 is generally regarded as an important date in Madagascar's history because it was in this year that the first Europeans visited the island. At this time the Malagasy were still divided into numerous small clans and there had been little movement towards higher forms of political organisation. But as we have seen, significant developments were already in progress which during the next hundred years or so would lead to the establishment of various kingdoms, two of which were destined to play a major role, the Sakalava in the seventeenth and eighteenth centuries and the Merina in the nineteenth century. It would be several hundred years before Europeans would have a comparable impact on the history of the island.

PART 2   EARLY EUROPEAN CONTACTS

Chapter 4

The arrival of the Europeans

Sailors from the Mediterranean, with a bit of luck, might have got to Madagascar before the Indonesians. Herodotus tells us that around 600 BC the Egyptian Pharaoh Necho sent a Phoenician expedition down the Red Sea with instructions to circumnavigate Africa. Three years later they returned via the Straits of Gibraltar having apparently carried out their orders. If so they must have passed within a few hundred miles of Madagascar, but it is highly unlikely that they ventured far from the shores of Mozambique. Three or four centuries later Greek ships came down the Red Sea to the East African coast to obtain ivory. Afterwards a Graeco-Roman trade, mainly in spices, developed with East Africa and India. But again it is improbable that any of these traders got as far as Madagascar. The Geography published in the second century AD by Ptolemy mentions an island of Menouthias which some scholars have identified as Madagascar; but expert opinion1 now favours an identification with Zanzibar or Pemba. The rise of Islam in the seventh century effectively denied European access to the Indian Ocean during the Middle Ages. Individual travellers such as Marco Polo journeyed across Arabia and as far east as China. But no European ship penetrated the Indian Ocean until the first Portuguese caravels rounded the Cape of Good Hope in their search for spices and the mysterious realms of Prester John.

When Vasco da Gama led the first fleet to India in 1498, he must have known that there was a large island opposite Mozambique known to the Arabs as the Island of the Moon, but he kept close to the East African coast on both the outward and return journeys. The second Portuguese fleet which left for India in 1499 intended to follow the same route. However, near the Cape the fleet was scattered by a tremendous storm which sank four of the ships. A fifth ship, commanded by Diogo Dias, was driven round the Cape and far to the east. When the storm abated Diogo sailed to the north until on August 10, 1500, he made a landfall which he assumed to be the coast of Mozambique. Only when the land ended in the north did he realise that he had come across a large island, which he named São Lourenço after the saint on whose feast day the island had been sighted. When the news was brought back to Portugal by the returning fleet it was assumed that the island was the Madagascar of Marco Polo, and as early as 1502 it appeared on a Portuguese map with the name of Madagascar. But sailors continued to refer to it as St Lawrence's Island and it was not until well into the seventeenth century that the name Madagascar came into general use.

The early voyages to India convinced the Portuguese that in order to take over the spice trade of the Indian Ocean they would have to eliminate their Arab competitors by force. As part of this process Tristan da Cunha in 1506 and Alfonso d'Albuquerque in 1507 attacked and destroyed Arab trading settlements on the northwest coast of Madagascar. During the following year various sporadic attempts were made to explore the coasts of the island with a view to establishing a trading settlement or at least a supply station on the route to the Indies. But it soon became apparent that the island had nothing to offer which would justify any diversion of effort from India and the Spice Islands. There was little sign of indigenous gold, silver or precious stones and not much in the way of spices: an encouraging heap of cloves in one port turned out to be the cargo saved from a shipwrecked Javanese junk. The uncertain temper of the inhabitants discouraged permanent settlement; and the idea of using Madagascar as a regular staging post was soon abandoned in favour of the Portuguese settlements on the African mainland.

During this period a fair number of Portuguese sailors were shipwrecked on the coasts of Madagascar, which are surrounded by reefs and are particularly dangerous during the cyclone season. In 1527 some 600 men were cast ashore on the southwest coast. Most of them probably died of disease or were killed by the inhabitants. One party may have penetrated the interior and sought refuge in the fantastic ruiniform limestone rocks of the Isalo massif, where a cave is still known as *la grotte des portugais*. Another group of about seventy is known to have reached the southeast where they built a stone fort on an islet in Ranofotsy Bay, to the west of Fort Dauphin. But the local Malagasy attacked them during a feast to celebrate the completion of the fort (the ruins of which can still be seen) and massacred all but eight. The survivors managed to hold out in the besieged fort until they were picked up by a passing ship. Elsewhere small groups of shipwrecked Portuguese appear to have integrated with the local population. The important journeys round the coast of Madagascar by the Jesuit Father Luis Mariano between 1613 and 1619 were undertaken partly to obtain news of these shipwrecked survivors; and also to carry out a more thorough exploration with a view to establishing Christian missions. But Mariano and his fellow-missionaries failed to persuade the Malagasy to believe in Hell and he eventually departed, convinced that the inhabitants would never be converted to Christianity. His departure marked the end of Portuguese involvement in the island, of which virtually the only trace remaining is the name of Diego Suarez, the magnificent natural harbour at the north end of the island.

The early Portuguese explorers were soon followed by French sailors from Dieppe. Many of these were pirates attacking Portuguese ships on their way home. A few more legitimate trading expeditions to the East Indies took place, notably two under the leadership of Jean Parmentier who called at Madagascar in 1527 and again in 1529. It was on the latter occasion that the first native of Britain set foot on the shores of Madagascar. He was a Scotsman, known to his shipmates as Jacques l'Ecossais – no doubt he was christened James. On July 26, 1529 the two ships of the expedition anchored at the mouth of the Manambolo river on the west coast of Madagascar. James volunteered along with a certain Vassé to go ashore. They were given a friendly reception by the Malagasy, and on the next day the crews traded some hats, buckram and paternosters in return for a goat and some fruit before the captains decided to sail further north to find a more suitable anchorage.

On the following day the ships anchored opposite what appeared to be a better landing-place and two boats were sent ashore with merchandise for barter. The crews were warned to take no risks but, encouraged by their friendly reception on the previous days, they carelessly left their weapons in the boats. The Malagasy indicated by signs that they would take them to a place where ginger, gold and silver could be found. James and Vassé and a third man called Bréant, went off with them. But they had hardly got out of sight when the others heard James give a great cry and then saw Vassé and Bréant running back pursued by men brandishing spears. Vassé and Bréant were overtaken and killed and the others pursued to the water's edge. On the next day a strong party was sent ashore to bury the dead, and found James' body riddled with spear wounds; but they again had to retreat hastily in the face of further attacks by Malagasy spearsmen. The ships sailed away after naming a nearby point Cape Treachery.[2]

Shortly afterwards King Francis I, in serious financial embarrassment, secured the cancellation of substantial debts to the king of Portugal in return for a decree forbidding his subjects to visit any of the lands claimed by the Portuguese. The interdict appears to have been lifted in 1547 for a voyage to India by Jean Fonteneau who called in briefly at Madagascar. But this was the last French voyage into the Indian Ocean for over half a century.

The English came rather late on the scene. They were as keen as any nation to share in the riches of the East but their geographical position gave them a special interest in the possibility of a northwest passage to India around the north of Canada. The fruitless search for this passage occupied much of the energies of their best navigators, while the freebooting element found consolation in pillaging the Caribbean possessions of the arch-enemy, Philip II of Spain. It was not until 1580 that the first English ship appeared in the Indian Ocean and it came not round the Cape of Good Hope but westward from Indonesia. It was of course Francis Drake's *Golden Hind* completing his circumnavigation with his holds full of Spanish treasure and East Indian spices. His achievement was repeated eight years later by Thomas Cavendish in a voyage which is now almost forgotten. Neither Drake nor Cavendish dallied in the Indian Ocean. From the East Indies they steered southwest and then west to pass well to the south of Madagascar on their way home round the Cape. But their voyage led directly to English involvement in the Indian Ocean and to the first contacts with Madagascar. Their successful breach of the Portuguese monopoly (which since 1580 had passed to the Spanish crown) persuaded a group of English merchants to seek authority to trade with the East Indies by the sea-route round the Cape of Good Hope. But the first English voyage to the Indies was a disaster. Of three ships which set off in April 1591 one had to be sent back with sick men at an early stage and the flagship sank in a storm. The third ship, commanded by James Lancaster, limped home after more than three years with only a handful of its crew and a cargo of pepper, which hardly compensated for the loss of the flagship and more than three-quarters of the original crews.

English plans for trade in the Indian Ocean took some time to recover from this setback. Meanwhile the Dutch, excluded from the Lisbon spice market by their rebellion against Philip II, initiated in 1595 the voyages which were soon to win them a dominant position in the East Indies. The first Dutch expedition to Sumatra and Java, commanded by Cornelius van Houtman, called in at St Augustine's Bay in the southwest of Madagascar where Houtman appears to have treated the local people with great brutality. Although beset by almost as many disasters as Lancaster's, the voyage was judged sufficiently successful to justify the launching of two more expeditions in 1598 with Houtman in command of the second. With him travelled the first Englishman known to have landed in Madagascar (the first known because Portuguese ships in the sixteenth century often had Englishmen among their crews and some of these might well have set foot in Madagascar).

John Davis of Sandridge, Devon, was worthy of the distinction. Although lacking the glamour and reputation of his freebooting contemporaries – Drake, Hawkins, Frobisher and Raleigh – he was perhaps the most skilful English seaman of his time, the author of several highly regarded books on navigation. When news of the plans for further Dutch voyages to the East Indies became known in London, the Earl of Essex suggested that Davis should offer himself as pilot with a view to picking up information which could be useful to future English voyages. Such was his reputation that the Dutch were glad to accept him. Accordingly when Houtman's second fleet anchored in St Augustine's Bay in February 1599 Davis was a member of the party sent ashore to barter for provisions. But the Malagasy, remembering Houtman's brutal behaviour on the previous journey, fled into the bush with their livestock. After a week the Dutch managed to buy one cow and a little milk; but another month's stay produced nothing more in the way of provisions. They left hungry and in ill-humour, giving the bay the name Bay of Hunger.

Back in London the successful Dutch voyages revived the cupidity and optimism of the merchant adventurers. In February 1601 the newly formed East India Company despatched a fleet of four large and powerfully-armed vessels on its first trading venture. John Davis of Sandridge[3] was the obvious choice as chief pilot and the commander was the surviving captain from the first expedition, James Lancaster. After calling at the Cape of Good Hope Lancaster, who was making for Sumatra, intended to proceed to Mauritius. But the steady easterly trade winds made progress difficult, and with scurvy increasing among the crew he decided to make for the northeast coast of Madagascar to replenish his stock of oranges and lemons.[4]

The fleet anchored off St Mary's Island where they were able to obtain oranges and lemons, but little else. A great storm blew the three ships from their moorings and the fleet sought more sheltered waters in the Bay of Antongil where they dropped anchor on Christmas Day 1601. During a stay of some ten weeks they bought "Fifteen and a quarter tunnes of rice, fortie or fiftie bushels of their peese and beanes, great store of oranges, limons and plantans, and eight beeves (oxen) with many hennes"[5] in return for their manufactured articles, mainly beads which were highly prized by the Malagasy. There were no signs of hostility; the Malagasy were by now accustomed to trading with European ships and the main problem was their skill in playing one buyer off against another to force up the price of their produce. Lancaster found it necessary to fix in beads the price of the various items of local produce which were offered for sale. Scurvy diminished with the availability of fresh fruit in the Bay, but some sixteen officers and men died of the flux (dysentery) which was attributed to the water which they drank.

These casualties were slight compared with those of a Dutch fleet of five ships, which had rested in the Bay two months earlier. They had left behind an inscription on a stone recording the deaths of nearly two hundred sailors during their stay. Cornelius van Houtman, who lost 122 men during his first visit to St Augustine's Bay, had already dubbed Madagascar *Coemiterium Batavorum* – the graveyard of the Dutch. Small wonder that the Dutch tended to avoid Madagascar and preferred to make Mauritius their staging-point. This beautiful and healthy island had been discovered by the Portuguese a century earlier. But it was still uninhabited when the second Dutch expedition to the East Indies stopped there in September 1598 and took possession of the island for Holland, naming it Mauritius after Maurice, the Prince of Orange.

The second English expedition missed Madagascar and called in at the Comoros. The third East India fleet put in at St Augustine's Bay in 1607. Thereafter expeditions to the East became almost annual affairs. At first they found calls at Madagascar most convenient for reprovisioning, usually at St Augustine on the way out to the East and less frequently at Antongil Bay on the return journey. Later they came to prefer the Comoros, especially during the heyday of the pirates around Madagascar. But for two centuries a call at either Madagascar or the Comoros was almost obligatory for British ships until Britain acquired Cape Colony and Mauritius during the Napoleonic Wars.

In time the Malagasy became accustomed to these visits and a regular trading pattern developed. But in the early years the British ships could never be sure of their reception. The experience of one captain, Richard Rowles, was particularly unfortunate. At the beginning of 1609 he became separated from the main East India fleet and called at St Augustine's Bay, where two of his crew were killed and one merchant captured by hostile Malagasy. He then made for the Comoros but contrary winds compelled him to put in at a bay in northwest Madagascar. Here the local king appeared to be friendly and Captain Rowles with five others went ashore to visit him. But as soon as they landed they were surrounded and carried off by force. The crew of the sloop rowed for their lives, pursued by Malagasy canoes which attacked the main ship with arrows and javelins and had to be driven off by cannon-fire which sank seven canoes. Samuel Bradshaw, who assumed command, waited for two weeks in the hope of freeing the prisoners. But a further attack by canoes and the sudden death of seven sailors, possibly from poisoned arrows, led him to abandon hope. Before leaving he moved the ship imperceptibly towards the shore until he was within cannon-range, when he delivered a broadside which littered the ground with corpses. Captain Rowles and the other prisoners were never heard of again and were presumably killed. Several years later the missionary–explorer Luis Mariano heard that the king had killed the captain and several sailors of a British ship because the ship had carried off his son. Perhaps Rowles paid the penalty for the misdeeds of someone else.

No doubt there was good cause for suspicion on both sides. For a number of years after British ships had been calling regularly at St Augustine the Malagasy tended to flee into the bush as soon as they came in sight. Only when they were persuaded of the visitors' good intentions would they return and begin trading. They appeared to be well supplied with spears and daggers and were not interested in iron as a trading commodity. At first they sold their produce only for silver, sheep costing twelve pence and oxen, the meat of which was reported to be excellent, between two and five shillings a head. Later they developed a special taste for red cornelian beads from India. In 1638 Peter Mundy noted that in St Augustine seven or eight of these beads would buy a good bullock and nine or ten when they were dear – "and nothing butt the said beades will goe for beeves. As for sheepe, hennes, fish, milke, oranges, etc, they may bee had for bigge brasse wyre... to hang in their eares, about their neckes and armes."[6]

Impressions of Madagascar recorded during these early voyages varied considerably. Some were soured by the hostile attitude or "treachery" of the local people. Others were disillusioned by the dangers of fever and dysentery and the uncertain availability of provisions. Those who called during the cooler, dry months of the southern winter usually had happier memories. And a number were favourably impressed by the physique of the Malagasy. Sir Thomas Herbert, who called at St Augustine in 1626, noted that:

"The people are generally strong, couragious and proper; the male sort, from their infancy practising the rude postures of Mars

... they are black, at no time shading their bodies from the parching sunne, rather delight to rub and annoint all over with grease and tallow, proud to see their flesh shine, the stinck never offending them ... bigamy is tolerated; they affect copulation very early, the youth scarce knowing 12, the maiden 10 yeeres in the world the name of Virginity."[7]

Two influential accounts, which were later published, were written by employees of the East India Company who visited St Augustine's Bay on the same voyage from June to September in 1630. Even allowing for the advantage of the cool season it is difficult to account rationally for the extravagance of their praise. Walter Hamond, a surgeon, published two pamphlets whose titles give a good indication of their content: *A Paradox proving that the inhabitants of the isle called Madagascar or St Laurence (in Temporall things) are the happiest People in the World;* and *Madagascar, the Richest and most fruitful island in the World.* Richard Boothby, a merchant, gave a glowing account of the wealth and resources of the island, marred only by frequent indications that it was based largely on hearsay.

As to the climate Boothby stated that throughout the three or four winter months that he was at St Augustine he was able to wear a suit of English cloth without discomfort; and that during this period not one of the ships' companies of 460 men died and there were not even any cases of sickness. Improbable but not impossible in an unusually cool winter – and Hamond's account confirms the absence of sickness. Boothby proceeded logically to advocate the establishment of a "plantation" or colony which could not only exploit the wealth of the island – "the chiefest paradise this day upon earth" – but from its strategic position dominate the whole East Indies trade.

Was this mere wishful thinking or was Boothby deliberately deceiving his readers and listeners (we know that he was propounding his views in London and Whitehall for a number of years before his pamphlet was published in 1646)? In fact he had a motive for exaggerating the attractions of Madagascar. He was nursing a grievance against the East India Company which he pursued over thirteen years by litigation and petition to Parliament. One must suspect that his aim was at least partly to encourage potential competitors to break the East India Company's monopoly and take away their trade. But whatever the motive Boothby, Hamond and other advocates of the Madagascar plantation found many listeners eager to be convinced.

Chapter 5

The dream of Madagascar

Both in Whitehall and in the City of London the climate was favourable for new ventures. Charles I had embarked on his prolonged period of personal rule without Parliament and was constantly seeking new sources of funds, but he was also casting around for more legitimate enterprises to supplement the rather disappointing revenue accruing to the Crown from the operations of the East India Company.

The Company had enjoyed mixed fortunes during its early years. When good cargoes were brought back profits were most gratifying. But at times heavy losses had been sustained from storm and shipwreck and also at the hands of their competitors. The Company was criticised for excessive caution and lack of vision in exploiting its charter. Its reluctance to sink capital in permanent establishments in the East was contrasted unfavourably with the Portuguese and Dutch practice of building forts and trading stations which gave them a considerable local advantage over the English. These arguments and the hope of greater royal profit persuaded the king in December 1635 to give his assent to the creation of a rival company to trade in the East. This was known as Courteen's Association from its leading member Sir William Courteen (who died in the following year and was succeeded by his son William, known as Squire Courteen to distinguish him from his father).

The new Association's first concern was to fit out a fleet to trade in the East. But the Royal Commission specifically referred to the East India Company's failure to establish forts and settlements and authorised the new Association "to settle factories and to plant colonies after the Dutch manner." From the outset a settlement in Madagascar was envisaged. King Charles was persuaded to lend his support and he nominated his own nephew, Prince Rupert, to lead the expedition and govern the settlement.

Prince Rupert was only seventeen at the time and his mother the exiled Queen Elizabeth of Bohemia (then living in The Hague) wrote to an old friend in London, Sir Thomas Roe, urging him to dissuade the prince from taking part in such a wild scheme. Rupert was not easily dissuaded. In the spring of 1637 he tried to raise funds to send a shipload of colonists to Madagascar under a Captain John Bond, who would prepare the way for Rupert to follow in the autumn. But funds were not forthcoming in sufficient quantity. The scheme collapsed and Sir Thomas Roe was able to write to Queen Elizabeth: "The dreame of Madagascar, I think, is vanished and the Squire must conquer his own island."

But the dream of Madagascar lingered in other minds. Two more schemes for a settlement in Madagascar to be led by Captain Bond were abandoned for lack of funds before the persuasive advocacy of Boothby and Hamond at last bore fruit. Despite the distractions of the Civil War, the project was now taken up vigorously by the Courteen Association. John Smart was appointed commander of the proposed settlement. One hundred and forty settlers, men, women and children, were collected and embarked on three of Courteen's outgoing fleet, the *Sun*, the *Hester* and the *James*, which sailed in August 1644.

The Bay of St Augustine had been chosen as the site for the colony. The expedition arrived there on March 3, 1645 and John Smart began energetically to organise the settlement. A fortified camp was constructed at Soalara on the south side of the bay, wheat and other crops were sown and contact established with the Malagasy with a view to trade. Looking to the future, Smart despatched the *Sun* on a voyage of exploration round the south and east coasts of the island. The captain was to call particularly at Sainte Luce in the southeast and Antongil Bay in the northeast. His instructions were to try to obtain land for another settlement, to enquire about minerals and products for trade and to seek exclusive trading concessions.

The *Sun* sailed in May (at the same time the *Hester* departed for the East) and returned in July with a discouraging report. The Dutch had already set up a fort and settlement at Antongil. The French were strongly established at Sainte Luce and at three other points on the east coast and had threatened hostile action if the English tried to trade with the Malagasy. In any case the trading prospects seemed poor, as a French ship had been on the east coast for over a year and its hold was only a third full. With hopes of trade or settlement on the east coast dashed, Smart sent the *James* northward along the west coast to purchase slaves, rice and other commodities to be traded in India for supplies for the colony; and to explore the possibilities of establishing a settlement at Assada (modern Nossi Be, "big island", more correctly spelt Nosy Be). The *Sun* was also despatched to India and Persia to seek a cargo for

England, or failing that supplies for the colony.

Supplies were desperately needed, for the colony was already in a bad way. Despite its natural beauty, St Augustine's Bay was a disastrous choice for a settlement. Its hinterland is one of the least hospitable parts of Madagascar. The climate is hot and arid and the thin covering of soil on a porous calcareous base supports only a dry thorny scrub with a few scattered baobabs. The settlers had arrived at the end of the short rainy season, so that their crops were planted at the wrong time and perished for lack of water; and what pasture there was for cattle soon dried up. There was no sign of the minerals they had been led to expect. The expedition had been badly fitted out and many necessaries forgotten. But above all they had failed to establish good relations with the local Malagasy. By a lamentable oversight they had not been provided with the cornelian beads which the Malagasy were accustomed to receive for their produce. And the Malagasy, who were usually friendly and willing to trade, understandably changed their attitude and became either non-cooperative or openly hostile when they realised that the visitors intended to settle and take some of their land.

In August 1645 a Courteen ship returning from India called in with a few supplies and gave Smart the opportunity to send a gloomy report to his principals.[2] The settlers had suffered every sort of privation and their numbers had been reduced by dysentery and fever. Only forty men were left fit to bear arms, the remainder being "old, ignorant, weake fellowes". As for the women, they were of "no other use but to destroy victuals" and he wished he could be rid of such "she-cattle". The inhabitants were "of soe base and falce a condition that they have not their fellowes in the whole world." The coastal people had refused to supply cattle, and when cattle were eventually obtained from further inland they were constantly being stolen.

Cattle stealing has always been, and still is, a major sport and a required proof of manhood in the south of Madagascar. But the faults were not all on one side. In November a local chief, Dian[3] Brindeth, offered to supply cattle to the settlers if they would fight for him against a hostile group threatening invasion. Apparently the settlers had earlier lent military support to this chief but he had not produced the cattle he had promised; on the contrary his followers had been active in stealing the settlers' cattle. Smart accordingly decided to teach them a lesson and at the same time obtain the cattle he needed. He agreed to give the required help and took his forty able-bodied men, well-armed, by sea to land near Dian Brindeth's village in the area of Tulear. The chief was delighted and next day came with three of his sons unsuspectingly into the

English camp. He was made drunk on liquor and abducted with his sons in the boats which returned to St Augustine's Bay, where they were eventually released in return for a ransom of 200 head of cattle. Smart reported that a complete reconciliation ensued but this seems doubtful, and the subsequent acts of "treachery" of which he complained had at least some excuse.

The relief thus afforded to the food situation proved to be only temporary. Two Courteen ships which had meanwhile arrived from England were found to be almost destitute of supplies, reducing the sorely-tried Smart to exasperated fury against his masters; and some of the meat had to be used to reprovision one of the ships for its onward journey to the east. By the end of the year the settlers had no food apart from the remaining cattle which were half-starved for want of pasture. Fever had increased with the onset of the rains and the supply of medicines was exhausted.

Over the following few months, the number of settlers declined from 100 to 63, mainly from sickness but also at the hands of the Malagasy, with whom relations had deteriorated to a state of open warfare. Only four days' rations of salt beef were left and the settlers were reduced to eating hides – "very good meat" according to Smart, "if well drest." It was clear that the settlement would have to be abandoned. A small stock of beads remained and Smart, who appears to have kept his health and energy, used this to buy a few more animals to be salted down for ships' provisions. The "many and well-built" settlers' houses were burned except for one which was left for the use of passing ships. The king's colours were left flying to mark the spot where letters were buried explaining what had happened. Then, full of joy at leaving "this most accursed place" the surviving settlers sailed away in the *Friendship* and a shallop on May 19, 1646[4].

After a short stay in the Comoros Smart ordered the party to re-embark for the Courteen station at Achin in Sumatra, but most of them, including all of the women, insisted on staying in the hope of being picked up by a ship returning to England. Only 23 settlers accompanied Smart to Achin where, after struggling with his customary zeal to put the factory in good order, he finally succumbed to dysentery and died, a worthy but unlucky pioneer. Those who remained at the Comoros were picked up shortly afterwards by an outward-bound ship which took them to India. Most were compelled by lack of means to stay there. Less than a dozen of the original 140 succeeded in returning to their native country. Among those who returned was one Powle Waldegrave. In 1649 he published a bitter denunciation of Boothby with a point by point refutation of Boothby's catalogue of the attractions of Madagascar.

He concluded: "I could not but endeavour to dissuade others from undergoing the miseries that will follow the persons of such as adventure themselves for Madagascar ... from which place, God divert the residence and adventures of all good men."[5]

This diatribe came too late to prevent the launching of another colonisation scheme. Early in 1649 a party of settlers under Colonel Robert Hunt had sailed in the Assada Merchant to establish a plantation on the island of Assada or Nosy Be. In a pamphlet which was not published until over a year later, Colonel Hunt explained that his aim in settling a colony there was at least as much to spread the Gospel and instruct the heathen as it was to increase trade. He attributed the failure of the earlier attempt largely to the poor choice of St Augustine's Bay as the location. As to the island of Assada; "I do believe, by God's blessing, that not any part of the World is more advantagious for a Plantation. being every way as well for pleasure as well as profit, in my estimation".[6]

Hunt's estimation was much nearer the mark than Boothby's. An island about the size of the Isle of Wight a few miles off the northwest coast of Madagascar, Nosy Be is a delectable spot, a true earthly paradise. Forest-clad volcanic hills sweep down to white sandy beaches fringed with coconut palms. Clear turquoise seas where rainbow-coloured fish disport in the fantasy-world of coral reefs provide an additional attraction. The fertile volcanic soil and equable tropical climate favour the growth of a wide range of products. Today the island exploits profitably sugarcane, cloves, pepper and the fantastically shaped ylang-ylang tree whose headily fragrant flowers are an important ingredient of many French perfumes. But despite the better choice of location the second attempt at colonisation fared no better than the first; and by the time Colonel Hunt's pamphlet appeared it was already posthumous.

Two ships, the *Bonito* and the *Lioness*, were despatched with settlers to reinforce Hunt's first party. But as they approached Nosy Be at the end of June 1650 they encountered a small boat containing the only survivors of the expedition. Apparently Colonel Hunt had decided to settle not on the main island but on a small island nearby which they called Goat's Island (probably Nosy Komba). But the inhabitants were hostile and fever rampant, and the Colonel and many others had died. The remainder had sailed on the *Assada Merchant* for the mainland of Madagascar, where the master, the purser and nine others were enticed ashore with promise of ambergris and murdered. The few left put to sea and were lucky to meet the *Bonito* and the *Lioness*. After a conference it was decided to attempt a further settlement on the main island of Nosy Be and the new settlers under the command of one of the survivors Major Hartley were landed there with six months' supplies. But the inhabitants maintained their hostile attitude and cut off any who strayed into the woods. Others fell victim to "the contagion of the place". The remainder decided after only seven weeks to abandon the settlement and sail for Surat. During the next year several more ships turned up with more would-be settlers but they also proceeded to India when they found the settlement abandoned.

Thus ended ignominiously the plans for an English plantation in Madagascar. It is tempting to speculate whether with better planning and preparation, a better location and more vigorous support from home a more permanent English colony might have been established. But in the existing state of medical knowledge the prevalence of malaria and dysentery in all the coastal areas was a serious obstacle, and the survival of a colony in the face of the hostility of the inhabitants would have required a substantial armed force, entailing expenses which would have been difficult to justify when the limited resources of the island were set against the greater riches of India.

The timing as well as the location of the colonisation attempts was unfortunate. The middle of the seventeenth century saw the foundation of the Sakalava military empire which was to be the most powerful force in the island for nearly two centuries. The rulers were drawn from the Maroserana dynasty which appeared in southwest Madagascar around the middle of the sixteenth century. In the early part of the seventeenth century a prince of this dynasty called Andriamisara appears to have established himself on the banks of the Sakalava, a small tributary of the Mangoky river and the most likely of several origins suggested for the name subsequently given to the people of the west coast. According to one tradition he had first to vanquish his brother Andriamandresy who then migrated eastward with his followers to found the Antesaka clan on the southeast coast in the region of Vangaindrano. Around 1650 Andriamisara was succeeded by his son Andriandahifotsy ("Prince White Man"). Lahifotsy, to use the more convenient shorter form of his name, conquered within a relatively short period of time a vast territory, stretching some 400 miles (640 km) north from the Fiherenana river, which became known as the Menabe kingdom of the Sakalava. According to one tradition the name Menabe, meaning "big red", derives from Lahifotsy's first victory against his northern neighbours. The night before the battle his troops dug a large ditch between the two camps, put in a huge red-coloured ox and covered it up with branches and earth. The animal uttered fearful bellowings which, coming from under the ground, appeared supernatural to the enemy who fled in terror.

But the name might more simply and plausibly derive from the symbolism of the colour red which in Madagascar was generally associated with royalty.

By the 1660s Lahifotsy's reputation was already well known to the French settlement at Fort Dauphin on the other side of the island. In 1669 he sent an embassy to Fort Dauphin with a view to preventing French aid to chiefs south of the Onilahy river, which would have forced him to abandon conquests in the north in order to protect his southern flank. Two years later a French trader from Fort Dauphin visited Lahifotsy to buy cattle and to ensure continued good relations with him. He found him with an army of 12,000 men (some of them would already be armed with flintlocks) and a vast herd of some 126,000 cattle. There seems little doubt that, even if the English colony at St Augustine had been able to establish itself more firmly, a warrior prince of this stature would never have allowed a foreign settlement to flourish on his doorstep.

Little is known of the Dutch fort which the *Sun* found at Antongil in 1645 except that it was abandoned after only a few months. Here as elsewhere on the east coast, there was abundance of water and ample food supplies – rice, yams, taro, sugarcane, poultry and a great variety of fruit. The local population, divided into numerous small clans, was by now accustomed to visits from Europeans and happy to trade with them; and in 1642 the king of Antongil had signed a treaty with the Dutch submitting himself and his people to the authority of the States-General of the Netherlands. One can only assume that the area lived up to its reputation as a graveyard for Europeans and that the Dutch decided that a permanent establishment was not necessary for their main purpose, which was to obtain supplies and slaves for their colony in Mauritius.

The French settlement in the southeast of the island proved to be more durable. In 1642 Richelieu granted a monopoly charter to a *Societé Française de l'Orient*, which immediately despatched a small party, under the command of Sieur Pronis, to Madagascar to establish a settlement there. In September 1642 Pronis hoisted the *fleur de lys* at Sainte Luce, near the southern end of the east coast, and laid claim to the whole island on behalf of His Most Christian Majesty. He sent agents to other points on the east coast to investigate possibilities of trade. But losses from fever and hostile inhabitants were so heavy that at the end of 1643 he abandoned Sainte Luce in favour of a narrow peninsula further south which appeared both more defensible and healthier. A fort was constructed and named Fort Dauphin in honour of the infant prince who had in fact already succeeded to the throne as Louis XIV.

The new site was in many respects well chosen. Apart from its advantages for defence it was one of the healthiest, or at any rate least unhealthy, spots on the whole coastline, sufficiently far south to enjoy cool weather, and exposed to winds from both east and south. It is also one of the loveliest places on an island with many beauties. To the east of the fort a wide bay, providing a shallow anchorage and some protection from the winds, terminates in a long spit of land crowned with four shapely hills. To the west lies another fine bay, useless for shipping because of reefs but with a splendid beach. To the north the great mountain range which runs down the east coast terminates in the Pic Saint Louis which rises over 1700 ft (530m) to preside with sombre dignity over the whole idyllic setting. The mountains form not only a watershed but also a climatic division between the tropical humidity of the east coast and the drier climate of the Mandrare basin so that a wide variety of cultivation is possible within a short distance of Fort Dauphin.

The local people, the Antanosy, were at first well-disposed. They already had some experience of European visitors and some of them were light-skinned descendants of shipwrecked Portuguese sailors. The chief ruler, Dian Ramaka (Andriandramaka in modern spelling), spoke fluent Portuguese, having spent three years of his boyhood in Goa, where he was baptised a Christian. On returning to Anosy his Christian faith lapsed under pressure from his father but he remained very friendly to Europeans.

The new colony started with high hopes. Trading relations were established with the Antanosy and with various points on the east coast; and ebony, hides and beeswax were exported to France. Pronis' deputy made an exploratory journey through the territory of the Antandroy, the Mahafaly, the Masikoro and the Bara and returned with thousands of cattle. Good relations with Dian Ramaka were cemented when Pronis married the chief's niece, with whom he had been living for some time.

Unfortunately the marriage was less well viewed by the colonists. As a Huguenot, Pronis was already the object of some hostility from the Catholic majority. They now resented in particular the expenditure of the Company's stores on the bride's relatives who, in accordance with a custom widespread in non-Western societies, moved in to share her good fortune. In 1646 the settlers mutinied. Pronis was clapped in irons where he remained for six months until released by the captain of a Company ship which arrived with new settlers. Although an amnesty was promised, Pronis took his revenge on twelve of the mutineers by exiling them to the uninhabited island of Bourbon (modern Réunion). He also arranged the killing of a local chief who had had relations with his wife during his imprisonment. Less excusable than this *crime passionnel* was his reward to the ship's captain who freed him: 73 Malagasy who had been enticed to the fort with promises of meat were seized and handed over to him as slaves to be sold to the Dutch in Mauritius. From this time, fear and hostility replaced the friendly relations which the settlers had enjoyed with Dian Ramaka and the Antanosy.

When news of these troubles reached Paris, the Company decided to send one of their leading members, Etienne de Flacourt, to investigate and restore the situation. He arrived at Fort Dauphin in December 1648 with forty-six new settlers and two missionaries. His first act was to send Pronis' wife back to her people, but he treated Pronis fairly leniently, retaining him as an assistant until an opportunity came to send him back to France. The situation of the colony proved however to be intractable. Trade had dwindled away while the settlers had squabbled among themselves. With France in a state of civil war, the Company was in no position to send trading goods or more settlers, and for five whole years no Company ship called. Without reinforcements the number of settlers declined steadily from fever, while isolated individuals or even groups were attacked and killed by the Antanosy. Flacourt was obliged to mount punitive expeditions and to indulge in cattle raiding which, in the absence of trading goods, was essential for feeding the settlers. Their former friend, Dian Ramaka, launched a major attack on the fort with thousands of men who were driven off only by cannon-fire. Flacourt retaliated with an assault on Dian Ramaka's village in which the village was completely destroyed and Dian Ramaka himself killed. Reduced to a policy of military domination Flacourt secured the submission of Ramaka's son and other chiefs, but in the absence of any support from France the colony's position became desperate.

Finally in 1654 a ship appeared, but it brought no supplies or settlers, only two missionaries and Pronis; and it was sent not by the Company but by the Duc de la Meilleraye, who appeared to have founded a new company on the ruins of the old. In February 1655 Flacourt left the colony to return to France, leaving Pronis once again in charge. Flacourt spent the next few years in litigation over the assets of the Company and in writing two remarkable books: a History of the Great Island of Madagascar containing a detailed description of the country, its flora and fauna, the inhabitants and their customs and beliefs; and a Relation of events within the colony together with a statement of the reasons for its failure. But an annex to the second edition of the Relation, listing the advantages of establishing colonies in Madagascar, showed that he had not lost hope. In 1660 he embarked again for Madagascar, but his ship was waylaid by Barbary corsairs and in the ensuing battle was blown up with the loss of nearly all on board, including Flacourt. Although his work at Fort Dauphin came to nothing, his reputation was assured by his books, especially his History which was for a century and a half the main fount of information about the island and is still a valuable source work for the historian.

Meanwhile the fortunes of the settlement had sunk to a new low. Shortly after Flacourt's departure the fort was destroyed by fire and Pronis died of fever. The brief governorship of his temporary successor was marked by robbery and violence on both sides culminating in the arrest and execution of Dian Ramaka's son and another chief after they had been piously baptised. In 1656 de la Meilleraye sent out a small fleet with reinforcements and a new governor, Champmargou. A competent military commander and a religious zealot, Champmargou proved incapable of conducting any policy other than war and repression and the colony was reduced to a beleaguered fort. The arrival in 1663 of eighty more settlers and a Lazarist missionary priest revived Champmargou's confidence and he unwisely encouraged the missionary in an attempt to convert Dian Manangue, the most important chief remaining in the area. Dian Manangue was not unsympathetic to the idea but was adamant in refusing to reduce the number of his wives. The missionary persisted and his excessive zeal led to his death after a confrontation during which he tore Manangue's *oly* (idol or talisman) from his neck and threw it on the fire. Champmargou led an expedition to avenge the missionary but found himself ambushed by 6,000 Malagasy. He was saved only by the intervention of La Case, a Frenchman who after quarrelling with Champmargou had married the daughter of a chief and become accepted as an important Malagasy prince himself. He now arrived on the scene with a force of his own men just in time to rescue Champmargou and ensure the survival of the colony for a little longer.

Little news of these melancholy events reached France, where Flacourt's books had revived interest in the colonisation of Madagascar. The young Louis XIV was looking for new worlds to conquer and on the death of de la Meilleraye his rights in Madagascar were ceded to the Crown. A royal charter was granted in 1664 to a new *Compagnie des Indes Orientales* which was sustained by much greater resources than the previous companies. Over the next few years the new Company sent out thousands of settlers and soldiers. Control was extended over a much wider area in the south, and trading posts were established or re-established at Sainte Marie and points on the east coast. A series of high-ranking governors came and went, with the durable Champmargou taking charge in between, but the colony fared no better than before. Fearful mortality from battle and disease kept the settlement dependent on regular reinforcements.

A lack of a clear policy and sheer incompetence in the colony's administration compounded the problems caused by native hostility, the climate and the isolation. The posts on the east coast had once more to be abandoned. After five years trading profits were so poor that the Company asked to be relieved of responsibility for Madagascar and henceforward concentrated its efforts on India. The Company's rights in Madagascar reverted to Louis XIV, who was reluctant to abandon the colony and sent out Admiral de la Haye to see what could be salvaged. He restored the local situation to some extent and appointed Champmargou again governor with La Case as his deputy. But on returning to the settlement in 1671 he advised the king that Fort Dauphin should be abandoned and he took away with him a large number of the colonists. Meanwhile both Champmargou and La Case had died. A residue of some 200 settlers was left under command of a Major La Bretèche, abandoned by their mother country and surrounded by a hostile population, which was in a state of anarchy after years of incessant raiding and warfare. But the event which finally sealed the fate of the colony was the arrival of a ship carrying fifteen young French girls.

Louis XIV had recruited these girls in an orphanage to be sent out as brides for the settlers on the island of Bourbon, which was now attracting his favour as a more suitable site for a colony. After a stay during which the ship's captain exploited the colonists' desperate need for supplies, the ship was wrecked on a shoal while leaving Fort Dauphin. The stranded girls, fearful of further dangers and privations, begged to be married to some of the settlers on the spot, and La Bretèche finally agreed. But this news was most unwelcome to the Malagasy women who had been living with the settlers and who now saw themselves being supplanted. With the fury of women scorned they turned against their lovers and betrayed them to the Malagasy warriors who were ever watchful for an opportunity to attack the settlement. On August 27, 1674 in the middle of the marriage festivities, half of the settlers were massacred. The remainder begged La Bretèche to abandon the colony, and a recently arrived ship provided the means of escape. So after spiking the fort's cannon and burning whatever stores could not be taken with them the survivors sailed away on September 9, 1674. Over thirty years of struggle and effort and the expenditure of thousands of lives thus ended in complete failure.

Yet the years were not entirely wasted. The Fort Dauphin adventure led directly to French occupation of Bourbon and later of Mauritius after this island was abandoned by the Dutch. This ensured continued French interest in Madagascar as an essential source of rice, beef and slaves for the settlers on Bourbon and Mauritius. The Mascarene islands acted as a base for a further attempt at a colony at Fort Dauphin in the eighteenth century and for more successful efforts to establish trading posts on the east coast. After the loss of Mauritius to the British, Bourbon (Réunion) remained the essential base for the pursuit of French ambitions in Madagascar; and links between the French communities in the two islands have always been very close. In the nineteenth century the French based their claims to a pre-eminent position in Madagascar on the "rights" established by Pronis in 1642. Although this claim appears somewhat absurd to modern eyes in view of the long periods when there was no official French presence on the island, there is nevertheless a direct line of descent from the pioneering work of Pronis and Flacourt to the French occupation and annexation of Madagascar two hundred and fifty years later.

Chapter 6

The shipwrecked sailor

The Fort Dauphin disaster ended official European attempts to colonise Madagascar for nearly a century. Contacts continued in coastal areas as ships of various nationalities, but mainly English, called in for supplies in the course of voyages to India and the East Indies. But the coasts of Madagascar, surrounded by shoals and reefs and beset by violent storms in the cyclone season, claimed many victims. And so over the years a fair number of seamen who survived the wrecks of their ships were cast ashore for varying periods of time. Many no doubt were killed or died of disease. The more fortunate were rescued by passing ships and a few of these recorded their experiences of life among the Malagasy.

One of the best-known of all accounts of shipwreck and survival is Madagascar, or Robert Drury's Journal, first published in 1729. This was for long regarded as the main source work on Madagascar in the English language, occupying a position similar to that enjoyed by Flacourt's History among works in French. Suspicions were however aroused when it was noticed that some of the descriptions of tribal customs in Drury's book were almost literal translations of similar passages in Flacourt's. Moreover Drury's publisher also published many of Defoe's works, while the narrative is interspersed with philosophical reflections of the kind to which the great Daniel was prone. Was this not therefore another fiction in the mould of Robinson Crusoe by the master himself or one of his collaborators or imitators?

Whether Drury himself wrote down an original draft or dictated his story to an "editor", it is clear that the organisation and much of the writing is the work of a professional writer, possibly Defoe himself. But there can be little doubt that the story is substantially true. Robert Drury certainly existed. Modern research[1] has unearthed documentary evidence supporting the main facts of his existence before and after the Madagascar adventure, his account of the voyage of the Degrave and the main events at the beginning and the end of his time in Madagascar. There can be no documentary evidence for the central period of his captivity among the

Antandroy and the Sakalava; but most authorities who know the region well[2] are convinced that the story could only have been recounted by someone who had spent a long time living in the area. While the background may be at times embroidered, the basic events of this remarkable adventure are narrated with a directness and simplicity which have the ring truth. A point in favour of authenticity is that there is no attempt to present Drury as a heroic figure. After an initial protest, he acquiesces in the degrading custom of licking his master's feet; he frequently gives way to tears of despair; and whenever there is any fighting in the offing he does his best to keep out of it. One of the most convincing features of the Journal is the unusual transliteration of the Malagasy names which appear in the text and of the Malagasy vocabulary which appears as an Appendix. This is just what one would expect from a Cockney with limited education and an imperfect ear for language, converting the often complex Malagasy names into the orthography of eighteenth-century English. Thus "matahotra" (fear) becomes "mertawhoutchs" or "mertorhocks", "Mahafaly" becomes "Merfaughla", and the river Onilahy is spelt "Oneghaloyhe"; while some of the chiefs and princes – Deaan Frukey, Deaan Tredaughe, Deaan Mevarrow and especially Deaan Woozington – seem to have strayed from the pages of a Trollope novel.

Robert Drury's story is worth recounting at length, not only for its own sake but for the unique picture it gives of life among the Antandroy and the Sakalava at the beginning of the eighteenth century. He was born in London in 1687. When he was only thirteen, he sailed to India on an East Indiaman, the *Degrave*, commanded by Captain William Younge. High mortality during a stay in India left the ship in charge of a second mate, who was the captain's son Nicholas Younge; while the fourth mate John Benbow[3], son of the famous admiral of the same name, was promoted to second mate. On the return journey the ship developed a serious leak, which required constant pumping. They put in at Mauritius and tried to find and repair the leak, but without success. They continued in the direction of the Cape of Good Hope, having taken on extra lascars to help with the pumping. But as they passed to the south of Madagascar the ship sank lower and lower in the water, despite the jettisoning of several guns and some of the heavy cargo; and the crew persuaded the young captain to put back to Madagascar.

Somewhere in the region of Cap Sainte Marie, the southernmost point of the island, the order was given to abandon ship and a hundred and sixty of the ship's company managed to reach the shore, either on a raft or by swimming. Their landing had been observed and several hundred Malagasy soon appeared. They killed an ox for the white men to eat and began looting the merchandise which drifted ashore as the ship broke up. The castaways' spirits rose momentarily when an Englishman called Sam appeared, but were quickly dashed when he recounted his own story. He had been cast ashore on this same spot a few months earlier together with two Scottish ships' captains, Captain Drummond and Captain Steward, and some others who had been marooned by pirates on the east coast and had been trying to get to St Augustine. The local king had made them welcome and treated them well but had made it clear that he would never let them go, as the presence of Europeans would greatly increase his prestige among neighbouring rulers. Sam feared that the new arrivals would likewise not be allowed to leave.

This was confirmed when the king, Deaan Crindo (modern spelling Andriankirindra), arrived next day with two hundred well-armed warriors and invited the survivors of the wreck to accompany him to his village capital. A three days' journey across burning sand and through thorny bush brought them to the village which was protected by an impenetrable barrier of closely planted bushes bristling with sharp thorns. Young Robin was one of a small group, including the officers, who were given quarters in the village, the remainder sleeping outside under trees. Two days later the officers led a desperate bid for freedom. During a morning call on the king they suddenly seized him, his wife and his nephew, Deaan Murnanzack, together with a number of firearms, and threatened to kill the king unless the whole English party was allowed to leave his domains. The king ordered his people to agree and the party set off in an eastward direction with their hostages in the middle.

Their aim was to reach the territory of King Samuel of Fort Dauphin, who was believed to be friendly to the English[4]. But this was some 80 miles (130 km) away, across a waterless, treeless plain offering no shelter from the burning sun; and many of the English party had no shoes, while some were already weak from sickness. During a nightmare journey of several days, hundreds of armed tribesmen followed closely and slaughtered any stragglers. In a series of negotiations the royal hostages were exchanged for three headmen and a few guns, but the warriors continued to follow and cut down the stragglers. The surviving Englishmen, enfeebled by the heat and their overpowering thirst, managed to cross the Mandrare river which was the boundary of King Samuel's country, but the way forward was barred by the tribesmen. They agreed to release the hostages in return for being allowed to continue on their way the next day. But during the night Captains Drummond and

Steward and a number of others including the mate Mr Benbow slipped away in the darkness hoping to fetch help from King Samuel. When this was discovered Robin and several other youths were seized and bound and all the others, starting with Captain Younge, were slaughtered. When the butchery was finished, Robin was handed over as a slave to the king's grandson and they marched rapidly back to their own territory. Hardly had they departed when 2,000 of King Samuel's men, alerted by Captain Drummond, appeared on the scene but alas too late for their rescue attempt.

So Robin Drury began his prolonged period of captivity. He was separated from the three other captive youths, of whom one later died, another was killed and the third managed to escape quite early. At first Robin was quite well treated by his young master, Deaan Mevarrow (probably Andriamivarotra), who was an important chief in his own right. His master's grandfather, Deaan Crindo, was "absolute lord of this country" but an almost constant state of warfare existed with neighbouring peoples and even between clans of the same ethnic group. The people among whom Robin now found himself were the Antandroy who for long enjoyed the reputation of being one of the most war-like and fiercely independent of the Malagasy peoples. They were never conquered by the Merina in the nineteenth century and it took the French colonial government nearly ten years to "pacify" the region. This did not prevent subsequent outbreaks of inter-communal warfare (the last war between the Antandroy and the Mahafaly took place in 1932), and the continuation of the national sport of cattle stealing. Nowadays they are normally peaceful but in other respects their way of life and customs have changed little since they were described by Drury. Their arid, spiny homeland provides no resources beyond cattle and a few sparse crops and many Antandroy have emigrated elsewhere in the island to find work. Despite their extreme poverty they retain a proud dignity, and their dances are renowned throughout Madagascar.

After a few months Robin Drury was put to work in the "plantations", where "Guinea corn, carravances[5] and potatoes" were grown. He was then put to look after his master's cattle, a job which was more to his liking as it involved the companionship of other young cowherds. From them he learned the local country lore, such as how to extract honey and wax from a hive without being stung or how to dig for *tandraka* (tenrec), the hedgehog-like creature which constructed intricate burrows below ground. On the whole, an agreeable existence for a young man, marred only by the violent temper of Robin's master, Deaan Mevarrow. On at least three occasions he flew into a rage with Robin because of his lack of subservience or refusal to follow local religious customs, and was prevented from killing him only by the intervention of his brother Deaan Sambo (Andriantsambo), who advised Robin to conform. He did so sufficiently to acquire over the years a position of trust and the useful post of royal butcher. By custom only members of the royal family were permitted to slaughter cattle on the numerous ceremonial occasions – funeral, circumcision or wedding, etc – when it was necessary to make a sacrifice.[6] This was a tiresome chore for the royalty and often an inconvenience for villagers if they lived at some distance from any member of the royal family. However, a white man was regarded as an acceptable substitute, perhaps because, as Drury noted,[7] the Antandroy royal family had paler skins and longer, straighter hair than the common people. So Robin was given the job, which carried a certain prestige and a useful fee in the shape of a sizeable piece of beef on each occasion.

Drury appears to have spent about ten years with the Antandroy, and was able to witness and later take part in the endemic intertribal and interclan fighting which was usually provoked by cattle raiding. Fairly soon after his captivity, probably in 1704, the king of the Mahafaly people to the west, Deaan Woozington (Andriankosintany) invaded the Androy in retaliation for raids on his villages. In this situation, all the Antandroy clans rallied behind their chief Deaan Crindo, in the defence of his capital. Woozington stormed the town successfully and captured Crindo's wife and daughter, but peace was soon made and the wife and daughter given back.

Some years later, around 1709, interclan fighting broke out among the Antandroy. It appears to have started when Deaan Mevarrow, Drury's master, stole three cattle belonging to one of his uncles (i.e. sons of Crindo) Deaan Frukey (Andriampiroky). A series of raids and counter-raids left Frukey and another uncle who joined him in possession of nearly all Mevarrow's cattle, while Mevarrow had captured many of their wives, children and slaves. Deaan Crindo then intervened to reconcile his sons and grandson. But his proposal to exchange the stolen cattle for the human captives was not accepted by Mevarrow because his uncles refused to make up the numbers of cattle they had killed. Crindo attempted to impose his decision by force but had to break off when he heard that his territory had been raided in his absence by his nephew, Murnanzack (who had shared his brief period as a hostage of the shipwrecked English seamen). Murnanzack (Andriamananjaka), as the son of Crindo's elder brother, believed that Crindo had usurped his own rights to the paramount position and profited from the dis-

The shipwrecked sailor

sensions within Crindo's family to assert his claims.

There followed a confusing civil war of raid and counter-raid in which Mevarrow and his brother Sambo allied themselves with Murnanzack and his three brothers against Crindo and his sons. Peace was eventually established by mediation from outside. The king of Fiherenana, the area north of St Augustine, had decided to make war on the common enemy Deaan Woozington and sent an ambassador, Ry-Nanno (possibly Ranaona), on a successful mission to reconcile the Antandroy and seek their alliance. When calling on Deaan Mevarrow, Ry-Nanno noticed Drury and spoke to him in broken English, which he had learned from English sailors calling at St Augustine. He commented on how badly he was being treated and said that if he could make his way to Fiherenana, which was some twenty days' journey away, he would be well looked after and put on the first English ship calling at St Augustine. Robin's hopes were thus raised but were dashed again when Ry-Nanno offered to buy him but Mevarrow refused to sell at any price. However an event soon afterwards afforded him some measure of consolation and distraction from his troubles.

With peace restored among the Antandroy, Mevarrow took the opportunity to settle an old score with a petty chief to the north who had stolen some of his cattle and slaves. Robin took part in the punitive raid and captured the chief's wife and sixteen-year-old daughter. It was the custom to kill any adult male enemies caught in battle but to treat captured women and children as slaves. Drury, who by now must have been about twenty-five years old, presented the wife to Mevarrow but kept the daughter for himself. When they returned home, Robin improvised a private wedding ceremony, and he clearly became very fond of his wife: "She was very handsome, of a middle stature, straight, and exactly shaped, her features regular, and her skin soft, fine and delicate, as any ladies in Europe. Indeed, all the women are soft and fine-skinned, who are of any rank, and carefully brought up ... I will not pretend to prefer them to our Europeans: and yet I can't help confessing it is with pleasure I think of mine, and with concern I remember our parting; for as to their fidelity, behaviour to their husbands, good-natured dispositions and agreeable conversation, so far as their little knowledge extends, I think the Europeans must not compare with them."[8]

For an unspecified, but apparently not very long, period of time Robin enjoyed the pleasures and comforts of marriage. But the end of the idyll was foreshadowed when Deaan Mevarrow consulted an *ombiasy* who foretold Robin's departure to the north and ultimate return to England. To prevent this happening, the *ombiasy* cast a spell: Robin was compelled to eat a dish of carravances and scrapings of various roots which were supposed to make him ill if he tried to escape. From this moment Robin resolved that he must escape as a matter of urgency, since if he were to fall ill Deaan Mevarrow would think it was the result of the spell and might kill him for trying to escape.

A friendly captive from the north advised him to seek refuge with Deaan Afferrer (Andrianafarana), a brother of Murnanzack who lived in the Angavo hills some sixty miles (95 km) to the north, and await the arrival of warriors from Fiherenana who could take him back to St Augustine. Robin tried to persuade his wife to come with him, but she was fearful of the *ombiasy*'s spell. So reluctantly he said goodbye to her and, setting off in the early morning, reached Afferrer's country the same night. Afferrer agreed to harbour him and promised to treat him as a white man should be treated, that is as an honoured guest rather than a slave. For the next six months Robin lived in relative comfort with the principal duty of accompanying Afferrer on hunting trips. However Afferrer made it clear that he was not prepared to release him.

Meanwhile news came that the Fiherenana were now ready for the promised war with the Mahafaly. The Antandroy warriors assembled in the west of their territory under Deaan Crindo. Robin went along with Afferrer, very apprehensive about meeting his old master, but Mevarrow was kept at home with an attack of yaws. When they joined forces with the Fiherenana he told the latter's commander Deaan Trongha (Andriamitranga) that when the fighting was over he intended to escape and follow him back to his country. The combined force then invaded the Mahafaly country. Woozington retreated before them but eventually attacked and was defeated with heavy losses. The allies then spent some time plundering and capturing cattle before dispersing to their own lands. Deaan Afferrer, suspecting Robin's design, had him watched closely by two men to prevent his running away. But after two months this precaution was relaxed and his opportunity came when Afferrer took him on a hunting trip. When the rest of the party were sleeping off their gorging of the meat of wild cattle, Robin slipped away. By travelling fast all night and the following day he soon put the possibility of pursuit well behind him. Following directions given to him by Ry-Nanno he went north till he came to some mountains and then struck northwest towards the Onilahy river.

Twenty-three days after his escape he crossed the Onilahy river on an improvised raft. A few more days travelling westward along the north bank of the river brought him to his friend Deaan

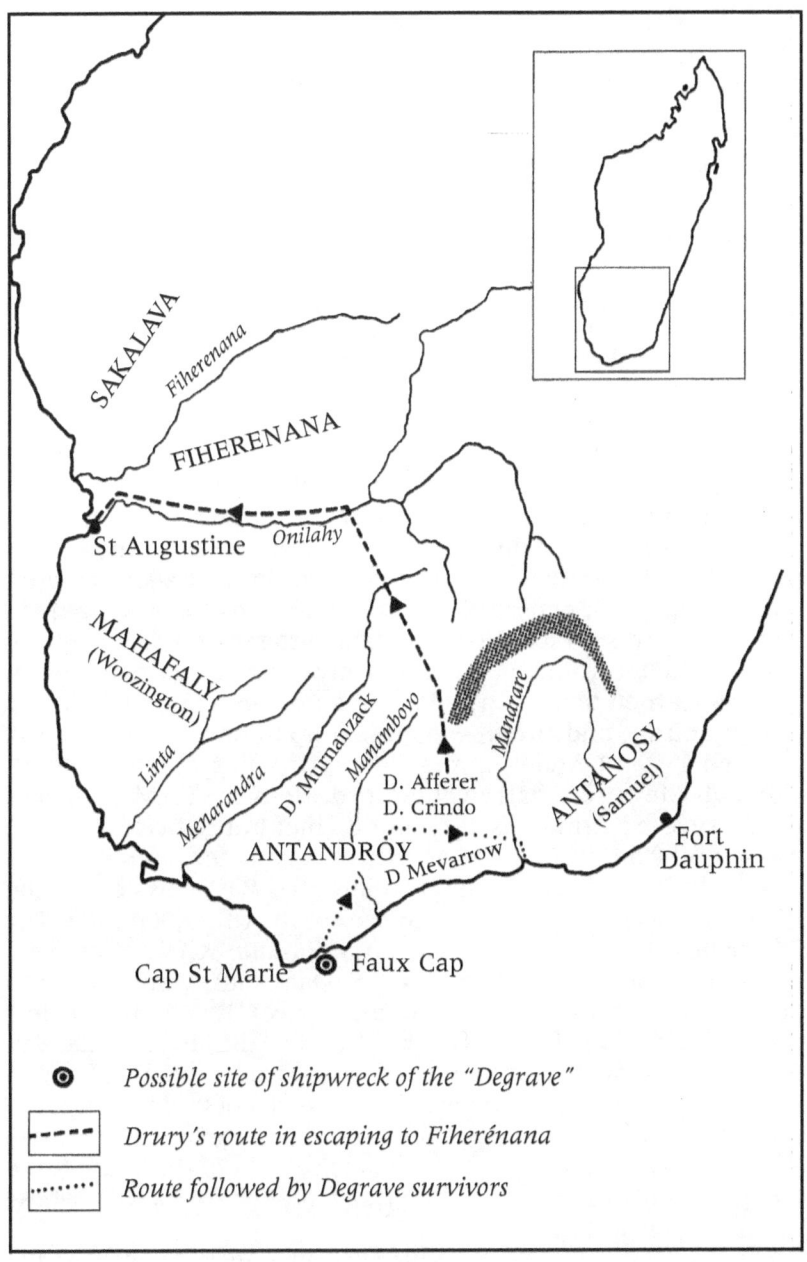

Drury among the Antandroy

Trongha who welcomed him warmly but gave him a gloomy picture of the state of the Fiherenana people. With Woozington and the Mahafaly a constant threat in the south, they were increasingly under attack from the powerful Sakalava, king to the north, Rer Trimmonongarevo (Ratsimonongarivo). The area was so impoverished by constant fighting that European ships now hardly ever called to trade.

This was depressing news for Robin, and indeed no ship came during the time he lived as Deaan Trongha's guest. He now learned with apprehension that a further campaign was being planned against the Mahafaly, involving another journey to Androy to link up with their allies. Drury hoped to be left behind, but a spiteful *ombiasy* prophesied that disaster would ensue unless the warriors were led by someone born outside Madagascar (Drury was the only candidate). So reluctantly he had to retrace his steps and face meetings with his two former masters. Afferer bore no ill will, but Mevarrow was more hostile and pressed Drury to return with him, mentioning that his wife had been inconsolable since his escape. Drury thought it expedient to promise to return to Androy after the fighting. He disappeared two days before the forces split up, to give the impression that he was escaping to return to Androy, but rejoined the returning Fiherenana army at an agreed rendezvous. He later learned that the wily Woozington had stealthily followed the Antandroy, and after they had split up to return home he had attacked Deaan Crindo's forces, killing Crindo and many others, although Mevarrow narrowly escaped. He believed Murnanzack would succeed Crindo as paramount chief but henceforward he was cut off from further contact with the Antandroy.

Shortly after the return to St Augustine's Bay, news came that Woozington was advancing from the south with 3,000 men. The Fiherenana retreated northward to Manombo where they were suddenly attacked in the rear by a Sakalava army and forced to flee in disorder back to the Fiherenana river. Drury was made a prisoner and handed over as a "slave" to the Sakalava commander, Rer Vove (Ravovy), a grandson of the king and a splendid figure 6 ft 8 in. (over 2 m) tall. But apart from the loss of freedom, Drury's status was far from that of an ordinary slave. He was well treated and housed and after a time was made captain of the guard, with the special duty of keeping a close watch on Rer Vove's wife, whose fidelity he suspected.

On his way home to his village a little to the north of the Morondava river, Rer Vove paid a ceremonial call on his grandfather the king, Rer Trimmonongarevo, at his capital Mahabo. Whether or not because of his fierce reputation, Robin thought him "a very odd and terrible figure". "His dress was such I had never seen any like it; his hair was twisted in knots, beginning at the crown of his head, making a small ring; then another ring of knots bigger than that, and so on downward, every circle larger than the upper. On several of these knots of hair hung some fine beads. He had a forehead piece of beads so low that some of them hung over his nose; among these were several gold beads. About his neck was a very fine gold necklace; over his shoulders, in the manner of an alderman's chain, hung two strings of beads, several of them gold; on each wrist about six mannelers of silver, seeming large enough to weigh near three dollars apiece, and four rings of gold on his fingers. On each ankle were near twenty strings of beads, strung very close, also fitting very close to his legs, a silk lamber, like a mantle, over his shoulders, and another, as usual, about his waist. He was an old man, not less, by what I could find, than fourscore years of age: yet of robust and hardy constitution. His colour rather tawny, like an Indian, than black; his eyes fierce, and his whole appearance frightful, or his singular habit and character made me think so."[9]

This is a fascinating glimpse of perhaps the most powerful Sakalava king at the height of the Sakalava empire. Ratsimonongarivo, or Andriamanetriarivo (the posthumous name[10] by which he is known in history) inherited the Menabe kingdom from his father Lahifotsy. With the aid of firearms obtained from pirates and slave traders he greatly strengthened the kingdom and succeeded in subjugating the Fiherenana; and by developing trade with the Europeans he increased prosperity. There was the customary dispute with his brothers over the succession. One brother, known posthumously as Andriamandisoarivo, was exiled to the north, taking with him relics (*dady*) of his father and grandfather to prove his descent from the Maroserana dynasty. With a small but well-armed force he conquered in a few short years a vast new kingdom stretching from the northern limit of Menabe at the Manambolo river right up to the Tsaratanana mountains at the north end of the island. Some tribes, like the Vazimba, submitted without fighting. One group refused to submit to Sakalava rule and customs, objecting in particular to the tradition by which men shaved their heads on the death of a ruler; they settled in the north centre of the island, between Majunga and Antongil, and became known as the Tsimihety ("those who do not cut their hair"). Andriamandisoarivo fixed his capital at Masselage in Mahajamba Bay and named his kingdom Boina after the Bay of Boina where he had achieved a victory against an Arab settlement. His influence extended well beyond the confines of Boina and he received trib-

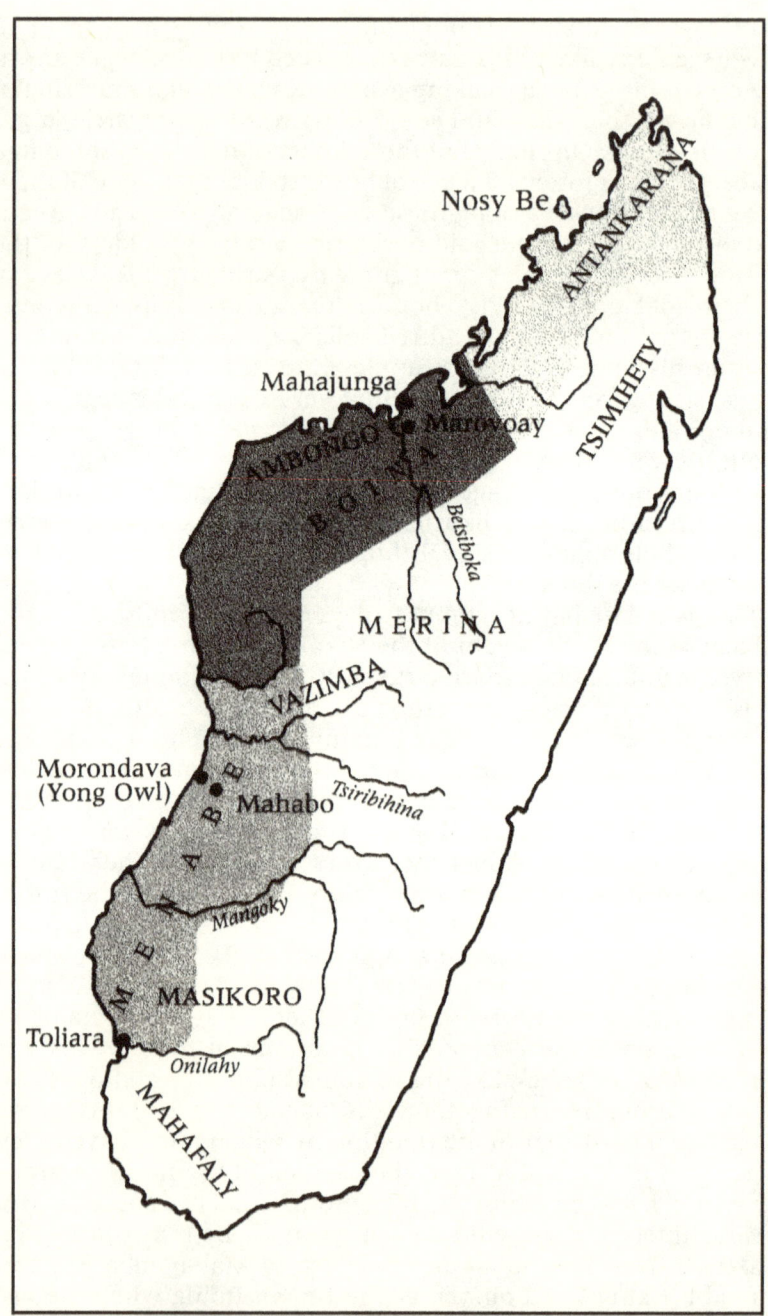

The Sakalava kingdoms in the eighteenth century

The shipwrecked sailor

ute from the Merina of the central plateau (who also paid tribute to the Menabe king), the Sihanaka from around Lake Alaotra and the Bezanozano from the forests to the east of Imerina. By the time of his death around 1710 the Sakalava kingdoms of Boina and Menabe were renowned and feared throughout Madagascar.

With his new master Rer Vove, Robin travelled to the area north of the Tsiribihina river where the great cattle herds of the Sakalava were kept, so numerous that the chiefly owners did not know within a few thousand how many they had. On the way they passed through a town of Vazimbas, one group of the relatively primitive people formerly thought to be the aboriginal inhabitants of the island but now believed to be descendants of the early proto-Malagasy immigrants. They also called on Vove's uncle, Rer Moume (Ramoma), the eldest son of the king and, according to Drury, "a very great prince and well beloved". After returning to Rer Vove's home, Robin was allowed to visit the capital Mahabo to see a fellow Englishman, William Thornbury, who had been marooned on shore nine years before when his ship had been blown away in a storm and who, like Robin, was awaiting an opportunity to leave on an English ship. On this occasion Robin also met two "ambassadors" from the Merina of the plateau. They told him that before the advent of firearms they had been more powerful than the Sakalava. The latter's easier access to firearms along the coast had reversed the position and Rer Trimmonongarevo maintained his superiority by refusing to sell any guns to the people of the interior.

Soon afterwards news came that an English ship had arrived at Yong-Owl at the mouth of the Morondava river. Robin heard that Will Thornbury had been taken on board. But when he asked if he could be sold to the captain Rer Vove was furious, pointing out that, unlike Thornbury, Robin was a slave legitimately captured in battle and that there was no question of letting him go. As a punishment for suggesting it, Robin was given menial slave work in the kitchen. Deeply depressed, he fell seriously ill with yaws and was sent to be cured by the Vazimba, who were skilled in herbal medicine.

When he recovered, he could not face returning to menial work under Rer Vove and took refuge with the king's son Rer Moume. Moume agreed to protect him and reproved his nephew for the folly of treating an Englishman as a slave when it was because of trade with the English that the Sakalava had become rich and strong. Robin was put in charge of Moume's substantial armoury of over a hundred muskets, given a house, some cattle, a plantation and a slave boy and persuaded, with little reluctance, to take a new wife. And so he lived in tolerable comfort for over two years, until news came that two English ships had arrived at Yong-Owl. The news was closely followed by two seamen bearing a letter from the captain of one of the ships, Captain Mackett, addressed to "Robert Drury, on the island of Madagascar." It stated that the captain had a letter on board from Drury's father (who had heard where he was from Will Thornbury) and instructions to secure his release at any cost.

Rer Moume, with many regrets, agreed to let him go, asking only for a gun as a present. When Robin appeared at Yong-Owl, half-naked, deeply tanned and with long matted hair and beard, the seamen took him for a "wild man". But a shave, a haircut and "a neat seaman's habit" so altered his appearance that his Malagasy friends did not recognise him when he paid a farewell visit to Rer Moume to present him with "a handsome and good buccaneer gun, also some powder and flints, and a case of spirits".[11]

Robin now embarked as a free man on Captain Mackett's ship, but he was not yet finished with Madagascar. The ship called in at Masselage to buy slaves from the Boina king, Deaan Toakoffu (Andriantoakafo), known to the English pirates and slave traders as "Long Dick" or "King Dick" (he was the son of Andriamandisoarivo, founder of the Boina kingdom). Captain Mackett then sailed for home via St Helena, Barbados and Jamaica, where the cargo of slaves was sold. They arrived in the Downs on September 9, 1717, sixteen and a half years after Robin had left on the *Degrave*. His homecoming was an anti-climax: his father and mother were both dead and his surviving relatives had almost forgotten him after such a long absence. He tried to settle down as a clerk and book-keeper but "things did not answer my expectation". After only a year he went back to sea on a slave-trading voyage to Madagascar.

Robin's knowledge of the language and the country were of course invaluable, and the ship traded successfully for slaves in the southeast of Madagascar and also at Yong-Owl, where Robin found that his friend Rer Moume had succeeded as king of Menabe. Robin's own experience of slavery does not seem to have turned him against the institution and he appears to have been perfectly content doing to others as they had done to him. His story ends with his return from this voyage in 1720, and little is known of him between that date and his death some time between the third edition of his Journal in 1743 and the fourth in 1750. It seems likely that he engaged in further slave trading or even piratical voyages. But he must have squandered or lost his profits since he appears to have finished up as a common porter at India House.

The shipwrecked sailor

In his last years he was to be found at Old Tom's Coffee House in Birchin Lane where he was ever ready to regale gentlemen visitors with authentic tales of adventure among the wild peoples of Madagascar.

Chapter 7

The pirates of Madagascar

For most people the word "pirate" is associated with the Caribbean and the Spanish Main in the sixteenth and seventeenth centuries. The Caribbean was indeed the great resort of pirates, mainly English and French, for over a century, drawn there by the fabulous wealth of the Spanish empire. While some were true pirates and outlaws, the majority regarded themselves as members of the honoured profession of privateer or corsair. They often held commissions from their government authorising them to attack and seize the property of their country's enemies and were required to hand over a percentage of their booty to the government. They also helped to protect the early French and English settlements from Spanish attack. But as Spanish power declined this protection was no longer needed and the privateers became an unruly nuisance who had to be tamed by the authorities. Many settled down to trade or plant sugar or tobacco. Others were recruited by their royal navies for the Wars of the League of Augsburg and of the Spanish Succession. Those whose lust for adventure and easy money was incurable turned to outright piracy. Some operated along the Pacific coast of South America, others along the Guinea coast of Africa. The most venturesome penetrated into the Indian Ocean to prey on the wealth of the East. These were the pirates of Madagascar.

It was not only experienced freebooters who were attracted to the Indian Ocean. As Lord Bellamont, governor of New York, reported to the Lords of the Admiralty in 1699: "The vast riches of the Red Sea and Madagascar are such a lure to seamen that there's almost no withholding them from turning pirates."[1] The prospect of easy riches, which lost nothing in the telling, was almost irresistible when contrasted with the hard and brutal lot of the average seaman; while the remoteness from European navies and the lack of a strong naval power in the Indian Ocean greatly reduced the risks of the profession there as compared with the West Indies.

The main hunting ground was the Arabian Sea, the Malabar coast and especially the Bab el Mandeb Straits at the entrance to the Red Sea where they hoped to intercept pilgrim ships from Moslem India on their way to Mecca. Their places of refuge included the Comoros and the Mascarene islands but above all Madagascar. This huge island offered ample supplies of meat, fruit and water and innumerable bays and inlets for concealment; and if hostile ships approached, the pirates could simply retreat inland. Long sloping beaches all round the island were suitable for careening their ships to scrape away barnacles, repair leaks and replace timbers riddled by the Teredo worm. With no European power established in Madagascar at that time there was no danger of interference from officious colonial authorities. The local population, organised for the most part in small clans, posed no threat to the well-armed pirates and were generally willing to trade and to seek the pirates' assistance in their local wars.

Thus for roughly forty years at the end of the seventeenth and the beginning of the eighteenth centuries, Madagascar was the principal centre where pirates congregated. This was in many respects the classic period of piracy in its brutal simplicity. It is less well known than Caribbean piracy, perhaps because it was on the whole unredeemed by any noble motives and therefore less amenable to romantic embroidery. In the early days of the Indian Ocean piracy there were half-hearted attempts to provide privateering cover. Ships leaving New England or the West Indies might carry a commission authorising them to attack, say, French establishments in west Africa. But once on the high seas the crews would, often with the connivance of the captain or even the owners, decide to go "on the account".

These early pirates made some claim to respectability on the grounds that they did not attack European ships and that plundering the heathen was a justifiable and even laudable operation. But their attacks on Indian ships jeopardised the position of the East India Company which was obliged to devote considerable resources to pirate hunting. Deriving no benefit or immunity from limiting the nationality of their prey, the later pirates attacked all shipping indiscriminately including ships of their own country. They became true pirates, outlaws of the sea, the enemies of the human race, liable to arrest and sometimes summary execution by any ship's company strong enough to overpower them.

We are fortunate in having an admirable contemporary account – *A General History of the Robberies and Murders of the most notorious Pyrates* by Captain Charles Johnson, one of the many pseudonyms employed by the indefatigable Daniel Defoe. Defoe gathered information over many years from accounts of voyages, conversations with ships' captains and reports of trials of pirates; and in most cases where it is possible to check with other contemporary accounts, his versions are substantially accurate. As with most of his writing there is an underlying didactic purpose and he uses the stories of the pirates to comment on the hypocrisy and injustice of contemporary British society. A basic theme is that the pirates' crimes differ only in degree from those of grasping merchants who exploit and plunder their fellow men. In the most remarkable section of the book he goes further and depicts a pirate community which is a veritable communist utopia run on lines which foreshadow and at times outstrip the most advanced ideas of the French Revolution. This is the pirates' Republic of Libertalia set up in the Bay of Diego Suarez by the French nobleman Misson and the Italian priest Carracioli and based on democratic representative government, equal sharing of profits, abolition of slavery and equality of all races. There was a basic contradiction in that this philosopher's paradise was sustained economically by the plundering of peaceful merchant ships and the murder of innocent seamen. The colony gradually declined and was eventually destroyed in a surprise attack by the local inhabitants who apparently had not been persuaded to adopt the precepts of international brotherly love.

A fascinating and instructive tale but alas mainly fantasy. Despite Defoe's skill in interweaving references to historical events and real people, including the English pirate Thomas Tew who becomes a leading member of the republic, this section of the book is now generally recognised as "one of Defoe's most remarkable and neglected works of fiction."[2] But the other pirates' tales are soundly based on fact, And Johnson/Defoe gives a sober and reasonably accurate account of the most famous pirates of the day Captains Avery and Kidd.

Avery and Kidd were not in fact typical of the Indian Ocean pirates, and neither spent much time in Madagascar. Avery's fame was based on a single voyage in 1694 which was crowned with spectacular success. After a brief call at Madagascar, probably in the Bay of Antongil, he sailed with three ships for the Arabian Sea to lie in wait for the pilgrim fleet to Jedda. There they captured two ships belonging to the Great Mogul (Aurungzebe) carrying important members of his court and possibly one of his daughters, as well as great quantities of gold, silver and jewels. Reports of this exploit inspired a number of romantic but largely fictional stories about Avery. In one of these he married the Mogul's daughter, who bore him a son, and then set himself up in oriental luxury as king of Madagascar and conquered the whole island. In reality he never returned to Madagascar but made his way back to England via the

West Indies. He appears to have hoped to use his wealth to buy a pardon, but the great outcry against him, inspired by the Mogul's anger and pressure on the East India Company, made this impossible. A huge reward of £1,000 was offered for the capture of each member of his crew; and 24 were arrested, tried and sentenced to either hanging or transportation as slaves to Virginia. According to Defoe, Avery managed to retire to Devon under an assumed name. But when he tried to dispose of his jewels, avaricious merchants gave him only a pittance and threatened to expose him when he protested; and he died in extreme poverty.

The dispersal of Avery's company still left many pirates at large in the Indian Ocean and it was necessary to take some action against them to appease the Mogul. Lord Bellamont had just been appointed as governor of New York and Massachusetts with the specific task of suppressing piracy and unlawful trading in which many New England merchants were involved. He persuaded some of the greatest officers of state – the First Lord of the Admiralty, the Lord High Chancellor, the Lord Chief of Justice and the Secretary of State – to join him in putting up £1,000 each to finance a privateering cruise of the Indian Ocean with the avowed objective of suppressing piracy but with the clear intention of picking up enough booty from captured pirates to provide a substantial profit on the investment. To command the enterprise Lord Bellamont recommended Captain William Kidd, who had held previous privateering commissions but had not always succeeded in maintaining a clear distinction between privateering and piracy. Kidd duly sailed from London in May 1696, calling in at New York on the way. However on arriving in the Indian Ocean he must have balanced the great risks and dubious rewards of attacking desperate pirates and the lesser risks and potentially greater rewards of turning pirate himself, and opted for the latter course.[3] He made no attempt to apprehend pirates around the coasts of Madagascar but proceeded north to the rich hunting ground of the north-west Indian Ocean. After six months with little success he captured a large Indian ship with a rich cargo which produced a dividend of £200 for each seaman, Kidd receiving 40 shares or £8,000. He then sailed for Madagascar where some of his crew joined another pirate ship and others decided to settle on the island, leaving a reduced crew to sail with Kidd back to America. On the way he learned that news of his actions had reached England and he had been declared a pirate. He continued on his way nonetheless, no doubt confident in the protection of his noble backers. But the uproar caused by his activities made it impossible to defend him. When he arrived in Boston in July 1699 he and his crew were arrested on the orders of Lord Bellamont. They were shipped to England and tried at the Old Bailey in May 1701. Kidd and six of his crew were hanged at Execution Dock and afterwards hung up in chains by the lower reaches of the Thames, where their bodies remained exposed for many years.

The fate of Avery and Kidd and their crews might lead one to conclude comfortably that piracy did not pay and that most members of the fraternity were likely to end on the gallows. But Avery and Kidd were far from being the most successful pirates. The more representative pirates of Madagascar plied their trade with a good deal of success over a number of years; and if they rarely attained a ripe old age they were more likely to die of disease or debauchery than at the end of a rope. Madagascar provided not only an ideal pirate base, but also a most agreeable environment and many pirates ultimately settled there, especially in the northeast. Most of the best anchorages were on the west coast in the estuaries of the major rivers. Pirates called in here, especially at St Augustine and Masselage, to obtain provisions. But the west coast was unsuitable for a permanent base because of the uncertain temper of the powerful Sakalava kings and because there was a greater risk of encountering warships on the main route to India. The Bay of Diego Suarez is one of the finest natural harbours in the world, but apart from the mythical Misson there is no record of any pirate establishing a base there; no doubt because the mountainous hinterland was then almost uninhabited so that provisions would not be readily available. The south had no ports, an arid, inhospitable interior and a hostile population. The almost straight southeast coast offers no protection against the trade winds and the powerful swell which surges against the narrow beaches and blocks the estuaries with sandbars. By process of elimination we are left with St Mary's Island, the coastline opposite and the Bay of Antongil, and it was this area which the pirates came to regard as their home.

The modern visitor has some difficulty in believing that St Mary's Island was at one time the greatest pirate stronghold in the world and that this idyllic, tranquil spot once reverberated with the violence, brutality and debauchery of pirate crews returning from successful expeditions. The island vies with Nosy Be and Fort Dauphin for the title of the most lovely spot on the coast of Madagascar, making up in peaceful, unspoilt charm what it lacks in spectacular scenery. It suffers by comparison with Nosy Be from a heavy rainfall, but this has the advantage of keeping tourists away, and anyone willing to risk a soaking will find the island little changed from the time when the pirates first came there. Riding, preferably on a bicycle, along the roads which are little more than tracks through the dense vegetation, one emerges suddenly on a sandy beach scattered with coconuts which are too plentiful to be worth collecting, and fronting a glassily smooth sea stretching to the mainland and the blue foothills of the eastern escarpment. At the south end of the island is a circular lagoon protected by a narrow and easily fortified entrance; in the middle of the lagoon is a small island which is still called Pirates' Island (*l'Ile aux Forbans*).

The fertility of St Mary's Island and the adjacent coast, and the friendliness of the inhabitants, assured the pirates abundant provisions, including beef, chicken, fish, turtle, yams, bananas, pineapples, coconuts, taro, oranges, lemons, palm oil, honey and sugar. St Mary's also became a market for the exchange of European manufactured necessities, especially ships' stores, powder and shot, against the pirates' booty. Merchant captains without too many scruples found this exchange highly profitable, as the pirates had few other trading outlets, but there was always the risk that if they tried to drive too hard a bargain the pirates might take the goods without paying or even seize the ship if it was in better condition than their own. The key figure in this traffic was Frederick Phillips, a Dutchman who had emigrated to New York as a young man and had made himself the richest man in the colony, mainly by acting as supplier and receiver to the pirates, first in the West Indies, and later in Madagascar. Lord Bellamont reported:

"'Tis the most beneficial trade, that to Madagascar with the pirates, that ever was heard of, and I believe there's more got that way than by turning pirate and robbing. I am told this Shelley (a captain of one of Phillips's ships) sold rum, which cost but 2s per gallon at N. York, for 50s. and £3 per gallon at Madagascar, and a pipe of Madeira wine, which cost him £19 at N. York he sold there for £300. Strong liquors and gunpowder and ball are the commodities that go off there to best advantage."[4]

Phillips's agent in St Mary's Island during the sixteen-nineties was one Adam Baldridge, who in a deposition made before Lord Bellamont when he returned to New York in 1699 gave some interesting details of his transactions and of the passage of pirate ships. Baldridge arrived at St Mary's Island at the beginning of 1691. His participation in an interclan war on the mainland earned him a working capital of seventy cattle and some slaves. He settled on Pirates' Island in the lagoon, where he built a house and later a Fort armed with "five great guns" which he obtained from a pirate ship in exchange for cattle. A section of his deposition[5] (quoted on the next page) gives an example of the extraordinary jumble of merchandise sent out by Phillips and an indication of the profits he made.

"*August 7, 1693*

Arrived the ship *Charles*, John Churcher Master, From New York, Mr Frederick Phillips, owner, sent to bring me several sorts of goods. She had two cargoes in her, one consigned to said Master to dispose of and one to me containing as follows: 4 pairs of shoes and pumps, 6 dozen of worsted and thread stockings, 3 dozen of speckled shirts and breeches, 12 hats, some carpenter's tools, 5 barrels of rum, 4 quarter casks of Madeira wine, 10 cases of spirits, 2 old stills full of holes, one worm, 2 grindstones, 2 cross-saws and 1 whipsaw, 3 jars of oil, 2 small iron pots, 3 barrels of cannon powder, some books, catechisms, primers and hornbooks, 2 Bibles and some garden seeds, 3 dozen of hens: and I returned for the said goods 1100 pieces of eight and dollars, 34 slaves, 15 head of cattle, 57 bars of iron."

Baldridge prospered and in 1697 was able to buy a three-quarter share of a visiting ship and set off on a trading voyage on his own account along the coast of Madagascar. Ten days after he left St Mary's the local Malagasy rose up and killed thirty white men, mainly pirates who had abused them and stolen their cattle, and took everything they or Baldridge possessed on the island. A ship met Baldridge returning from his voyage and told him it was not safe to go back to St Mary's. He accordingly sailed back to New York with only his share of the ship and the profits of his last voyage. However within a year or so pirates were once again installed on St Mary's Island.

Nearly all the pirate captains were English (many from New England or the West Indies) but a lot of the crews were French, Dutch or Scandinavian.[6] A leading pirate captain was John Bowen, who commanded a number of successful cruises around the turn of the century in different ships, with other well known pirates at times serving under him or in partnership with him. They included George Booth, who was killed by Arabs when leading a shore party at Zanzibar; Thomas Howard, who retired to settle in India after a successful joint expedition with Bowen along the Malabar coast; and Nathaniel North, a Bermudan whose whole life from boyhood was spent in privateering and piracy, and who served for some time as Bowen's quartermaster. But perhaps the most interesting of them was Thomas White, who may have indirectly made a significant contribution to Madagascar's history.

Like Bowen, White was one of many "involuntary" pirates, respectable merchant seamen who had the misfortune to be captured by pirates and given the choice of joining them or being abandoned to an uncertain fate, either set adrift at sea or left on a desert island. Though well qualified as a sea captain, he at first preferred to avoid positions of responsibility, perhaps hoping that if he was ever caught he could plead that he was a 'forced man'. Thus he served as a common seaman under Booth and Bowen and then under North, who took over Bowen's ship the *Defiance* when Bowen decided to retire in Mauritius. North sailed to Fort Dauphin where White and some 30 men went ashore to obtain provisions. A high wind blew the *Defiance* away from its moorings leaving the shore party stranded, and White as the most experienced seaman was obliged to assume command. After a hazardous journey in the ship's longboat up the west coast and round the northern cape they eventually reached St Mary's Island. They found that North and the crew of the *Defiance* had settled at Ambonavola (probably the modern Fénérive) on the coast opposite. They had built houses and forts in a number of separate settlements, the English, French, Danes and Dutch each having their own area. White and his group found that their share of the company's profits had been scrupulously preserved against their return. The amount was substantial enough for White to think of returning home. With some of this comrades he took the longboat round to the west coast looking for a ship to take them back to England. But at Masselage they met another group of pirates who persuaded them to join in another pirate cruise and elected Thomas White as their commander.

On his first, and indeed only, voyage as pirate captain White's behaviour did not conform to the bloodthirsty, ruthless stereotype but despite this the voyage was a financial success. In the Red Sea they successively captured a large and rich Indian prize, a Portuguese merchantman and an English ship, the *Dorothy*, which they kept for themselves as their own ship was damaged in the attacks. The pirates voted to give the Portuguese ship and cargo to the captain of the *Dorothy* together with whatever cargo he pleased to take from his own ship. Then after plundering the Indian ship, they gave it to the Portuguese and Indian prisoners to sail away. On the following day they captured a small English ship carrying a certain amount of money, including 500 dollars intended for bringing up two children who were in the charge of the ship's captain. According to Defoe, when White discovered this he not only persuaded his men to hand the money back to the children but organised a collection for them which raised another 120 dollars.[7]

The *Dorothy* now returned to Madagascar, touching first at Bourbon where several of the crew retired with their share of the booty, which came to £1200 a man. White and the remainder went ashore at Hopeful Point[8] on the coast of Madagascar near St Mary's Island. They made a settlement and set about refitting the *Dorothy* for another cruise in the Red Sea. Another pirate captain, John

Halsey from Boston, came in with a brigantine (the *Charles*) and found "Captain Thomas White and his Company, being about 90 or 100 Men, settled near the same Place, in petty governments of their own, having some of them 500 or 600, some 1,000 Negroe Subjects, who acknowledged their Sovereignty."[9] The fast-sailing brigantine being more suitable for their piratical purposes than the *Dorothy*, most of the crew of the latter threw in their lot with Halsey, the modest White enlisting before the mast as a simple seaman. Nathaniel North, by now bored with life on shore, despite the distraction of slaving wars against neighbouring clans, also joined up as quartermaster. In the Bab el Mandeb Straits the *Charles* came up with four English ships and, despite being heavily outnumbered and outgunned, captured two of them, with £50,000 in money on board. They returned to Madagascar to share out the loot but for White it was his last prize money, as he fell seriously ill of the flux. He was still alive on December 29, 1707 when he and his men handed in to a passing ship a petition for a pardon for past piracies for transmission to the queen by the President of the East India Company at Surat; but the same ship leaving on March 10, 1708 reported that about twenty of the pirates, including Captain White, had died of "fevers and fluxes" brought about by excessive drinking and other irregularities.

Of the other pirate captains not accounted for, Bowen had died "of the dry belly ache" six months after his retirement in Mauritius. Howard, put ashore on the Malabar coast, "married a Woman of the Country, and being a morose ill-natur'd Fellow, and using her ill, he was murder'd by her Relations".[10] Halsey, after a further successful voyage, died of fever shortly after White. North survived for a number of years but did not undertake any further pirate cruises. He returned to his old settlement at Ambonavola, became involved in endless interclan warfare and finally was murdered in his bed by his enemies.

The central period of Madagascar piracy had already come to an end with the death of White and Halsey in 1708. Thereafter there was a lull, probably because potential recruits to the trade were absorbed in the national fleets which were engaged in the War of the Spanish Succession. The revival of piracy in the West Indies at the end of the War had its repercussions in the Indian Ocean where it led to a brief but spectacular resurgence associated especially with the names of England and Taylor.

Edward England was a leading member of the pirate community which flourished on New Providence Island in the Bahamas from about 1713 until the island was occupied by the British in 1718; so much so that he was one of those specifically excluded from an amnesty for pirates proclaimed by the government in the latter year. With no hope of pardon, England went off marauding along the African coast and in the South Atlantic, capturing over a score of ships. In 1720 he led a squadron of two pirate ships via Madagascar and the Comoros to the Malabar coast where they captured several Indian ships. However England's authority began to decline in favour of the captain of the other ship, Taylor, "a Fellow of a most barbarous Nature, who was become a great Favourite amongst (the pirate crew), for no other reason than because he was a greater brute than the rest."[11] England was in due course demoted and later put ashore with three companions on Mauritius which had reverted to being a desert island, the Dutch having abandoned it in 1710. He and his friends then built a boat which took them to Madagascar, where they joined the pirate community in and around St Mary's Island. England died a year later, apparently full of remorse at his past misdeeds and urging his friends to give up their wicked career.

Taylor had meanwhile completed the last and probably the most successful of all the pirate cruises in the Indian Ocean. Returning from the Malabar coast, where they captured several Indian prizes but had some narrow escapes from fleets of armed East Indiamen, they called in at Bourbon on April 8, 1721. Here they found the answer to a pirate's prayer – a Portuguese ship disabled and helpless after a violent storm and carrying the Portuguese Viceroy of Goa and a fabulous treasure principally in diamonds which alone were worth three or four million dollars. With this enormous booty they sailed to St Mary's Island where the share-out yielded something in the region of £4,000 or £5,000 a man (about £500,000 or $800,000 in modern terms) including 42 small diamonds each, or the equivalent in larger stones. This was more than enough to persuade many of them to retire and settle in Madagascar. The others got ready to sail with Taylor on another venture to the Red Sea. But news of a strong British naval squadron rounding the Cape with instructions to hunt down the pirates caused them to alter their plans. In December 1722 they split up, some going back to Madagascar to settle there, and the rest under Taylor returning to the West Indies, where Defoe concludes the story with a typical reflection:[12]

"Here they sate down to spend the Fruits of their dishonest Industry, dividing the Spoil and Plunder of Nations among themselves, without the least Remorse or Compunction, satisfying their Conscience with this Salve, that other People would have done as much, had they had the like Opportunities. I can't say, but that if they had known what was doing in *England*, at the same Time, by the *South-Sea* Directors,[13] and their Directors, they would certainly have had this Reflection for their Consolation, *viz*: that whatever Robberies they had committed, they might be pretty sure they were not the greatest Villains then living in the World."

Chapter 8

The sons of the pirates

Taylor's last cruise was the final spectacular encore before the curtain came down on the pirates of Madagascar. His encounters with strong East India Company fleets and the appearance of a naval squadron in the Indian Ocean were clear signs that the risks were now becoming too great. The squadron consisted of four men-of-war under Commodore Thomas Mathews. He had been given the two-fold mission of helping the East India Company in their war with the Portuguese and of stamping out piracy. But Mathews's chief aim during his stay in the Indian Ocean seems to have been to acquire a quick fortune by trading and he had no scruples about using His Majesty's ships for this purpose. The squadron went first to India where, finding that an armistice had been agreed with the Portuguese, Mathews set about private trading to the great annoyance of the Bombay Council. He was then ordered to Madagascar to break up the private settlements and destroy their bases and harbours.

Mathews arrived with his squadron opposite St Mary's Island in April 1722. One of his midshipmen, Clement Downing, later published an account[1] which showed how he carried out his instructions. Finding the wrecks of several ships destroyed by the pirates, with their cargoes of "China Ware, rich Drugs and all sorts of Spices" lying on the beach with several guns, Mathews took on board the guns and the least damaged parts of the cargoes. A white man appeared called James Plantain who said he was a retired pirate living in a fortified settlement some miles away called Ranter-Bay.[2] Some officers who visited the fort "brought an Account of the great Riches the said *Plantain* was possessed of, and how he was homaged by the Natives, and called king of *Ranter-Bay*, had a large Number of Slaves under him; and that there were also one *James Adair* a *Scotsman* and a *Dane*, who were fortified there as well as he, and that they lived a very profane and debauch'd Life, indulging themselves in all manner of Wickedness." Deciding that Plantain's fort was too strong and well guarded to be attacked, Mathews instead sold the pirates large quantities of alcohol for a very high price in diamonds and gold pieces and traded clothing and other goods for several cattle. He made no further effort to seek out pirates elsewhere in Madagascar but returned to India to engage in further trade for his private profit. His behaviour eventually led to a court martial, but as his punishment was only a fine of four months' pay he probably had few regrets.

Plantain, Adair and the Dane were members of the crews of England and Taylor who preferred to settle in Madagascar rather than return to the West Indies. When Midshipman Downing's account of Commodore Mathews's expedition was published in 1737, it included a long narrative of Plantain's romantic adventures in Madagascar, which was probably written a long time after Downing's visit to St Mary's Island. The central theme is Plantain's passion for Eleanor Brown, the offspring of an English seaman and a daughter of the king of Boina, King Dick. Wishing to have a wife of English extraction, Plantain sent to ask King Dick for his granddaughter's hand, but King Dick was persuaded by some other pirates living at Masselage to refuse. Plantain, with the support of his fellow-pirates, some native rulers who had grievances against King Dick, and a powerful half-caste known as Mulatto Tom and said to be the son of Avery, then invaded the Boina, defeated King Dick's forces and captured Masselage along with King Dick. He found his lady-love already pregnant by one of the pirates living at Masselage, and in his rage had King Dick put to death. But he married Eleanor notwithstanding and appears to have lived reasonably happily with her, despite her habit of lecturing him on religion, having been well brought up as a Christian by her father. Plantain subsequently made himself king of all Madagascar after two victorious overland campaigns with Mulatto Tom to subdue unfriendly kings at Fort Dauphin and St Augustine!

Sheer fantasy, of course, as anyone familiar with the distances and the difficulties of terrain will realise, and totally unsupported by any other evidence. It is unlikely that Plantain was ever king of anything much more than the village of Rantabe containing perhaps a few hundred souls. He was probably only one of perhaps several dozen pirates living as princelings or village chiefs in little communities along the northeast coast or some little distance in the interior, owing their position to their martial reputation and their ill-gotten wealth which often enabled them to marry the daughters of Malagasy chieftains. Small pirate communities existed for short periods of time at other points on the coast, such as Masselage, St Augustine and Matitanana; but the favoured area for settlement was the stretch of coast from Tamatave to the Bay of Antongil. Here the struggle for existence is greatly eased by the warmth of the climate and the abundance of the vegetation. For the average pirate, starting life perhaps in a riverside slum on the Thames and having survived years of brutality and privation at sea, his "retired" existence among the bamboo and the coconut palms, surrounded by his Malagasy family and ample supplies of meat, fish, exotic fruits and potent home-brewed alcohol, must have seemed closer to paradise than he ever expected to see.

Many of the ex-pirates were content to sink into the agreeable apathy of this Malagasy *dolce vita*, to become integrated into the Malagasy way of life as so many previous immigrants had done. Others more energetic took part in interclan raids and wars either as mercenaries or on their own account in order to obtain slaves to sell to the visiting slave ships, aboard which they were quite likely to find some former shipmates. There had often been a link between piracy and slave trading, and when the risks of piracy became too great, a number of pirates, whose anonymity provided some guarantee against prosecution, enlisted on slaving ships. But it would be wrong to attribute to the pirates major responsibility for the Madagascar slave trade. This was already flourishing before Madagascar became an important scene of pirate activity. A colonial report[3] dated 1676 mentions that Barbados already had a population of over 32,000 slaves from Guinea and Madagascar; Malagasy slaves were also exported at that time to Jamaica and the Carolinas[4] and even to Boston,[5] where there were 200 African and Malagasy slaves in 1676. Nor can we blame the pirates for the fearful scourge of the interclan or intertribal wars which were often provoked for the sole purpose of capturing slaves. Drury's evidence shows that in the Mahafaly and Androy countries, where the absence of ports ruled out an external slave trade and inhibited any other European involvement, internecine warfare was almost the normal state of affairs. But the brutality of many pirates and their skill with firearms probably added a new element of ferocity to slave raiding so long as they were actively engaged in this business.

We have little direct evidence of what happened to the ex-pirates living in Madagascar during the years following the visit of Commodore Mathews. It is unlikely that many of them survived for very long. Malaria and dysentery would certainly exact their customary heavy toll. Some may have been killed during interclan fighting or slave raids; some may have been murdered like Nathaniel North, by enemies made in the course of such fighting. Others who were foolish enough to treat their wives brutally may have been poisoned by their wives or otherwise put to death by their wives' relatives with the added incentive of laying their hands on whatever remained of pirate booty. One report describes the wives and widows of the pirates of St Mary's Island wearing dresses of the most beautiful Indian materials embroidered in gold and silver, with golden chains, rings and bracelets and even diamonds of considerable value.

For all these reasons it is doubtful whether more than a very few of the original pirates were still living in Madagascar by about 1730. Being by nature destroyers rather than builders they left no permanent memorial in the way of buildings (apart from the ruins of Baldridge's fort) or political organisation. Except in one respect they had no more effect on the course of Malagasy history than a meteor flashing across the sky and expending itself in a shower of sparks. But both those who settled in Madagascar and others who consorted with Malagasy women during briefer stays in the island fathered numerous children who came to be regarded as a separate clan known as the Malata (mulattos) or Zana-Malata ("children of the mulattos"). Although no longer a cohesive group their descendants are still identifiable today, sometimes with reddish hair or blue eyes as visible evidence of their origin. In the eighteenth century they were destined to play an important role in the history of their region.

While important kingdoms were being forged elsewhere in the island in the sixteenth and seventeenth centuries, the people of the northern half of the east coast, now known as the Betsimisaraka, remained divided into many small clans. The geography of the east coast as a whole – a narrow coastal strip split into small segments by numerous rivers rushing down from the eastern escarpment – did not favour large political groupings; and this factor probably helped to limit the size of the kingdoms formed further south by late "Arab" immigrants – the Antambahoaka, the Antemoro and the Antanosy. The small clans of the northern sector were at first an easy prey for the Sakalava warriors of the Boina, raiding for slaves. But from the end of the seventeenth century the growing trade with European merchant-men and pirates brought them wealth and firearms which enabled them, with the occasional help of the pirates, to repel the Sakalava and eventually to raid successfully for slaves into their territory. The wealth of the region between Tamatave and the Bay of Antongil, based on the European and pirate trade, aroused the envy of the people further south; and a struggle developed between the Antatsimo ("people of the south") and the Antavaratra ("people of the north") for the control of the ports – Tamatave, Foulpointe and Fénérive – where this trade was principally carried on.

An important chief of the Vatomandry region called Ramanano grouped together some twenty clans of the Antatsimo in an al-

The sons of the pirates

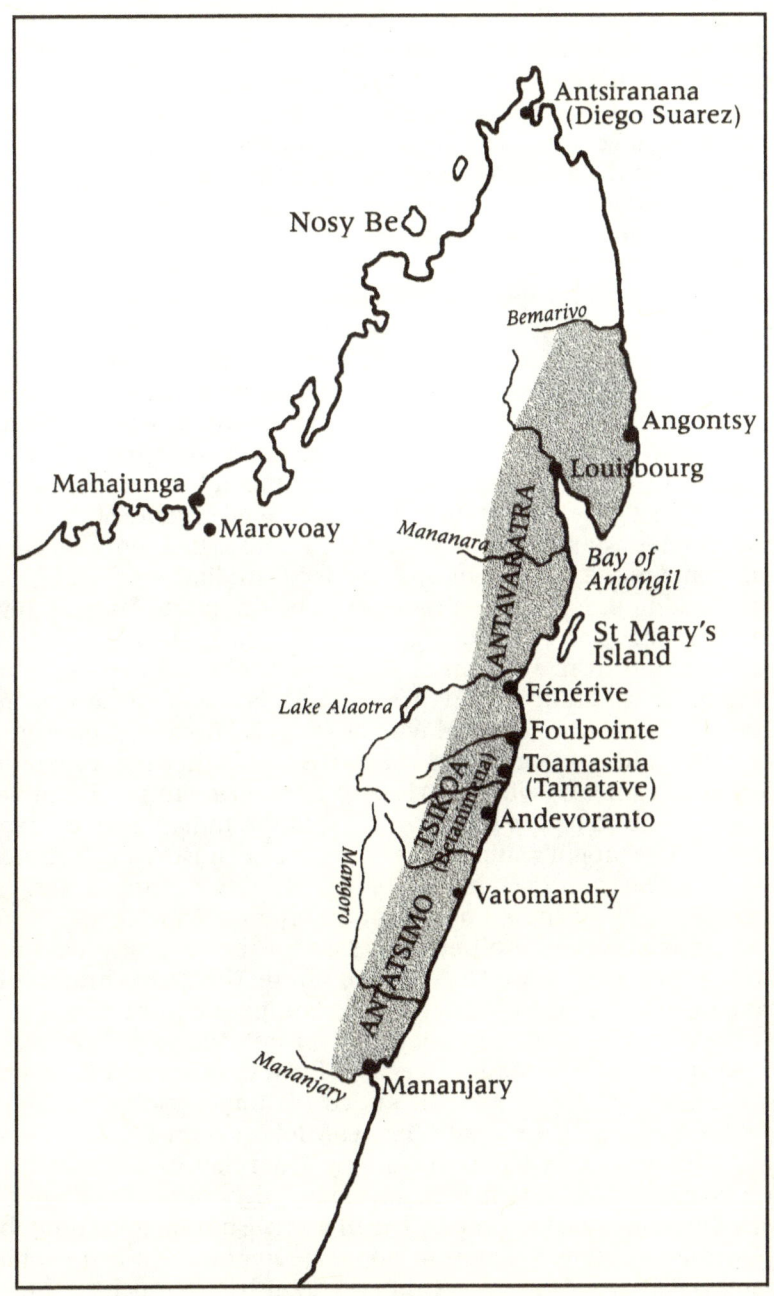

The Betsimisaraka region
Approximate modern limits of the Betsimisaraka

liance which took the name of Tsikoa ("the invincible"). With a numerous army he marched north and seized control of Tamatave, Foulpointe and Fénérive. The Tsikoa behaved as brutal conquerors to the Antavaratra, burning their villages and crops, selling many of them as slaves and even desecrating tombs, a deadly and unforgivable act to the ancestor-venerating Malagasy. The oppressed Antavaratra turned for help to the Zana-Malata, among whom a new leader emerged. His name was Ratsimilaho.

The identity of Ratsimilaho is still the subject of dispute. Our main source of information is the account written some sixty years later by the French trader and explorer Nicolas Mayeur and based on oral traditions of events which were still recent. Mayeur put the date of Ratsimilaho's emergence as 1712 when he was a young man of eighteen. He was said to be the son of an English pirate Tom (Tamo to the Malagasy) and Rahena, a Malagasy princess daughter of a chief of Fénérive. Tom had taken his son to London to give him a good education but the boy, aged seventeen, had become homesick after three months so his father had sent him back with some money, weapons and goods for trading.

For a long time Tom was thought to be the pirate Thomas Tew who was active around Madagascar in the early sixteen-nineties, which would fit in with an eighteen-year-old son in 1712. But there is no mention of Tew having a Malagasy son; he was an American from Rhode Island who as far as is known never visited London; and he was killed at sea in 1696. Another theory would identify Ratsimilaho with the Mulatto Tom of Downing's narrative, who was said to be the son of Avery and the Indian princess captured on the Mogul's ship. But as we have seen Downing's narrative is highly suspect and the story of Avery siring a son in Madagascar by an Indian princess entirely mythical.

There is however another candidate for the paternity who fits the requirements more closely. The pirate Thomas White spent some time in the area of Fénérive and Foulpointe towards the end of his life, and a son is mentioned in Johnson's *History of the Pyrates*:[6]

"At his return to Madagascar, White was taken ill of a Flux, which in about 5 or 6 Months ended his Days; finding his Time was drawing nigh, he made his Will, left several Legacies, and nam'd three Men of different Nations, Guardian to a Son he had by a Woman of the Country, requiring he might be sent to England with the Money he left him, by the first English ship, to be brought up in the Christian Religion in hopes he might live a better Man than his Father ... Some Years after an English Ship touching there, the Guardians faithfully discharged their Trust, and put him on board with the Captain, who brought up the Boy with Care, acting

The sons of the pirates

by him as became a Man of Probity and Honour."

This story fits in with our picture of White as a somewhat reluctant and bourgeois pirate. The main drawback is that a son of White could not have been born in Fénérive much before 1704 or 1705 and so could not have played the role attributed to him by Mayeur in 1712. However the date of 1712, when the pirates were still active, seems too early for the important events in which Ratsimilaho was involved; and his rise to power is not reflected in any of the European accounts of this period. A date in the early or mid seventeen-twenties, when a son of White would have been in his late teens, is in many respects more plausible. Although only eighteen when he returned from England, Ratsimilaho had inherited courage and audacity from his father as well as money with which arms could be bought. His first move was to send an ultimatum to Ramanano, calling upon him to give up Fénérive and Foulpointe, while graciously permitting him to keep Tamatave for his trading needs. Ramanano angrily expelled the upstart from his domains on pain of death and Ratsimilaho withdrew to the Bay of Antongil, announcing that he would return. Having thus boldly captured the imagination of the downtrodden Antavaratra he summoned their chiefs to a meeting with some of the Zana-Malata and made a great speech or *kabary*. After deploring their submission to the Tsikoa tyranny he urged them to join him in throwing off the yoke, offering to lead them and to ensure an adequate supply of arms. The other chiefs then spoke, the older ones cautious for peace, the younger ones enthusiastic for war. Youth prevailed, Ratsimilaho was elected leader and all swore an oath of blood brotherhood before dispersing to raise the standard and recruit warriors. A sizeable army was collected, Ratsimilaho distributed 200 muskets and then advanced on Fénérive.

Although the Tsikoa were taken by surprise, their defences at Fénérive were too strong to be taken by assault. Resorting to subterfuge, the attackers withdrew and pretended to disperse. After a time the Tsikoa resumed their normal occupations, which at that season included ploughing the rice-fields by the traditional method of trampling by cattle urged on by shouts and blows from the men. At the end of the day when cattle and men were exhausted and covered in the rich red laterite mud, Ratsimilaho launched his attack and captured Fénérive with little difficulty. He dubbed his defeated opponents the Betanimena ("much red earth"), a name by which their descendants living around Vatomandry and Brickaville are still known today. Ramanano was forced to sue for peace and to abandon Fénérive and Foulpointe, but he was allowed to keep Tamatave. The victorious Ratsimilaho was elected king of the northern people who now took the name Betsimisaraka ("the many inseparable"); while he himself changed his name, in accordance with the general practice of Malagasy kings on accession, and was henceforth known as Ramaromanompo ("he who rules over many").

The peace proved to be only a truce. Ramanano continued to oppress the people in the hinterland of Tamatave, and denied them access to the port. Ramaromanompo supported the inland people and besieged Tamatave, forcing Ramanano to retreat to the south. Finding himself unable to defeat Ramanano unaided, Ramaromanompo formed an alliance with Kalaheka, chief of the most southerly Antatsimo, by marrying his daughter and promising him the port of Fénérive. The allies finally subdued Ramanano who had to pay an annual indemnity of fifty cows and five slaves for five years. Unfortunately opposition from his own supporters prevented Ramaromanompo from keeping his promise with regard to Fénérive. Kalaheka rebelled against him and was killed in battle; but Ramaromanompo won over his people by unusual magnanimity in freeing his captured warriors. He was now undisputed leader of a confederation stretching nearly 400 miles (640 km) from somewhere to the south of the Mangoro river to well beyond the Bay of Antongil. This Betsimisaraka group, formed by the son of an English pirate, has retained its identity, if not its cohesion, and counts today as the second largest ethnic group in Madagascar.

Ramaromanompo gave further proof of his broadness of vision by seeking an alliance with the powerful Sakalava king of the Boina, which was sealed by his marriage to one of the king's daughters with the rather unappetising name of Matavy ("the fat one"). However she clearly had some attractions since she subsequently bore a son by another man. Ramaromanompo, not wishing to jeopardise his relations with the Sakalava, accepted the boy as his own son, giving him the pretentious name of Zanahary ("God, the Creator") and recognising him as his heir.

There is a curious echo here of Plantain's paramour Eleanor Brown, who likewise was a Sakalava princess from the Boina and who was already pregnant by another man when Plantain bore her off. This prompts the thought that Downing's highly coloured account of the adventures of Plantain and Mulatto Tom might be a garbled version of Ramaromanompo's career, with his military campaigns against the Antatsimo inspiring the more extravagant tales of Plantain's conquests. And leaving aside the supposed link with Avery, the character of Mulatto Tom might well be based on Ramaromanompo, who to the end of his life was known to European traders as Tom Similo.

The sons of the pirates

Despite Ramaromanompo's work of unification, the Betsimisaraka remained essentially a confederation of small groups rather than a united kingdom. Ramaromanompo does not seem to have assumed the divine and absolute powers of the African style of kingship as practised among the Sakalava. He was rather the paramount chief among a number of important chiefs, *filohabe*, along the coast. The geographical factors continued to inhibit the development of a strong central authority. The Zana-Malata, inheriting some of the restlessness and energy of their fathers, were unruly and difficult subjects. The depredations of the slave trade were a constant weakening factor. And towards the middle of the eighteenth century local sovereignty was threatened by the trading interests of the French, based on their settlements in the islands of Bourbon and Mauritius, which they had occupied and renamed Ile de France after its abandonment by the Dutch. So long as Ramaromanompo remained alive, his intelligence, strength of character and great prestige enabled him to resist these pressures and maintain his authority. But after his death in 1750 the kingdom he had created disintegrated under his successors.

Matavy's son Zanahary, known to the French as Jean Harre, succeeded to the main inheritance, but was able to maintain only a tenuous authority in the northern part of the kingdom. St Mary's Island, or Ile Ste Marie in French, was bequeathed to Bety, a favourite daughter of Ramaromanompo by another wife. She was a young lady of great charm (the correct form of her name is Betia meaning "much loved") celebrated mainly for her romance with a Gascon corporal Jean-Onésime Filet or Fichet, known as La Bigorne (meaning "anvil horn" an obvious allusion to his sexual prowess). Most history books record that for love of her corporal she ceded her island to France; but it is extremely doubtful that he appeared on the scene before the cession took place.[7]

Even while Ramaromanompo was alive the French *Compagnie des Indes* was casting covetous eyes on Ile Ste Marie. Their possessions in Bourbon and Ile de France, devoted largely to sugarcane and coffee plantations, needed regular supplies of food, mainly beef and rice, and slaves to work on the plantations. The northeast coast of Madagascar supplied all these commodities, and Ile Ste Marie was an ideal offshore base for the trade. The Company appointed an agent, Guillaume Gosse, to negotiate the cession of the island with Ramaromanompo, but his death intervened and negotiations were pursued successfully with Bety. On July 30, 1750 Bety and twenty-nine chiefs of the island went on board a French frigate and signed with a cross opposite their names a treaty ceding sovereignty over the island to France. In the following weeks, however, Gosse and other members of the Company who were with him seem to have committed all kinds of excesses and even violated the tomb of Ramaromanompo; and on September 14, 1750 the population rose up and massacred Gosse and fourteen other Frenchmen.[8]

As a reprisal for this massacre, the governor of Ile de France sent a warship to burn a few villages on the coast of the mainland; and it was probably at this stage that La Bigorne was sent to Ile Ste Marie as the Company's delegate to restore the situation. The French reprisals gave an excuse to some of Zanahary's unruly subjects to rebel against him. Zanahary accused his half-sister of stirring up the trouble, and to reassure him Bety, accompanied by La Bigorne, visited him at Foulpointe to conclude a blood pact (*fatidra*) with him. Over the next decade La Bigorne, who appears to have married Bety, efficiently promoted the interests of the Company and of France, partly by stirring up trouble between the Betsimisaraka of the coast and those of the interior, known as the Ambanivolo. In 1762 he took up arms against his brother-in-law Zanahary, driving him from Foulpointe to take refuge in the Bay of Antongil, where he was assassinated in 1767.

The disintegration of the Betsimisaraka continued under Zanahary's son Iavy. With the help of the slave traders he resumed possession of Foulpointe and effective control of some 150 miles (240 km) of the coast. He could still muster 25,000 warriors and by means of constant raids against the Ambanivolo of the interior he became the principal supplier of slaves. His period of rule is notable mainly because of the extraordinary episode of Baron Benyowsky.

A Polish–Hungarian Count in the service of the Polish king Stanislas Poniatowski, Benyowsky was captured by the Russians and exiled to Siberia. In a series of romantic adventures which became more remarkable in his telling of them, he escaped eastwards to Kamchatka and thence to Macao where he found a ship which took him to the Ile de France (Mauritius). Here his fertile imagination was fired by what he heard of Madagascar. Proceeding to France in 1772 he captivated the Versailles court with his extravagant tales and equally extravagant plans to build a French colony in Madagascar. The moment was propitious, as only the previous year another attempt to set up a colony at Fort Dauphin had come to nothing. Count Maudave, an early exponent of "*la mission civilisatrice*", had landed there in 1768 with enlightened philosophical ideas of governing the country in partnership with the Malagasy. But lack of resources and the indifference or hostility of the inhabitants proved insurmountable, and after less than two and a half years Fort Dauphin was once again evacuated. The French government now rashly entrusted the glamorous Baron with the task of establishing a settlement in Madagascar.

In February 1774 Benyowsky, with a company of troops called "Benyowsky's volunteers", established himself in the Bay of Antongil, building a small town which he named Louisbourg near the site of the modern Maroantsetra. Six months later he reported to the minister at Versailles that he had subjugated the whole island and built up a highly profitable trade. Reports from the Ile de France were however less enthusiastic and in 1776 two commissioners were sent out to investigate the Baron's work. They found trade at a standstill, the "capital city" of Louisbourg a collection of miserable huts, the country round about depopulated by Benyowsky's wars and nothing to show for the expenditure of two million *livres* and the death of three hundred men from fever. Benyowsky was sent back to France where his inventiveness in presenting his version of events failed to explain away the disaster or persuade the new king, Louis XVI, to give him a second chance. He journeyed to Vienna and London to "offer" Madagascar to the Emperor and King George III, but they had other preoccupations. Crossing the Atlantic this prince of confidence men obtained some private backing in the newly-created United States which enabled him to charter a ship and return to Madagascar in 1785. He seized a small French trading post at Angontsy near Cap Est and tried in vain to rouse the local chiefs to drive out the French traders. This threat to the economic interests of the Mascarenes could not be ignored, and the governor of the Ile de France sent a small military detachment to arrest Benyowsky. When he refused to surrender he was killed in an assault on his small fort in May 1786.

Meanwhile French trading activities had increased with the steady expansion of the settlements on Ile de France and Bourbon. Having at first operated mainly from Ile Ste Marie, they now maintained several posts on the mainland, notably at Tamatave and Foulpointe. At the latter port in 1792 there were eight official agents, buying mainly cattle and rice on behalf of the French authorities in the Mascarenes, and twenty-two independent traders, dealing mainly in slaves. Other items bought in less quantity were pigs, raphia palm and timber for building. In return the traders supplied various manufactured articles – cloth, knives, mirrors, brandy and rum – but principally gunpowder, muskets, flints and bullets.[9] Their activities, especially the supply of munitions, were undoubtedly an important factor in the unsettled atmosphere of the coastal strip in this period and contributed to the disintegration of the Betsimisaraka kingdom.

Zakavola, who succeeded Iavy in 1791, at first continued his father's policy of cooperation with the French slave traders, whose leader Dumaine enjoyed a quasi-consular status. But after the departure of Dumaine, Zakavola turned against the French and attacked their installations. The governor of Ile de France sent an expedition against him in 1802, and in the following year he was murdered by his own subjects. Anarchy ensued, with two sons and two uncles of Zakavola disputing the succession with other chiefs. Members of a later group of Malata, sons of French traders rather than English pirates and themselves engaged in the slave trade, now came to the fore: the chief was Jean René, together with his brother Fiche (Fisatra) and a cousin Coroller. But the real power along this coast was by 1810 in the hands of the French, represented at Tamatave by their agent Sylvain Roux.

The Malata dynasty founded by Ramaromanompo thus survived his death by little more than fifty years. But the pirate blood of the Zana-Malata was still manifesting itself in an extraordinary series of sea raids against the Comoros and the Mozambique coast. These appear to have started around 1785 and according to one account Baron Benyowsky was indirectly the cause. On his return to Madagascar that year the ship that brought him from Baltimore landed him at Cap St Sébastien near the northern tip of the island. It then unexpectedly sailed away in the direction of the Comoros leaving him stranded, so that he had to make his way by land to Angontsy, the scene of his last stand. Before he did so he sent a canoe to the Comoros to ask the Sultan to detain the ship. By the time the canoe reached the Comoros the ship had already left. But the canoe returned with news of the wealth and defencelessness of the Comoros and knowledge of how to navigate there. Another version, current on the west coast, was that some Malagasy from Angontsy were taken to the Comoros in a pirate ship and left there. They became involved in a local war and helped one side win, and as a reward were sent back to Madagascar. One of them called Rassiriki had noted the direction of the journey and the position of the stars. Back in his own country and looking for slaves to sell he conceived the idea of taking some from the Comoros and so led the first expedition which was later followed by many others.

In fact the people of the northwest coast would have known a good deal about the Comoros and how to get there. And the Zana-Malata must have heard about the islands from their pirate fathers, for whom the Comoros were a favourite resort. The impetus to go raiding there was almost certainly the need to find another source of slaves to sell to Ile de France and Bourbon as it became more difficult to obtain them by raids into the interior. They were however inhibited by the lack of sea-going craft. The outrigger canoe which is used on the west coast is not found at all on the east coast. The craft used in rivers and in sheltered coastal waters was, and indeed still is, a simple hollowed out tree trunk without a keel, propelled by shovel-shaped paddles. If it was necessary to venture out into the ocean, for example to hunt whales (a popular east coast occupation in the eighteenth century) the sides were raised with planks tied on with creepers; and a hole was pierced in the forward bench-seat to support a small mast and sail when the wind was from behind. Probably the first step was to use these modified canoes to raid for slaves further down the east coast. The success of these raids, and possibly the difficulty of repeating them once the element of surprise was lost, may have inspired the more ambitious venture of raiding across the seas to the Comoros.

For this purpose larger canoes measuring something like 45 ft long by 10 or 12 ft wide (14 x 4 m) were constructed from planks bolted together with wooden pegs or sewn with raphia fibres, using techniques inherited from the pirates. Such craft, carrying thirty to forty men each, were ill-designed for the open sea. It was the practice to lash two together for greater stability in rough weather but even so many capsized in high seas. With little manoeuvrability they were at the mercy of the wind and the timing of the raids was crucial. The outward journey to the Comoros was favoured by the prevailing trade winds and the east–west current which dominates these waters for most of the year. The return journey was only feasible during the monsoon season around the beginning of the year, although it was always difficult and often hazardous owing to cyclones.

The normal pattern was therefore to set out in October and return early in the following year. During the preceding months, Zana-Malata chiefs would journey along the coast, extracting promises of participation sealed by solemn oaths. The first canoes would start from Tamatave and proceed north, picking up contingents at Foulpointe, Fénérive, Tintingue and other ports. The Betsimisaraka coast would thus be denuded of its canoes and much of its male population, bringing to a standstill the export trade in rice and other commodities to the Mascarene Islands. At Vohemar the fleet was expanded by further contingents from Antongil Bay and the coast to the north. They then continued round the northern cape to Nosy Be or one of the bays on the neighbouring mainland, where they were joined by a party from the Sakalava coast whose main motive was probably to obtain slaves for agricultural labour. A major expedition, which took place usually every five years, consisted of between 400 and 500 canoes, carrying perhaps 15,000 to 18,000 men. In the intervening years a much smaller

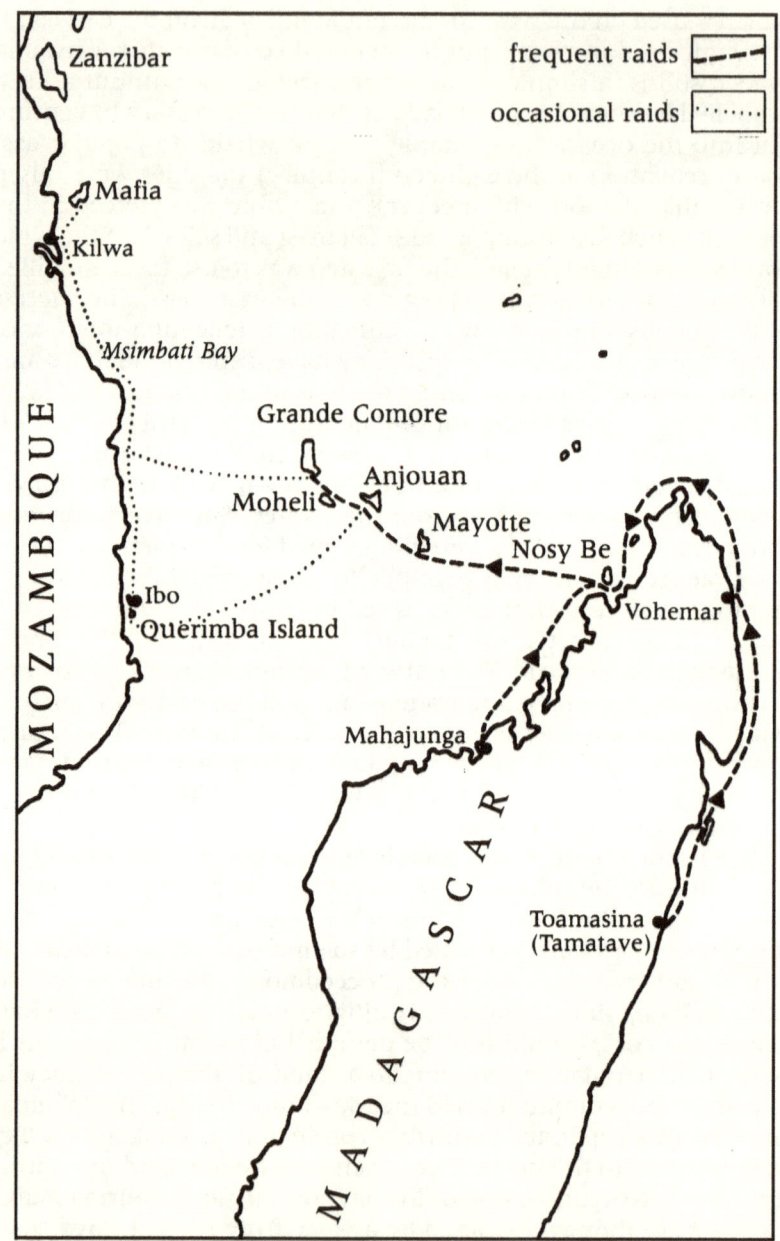

The raids of the Malagasy pirates 1756–1820

raiding party of about 50 canoes would be sent, which would allow the battered Comorians to re-establish their plantations and build up their wealth in time for the next major invasion.

From Nosy Be or thereabouts it was an easy journey due west to the Comoros. In the raiding season a lookout was kept on Pic Valentin on Mayotte island and a great fire lit to signal the approach of the enemy. The grand fleet of nearly 500 canoes, surging across the sea like a swarm of locusts, was a sight to inspire fear. The warning was passed to the other islands and especially Anjouan, the richest and therefore the main target. The Comorians who were warned in time would barricade themselves in the main towns, leaving the countryside open to plunder. A group of the invaders would build huts round the towns they wanted to besiege while the others would roam the islands for provisions and prisoners who could be sold as slaves. The siege of the towns would often last until the wind changed to favour the return journey to Madagascar. If the change were long delayed the Comorians would suffer the horrors of famine which in 1808 reduced some women in Anjouan to eating their own children and others to blowing themselves up in the powder magazine where they had taken refuge.

In a period of over thirty years the Comoros were spared an annual visitation only when bad weather prevented an expedition or the raiders attacked other targets on the African coast. For a long time it was thought that these diversions to Africa were accidental, resulting from an error in navigation or a change in wind sweeping the raiders past the islands towards Mozambique.[10] It now appears more probable that the raids on the African coast were deliberate. Some at least may have been carried out at the behest of deposed Comorian princes pursuing personal ambitions or vendettas, with the Malagasy raiders acting as mercenaries rather than on their own account.[11] The raids on Africa were carried out by substantial expeditions which attacked African, Arab and even Portuguese settlements along the coast. European ships were not safe from the voracious pirates. A Portuguese vessel was sacked and a Portuguese corvette of 16 guns sent to punish those responsible was destroyed with all its crew; and a French slaving vessel was also seized and destroyed.

The main sufferers on the African coast were the Querimba islands and the Portuguese station at Ibo. In 1808–9 the pirate attack made a desert of these fertile islands, destroying houses and plantations and killing or capturing all the inhabitants who fell into their hands. After years of rumours of further attacks the next major assault took place in 1816–17 when the pirates were so numerous that they were divided into two expeditions, one commanded by a Comorian prince and the other by a "Moor" called Nassiri. However they suffered heavy losses from bad weather, and although they successfully raided unprotected points on the coast they were easily repelled by the Portuguese at Ibo and by the Arab Sultan of Kilwa on the Tanzanian coast. Another expedition to the Tanzanian coast the following year captured 3,000 slaves and much booty from Kilwa and the Mafia island group, but ended in total disaster. Word quickly reached Zanzibar and the Sultan sent twenty sloops armed with cannon in pursuit. After a chase of sixteen days the Malagasy were caught in Msimbati Bay just north of the Ruvuma estuary where, trying to pass through a shallow channel between an island and the mainland, they ran their canoes aground. The Arabs came up and with their superior armament (the Malagasy were armed only with spears and muskets) slaughtered the pirates to a man.

Losses on this scale would have eventually discouraged further assaults on the mainland, but raids on the Comoros continued to show a profit. The Comorians made frequent appeals for protection to the British and French settlements in the Indian Ocean, but so long as the Napoleonic Wars lasted there was little they could do. In 1812 the British governor of Cape Colony, responding to an appeal from the Sultan of Anjouan's emissary known as Bombay Jack, ordered a frigate to visit Malagasy ports to discourage the raids; but, the cyclone season making Malagasy waters dangerous, the captain limited himself to delivering arms and munitions to the Sultan. These were not much help as the Comorians were too pusillanimous to make effective use of them. So in 1814 Bombay Jack travelled to Mauritius to appeal to the governor, Sir Robert Farquhar, who was already taking a close interest in Madagascar. As we shall see later this appeal led finally to the cessation of the raids in the context of the Anglo-Malagasy Treaty for the abolition of the Malagasy slave trade.

Thus ended a remarkable episode which seems like a distant echo of the period in the ninth century when the high-prowed ships of the Norsemen crossed the North Sea every spring to ravage the coasts and estuaries of Britain. And it is not too fanciful to suggest that Norse blood still flowed in the veins of some of the Zana-Malata via the Normandy seamen from Dieppe who were prominent among the pirate crews who frequented the coasts of Madagascar a century earlier.

Chapter 9

The rise of the Merina

Up to the end of the eighteenth century European knowledge of Madagascar remained, with very few exceptions, limited to certain areas of the coast. In the north the splendid harbour of Diego Suarez was still unexploited; while the sparse population of its mountainous hinterland the Antankarana ("people of the rocks") had little contact with the rest of Madagascar or the outside world. On the east coast the French, as we have seen, had acquired possession of Ile Ste Marie and had established trading posts along the coast opposite the island. Although the colony at Fort Dauphin had been abandoned, a trade mainly in cattle continued with the French settlers at Bourbon.

Difficulty of access and the extreme poverty of the country kept the Antandroy isolated from European contact. But we know that during the eighteenth century they suffered repeated attacks from the Mahafaly, the Sakalava, the Bara and the Antanosy which eventually destroyed their ruling dynasty and reduced them to a collection of individual clans. The last intertribal fighting recorded by Drury, when the Antandroy paramount chief Andriankirindra was killed by the Mahafaly under Andriankosintany, may have been the beginning of this process of disintegration. The Maroserana dynasty of the Mahafaly retained its authority, but at some stage split up into four branches.

Towards the end of the century the rising power in this area was the Bara people, expanding into the south central region between the Isalo Massif and the eastern escarpment. Their height and dark skin indicate that they have closer links with Africa than the other Malagasy peoples apart from the Sakalava; and it is possible that they are descended from some of the Africans who were found along the west coast by Luis Mariano at the beginning of the seventeenth century but who disappeared from the coast during the following century. Their ruling family, the Zafimanely, was an offshoot of the Maroserana dynasty. They are an essentially pastoral people and their semi-nomadic existence may well have developed their warlike qualities. They first appear as an identifiable group in the early seventeenth century in the region of the Ivohibe depression: this remote and beautiful valley, resembling a smaller version of the Kenya rift valley, appears to have served as a refuge and cradle of several tribal groups in the south. As they expanded from their original homeland their raids became a considerable harassment to the Antandroy and the Mahafaly in the south, the Masikoro to the west and the Betsileo to the north. But their dispersal over greater areas of the vast arid plains made it more difficult to maintain any central authority; even today it is virtually impossible to police this area effectively against cattle thefts and the *feu de brousse*, the widespread though now illegal practice of burning old grass which is gradually turning the whole of the south into a desert. During the nineteenth century the Bara split up into numerous small clans under separate chiefs, but they retained their common identity and remained a military threat to their neighbours until some time after the French occupation.

Along the west coast the Sakalava kingdoms extended their authority to the north and reached the height of their power in the middle of the eighteenth century before entering a period of gradual decline. The Boina king Andriantoakafo whom Drury knew as King Dick expanded the kingdom northwards along the coast as far as Nosy Be. Known posthumously as Andrianamboninarivo, he was successful in holding his widely scattered kingdom together, but after his death it was split up among his four sons. His eldest son moved his capital some way up the river Betsiboka to Marovoay ("many crocodiles") which remained the residence of the Boina kings up to modern times. Two other sons established vassal kingdoms in the western part of the Boina. A fourth son Tsitavana went north and extended his father's acquisitions inland up the valleys of the Sofia and Sambirano rivers. He secured the submission of the Antankarana and ruled in this area for some time before succeeding to his brother's throne at Marovoay around 1750. He was succeeded around 1780 by his great-niece Ravahiny, the first and greatest of the Sakalava queens. She ruled capably until her death in 1808, successfully maintaining the unity of the Boina against rebellions both in the north and the south, and her memory is still venerated in the northwest of Madagascar. The richness of her court, sustained by the overseas trade centred on Majunga, excited the admiration of foreign visitors and the envy of other Malagasy tribes. She made an official visit to the Merina kingdom of the central plateau and treated on equal terms with the rising power which after her death was to be largely instrumental in the disintegration of the Boina.

Further south, the prestige of the Menabe kingdom of the

Sakalava declined somewhat after the death of the terrible Ratsimonongarivo described by Drury. His son Ramoma, whom Drury described as "a very great prince and well beloved", kept the kingdom together despite the handicap of being paralysed so that he had to be carried everywhere. He appears to have merited Drury's description, being as much loved as his father was feared, and his posthumous name can be translated "father of his people". After his death around 1740 his son Ramiteny succeeded to the throne but was soon murdered by his brother Ratoakefo who set himself up as king at Mahabo. A son of Ramiteny called Ratrimolahy established a separate kingdom in the Tsiribihina valley. He appears to have inherited some of the qualities of his fierce great-grandfather Ratsimonongarivo and in due course he attacked and conquered the rival kingdom at Mahabo and re-established the unity of Menabe. But internal disputes over the succession broke out again after his death so that it was a considerably weakened Menabe kingdom which had to face the rising power of the Merina early in the nineteenth century.

With their numerous ports facing the Mozambique Channel, the Sakalava had wider contacts with the outside world than the rest of the Malagasy people. Arab traders continued to be active in the north-west where Majunga developed into a thriving trading centre. There was some contact with Africa, the most spectacular being the raids on the East African coast in which Sakalava of the north participated. European ships, mainly English but also Dutch, French and Portuguese, called in occasionally at Sakalava ports on their way to India. The English as always favoured St Augustine's Bay, and their visits were sufficiently frequent for the inhabitants to pick up a smattering of English and occasionally to adopt English names.

In July 1754 a fleet of six ships of the Royal Navy on its way out to India anchored in St Augustine's Bay. The commander was Admiral Watson and his fleet was to play an important role in collaboration with Clive in destroying the French position in India during the Seven Years' War. Their call at St Augustine's was necessitated by the high degree of sickness on board. One hundred and fifty of the crew on the flagship alone were sick, mainly of the scurvy, but thanks to fresh food and the coolness of the weather they nearly all recovered in less than three weeks. Edward Ives, the surgeon on board the flagship, made a detailed record of the visit. As soon as the fleet anchored, several local notables from the court of the king of Baba came on board, led by "old Robin Hood" who appeared to act as the king's prime minister and negotiated the king's transactions with the fleet's agent-victualler. There was also the king's general called Philibey, and two captains, John Anderson and Frederick Martin. "And the king's own family likewise, in imitation of the court of England, is not without a Prince of Wales, a Duke of Cumberland, a Prince Augustus, and Princesses distinguished by English names".[1]

The prevalence of English names indicates fairly frequent calls by English ships and is explained by Ives in the following passage: "The men are allowed to have as many wives as they please or can support. The king has three; the Duke of Baba (the king's nephew) but one; John Anderson two. Their children they often name after any English officers who happen to be there at the time of their wives' pregnancy, or delivery. One of John Anderson's wives was with child, while we were there; and he assured Sir William Hewet, that if she brought him a boy, he would give the child his name and title."[2] A similar practice in the plateau area in later times led to a number of Malagasy children being named after British missionaries giving rise to modern family names like Rajohnson, Randavison, Raharijaona (Harry Jones) and Robinson.

The king of Baba lived in a town of mud huts up country some 12 miles (20 km) from the Bay. We do not know his Malagasy name but he was presumably an important Masikoro chieftain, related to or descended from the Fiherenana chiefs who befriended Robert Drury, and a tributary of the Sakalava king of Menabe. He had a well-developed sense of protocol and refused to visit the fleet until the admiral had called on him first. Admiral Watson accordingly visited him accompanied by Ives: "The king was about sixty years of age, very corpulent and had at that time a violent fit of the gout. He was sitting on a grass-mat spread on the ground, with a wrapper round his middle, and on his head he wore a Dutch grenadier's cap, a foot and a half high, faced with the arms of the Dutch East India company cut in brass. He took the Admiral by the hand, and enquired how King George did: when he was told that he was now in health, but had lately been in great affliction on account of the death of his eldest son, he feelingly replied, "Ay, I have likewise lost my Prince of Wales".[3]

On learning that Ives was a doctor the king asked if he would treat him for gout. But he died shortly afterwards, fortunately before Ives had given him any treatment. A decision on the succession had not been taken when the fleet left, but Ives learned later that the king's sixteen-year-old second son Raphani had been preferred to his older nephew the Duke of Baba. It was no doubt a son or nephew of Raphani who appears as king of Baba in our next adventure.

In May 1792 an East Indiaman, the *Winterton*, sailed from England for Madras and Bengal with 280 people on board, ten of them women. In the darkness of the early morning of August 20, she went aground on the reefs about 6 miles (10 km) from the shore north of Tulear. Attempts at refloating failed and the ship began to break up. Over the next few days most of the crew and passengers got ashore on makeshift rafts, but about forty were drowned in the process. The exhausted survivors took eight days to reach Tulear, only 50 miles (80 km) away, where the king of Baba received them with affection and promised to protect them. Ten days later the Third Officer, Mr Dale, and some of the crew set off in a yawl to make for Mozambique in the hope of finding a ship which would take the shipwrecked party to the Cape of Good Hope. The remainder settled down for a long and tedious wait. They had ample time to observe life at the king of Baba's court. One of the passengers, George Buchan later published a detailed account.

On the structure of society, Buchan commented:

"The scale of society seemed pretty much arranged in three classes; the highest class, next to the king, and what I may call the officers of state, being those whose occupation was the profession of arms, who rank probably according to the extent of their possessions in slaves and cattle; the next, fishermen, who remain on the sea coast, and are engaged in the management of their canoes and fishing; and the last, the slaves. The king, though held in habitual reverence and, so far as we saw, promptly obeyed, cannot be considered wholly despotic; for in the event of any undue severity, his subjects will leave him and migrate to another state ... The practice which seems to exist of making all weighty questions matter of public deliberation, must have a powerful effect in upholding independence and elevation of mind. I remember being quite struck with the fluency of speech and oratory which we sometimes heard ...

"Their huts are commonly built of reeds and rushes, from 13 to 15 ft in length, the fire being kindled in the middle. The furniture consists of a bed made of reeds, covered with a mat, a few calabashes, some wooden spoons, and two or three earthen pots, which they pack up and move from place to place at a moment's warning. I think I may call them, among themselves, a social and happy people ... They enjoy apparently much domestic harmony. Polygamy is allowed, but it is far from being generally practised. Their kindness to their slaves is quite remarkable ... Their general turn of mind appears that of lively quickness, accompanied by a thirst for knowledge ...

"There were one or two besetting sins to which our Madagascar friends were certainly particularly prone; the first was the desire of intoxication, from which few, from the highest to the lowest rank, was exempted ... The next failing was a liking for *spulzie* or, in humbler terms, a thievish disposition ... Plunder is a part of their system."[4]

A frank but attractive picture is painted of the young king of Baba: "He seemed to be about 25 years of age; not tall, and rather slimly made, but well-proportioned. His countenance did not indicate any striking ability, but much liveliness and benignity. His complexion was remarkably white, approaching copper colour.[5] When occasion required it, he appeared with a good deal of what might be called in their way magnificence, having around him a large body of armed men and attendants; but he did not seem fond of the royal state, and generally went about with very few people ... The palace was little more than a hut on a larger scale."[6]

The king shared the general fondness for alcohol, although he never seemed to lose recollection and always maintained a certain dignity. The overriding impression is of the young king's generosity towards his involuntary guests. The burden of feeding them was considerable, and the number of cattle killed for them caused some discontent among the people. Although he would normally have travelled to other parts of his country, he stayed at Tulear all the time they were there, at considerable personal inconvenience, knowing that in his absence their safety was uncertain. The treasure on the *Winterton* had been recovered from the wreck by fishermen who had presented it to the king; and he would have been perfectly entitled to keep it all as salvage. Instead he gave 20,000 dollars to the ship's officers for distribution among the passengers and crew; he also gave them clothes which had been salvaged and which were particularly welcome to the women. Altogether, as a report from Calcutta later acknowledged, they received "such disinterested attention as would have done honour to the most civilised Christian".[7]

There was, however, nothing that the king could do to mitigate the oppressive climate and the dangers of disease. Wrecked at the end of the cooler season, they had to endure the full heat of summer and the discomfort and humidity of the rainy season. In six months some ninety of them died of malaria, aggravated in some cases by the extraordinary remedies (including tobacco juice and sea water) to which they resorted in the absence of more orthodox medicines. Mr Dale and his party finally turned up in March 1793 with a small ship on which the hundred or so survivors embarked. After further adventures including capture by a French privateer they managed to reach Madras. It is pleasant to record that the

East India Company took the first opportunity to send a handsome present to the king at Tulear.

The action of the French privateer was one of the earliest echoes in the Indian Ocean of the twenty years' war between Britain and France which was to have a profound effect on Madagascar's relations with the outside world and to lead to a decisive shift of European interest from the coasts to the central plateau. But for the time being the mountainous interior remained shrouded in almost impenetrable mystery. At the time of the first French occupation of Fort Dauphin, La Case roamed deep into the southern interior, perhaps as far as the edge of the southern plateau. During the same period François Martin, who was later to win fame as the founder of Pondicherry, was in charge of a trading outpost at Fénérive. Looking for fresh supplies of cattle, he led a large expedition up into the lower plateau region around Lake Alaotra, the home of the Sihanaka ("the people of the marshes"). But he found the Sihanaka numerous, well armed and hostile and had to beat a hasty retreat. No other Europeans got as far into the interior for over a century, and the high plateau remained completely unknown. In 1776, a map[8] prepared on the orders of Baron Benyowsky and showing the location of the various tribes, made no mention of the important peoples living in the centre. Nevertheless, Benyowsky was responsible for the initiative which led to the first breach in this wall of ignorance.

At the beginning of 1777 Benyowsky, possibly inspired by the lacunae revealed by his map, dispatched Nicolas Mayeur on a secret mission to investigate trading opportunities in the interior. Mayeur, who had emigrated to the Ile de France as a boy, had already travelled and traded in many parts of Madagascar and spoke the language well. Starting from Foulpointe with forty porters laden with provisions, ammunition and merchandise, he travelled south along the coast until he reached the Mangoro river. Turning west he followed the river valley inland, climbing through the eastern escarpment until he reached the country known as Andrantsay in the central plateau somewhere in the region of the modern town of Antsirabe. The ruler of Andrantsay, who had traded with Mayeur on a previous visit, did not wish to share the benefits of this trade with his powerful neighbours to the north in Ankova ("the country of the Hova"), and tried to prevent him from travelling there. However, after a secret meeting with the king of Ankova (Andrianamboatsimarofy), who had crossed the border in disguise, Mayeur pretended to leave for the coast and then doubled back further north into the Hova country. Here he found a numerous, thriving and industrious population under an organised government, living in well-built stone and earth houses and manufacturing a wide variety of iron implements, weapons and utensils. On his return to the coast he wrote a report which concluded: "The Europeans who have frequented the Island of Madagascar and who read these memoirs, will have difficulty in persuading themselves that in the interior of this great island entirely surrounded by savage peoples there is more enlightenment, more industry and a more active administration than on the coasts where the inhabitants are in constant relations with foreigners." This report, along with a more detailed report of a further visit by Mayeur to Antananarivo in 1785, seems to have attracted little attention at the time. The two reports languished in the archives of Ile de France for a generation but were unearthed after the British occupation in 1810 and were to have an important influence on subsequent events.

The people "discovered" by Mayeur are, by accepted modern usage, known as the Merina, although most early accounts and oral traditions refer to them as the Hova. As we have seen, the origin of the Merina/Hova is clouded in doubt and mystery. Yet we have a lot of information about the beginnings of the monarchy, thanks to some extraordinarily vivid and detailed oral traditions collected at the end of the last century by a Jesuit missionary, R P Callet, and published as *Tantaran'ny andriana*.[9] These trace the line of monarchs back to the fourteenth century where tradition becomes legend, with the first king said to be the son of God. But they also recount complex genealogies of many families, together with events in which they were involved and details of numerous old customs and beliefs. Though far from entirely reliable (there are sometimes conflicting versions of the same event) they are a most valuable source of information and from the sixteenth century onwards the existence of the principal characters is confirmed by the presence of tombs which can still be visited.

It was around the middle of the sixteenth century that various changes took place which were to lead eventually to the emergence of the powerful Merina monarchy. The *Tantara* tend to support the view that the group responsible for these changes, the Hova, emerged from within the existing population of the highlands rather than from outside the area, whether recent immigrants from Java/Malaya or less probably an old Malagasy tribe which had moved slowly to the centre from the southeast. Modern histories usually present the birth of the Merina monarchy as resulting from a conflict between immigrants (Hova) and the existing population (Vazimba) who were pushed out or absorbed. But the *Tantara* give the impression that the Hova were originally only one

The rise of the Merina

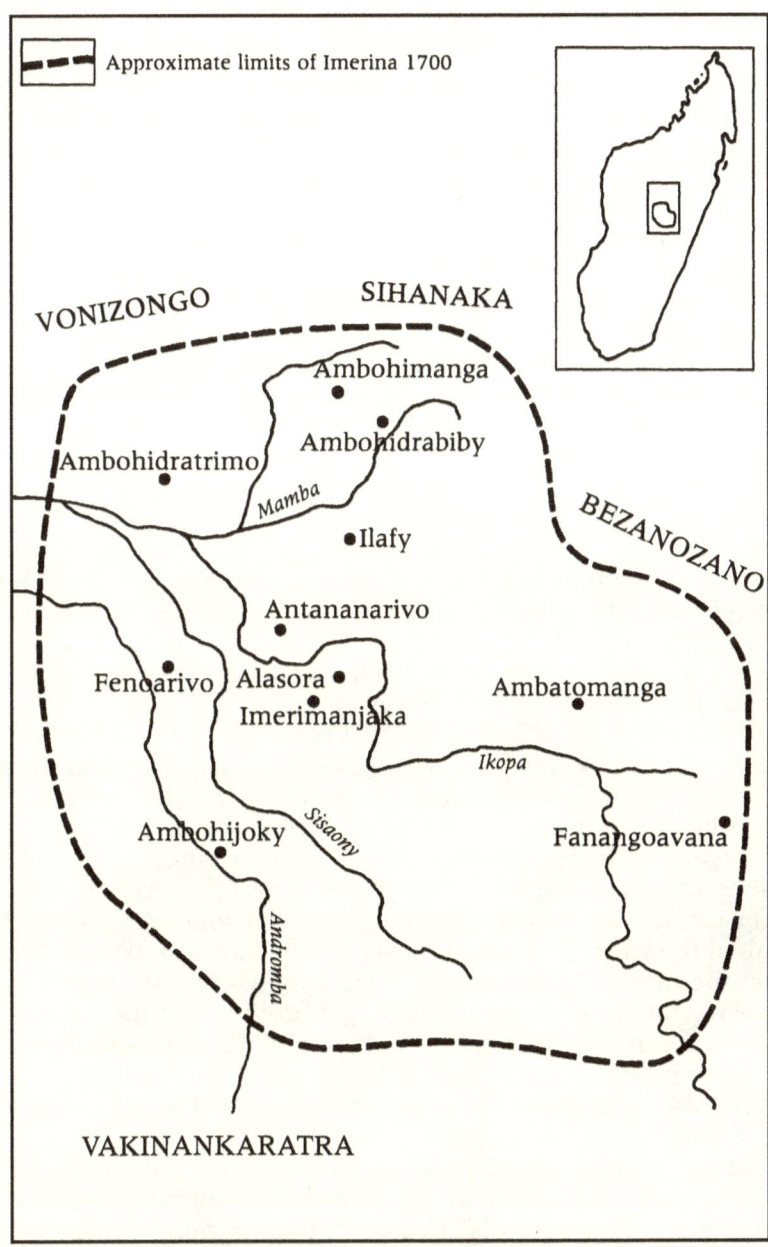

The Merina kingdom under Andriamasinavalona

group of Vazimba, occupying one village or group of hamlets.

There are however other oral traditions which record a movement of the Hova from the southeast down the valleys of the Sisaony and Ikopa rivers. These traditions lend support to the view that the Hova were late immigrants from the east coast, ascending to the plateau up the valley of the Mangoro; and are not incompatible with a suggestion that they were an *émigré* group of Betsileo from the southern plateau, whose noble class were called Hova. It is possible that the *Tantara* traditions were altered by later Merina kings to emphasise their descent from the Vazimba and thus strengthen the legitimacy and title to rule of a group who might otherwise be regarded as immigrant upstarts.

For the time being the precise origin of the Hova must be regarded as unproven. Fortunately their history from the time of their emergence in the central plateau around the middle of the sixteenth century is reasonably clear and straightforward. In the Vazimba period, up to the sixteenth century, every village had its own chief or king. The earliest of the Merina kings of what we might call the post-Vazimba period was Andriamanelo, who was born in the little village of Imerimanjaka, a few miles to the south of Antananarivo. But his mother was a Vazimba queen, descended from several generations of Vazimba chiefs. She was either Rafohy or Rangita, according to which version of the *Tantara* is followed,[10] and she was responsible for the first essential step in creating the monarchy. Having two sons, she decreed that her succession would pass first to the elder, Andriamanelo, and then to the younger. Previously the inheritance had been divided among all sons, or younger sons had gone off to found a separate village, thus adding to the fragmentation. By establishing an orderly succession to an intact inheritance Rafohy or Rangita (or in some versions both) halted the fragmentation and gave an incentive to expansion. In fact the queen's decree did not prevent rivalries developing between Andriamanelo and his younger brother, and the latter was put to death by the people "to please the king". Thus a kind of precedent was established by which a successor was nominated (not always the eldest son) and other possible claimants were assassinated to avoid disputes.

Andriamanelo moved his capital a few miles to the east to the village of Alasora, where four hundred years later his tomb is still a place of pilgrimage. His great contribution to the expansion of the Hova was the introduction of new iron technology – iron spades (*angady*) with which to improve agriculture and to dig a defensive ditch around Alasora, iron axes and other tools with which to build better houses and to hollow out canoes from tree trunks, and a new weapon described in the traditions as "flying iron" (probably the crossbow) which gave his warriors a decisive superiority over neighbouring Vazimba.[11] How he acquired this iron technology is still obscure. But various concurrent cultural innovations, such as the Arab calendar, divination (*sikidy*) and perhaps circumcision, suggest the presence of sorcerers or diviners (*mpisikidy*) possibly of Zafi-Raminia origin who could have brought new knowledge of iron with them; one of these may even have been his father, since there is a suggestion that Rafohy married a "foreigner", and one tradition specifically attributes the introduction of the new iron technology to him.

With the aid of his iron weapons Andriamanelo extended his domain several miles to the east and northeast of Antananarivo, then called Analamanga ("the blue forest"). He married the daughter of Rabiby, a Vazimba chief living at Ambohidrabiby ("Rabiby's village") a few miles to the east of Ambohimanga. After six children had died young, the *mpisikidy* were consulted to recommend the most favourable circumstances for the birth of the seventh; and, a wild boar (*lambo*) passing by at the moment of birth, the child, a boy, was named Ralambo. To ease the succession, Andriamanelo arranged a marriage between Ralambo and his great-niece, the grand-daughter of his murdered younger brother, thus fulfilling after a fashion his mother's wish that the succession should pass in due course to the younger son.

Ralambo, who succeeded his father towards the end of the sixteenth century, moved his capital to Ambohidrabiby which he had inherited through his mother. He extended his kingdom in the course of several successful campaigns against neighbouring Vazimba and he also repelled incursions from other tribal groups. He was responsible for naming his country Imerina ("the land where one can see far", an allusion to the extensive views from the villages built always on hill-tops). His success in battle was attributed partly to the appearance within his ranks of the first firearm (probably an arquebus[12]) to be used in Imerina; and partly to a royal idol or talisman named *Kelimalaza* ("small and famous"), which in one battle caused huge hailstones to fall and kill many of the enemy.[13] Ralambo was the first Merina to eat beef which was previously considered unhealthy and, possibly to get round a verbal taboo, he changed the name of cattle and beef from *jamoka* to the Bantu *omby*. He was also responsible for other innovations, such as the annual royal bath festival to mark the new year, and the establishment of a hierarchy of four classes among the *andriana* or nobles, depending on the closeness of their relationship with the royal family.

Ralambo chose as his successor his second son (though by his first wife) Andrianjaka ("the prince who rules"), who had proved himself as a courageous and intelligent leader in several of his father's campaigns. He extended the kingdom to the north and west and probably had trading connections with the west coast since he acquired fifty muskets and three barrels of powder. His lands now hemmed in on three sides the Vazimba stronghold of Analamanga, with its great rock rising from the marshy plain like Gibraltar from the sea. This natural fortress fell to him without a blow when he advanced with an army so numerous that the defending Vazimba took fright and fled at the sight of the smoke from their camp fires. But Andrianjaka dealt magnanimously with the Vazimba chiefs, giving their family an honoured position in his kingdom; he also originated the cult of Vazimba ancestors. Taking possession of Analamanga he renamed it Antananarivo ("the town of a thousand") and built his *rova* or royal enclosure on its highest point: his simple wooden hut, somewhat restored, can still be seen there. His occupation of this strong position, controlling a great expanse of marshy plain with its potential for rice growing, crowned the work of his predecessors and established a firm foundation for Merina power. The rest of his reign was mainly engaged in the construction of dykes and canals to transform the marshes into the rice-fields which were to enable the Merina to become the most numerous people in the island.

The rice-fields were further extended under Andrianjaka's son and grandson, who were otherwise remarkable only for the length of their names. Andrianjaka's grandson was called Andriantsimitoviaminandriandehibe, meaning "the prince not equalled by the great princes". His elder son succeeded him but proved to be inadequate and was overthrown by a group of chiefs who placed the second son, Andriamasinavalona, on the throne. During his reign the kingdom was further extended, by the submission of various chiefs, to cover the whole of central Imerina, roughly within a radius of 20–25 miles (30–40 km) from Antananarivo. He was a contemporary of two great Sakalava kings, Drury's Ratsimonongarivo in Menabe and Andriamandisoarivo who created the Boina kingdom. But despite its much smaller area, the Merina kingdom was probably more powerful than the Sakalava at this time, thanks to its dense population sustained by the expanding ricefields. In the eighteenth century the position was to be reversed owing to the Sakalava control of the west coast trade, particularly in arms, and to divisions within the Merina kingdom. For these Andriamasinavalona was to blame. An excess of paternal affection led him to divide his kingdom into four principalities for his four sons, with the promise that they would become independent kingdoms after his death.

In vain did a faithful counsellor, Andriamampandry, who had played a leading part in putting him on the throne, inveigh against the dangers of dividing the kingdom, reinforcing his arguments with symbolism in typically Malagasy fashion. Four fighting cocks, released in the king's presence, immediately flew at each other; four hawks, released inside the king's modest hut, spread dust and confusion everywhere as they fluttered frantically seeking an exit. But the king uneasily maintained his decision. Even during his lifetime a dispute developed with one of his sons, established at Ambohidratrimo, who captured Andriamasinavalona and held him prisoner for seven years. After Andriamasinavalona's death around 1710, Imerina split up into four kingdoms based on Ambohimanga (the north), Ambohidrabiby (the east), Ambohidratrimo (the west) and Antananarivo (the south). The unfilial son at Ambohidratrimo died about the same time, and his kingdom declined in importance; and the kingdom of Ambohidrabiby soon became subordinate to Ambohimanga. But Andriamampandry's fears proved to be only too well founded. Rivalry and often open warfare continued between Antananarivo and Ambohimanga for most of the eighteenth century, with the smaller kingdom of Ambohidratrimo sometimes taking sides and the Sakalava being called in from time to time in aid of one side or the other.

From this point the *Tantara* concentrate on the Ambohimanga branch, which was to become the main line of the Merina succession. In Antananarivo, the succession passed through Andriamasinavalona's eldest son to a grandson, a great-grandson, another great-grandson and finally to a nephew of the latter, Andrianamboatsimarofy, who was the "king of the Hova" visited by Mayeur in 1777 and again in 1785. Mayeur noted that as the descendant of the eldest line he had a theoretical primacy in the whole of Imerina; but in fact he was having difficulty in asserting authority over his own domains. During Mayeur's visit in 1785 he was engaged in war against a cousin established at Alasora, only a few miles south of Antananarivo. Mayeur witnessed three attacks by substantial forces against Alasora; during the second battle a cloud of locusts caused the fighting to be abandoned with both sides engaging the common enemy and women and children emerging to carry off basketfuls of dead locusts to be eaten. Despite a considerable superiority of numbers Andrianamboatsimarofy was unable to capture Alasora even on the third attempt. He was to be the last king of Antananarivo before the northern branch took over.

At Ambohimanga an important role was played by Andriambelomasina who ruled this small kingdom from about 1730 to 1770. He consolidated his own territory, extended it somewhat by marriage alliances and fought off incursions by the Sakalava. But he is remembered mainly for the arrangements he made for the succession. He named his eldest son Andrianjafy as his immediate successor and set him up at Ilafy, a village half-way between Ambohimanga and Antananarivo; but he ruled that the succession should thereafter pass to Ramboasalama, the son of his eldest daughter. Ramboasalama ("healthy dog"), a deliberately unattractive name so as not to arouse the interest and jealousy of evil spirits, was auspiciously born, probably around 1745, on the first day of the new moon of the first month, the same day as Ralambo; and other signs and portents marked him out for a great destiny.

When Andrianjafy succeeded his father around 1770 he soon earned the hatred of his subjects by his brutal and tyrannical behaviour. He became jealous of his young nephew and conceived various plots to kill him so that the succession could pass to his own son. Ramboasalama was warned in time and fled to the north, but a famous diviner persuaded him to return and set himself up as an independent ruler at Ambohimanga. Twelve chiefs of northern Imerina supported him, and although Andrianjafy was allowed to retain Ilafy for a short time he was eventually overthrown and killed, probably in 1787. Ramboasalama was now proclaimed king of Ambohimanga and took the name of Andrianampoinimerina ("the prince in the heart of Imerina" or "the prince desired by Imerina"). Nampoina, as it is more convenient to call him, now assured himself a period of peace by concluding a treaty with the two other Merina kings, reinforced by a double matrimonial alliance with Andrianamboatsimarofy of Antananarivo, who promised to give a young daughter as wife to Nampoina in return for one of Nampoina's sisters as wife to himself. During the next seven years Nampoina consolidated his power and prepared to fulfil an ancient prophecy that a prince would come down from the north to reunite the Merina. He was to do much more than that.

To appreciate fully the achievement of this remarkable man, it is necessary to visit the base from which he started, the little village of Ambohimanga, which has altered little since his time. Situated only 12 miles (20 km) to the north of Antananarivo, Ambohimanga is, like most other villages on the plateau, built on a small hill. Its name, meaning blue hill or blue village,[14] derives from a dense clump of primary deciduous forest on the steepest side, which appears blue at a distance, and which has survived because the sacred nature of the village made it *fady* to destroy the trees there. The approach to the village on the less steep side is through the original gateway, surmounted by a lookout post and protected by a huge round flat stone, some 15 ft (4 m) in diameter and weighing 12 tons, which used to be rolled over to block the entrance at night. Higher up the hill is the *rova* or royal enclosure, surrounded by a high wall, with watch-towers at the four corners. In front of the *rova* is an open space where the people gathered to hear the king deliver a *kabary*, and containing the sacred stone (*vatomasina*) on which the kings of Ambohimanga took the equivalent of the oath of office on ascending the throne. Within the *rova* is Nampoina's "palace" almost as it was – a simple rectangular wooden hut of pitch-painted planks with a steep pointed roof originally thatched with rice-straw. Inside, a single room some 20 ft by 12 (6 x 4 m) serves as kitchen, sitting room and bedroom. In the centre of the room a few stones make a fireplace with no chimney save a hole in the roof; the walls are hung with simple utensils, spears, javelins and targes. In one corner the king's narrow wooden bed is set 8 ft (nearly 3 m) high as protection against a surprise attack by an assassin, and is reached by a ladder carved out of a solid piece of wood. In contrast the vast bed for his twelve wives[15] in the adjacent corner is raised only a few inches from the earthen floor. Behind the *rova* one can climb to the highest point of the hill from which the sacred trees fall away to the south. The eye travels along a shallow valley to where the great rock of Antananarivo rises in the distance, crowned with its royal palace. It is easy to imagine Nampoina gazing across at his future capital and brooding and planning his great designs.

Nampoina displayed most of the qualities of great leaders throughout history. He had the gift of inspiring and retaining the affection of his people, and was generous in rewarding those who served him. He was a skilful organiser and administrator who developed a complex social and administrative structure without benefit of written records and therefore of bureaucracy. He must have been a spell-binding orator; details of many of his speeches, full of the imagery which the Malagasy love, were preserved in folk memory long after his death. As a military leader he was not perhaps in the front rank, owing his victories less to strategic or tactical skill than to his ability to organise, train and arm his troops. Whenever possible he preferred to gain his objectives by diplomacy rather than by armed force; and although he could be ruthless in destroying those who opposed him he knew when magnanimity would serve his purposes better.

After so many years of anarchy, however, military force was an essential requirement for the re-unification of Imerina. During the years of peace Nampoina established fortified villages on the limits of his territory, obtained large quantities of firearms and organised and trained his soldiers. The core of his army was an élite "imperial guard" of fifty, later seventy, warriors, including the twelve chiefs who had placed him in power; but when battle called, all able bodied-men were expected to exchange their spade for a spear or musket. The opportunity came when Andrianamboatsimarofy, who in his later years reverted to a youthful addiction to alcohol, broke his word by giving in marriage to the king of Ambohidratrimo the daughter he had promised to Nampoina. Nampoina's attack on Antananarivo was successful. But a smallpox epidemic weakened the garrison he left in charge, and the town was recaptured by the Manisotra, a famous warrior clan from the village of Ambohijoky who remained loyal to Andrianamboatsimarofy. When the Manisotra returned to their village, Antananarivo again fell to Nampoina's troops; only to be retaken again by the Manisotra, while Nampoina was in Ambohimanga for the New Year royal bath festival and the garrison at Antananarivo were comatose from the gorging of sacrificed cattle. Nampoina now took Antananarivo a third and final time by siege and ensured permanent occupation by taking up residence himself and establishing a proper system of defences and look-outs. This protracted struggle for Antananarivo seems to have lasted from 1792 or 1793 to 1795 or 1796. The defeated Andrianamboatsimarofy died shortly afterwards at Fenoarivo, to the west of Antananarivo, and he is buried at a little village a few miles to the south.

Nampoina obtained the peaceful submission of Imamo, the area to the west of Imerina as far as Lake Itasy, by returning to the king of Imamo two of his daughters who had been caught in the siege of Antananarivo. Over a period of years he proceeded to subdue the rest of Imerina and to extend its frontiers to the east, where he captured Ambatomanga from the Bezanozano, and to the northwest. All possible rivals were eliminated by the capture of Ambohidratrimo, where the king fled leaving Nampoina to take the young wife originally intended for him; and of Fenoarivo, where Andrianamboatsimarofy's son had been allowed to rule for a few years. The last and most formidable obstacle to his progress was the "eagle's nest" of Ambohijoky, stronghold of the fierce Manisotra and their even fiercer wives, who took up muskets and played an active part in the defence. Four separate attacks, the last in the presence of Nampoina himself, were driven back with heavy losses. Despite their successful resistance, some of the Manisotra recognised that they could not hold out indefinitely and were in favour of submitting; but the women would not countenance it. Finally they were forced to submit by the threat of famine after some of Nampoina's men had destroyed their rice crop just before harvest time. Some of them fled to the south to the country of the Betsileo, who soon afterwards became themselves the object of Nampoina's ambitions.

The Betsileo are one of the most important, and probably one of the oldest, of the Malagasy peoples. Their traditions suggest that the first inhabitants of the southern plateau region were Vazimba or proto-Malagasy who came up the valleys of the Matsiatra and Mania rivers, tributaries respectively of the Mangoky and the Tsiribihina. Later immigrants from the east coast included "Arabised" elements, probably Antemoro, who became chiefs. The word "plateau" is even less appropriate for the Betsileo region than for Imerina; it is rather an elevated range of hills and valleys with hardly any flat areas. The landscape is one of the most picturesque in Madagascar, with many trees, mainly recent growths of eucalyptus, softening the outline of the hills, in contrast to the bleak and barren *tanety* of Imerina. The Betsileo are the best farmers and probably the hardest workers in Madagascar, and the scenic beauty is enhanced by the skilfully terraced rice-fields, reminiscent of Ceylon or Java, on all but the steepest slopes. The highly accidented relief was however an obstacle to political development and the Betsileo were never united under one king. For brief periods the two main provinces of the Betsileo, Isandra and Lalangina, each achieved unity under their more important kings. But they soon declined again into groups of petty principalities and they could put up no effective resistance to the expansion of the Merina under Nampoina.

The most northerly of the Betsileo kings was Andriamanalina who ruled in the Andrantsay region near the modern town of Antsirabe. The story of how Nampoina dealt with him is a classic of Malagasy oral tradition, illustrating both Nampoina's subtle diplomacy and the Malagasy love of imagery and symbolism. Nampoina first sent emissaries to invite Andriamanalina to become his son, i.e. to accept his overlordship. When this had no effect he sent a *lamba* (a toga-like cloak which is the main feature of traditional dress in the highlands) in which a small hole had been cut, symbolising Andriamanalina's isolation in a country otherwise dominated by Nampoina. In reply Andriamanalina sent a cane cut to his own height and invited Nampoina to measure himself against it; the implication was that whoever was the taller would be recognised as overlord of the other, while if they were of equal height the issue would have to be settled by war. Nampoina proved to be an inch taller and accordingly claimed the other's submission. Andriamanalina asked for time to consult his people and then sacrificed an ox, announcing that if the ox died quietly he would go to war with Nampoina, but that if it bellowed he would submit. The ox bellowed but still he hesitated. He was finally persuaded to submit when he found that his son had secretly come to an understanding with Nampoina and that he was further isolated by the submission of a Betsileo king to the south.

The remaining Betsileo kings also submitted in due course. Most of them did so peacefully and were allowed to continue to rule as Nampoina's vassals. Those who resisted were no match for the Merina troops and were quickly subdued. Nampoina had thus in little more than a decade extended his control from the few square miles of his fief at Ambohimanga to all the inhabited area of the high plateau – an area twice the size of Wales, and not unlike it in physical features. It may have been at this stage that he expressed his ultimate ambitions in a famous phrase: "The sea shall be the limit of my rice-fields".

But the sea was still some distance away and the road to it passed through difficult and desolate country; while the Sakalava were still a force to be reckoned with on the west coast. Nampoina had a diplomatic success in persuading Queen Ravahiny of the Boina to visit Antananarivo; but she did so as an equal, and although the Merina subsequently claimed that the visit implied acceptance of Merina suzerainty, the Sakalava maintained that Nampoina's presents to the queen were an acknowledgement of the vassal status to which the Merina had been reduced in the eighteenth century. The divided and weakened Menabe was less capable of standing up to Nampoina; but for the time being the Merina lacked the resources to impose any effective control over this vast region. Emissaries sent by Nampoina obtained only the submission of a few minor chiefs and permission to establish a small garrison at Mahabo.

Nevertheless, Andrianampoinimerina had raised the Merina from a squabbling group of petty princes to the foremost military power in the island. Like his contemporary Napoleon, he was a notable administrator as well as a military leader and imposed major reforms on the administrative and social structure of his kingdom. While consolidating the best of the old customs he imposed a new organisation which resembled in many ways the feudal society of medieval Europe. At the centre was the all-powerful, semi-divine figure of the king, the link with God and the ancestors, the source of all authority and the owner of all land. Some of the land was crown land (known as *menabe* ("big red"), red being the royal colour) depending directly on the king; the remainder was divided into *menakely* ("little red") – small fiefs held by feudal lords and each consisting of one or more villages. In each village the people grouped in an assembly known as the *fokonolona* ("the people of the clan or village") were made responsible for law and order, the settlement of petty disputes, the organisation of unpaid labour for public works such as roads and irrigation ditches, and the collection of taxes, known as *vodihena* (literally "rump meat" from the time when Ralambo, in authorising the slaughter and eating of beef reserved the hump and the rump for royalty).

There was a rigid class structure with strict rules about intermarriage. At the top the *andriana* or nobles were divided into several grades, based on those established by Ralambo with additions by later kings. The middle class of free men was divided into two: the genuine *hova*, sometimes known as the *folovohitra* ("ten villages") from the ten villages of central Imerina; and the class of freed slaves and royal servants known collectively as the *mainty* ("blacks"). At the bottom were the *andevo* or slaves, including members of other tribes captured in battles or raids, imported African slaves known as Masombiky (from Mozambique) and local people reduced to slavery for certain offences.

Despite this rigid structure, the king was not isolated from the people. His main channel of communication was not the feudal nobles but seventy royal agents known as *vadin-tany* ("husbands of the earth"). They formed a general council to advise the king, along with an inner council of twelve great chiefs; and they travelled throughout the kingdom conveying the king's wishes, judging the more serious disputes, collecting taxes and ensuring that the public works were carried out. But the king also communicated directly with the people by means of his famous *kabary*. He used these to ensure the support of the people for military expeditions and their cooperation in irrigation and other public works; and to promulgate a complex series of laws. Theft and banditry, which Mayeur had noted as a serious scourge in Imerina, were suppressed by severe laws rigorously applied. Agriculture and especially rice-growing was encouraged by an almost mystical attitude to rice, with which Nampoina personally identified himself "rice and I are one". Hard work was expected of everyone: the lazy were beaten and those who applied to the king for assistance had a spade thrust into their hands. Trade was promoted by the establishment of markets in localities named after the day of the week on which the market was held, by the regulation of prices, weights and measures and by a law making the smallest theft within a market punishable by instant death.

With a wide range of livestock and agricultural products and an iron industry based on ample supplies of ore and wood from the forests of the Bezanozano, Imerina was self-sufficient in everything except firearms and ammunition. These were obtained from the coast in exchange for slaves captured during military expeditions; during the latter years of Nampoina's reign, an average of 1500 to 1800 slaves were exported each year from Imerina. This trade was now almost entirely in the hands of French traders from the east coast who shipped the slaves to the plantations of the Ile de France and Bourbon. Nampoina had a healthy mistrust of Europeans, and only a few privileged slave traders were permitted to enter Imerina further than the border village of Ambatomanga. In 1808 one of them, Barthélémy Hugon, was allowed to visit Antananarivo, and he appears to have been the only European to have left a written account of Nampoina. He describes him as "perhaps fifty years old (more probably he was over sixty), very ugly, with straight hair, having the appearance of a Malay. He is without doubt the richest, the most feared, the most enlightened, and has the largest kingdom, of all the kings of Madagascar."[16]

By 1808, Nampoina's work of expansion and consolidation was virtually complete. He had already chosen his young son Radama, born in 1793, as the successor most likely to carry on his work. While still a boy he had accompanied his father on some of his campaigns. Now at the age of only fifteen he was given command of two expeditions, one to part of the Betsileo which had rebelled and the other to the Boina, where the death of Queen Ravahiny appeared to offer new opportunities. The first was successful, but the advance into the Boina ended in defeat, although the capture of many cattle enabled Radama to return to a hero's welcome.

In 1810 Nampoina fell seriously ill and felt the end approaching. He summoned Radama and his counsellors to confirm the arrangements for the succession and to transmit his final recommendations and instructions. Above all Radama was to complete the conquest of the island: "Imerina has been gathered into one, but behold the sea is the border of my ricefields, O Radama". He then "turned his face to the wall" and died. His body, wrapped in eighty silk *lambas*, was carried to Ambohimanga and buried in a canoe made of solid silver. At the end of the century his remains were reburied alongside the tombs of the earlier Merina kings in the *rova* at Antananarivo, from where, in the words of Hubert Deschamps, "he dominates the plains and hills of Imerina, as he has dominated, from a great height, the history of Madagascar."[17]

PART 3   TOWARDS A NEW CIVILISATION

Chapter 10

The king, the governor and the sergeant

The accession of Radama I to the Merina throne in 1810, the year of the British seizure of Mauritius from the French, marks the great turning-point in the history of Madagascar. The ambitions of the young king, coinciding perfectly with the plans of the first British governor of Mauritius, Robert Farquhar, were to lead to the Merina conquest of most of the island and to bring Madagascar firmly into the world of the nineteenth century.

A well-known portrait by the French painter Coppalle and numerous descriptions in letters and journals give us a good idea of Radama's appearance and character. One French traveller, Leguével de Lacombe, described him as "short and slender but well-proportioned and of pleasing appearance; his features were those of a Malay but more delicate; his skin was also whiter and smoother, his eyes lively and sparkling. His nervous tics and his quick, jerky speech revealed straightaway the petulance of his character."[1]

He was indeed very much a spoilt child. The favourite son of an autocratic despot, he was accustomed at an early age to having his slightest whim gratified. He could be casually cruel, and was ruthless in destroying any opposition to his wishes. Self-discipline and restraint were totally foreign to him, and indulgence in alcohol and his sexual appetites undoubtedly contributed to his premature death. But his lack of inhibitions had its endearing side, shown in the childish delight with which he received new gadgets from abroad. And his weaknesses were more than outweighed by his capacity for warm friendship and above all by his high intelligence and adaptability which enabled him to lead a profoundly conservative people into a new era.

His first task was to consolidate the kingdom left by his father. The replacement of the formidable Andrianampoinimerina by a seventeen-year-old boy encouraged rebellions by the Bezanozano at Ambatomanga and some of the Betsileo at Ambositra. These were put down with some difficulty and both towns were destroyed. Radama then turned his mind to the conquest of other parts of the island, in fulfilment both of his father's wishes and of his own ambitions to become a great conqueror in emulation of Napoleon, whose exploits were related to him by French slave traders. But for the time being he lacked the military means to achieve his aims.

From the relatively densely populated Merina kingdom Radama had no difficulty in raising an army larger than that of any possible adversary. In his early campaigns his troops probably numbered between forty and fifty thousand, the majority armed with muskets acquired through the slave trade, the remainder with lances. They were far from being an undisciplined horde: at gatherings of the whole army a slight gesture from Radama would command instant silence; and there was a rudimentary organisation with the nobles and chiefs of the civilian administration assuming appropriate military commands. But the soldiers were virtually untrained in military manoeuvre and the use of their weapons; and commissariat organisation was almost completely lacking. The soldiers carried a minimum supply of rice but were expected to live off the country. Their great numbers then became a serious handicap when they invaded the more desolate parts of the island. Several expeditions into the bleak plains of Menabe ended in disaster as the Sakalava king Ramitraho retreated into yet more inaccessible bush until the Merina army was forced by starvation to return home many thousands fewer.

Another expedition through the more fertile lands of the Betsileo succeeded in subduing Vohibato, an area at the extreme south of the Betsileo which had never submitted to Andrianampoinimerina. The defenders took refuge in the village of Ifandana, perched on a precipitous rock and approached only by a steep and narrow pathway easy to defend. Assault was out of the question and Radama's army settled down to a long siege. But the starving defenders refused to surrender, preferring to commit collective suicide by dancing blindfold on the edge of the precipice until one by one they fell to their deaths on the rocks below. A crumbling pile of human bones still marks the place where some three thousand died in this way.

It was about the time of this macabre episode that Radama's destiny became linked with that of Robert Townsend Farquhar. Born in 1776, the son of a well-known physician and grandson of a Presbyterian minister, Farquhar entered the service of the East India Company at the age of twenty. The repercussions of the European wars gave ample scope for his zeal and initiative and within a few years he became governor of the Moluccas. When these islands were restored to the Dutch by the Treaty of Amiens, Farquhar returned to India where he continued to earn the esteem of his superiors. His great opportunity came in 1810 when he was appointed to accompany a naval and military expedition against the French islands in the Indian Ocean in order to assume the government of the islands after their capture.

The only surprising thing about this expedition is that it was not undertaken sooner. French privateers based on the Ile de France had for a number of years caused heavy losses in Britain's East India trade. Between 1807 and 1809 the East India Company lost at least forty ships, whose cargoes alone were worth more than one million pounds. Another reason for the expedition was the Government of India's fear that Ile de France might be used as a forward base for a French invasion of India, as in the days of Hyder Ali in 1782. The British moved first against the island of Bourbon,[2] which was captured after a stubborn resistance on July 8, 1810. Plans for the attack on Ile de France were disrupted by a disastrous naval action at the entrance to Grand Port in which several British ships were lost. But the arrival of naval squadrons from the East Indies and Cape stations restored the situation and gave the attackers an overwhelming superiority. The French governor capitulated on December 3, 1810 and the British commander-in-chief, Major-General Abercrombie, agreed to astonishingly lenient terms. The French garrison and naval personnel were not made prisoners but were returned to France at British expense. The civilians who decided to remain were guaranteed respect for their language, religion, customs and laws; and compensation was paid for any damage done by the British troops. It is not surprising that Farquhar, who had immediately been appointed governor, could report at Christmas that the take-over had been smooth and that the island, now renamed Mauritius, was all quiet.

Nevertheless Farquhar was faced with a tricky situation. Among the local customs guaranteed by the capitulation terms, slavery was perhaps the most important. The plantation economy of the islands was completely dependent on slave labour, and slaves were in short supply. But the importation of slaves into British territories had been made illegal by the Act of 1807 abolishing the slave trade. Local planters in Mauritius maintained that 40,000 new slaves were needed to cultivate the available land, and Farquhar was sufficiently persuaded to write to Lord Liverpool in February 1811 to ask that an exception be made in the case of Mauritius. Lord Liverpool's reply,[3] starting "I cannot sufficiently express my surprise that you should have supposed it possible ... ", left him in no doubt that, while there was no intention to change the condition of slaves already on the islands, British public opinion would not tolerate any continuation of the slave trade.

There is no reason to doubt Farquhar's personal opposition to slavery. But despite Lord Liverpool's rebuke he continued to believe that the special situation in the islands justified a cautious approach; and he delayed for several years the registration of slaves and the setting up of a special Admiralty court as required by the 1807 Act. It was in any case impossible to prevent all smuggling of slaves into the islands. The Royal Navy in the Indian Ocean had many other commitments and could only spare a frigate or sloop for an annual visit to the area of Madagascar and the Mascarenes. In the end it was Farquhar who struck the most effective blow against the slave trade by tackling the main source of supply, which was Madagascar. Shortly after the occupation of Mauritius, a small naval squadron of two corvettes was sent to take possession of the French establishments on the coast of Madagascar. The squadron appeared off Tamatave on February 18, 1811 and Captain Lynne called upon the French Agent Sylvain Roux to surrender. There was a small garrison which might have put up a resistance, but lack of pay and clothing had caused the troops to refuse to obey orders, and Roux had no choice but to accept the capitulation terms offered. Together with his garrison and the handful of French traders scattered along the coast he was deported to Mauritius, and a small British garrison was left behind in Tamatave. As Farquhar reported to Lord Liverpool: "This has freed these seas from the last French flag, and secured to us an unmolested traffic into the fruitful and abundant island of Madagascar."[4]

The prospects for a further expansion of British influence must have seemed enticing. Farquhar sketched an ambitious plan for establishing a British settlement on Madagascar which, echoing Walter Hamond, he described as "the most fruitful country in the world". But his enthusiasm evoked no response in London, and the garrison at Tamatave was soon withdrawn on the orders of the local military commander. Farquhar's hopes appeared to receive a further setback from the Treaty of Paris of May 30, 1814 which, while ceding to Britain "the Isle of France and its dependencies, especially Rodriguez and the Seychelles", restored Bourbon to France. There was however no mention of Madagascar, and Farquhar was quick to exploit this apparent oversight and the ambiguity[5] of the word "especially" which seemed to imply that there were other dependencies. Arguing with some justice that the French trading posts in Madagascar had been dependencies of Mauritius, and that the treaty required that only the establishments in Bourbon be handed back to France, Farquhar proceeded to treat Madagascar as being within the area of his governorship.

In 1815 a small British trading depot was established at Port Loquez in the Bay of Antongil. It lasted only a few months before a quarrel with a local chief called Tsitsipy led to a massacre of all but one of the traders. A punitive force sent from Mauritius under Captain Le Sage obtained the submission of most of the chiefs of Port Loquez, who executed Tsitsipy and ceded a large tract of land to the British as compensation. But no one in Mauritius was keen to return to Port Loquez, and Tamatave henceforth became confirmed as the chief port on the east coast and the main channel for trade between Madagascar and Mauritius.

Meanwhile, the French authorities both in Bourbon and in Paris had protested vigorously against Farquhar's assumption of authority over Madagascar. The arguments they used were contradictory: the governor of Bourbon argued that France had never exercised sovereignty over Madagascar and that therefore Britain could not inherit any such sovereignty; while the French government maintained that French sovereignty dating from the seventeenth century had not been affected in any way by the Treaty of Paris. But in the last resort legal arguments over sovereignty and the interpretation of the treaty were of secondary importance. The deciding factor was the attitude of the British government. In Westminster there was little interest in acquiring new responsibilities in Madagascar, and even less willingness to have a row with the French over the issue. In vain did Farquhar point to the danger of a revival of the slave trade if the administration of Bourbon, where the trade had not been abolished,[6] were to take possession of the trading posts in Madagascar. He was informed that the British government agreed with the French interpretation of the treaty and that the former French establishments in Madagascar must be handed back.

Farquhar was checked, but not mated. He continued to find excuses for not returning the trading posts to the French. And meanwhile his fertile mind had already evolved an alternative plan for securing his aims, based on a careful study of the situation in Madagascar.

Soon after taking over in Mauritius, Farquhar commissioned a former French officer, Barthélémy de Froberville, to make a comprehensive survey of all available information about Madagascar, "in order to assist the governor to discover the best means for immediate measures to extend British rule in this dependency of Mauritius". The resultant collection[7] of reports and memoranda, supplemented by a Malagasy dictionary compiled by Froberville, is an invaluable summary of European knowledge of the island at that time. From it Farquhar obtained a picture of a country divided into numerous squabbling tribes which had nevertheless resisted successfully all previous attempts at European settlement. Military conquest was clearly out of the question. But it would be an endless task to try to secure the separate submission or alliance of all the different tribes. Some sentences in an unsigned memorandum pointed the way to a solution: "Can it be hoped that the chiefs and the inhabitants will submit of their own free will to the English? This cannot be hoped for. If a single monarch were in authority over the whole extent of the island, he might possibly be won over to yield his crown to the king and people of Great Britain."[8]

In view of the British government's attitude the idea of acquiring sovereignty over Madagascar was no longer feasible. But the essential aims of British policy could be achieved by alliance with a "single monarch". Where was this single monarch to be found? The reports of Mayeur and Hugon pointed clearly to the Merina as the most advanced and dynamic people on the island; while more recent information from traders who had visited the plateau indicated the intelligent and ambitious Radama as the ideal partner for the governor's designs. The plan which Farquhar now evolved had a beautiful simplicity. He would seek to establish an alliance with Radama and then help him to extend his dominion over the rest of the island. In this way the whole island would become open to British influence and trade; while the French would be prevented from returning, not by a dubious British claim to sovereignty but by the firmly established power of a native kingdom. At the same time Farquhar hoped to kill the slave trade by persuading Radama to prohibit the export of slaves from his present territory and ultimately from the whole of Madagascar. Contemporary French writers tended to sneer at the anti-slavery argument as a sanctimonious cover for the further expansion of British power. But no one who reads Farquhar's correspondence can doubt the sincerity of his opposition to the slave trade. And his personal feelings were no doubt reinforced by the need to show himself especially zealous in the anti-slavery cause to erase the unfortunate impression created by his initial defence of slavery in Mauritius.

The execution of Farquhar's plan matched the brilliance of the concept. It was indeed an object lesson in how to win over a powerful, suspicious ruler in a remote and almost unknown territory. The approach to Radama was carried out in three stages: first an unofficial mission to establish contact and gain information; then an official mission to secure a general treaty of friendship and alliance; and a final official mission to obtain the more detailed objectives of British policy.

For the first unofficial mission Farquhar chose Jacques Chardenoux, a former French slave trader now settled in Mauritius. He had made several previous journeys to Antananarivo and knew Radama well, having earlier established friendly contact with Andrianampoinimerina. He was now given detailed instructions to note down all possible particulars of the country and its people – the climate, size of population, state of health, life expectancy, customs, laws and usages, natural history, methods of agriculture and warfare etc – and to bring back samples of minerals, animal life and local products. He conveyed presents from the governor and was instructed to offer alliance and friendship and to persuade Radama to send some of his leading men to visit Mauritius and if possible some members of his family to be educated there. He was also to suggest the substitution of useful commerce for the slave trade which was depopulating the island.

At the end of June 1816, Chardenoux set off from Tamatave along the road which was to be followed by thousands of Europeans – traders, missionaries, soldiers and diplomats – during the next century until the railway was built. For the first three days the route was southward along the *pangalanes*, a series of lagoons formed by the great line of sand dunes piled up by the relentless swell and trade winds from the east. This was easy going in canoes, with brief overland passages between the lagoons. At Andevoranto the road turned inland, and after a short canoe journey upriver the remainder of the journey was on foot or, for the privileged traveller, by *filanjana*. This was the Malagasy version of the sedan chair, consisting of a simple seat slung between long poles and carried by four bearers or runners. In close support were four more bearers who at intervals of a few minutes would take over from the other four without breaking the rhythm. On level ground a good *filanjana* team could maintain a speed of six miles (10 km) an hour. But once the coast had been left behind there was little level ground on the way to Antananarivo.

The path soon climbed into the foothills, clothed with bamboo, raphia palm, the travellers' tree and other secondary growths, where the bearers slithered on the clay slopes made slippery by the rain which falls at all times of the year on the east coast. At times the path followed valleys of spectacular beauty with rushing streams cascading down from the escarpment. From time to time the party would pass by a small, silent village of a few miserable huts with chickens and dogs roaming about and the villagers watching apprehensively. The larger villages served as staging posts. On the sixth day the travellers had their last glimpse of the sea at the sadly-named village of Taniankova ("the weeping-place of the Hova") where Hova slaves being brought down from the plateau had their first glimpse of the sea which was to take them to permanent exile and death in a strange land.

Now the way became even steeper as they climbed the first escarpment and entered the silence of the dense primary forest, broken only by the shrill chattering of cicadas and the occasional weird cries of the lemurs for whom this is the last great stronghold. Here the abundant wild life is supplemented in the Malagasy imagination by terrible monsters lurking in the woods, possibly inspired by folk memories of giant lemurs now extinct.

Around Moramanga the bearers had a respite as the road levelled off on the lower plateau, a narrow depression running north-south between the two escarpments and cradling to the north Lake Alaotra, the country's largest lake. A short final climb through the steep upper escarpment brought the travellers to the high plateau, the heartland of Madagascar and the home of the Merina. The silence and gloom of the forest was now replaced by bare rolling hills under wide, open skies, with frequent bustling villages and markets interspersed with the vivid green of the rice-fields. After a last night's stop at Ambatomanga, it was only a short day's journey to where the great rock of Antananarivo, visible for many miles around, lifted itself some 600 ft (180 m) above the rice plains. To reach the royal *rova* on the summit involved the steepest climb of the whole journey up "streets" which were no more than narrow tracks or steps among the disorderly clusters of wooden houses clinging to the hillside.

Radama greeted Chardenoux with the affection of an old friend and the cautious respect due to the representative of a relatively unknown power which had defeated his hero Napoleon. He was however suspicious because of rumours that the British intended to prevent him from continuing the slave trade. Chardenoux thought it prudent not to pursue this point of his instructions, but he reported to Farquhar that Radama's source of slaves was drying up as there were not many territories left to conquer, and that he might therefore be interested in alternative sources of income. Radama did agree to send some of his ministers to visit Mauritius and his two young brothers Ratafika and Rahovy to be educated there.

He also agreed to an alliance which was sealed by an oath of blood brotherhood (*fatidra*) between Chardenoux and one of his companions on one side and six ministers, including the prime minister Ratala, and the two young princes on the other. Water was poured into a large dish containing a gold piece, gunpowder, stones, bullets, salt and a piece of ginger. All the participants made a small incision in the stomach to produce a drop of blood which was mixed in with the rest of the ingredients. The point of a spear was plunged into the mixture and everyone held the shaft of the spear in the left hand with the prime minister beating it with a piece of iron in his right hand. All then swore faithful alliance on behalf of their two governments after which they drank a little of the liquid in the bowl. Finally they placed their hands one on top of the other and the remaining contents of the dish were poured over.

Chardenoux returned to Mauritius with the ministers and the two princes in September 1816. Farquhar was well pleased with this initial contact, and although the cool season which was regarded as the only safe time to travel in Madagascar was almost over, he decided to follow up at once with an official mission. As leader he chose his *aide-de-camp* Captain Le Sage, who had recently returned from the punitive expedition to Port Loquez. Most writers have assumed from his name that Le Sage was a French Mauritian, but he was in fact a British army officer born in London. He was now put in charge of a mission numbering about a dozen, including Chardenoux, a doctor and an interpreter, with an escort of some thirty soldiers, both British and sepoys from Bengal.

The mission landed at Tamatave on November 17, 1816. After some negotiations with Jean René, the half-caste chief of Tamatave and his brother Fisatra (known to the British as Fish) they set off for the interior on November 28. The season of tropical storms had already started and progress was slow because of the weather and the high incidence of sickness: malaria and dysentery were to carry off more than a third of the party before they returned to Mauritius. By the time they reached Antananarivo on December 21, Le Sage was himself seriously ill and had to be carried in a litter. Radama sent some ministers and members of his family to escort him, and a special *filanjana* for Le Sage to be carried by a dozen Malagasy soldiers. A procession formed up with the British soldiers in front, followed by the civilian members of the mission, the Malagasy ministers, then Le Sage in the *filanjana* with the Bengali sepoys in blue trousers and red turbans bringing up the rear. Crowds of Malagasy lined the road. When they reached the foot of Antananarivo, thousands of soldiers came dancing down the hill, brandishing their weapons and firing their muskets into the air. An incessant crackle of musketry fire accompanied their final approach up the narrow streets densely packed with people, while at each halt Le Sage's own soldiers fired a volley. At the top of the hill they came to the palace where Radama, seated on a throne, gave them a warm welcome; but seeing how ill and exhausted Le Sage and most of his men were he cut short the initial ceremonies and sent them to the houses assigned to them.

Le Sage was now desperately ill with malaria and soon fell into a coma which lasted seventeen days. He managed to stagger from his sick bed to seal the oath of blood brotherhood with Radama personally, and before his departure on February 5 he concluded a general treaty of friendship and peace. He did not try to carry out Farquhar's secret instructions to raise the question of the abolition of the slave trade, believing himself to be too feeble for the lengthy discussions and negotiations which would be needed. But he made an important contribution to future developments by leaving behind Sergeant Brady (a Jamaican mulatto) and another non-commissioned officer (who did not stay long) to train the Merina troops in the European style.

The failure to broach the subject of the slave trade was a disappointment to Farquhar. But the ground was now thoroughly prepared for a more determined effort. The time had come to return Radama's two brothers. Thomas Pye, who had been sent to Tamatave as British Agent for Madagascar, was now instructed to accompany the two princes to Antananarivo and propose to Radama the abolition of the slave trade. The object was "to convince a semi-civilised despot that it is more advantageous to him to keep his people in his dominions, and by their labour to provide those articles which his country produces in sufficient quantity to exchange for the merchandise of Europe and India which he requires, than to depopulate his country by the sale of his subjects, and of his unfortunate neighbours, whose country he lays waste in order to gratify his desires".[9] The boys' tutor, Sergeant James Hastie, was to act as Pye's deputy and to assume charge of the mission if, as proved to be the case, Pye's health did not permit him to make the journey.

James Hastie was destined to make the major contribution on the British side to the Anglo-Merina alliance. He was born in 1786 in a Quaker family in Cork, where his father was a miller. He received a good education but the pious restrictions of life at home drove him to run away to become a soldier in India. He served in the Mahratta War, was promoted sergeant, and was sent to Mauritius in 1815. He came to Governor Farquhar's attention in September 1816 when a fire ravaged half of Port Louis. The other half was shielded from the blaze by Government House but at one time its roof caught fire, threatening to spread the flames to the rest of the town. Hastie, a big and powerful man, climbed four times on to the roof with a bucket of water and succeeded in extinguishing the fire.[10] As a direct consequence Farquhar appointed him as tutor to the two young princes who had just arrived and whom Farquhar had taken into his own house.

When Hastie arrived at Tamatave at the beginning of July 1817 with the princes, he found the whole area in a turmoil. Radama was advancing on the town with an army of 30,000 which was laying waste the countryside; he was combining a trip to greet his brothers with a military expedition to impose his authority on Jean René and Fisatra, who had foolishly referred to him as a beardless boy. René turned to the British for protection. Pye acted as intermediary and agreement was reached by which René was confirmed as governor of Tamatave but acknowledged Radama as his overlord.

Hastie, taking with him various presents including several horses, now accompanied Radama on the return journey to Antananarivo, and witnessed the pitiful sufferings of the Merina army as they passed through the country they had already stripped of all foodstuffs. He found that although July was the cool season for travelling it was certainly not a dry season on the east coast. His journal entry for July 20, reads: "Rain all night, hut leaky. The path is constant ascent and descent, not an acre of level ground. Passed six streams which are much swelled by the Rains. ... If this is the good Season for travelling this country, I assert it is impossible to proceed in the bad." And on the following day: "Rains incessant, paths not possible. I cannot paint the situation of the Ovas.[11] They are covered with dirt, half starved, half drown'd and naked. They eat anything they can get without cooking."[12] The steep, slippery slopes were particularly difficult for the horses which also suffered from lack of proper fodder. The best of them, intended for Radama, died on the way but the others survived to become the first horses seen on the plateau.

In Antananarivo Hastie set about winning the confidence of the king. The presents, including a compass, a map of the world and a chiming clock, were a great success. The clock was at first "a little deranged" but Hastie repaired it and Radama's "joy was unbounded. He sat on the ground by it an hour and danced when it struck."[13] And when he rode a horse for the first time he "laughed loud, screeched and danced, declaring that he never received so much pleasure".[14] Hastie also impressed Radama by his versatility, which included constructing a bedstead for the king, sowing a field with wheat, showing how bullocks should be trained to the yoke and giving medical treatment to Radama and some of his subjects for various ailments.

Hastie accompanied Radama on all ceremonial occasions, and noted everything down in his journal. At the annual royal bath festival, Radama "on the water first touching him he screeched, which was re-echoed by the crowd outside. – and on their commencing dry-rubbing him he screeched again and it was similarly re-echoed. He then put on his Cloth and went out throwing some of the water in which he was washed on the People."[15] There was also a military review where the precision of the drill was a great credit to Brady, now promoted captain by Radama, and an indication of the high quality of the Hova troops.

Hastie also witnessed the cruelty and barbarity of the administration of justice under Radama. One method of treating someone suspected of a serious crime was to cut off first the individual fingers, then the hands, then the limbs until the suspect confessed, when he was instantly executed; so that the poor unfortunate had the choice of being liquidated either at one blow or by instalments. More usual was the trial by ordeal using poison derived from the kernel of the fruit of the *tangena* shrub. The accused was made to swallow three pieces of chicken skin and some rice, followed by some scrapings of the *tangena* nut mixed in the juice of a banana. Then large quantities of rice water were drunk to promote vomiting. If all three pieces of skin were vomited up whole the accused was considered innocent, but often became seriously ill and sometimes died from the effects of the poison. Hastie saw the ordeal applied to the female attendants of one of the king's sisters who had fallen ill. Only one managed to bring up all three pieces of skin. The others had their ears, noses, legs and arms cut off and were then cast over a steep precipice just below the royal *rova*. Hastie's horror was increased by the evident enjoyment of the spectacle by his angelic-looking pupils who, despite continuing lessons with him, soon slipped back into the ways of their country.

Meanwhile, Hastie used every opportunity to argue the case for prohibiting the export of slaves from Madagascar. Radama appeared to be convinced of the desirability of this, but foresaw great difficulty in persuading his people to agree. If he did not export enemy soldiers captured in battle, what else was he to do with them? And without the revenue from the slaves how could he import the arms and other supplies he needed? Because of the remoteness of Imerina and the lack of roads to the coast there was nothing else his people could export. Hastie suggested that the slave labour if retained in the country could be put to productive use and in particular could build roads to the coast; but Radama was afraid that such roads could be used by future enemies to invade Imerina.

Eventually Radama offered to abolish the export of slaves if the British would provide him with the equivalent in arms and money of the proceeds of the slave trade. Hastie became convinced that this was the only solution, and set off to return to Mauritius to persuade the governor. But on arrival at Tamatave he found that Farquhar had already come to the same conclusion and had written a letter to Radama offering arms in return for the abolition of the slave export trade. Armed with this letter, Hastie hurried back to Antananarivo. Radama was delighted, but some time was still needed to persuade his people. At a *kabary* on October 9 held for this purpose some bold spirits even accused Radama of being the slave of the English. This infuriated Radama and made him even more determined to carry through his intentions. Agreement on the contents of a treaty and the amount of the "equivalent" was reached in a few days. As Hastie was too junior to be given plenipotentiary powers he now had to return with four envoys of Radama to Tamatave, where the treaty was signed on October 23 by Pye and Captain Stanfell RN on behalf of the governor of Mauritius.

Under the treaty Radama agreed to prohibit the export of slaves (anyone disobeying to be reduced to slavery!) and also to do everything possible to prevent the piratical raids on the Comoros from the coasts of Madagascar. In return he was to receive each year 1,000 dollars in gold, 1,000 dollars in silver, 100 barrels of gunpowder, 100 English muskets with 1,000 flints, 400 soldiers' uniforms, 12 sergeants' swords, 600 pieces of cloth, a full-dress uniform for himself and two horses. A cardinal point for Radama was that he was recognised in the treaty as "king of Madagascar" (a title never accepted by the French, who continued to refer to him as "chief of the Hovas"). He immediately issued a proclamation putting the treaty into effect and despatched emissaries to the east coast to stop the export of the latest batch of slaves who had left the plateau.

Having seen his policy crowned with success, Farquhar returned to Britain on leave, where he was rewarded with a baronetcy. Hastie was appointed Assistant Agent to reside at Antananarivo and watch over the execution of the treaty. Returning in the midst of a smallpox epidemic, he was able to save many lives by introducing vaccination. He also persuaded Radama to begin building roads to take advantage of horse transport which was now becoming available.

This happy interlude was interrupted by reports from the coast that the first payments due under the treaty would not be made. Hastie protested that the reports must be false, and Radama executed several of his own family for doubting the word of the British.[16] But when Hastie went down to Tamatave to investigate he found that the reports were true. The acting governor, Major-General Gage John Hall had refused to pay the "equivalent" without confirmatory orders from London, and now recalled Hastie from Antananarivo. Radama, understandably furious at this breach of faith, ordered the resumption of the slave trade, and Farquhar's carefully constructed policy was suddenly in ruins.

General Hall has been depicted by missionary writers as the unmitigated villain of this episode. But his motives seem to have been of the best. A blunt, straightforward soldier, he had disapproved of the lenient terms offered to the Mauritians and even more of Farquhar's cautious, not to say devious, policy regarding slavery and the slave trade in Mauritius. When slaves from Madagascar continued to enter Mauritius after the signing of the treaty with Radama (no doubt they were exported either before the treaty could be applied or from areas not under Radama's control) he assumed that either the treaty was another piece of fraudulent window-dressing by Farquhar or that the Malagasy were cynically disregarding it. He therefore refused to implement the treaty, and meanwhile set about enforcing the anti-slave trade legislation with the utmost rigour, even dismissing the Chief Justice and other officials who were lax in applying it.

It is impossible to question Hall's sincerity and later writers[17] have attempted to rehabilitate him by contrasting his firm opposition to slavery with Farquhar's equivocal attitude. But in certain situations sincerity and straightforwardness are not enough, and Hall stands convicted of the charge of stupidity. He completely failed to understand Farquhar's overall strategy. Whatever his motives, the practical effect of his action was to destroy Britain's credibility with Radama and to postpone for several years the measure which was to be the most effective weapon against the slave trade in the region. At the same time his high-handed behaviour within Mauritius aroused great resentment and led to demands for his recall. He left at the end of 1818, an honest man lost in the subtle toils of diplomacy and colonial administration.

Hall's blundering intervention gave the French an opportunity to recover some of the ground they had lost in Madagascar. Sylvain Roux was reappointed agent on the east coast and Jean René, abandoned by his new allies, thought it prudent to renew his links with the French. In Antananarivo a French army deserter, Sergeant Robin, turned up in 1818 and soon won the confidence of

Radama. He became the king's secretary and tutor, teaching him to read and write in French, and set up a classroom in the palace to teach some of the royal children. He also assisted Brady, who had stayed on despite the rupture with the British and was now made a general, in the training of the army. Thanks largely to Robin, France retained a foothold in the Merina capital during a period of British dominance.

Farquhar's home leave was prolonged by ill-health and he did not return to Mauritius until July 1820. He immediately set about repairing the damage caused by General Hall. Hastie was reappointed Agent and sent back to Madagascar, accompanied by a Welsh missionary, David Jones. At Tamatave, which had recovered its prosperity with the revival of the slave trade, they were warned not to proceed as Radama had ordered that no Englishmen should ever visit Antananarivo again. Hastie was not deterred and sent a message to Radama asking for permission to visit his capital. They set off without waiting for an answer, and on the way they received an encouraging message from Radama. When they reached Antananarivo, the impulsive Radama forgot his resentment at British perfidy in his delight at seeing Hastie again. Jones recorded[18] that "the king appeared as if he was lost in ecstasy and joy and mirth – overwhelmed with rejoicing and laughter, that he could hardly keep his seat – hugging and pulling about Mr Hastie in such a manner that I have never witnessed such a sight and such excess of joy on any occasion in all my life as this day on the reception of Mr Hastie".

Nevertheless Hastie's task in negotiating the renewal of the treaty was formidable. Contrary to Sir Henry Wootton's mischievous definition of an ambassador as "an honest man sent to lie abroad for his country", a diplomat's value depends on his word being trusted by the government to which he is accredited. Hastie's credibility had been completely undermined by Hall's repudiation of the treaty which he had negotiated. It is a remarkable tribute to his character and diplomatic skill that he was able to restore his credit and accomplish his task. But he could never have succeeded without the intelligence and sympathetic understanding of Radama, who needed the British alliance and was willing to overlook the past in the pursuit of his long-term aims.

But first Hastie had a lot of explaining to do. How was it possible for the treaty agreed with the great Farquhar to be overturned by a subordinate without the latter being severely punished? Hastie explained that General Hall had been recalled and that Farquhar was once again in control. But how could Radama ask his people to renew a treaty with a nation that had deceived them? There was already a new Malagasy proverb "as false as the English". Hastie pointed out that the treaty had now been endorsed by the king of England, that the arguments which justified the treaty in 1817 were still valid and that in any case the British Navy would be able to prevent at least the bulk of the slave traffic. Radama was soon persuaded but his counsellors remained strongly opposed, despite two assemblies where Hastie, supported by the king, argued the advantages of the treaty. It became clear that some additional inducements would be necessary. Radama asked for help in instructing his people – British artisans to teach useful crafts in Madagascar and training for ten Malagasy in Mauritius and another ten in England. Hastie was able to promise the British artisans (which the London Missionary Society was willing to provide) and the training in Mauritius, but had no authority to offer training in England. But to save the treaty he finally agreed to training in England on his own authority and if necessary at his own expense, as Radama shrewdly guessed. The treaty was accordingly renewed on October 11, 1820 and a proclamation ordered the immediate halting of the export of slaves. In a separate document Radama agreed to allow missionaries from the London Missionary Society to work in Madagascar. Hastie agreed to take an additional eight young Malagasy back to Mauritius to learn to play military band instruments and Radama generously waived his claim to the "equivalent" due to him for the period when he applied the 1817 treaty.

The next few years saw the high point of Anglo-Merina cooperation and the vindication of Farquhar's policies. By recognising Radama as king of Madagascar and providing him with the means to assert his title in the coastal areas, the British achieved their aims of suppressing the slave trade and excluding French influence from Madagascar: a combination of humanitarian motives and *realpolitik* to induce a virtuous glow of satisfaction in any diplomat.

The essential instrument of Anglo-Merina policy was the Merina army. By 1820 Brady had already trained a small élite corps to a high state of drill and discipline. The money, arms and uniforms supplied under the treaty enabled this professional nucleus to be expanded. A system of army ranks was established based on numbers of "honours", one honour for a private up to ten honours for a general.[19] Stricter discipline was enforced, and burning alive was made the penalty for a soldier deserting his post in the face of the enemy. Robin and Hastie were made generals along with Brady to assist in training and to command troops in various campaigns.

But first there were some lessons to be learned in the use of this new force. At the outset it was envisaged as merely the spearhead

The king, the governor and the sergeant

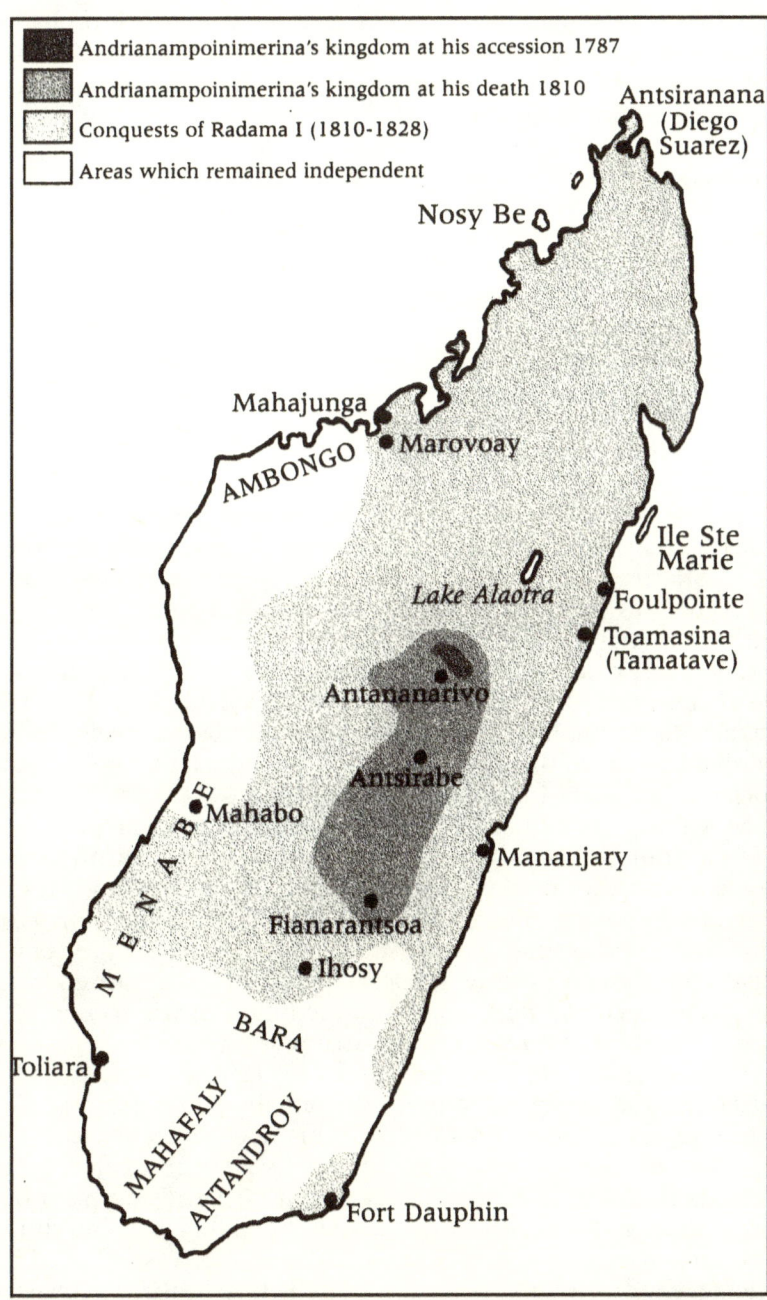

The expansion of the Merina kingdom 1787–1828

of the old-style armed mob. In 1820 a large force which probably included a few hundred trained soldiers was sent under Robin against the stubborn Sakalava king of Menabe, Ramitraho. After a prolonged but inconclusive battle, the Merina retreated in disorder. To avenge this defeat Radama, accompanied by Hastie, returned to Menabe in 1821 with a vast army of some 70,000 including a thousand professionals. Ramitraho's skilful guerrilla tactics and scorched earth policy led to enormous losses, mainly from disease and starvation, and Radama had to return without achieving any of his objectives. But the lesson had been learned. In the following year Radama led a much smaller army consisting only of trained troops, whose numbers had risen to 13,000 supported by 7,000 slaves to carry baggage and provisions. This force was able to move more rapidly and bring some of the Sakalava to battle. But the elusive Ramitraho continued to fade into the bush at the approach of the Merina troops, and Radama was again faced with serious supply problems. A diplomatic solution was suggested involving Radama's marriage to Princess Rasalimo, a daughter of Ramitraho, and the latter's acceptance of Radama's suzerainty. Peace was agreed on this basis and a string of Merina garrisons was left in southern Menabe and along the western plateau.

Radama next turned his attention to the east coast, with the active encouragement of the British. In 1822 Sylvain Roux had reoccupied Ile Sainte Marie and persuaded a number of chiefs on the mainland to make their submissions to France. Radama issued a proclamation declaring invalid any cession of Malagasy territory made without his ratification. In 1823 he organised a major expedition to impose his authority on the east coast. One army corps was sent north to the Bay of Antongil, while Radama and Hastie with another corps descended to Ivondro and then north to Tamatave. Here Radama heard for the first time military band music played by the young Malagasy who had just returned from Mauritius. Leguével de Lacombe's description of the scene[20] is a good illustration of Radama's high-strung sensibility:

"As soon as Radama heard them, all his faculties seemed to be suspended and for several minutes he remained in a state of complete immobility, with his eye fixed, his neck stretched and his head bent on the side where the musicians were concealed. Suddenly, as if he had been dreaming, he put his hands on his brow and withdrew them almost immediately, giving a great shout which startled us. This first explosion of pleasure was followed by dancing, shouts of laughter and tears which indicated to Hastie a complete success; the king embraced everybody and could not tell one person from another."

There was one disappointment at Tamatave. Sir Robert Farquhar had relinquished his post at Mauritius and on his way home had called in at Tamatave. He had expressed the hope that Radama might meet him there. But Radama could not get away from Antananarivo in time and so the two men, who together had altered the course of Madagascar's history, were fated never to meet. Back in Britain, Farquhar entered Parliament, where he had to undergo criticism from the abolitionists for his early policy in Mauritius. He died in 1830.

From Tamatave Radama and Hastie went north to Foulpointe where a British warship commanded by Captain Moorsom awaited them. In a great *kabary* Radama repeated his opposition to any cession of territory to the French. He pulled down a commemorative stone erected by the French and sent troops along the coast to enforce the submission of those chiefs who had rallied to the French. The new French Agent at Sainte Marie (Sylvain Roux had recently died) protested vigorously, but with only a weak garrison he was powerless to interfere, especially in the presence of a British warship. Captain Moorsom not only provided diplomatic support but actively assisted Radama's campaign by transporting Radama and 200 of his troops to rejoin the army corps at Antongil. But no attempt was made to dislodge the French from Ile Sainte Marie. French rights there were more firmly based on Queen Bety's cession in 1750 and it was no doubt considered that to drive them out would be too great a provocation to the French.

Radama now marched along the northeast coast, where the Antankarana accepted his suzerainty. He completed this remarkable campaign by marching south through the country of the Tsimihety, who submitted peacefully, and the Sihanaka, who put up a stubborn resistance on an island in Lake Alaotra before submitting. Meanwhile another force commanded by Jean René and Prince Ratefy extended the area of Merina domination along the east coast as far south as Vohipeno, where the Antemoro king was allowed to retain his throne but had to acknowledge Radama's overlordship. Garrisons were left in all these areas and by the end of 1823 virtually the whole of the east coast and most of the north and centre were under Radama's control. The only residual French presence was a derisory garrison of one officer and three soldiers at Fort Dauphin, which eventually surrendered to a Merina force of 3,000 in 1825.

The last important area where Radama's writ did not run was the Sakalava kingdom of the Boina in the northwest. Although there was little French political influence in the area French and Arab slave dealers were still active in Majunga, whence slaves were exported to Bourbon and Zanzibar. The British were therefore anxious for Radama to impose his authority and enforce the treaty of 1820. Circumstances were favourable, since the Boina kingdom had begun to disintegrate after the death of the great Queen Ravahiny in 1808. The process was hastened when Andriantsoly, a young king who succeeded in 1822, offended many of the traditionalist chiefs by becoming a Moslem.

This time the British Navy took action ahead of Radama's troops. Towards the end of 1822 a British squadron under Commodore Nourse appeared off Majunga. By combining a show of force with some blatant trickery, Nourse persuaded Andriantsoly to salute a flag which turned out to be Radama's flag, so that the Boina king appeared to be recognising Radama's authority. Andriantsoly naturally denied any such intention, but Radama's response was a brutal ultimatum – either submit or prepare for battle.

In 1824 Radama invaded the Boina with a powerful and well-disciplined army. Resistance would have been hopeless, and to avoid unnecessary bloodshed, Hastie went ahead of the main force to persuade the various chiefs to submit peacefully. In this he was aided by the lack of enthusiasm for Andriantsoly and by the disciplined behaviour of the Merina army, where looting was now punished by death. The Antalaotra governor of Majunga refused to change his allegiance and was executed. But the remaining chiefs, persuaded that resistance was useless and that they had nothing to fear from Radama's troops, were happy to accept his suzerainty. Andriantsoly himself was finally tracked down and persuaded by Hastie to submit. He was allowed to retain his kingly title, but henceforth the Merina governor who was appointed in Majunga was the real ruler of the Boina.

Thus within four years of the renewal of the treaty with Britain, Radama was the unchallenged overlord of most of Madagascar. The remote and desolate plains of the Androy and Mahafaly in the south-west remained outside his control, as did most of the Bara country, apart from a precarious Merina outpost at Ihosy. In the Sakalava kingdoms Merina rule never extended into the inaccessible northern half of Menabe or the southern part of the Boina known as Ambongo. And elsewhere among the Sakalava Radama's authority was tenuous. An attempt to disarm the population of Menabe led in 1825 to an uprising and the massacre of all the Merina garrisons there. This inspired Andriantsoly to rebel and attack, without success, the strong garrison at Majunga. A long and bitter campaign followed in which Andriantsoly was gradually driven north until in April 1826 he fled to the Comoros. His sister Oantitsy was elected queen in his place and was allowed to rule under Merina suzerainty in the north of the Boina, while the Merina governor at Majunga ruled directly in the central area. In Menabe a Merina army was able to restore the situation and re-establish the garrisons; but Ramitraho continued to elude capture and to maintain an effective independence away from the areas controlled by the garrisons.

If Radama's authority over the island was not complete, there was at least no effective challenge to his title of king of Madagascar. His conquests had owed much to the three foreign sergeants whose services he had rewarded with the ten honours due to a general. Brady's role was purely military. He was regarded as commander in chief and deserves most of the credit for the creation of the European-style army which was the instrument of Radama's success. The Frenchman Robin, who seems to have been less successful when given a military role, enjoyed considerable influence as the king's secretary, and was appointed marshal of the royal court. But James Hastie undoubtedly occupied the pre-eminent position as Radama's principal adviser on matters both military and politic.

There was a genuine affection between the slightly-built young king and the large Irishman. In his diary Hastie repeatedly expressed his admiration for Radama's qualities, without any of the condescension which has too often characterised the European view of the "native" right up to our own time. Radama's affection for and confidence in Hastie is attested by many contemporary accounts. Hastie was able to use his favoured position to promote numerous improvements, such as the building of roads, the cleaning of the streets, the introduction of new crops and the manufacture of sugar, and to lend general support to the work of the missionaries and artisans of the London Missionary Society. The ordinary people of Imerina benefited even more from his success in persuading Radama to abolish a number of harsh laws and customs. Thanks to him the rate of interest was reduced from something like 8 per cent a month to 30 per cent a year; and debts incurred in buying the expensive but socially necessary funeral shrouds (*lambamena*) were cancelled. Capital punishment for some offences was reduced to hard labour. He failed to secure the complete abolition of trial by poison, but henceforth the poison was usually administered on dogs representing the accused; and he persuaded Radama to forbid the sacrifice of infants born on unlucky days.

One is tempted to speculate on what Hastie and Radama might have achieved together if they had been allowed a normal span of life. But the strain of living in an often harsh climate, with constant travelling on military campaigns or to and from Mauritius eventually wore down Hastie's strength. In 1826 a series of accidents further weakened him and a fever led to his death on October 18 at the age of forty.

Hastie, now almost completely forgotten in his own country, is one of the most important and attractive figures in the history of Anglo-Malagasy relations. In nineteenth-century Madagascar it was rare for a Frenchman to speak well of an Englishman, or vice versa. But Coppalle, the French painter who spent some time at Radama's court, gave generous praise to Hastie's efforts to reform abuses: "It is thus that Mr Hastie (for it is he who is responsible for a large part of the good which is done in this country) destroys, little by little and one after the other, the numerous prejudices which stand in the way of the development of the minds of the *ambaniandro* (one of the names of the Merina) and leads these people towards the arts for which their natural talents seem so well suited."[21]

For Radama the loss of Hastie was irreparable: "He has surpassed every agent that preceded him; and never will any who may succeed him, prove his equal."[22] In a letter reporting his death to Farquhar, Radama wrote[23]: "By his wise counsels, and promptitude always to assist the needy and distressed, he not only attached myself to him more and more every year, but also my people, who lament his loss, as a friend and a father, who could conduct himself in such a manner as to attract the affections of persons of every rank among my subjects." Gun salutes were fired every quarter of an hour on the afternoons of the day he died and the day of his funeral. Malagasy grenadiers escorted him to his tomb and fired three volleys over it "according to the British custom". He left a widow[24] and a year-old son who was later brought up in England with the help of a British government pension.

Chapter 11

The missionaries

Of all the changes made during Radama's reign, the most far-reaching in its effects was the introduction of British missionaries. They were not the first Christian missionaries to arrive on the island. Jesuit missionaries from Portugal had appeared soon after the European discovery of the island, but their efforts bore no fruit. Lazarist missionaries had rather more success during the French occupation of Fort Dauphin in the seventeenth century, but after the abandonment of the colony the Christian converts reverted to paganism. The work of the London Missionary Society was however to have a profound and lasting effect on the history of the island.

The London Missionary Society, known as the LMS, was founded in 1795, the product of the evangelical revival of the late eighteenth century. At its foundation the LMS was an ecumenical body grouping most branches of the Protestant Church in England. But the Anglicans and the Methodists soon withdrew to form their own missionary societies, leaving the LMS to the more radical Nonconformists, especially the Congregationalists.[1] Its first missionary ventures were to Tahiti in 1796 and South Africa in 1798, but as early as 1796 the Society's attention was drawn to Madagascar. Various schemes to establish a mission there as an offshoot of the South African mission were not followed up for one reason or another. The British occupation of Mauritius opened up fresh opportunities. Early in 1814 Reverend Le Brun was sent to Mauritius, having been instructed that "an important object of this mission is to prepare the way to the great island of Madagascar". This fitted in admirably with the plans of Governor Farquhar, who wrote to the LMS warmly supporting the idea of a mission to Madagascar. When the Society seemed to be rather dilatory in responding, he used the visit to Mauritius of the rival Wesleyan Methodist Missionary Society to stir them into action. Discussions between the two societies led to agreement that both could operate in Madagascar. But the LMS was the first actually to recruit volunteers for Madagascar, and the WMMS turned its attention elsewhere.

The volunteers chosen by the LMS were David Jones and Thomas Bevan. Both were born in Cardiganshire in 1796 and had studied at a bible school run by Dr Phillips at Neuaddlwyd. After completing their studies at the missionary academy at Gosport they were ordained and appointed to open a mission in Madagascar. An unexpected hitch developed when the two young men refused to go unless they were first married. A subcommittee set up to consider the problem concluded, with some justice as it turned out, that married missionaries should not be sent to Madagascar, partly because of the rigours of the climate. Bevan withdrew his demand but Jones stubbornly maintained his attitude and in the absence of any other candidates the Society reluctantly agreed to the marriage condition.

The two young men, with their brides, sailed to Mauritius in February 1818. They arrived in July to find that all links with Madagascar had been broken by General Hall's reversal of Farquhar's policy. The general strongly advised them not to proceed and even Hastie thought that it would be a waste of time trying to establish a mission in Madagascar in the existing circumstances. Jones and Bevan decided nevertheless on an exploratory visit, without their wives, to Tamatave, and they landed there on August 18, 1818.

Their reception was reasonably encouraging. The slave-trading community was hostile but an English trader called Bragg was friendly and helpful in providing lodgings and servants. Jean René was pessimistic about the prospects of establishing Christianity on the coast and advised that they should seek Radama's permission to work in Imerina. But reports of Radama's anger at the breach of the treaty discouraged them and they decided to begin their work in Tamatave. They opened a small school to which Fisatra, René's brother, sent his son. They then decided to return to Mauritius to bring over their wives, who meanwhile had each produced a baby daughter. As Mrs Bevan was ill, the Bevans stayed behind for a time, while the Jones family returned to Tamatave, arriving there on October 19. The Bevans followed at the beginning of January. But by now the season of the dreaded Malagasy fever was well advanced, and a month later David Jones was the sole survivor of the two families.

Even the fevers of Madagascar were rarely as deadly as this, and poison was suspected at least in the case of the Jones family. Whatever the cause Jones would have been forgiven if he had abandoned the mission after such a calamitous start. But his faith remained unshaken. He recorded his gratitude to the Lord for sustaining him through his troubles, and his determination to carry

The missionaries

on and wait for other missionaries to join him. He was encouraged by a visit from one of Radama's generals who told him that Radama would welcome missionaries on the plateau and would like Jones to visit him. But he continued to suffer from attacks of malaria; and his health was further impaired by harassment from Bragg who now turned against him and looted his baggage while he was lying helplessly ill. In July 1819 he returned to Mauritius to recover his health and wait for a better opportunity to resume his mission.

This opportunity came with the return of Farquhar and the resumption of negotiations with Radama. Farquhar gave his full support to Jones and sent him to Antananarivo along with Hastie. The missionary was of considerable help in the negotiations by offering missionaries and artisans from the LMS to provide the education and training which were among Radama's major objectives. As Jones reported,[2] "King Radama is exceedingly kind and affable. He is a great advocate for education, and esteems the instruction of his people in the arts of civilization more than Gold and Silver." At Jones's instigation the king wrote a letter [3] to the LMS asking them to send as many missionaries as they could, provided that they included craftsmen such as weavers and carpenters as well as men of religion. At the same time Radama wrote to Bourbon rejecting an offer of Roman Catholic missionaries. He may have been influenced by Jones's account of the differences between the Protestant and Catholic religions, which no doubt included liberal references to the horrors of the Spanish Inquisition. But there were other good reasons: it would have confused his people to have rival missionaries advocating different versions of Christianity; and so long as the French maintained territorial claims in Madagascar Radama was bound to favour the British.

On December 8, 1820 Jones started his first school with three pupils, young nephews of the king, including the likely heir to the throne. Radama had a house built for him close to the royal palace and his class soon increased to twenty-two children of the royal family, one third of them girls. Teaching was in English, as there was no written Malagasy and Jones's knowledge of the language was still rudimentary. Conditions were primitive and teaching aids totally lacking. There were no desks, no blackboard, no books and very little paper. As a substitute for slates, smooth boards were soaked in fat and covered in charcoal ash on which letters and figures could be traced with a pointed wooden stick.[4] Fortunately the basic educational material was excellent. The children proved to be remarkably quick at their lessons and good at singing. Altogether the prospects for a Christian mission seemed to be very favourable. Jones commented that the people of the plateau were more advanced in civilization than many of the inhabitants of Wales.

He was however appalled by the general state of morality and deeply disturbed by the temptations to which this exposed him: "The greatest sins of all they are guilty of, are adultery and fornication which reach to the highest pitch among the people universally so that there are few husbands and wives who are not guilty of adultery and not one young person above ten years of age I believe free from fornication. When I arrived here at first many were expressing their wonder at me in not sending for a woman to sleep with me every night; and they thought me to be a very strange sort of a being acting contrary to what nature had given to men. Besides I have received messages sent me by women requesting me time after time to send for them to sleep with me. But thanks be to God who has given me strength to overcome their temptations hitherto and to keep my character blameless in this respect. These instances out of many I have witnessed in so short a time may show you how great are the temptations before Missionaries in this place particularly those who may reside here unmarried; for they are men of like passions with others and not angels."[5]

Jones clearly doubted his own ability to resist temptation indefinitely. The arrival of the first missionary reinforcement, Reverend David Griffiths, on May 30, 1821, enabled him to leave the school in his charge and return to Mauritius. He arrived there on July 13, and only a week later he married Miss Marie Anne Mabille, a French or creole girl who was a member of Le Brun's church. At the end of September he sailed back to Madagascar with his bride and also Mrs Griffiths and her baby son. Griffiths came down to Tamatave to meet them and accompany them back to Antananarivo where Radama had organised a special welcome for them. Huge crowds thronged the streets to gape at the first European women and child to be seen in Imerina.

It was agreed that Jones would continue with his school for royal and noble children, which was now referred to as the Royal Academy. Griffiths opened a new school, known as the "public school", for other children, and his first pupils, selected personally by Radama, again included a number of girls. The two wives set to work making clothes for the children, who demanded to be dressed in the European style; they also taught the girls sewing and other homemaking skills. On New Year's Day 1822 all the children, neatly dressed and singing beautifully, attended a baptism service for the Griffiths's little boy, the first Christian baptism to be held in Imerina. The following August the new Mrs Jones gave birth to a baby girl, the first European child to be born on the plateau.

The missionaries

Meanwhile Radama's brother-in-law, Prince Ratefy, had returned from a most successful visit to England, where he had accompanied nine Malagasy youths sent to be educated there under the treaty. He had been presented to King George IV and his intelligence and agreeable manners had made a favourable impression on everyone he met. He attended the general meeting of the LMS in May 1821 at which Radama's letter to LMS was read out and acted "like an electric shock on the immense multitude". As an eye-witness[6] commented: "The letter itself must give every impartial person a favourable opinion of the king, both for his discernment and liberality; and few could have expected to hear such sentiments from a despotic monarch of a supposed horde of barbarians". With renewed enthusiasm, the LMS took charge of the education of the youths in various trades and crafts. Another missionary, John Jeffreys, was sent out to Madagascar with his wife and four young artisans, a carpenter, a blacksmith, a weaver and a tanner.

These welcome reinforcements arrived in June 1822, but the carpenter died within ten days. The other artisans, after writing at Jones's insistence to ask for their lady friends to be sent out to marry them, set about teaching their trades to Malagasy apprentices. Jeffreys for his part opened a third school two weeks after his arrival. The foundations were now laid for a steady expansion of missionary work in three main fields: scholastic education, training in arts and crafts and, perhaps most important of all, the study of the Malagasy language leading to the preparation of dictionaries and the translation of the Bible.

After the initial enthusiasm, school education had to overcome a number of difficulties. Traditionalist opponents of Radama's policies circulated rumours, based on the continued absence of the youths who had accompanied Prince Ratefy to Britain, that the schools were devices to lure the children into slavery. The missionaries were even accused of cannibalism. Anxious parents sent their children away to remote villages or hid them in rice pits, where several died of suffocation. In the absence of Radama campaigning in Menabe, the queen mother summoned a *kabary* of the people to denounce the rumours and to order parents to send their children to the schools in accordance with Radama's wishes. Radama reinforced this on his return by a proclamation stating that he would grant noble rank to those who could read and write and employ them as his secretaries. In fact this offer was not as attractive as it sounds, since in general government service was unpaid. It therefore appeared to the people as an extension of the *fanompoana*, the compulsory unpaid labour which had traditionally been used in Imerina for building irrigation ditches and other public works. The same consideration dampened enthusiasm for learning any of the trades taught by the artisans, which usually led to unpaid work, for example helping to build a new palace for Radama.

For a time therefore the missionaries had difficulty in finding enough children for their classes. The situation changed dramatically around the beginning of 1824. This was due to the increasing use of Malagasy as the language of instruction, as the missionaries mastered the language and were able to write out lessons in Malagasy; and also to the Lancastrian method by which the more advanced pupils acted as monitors to teach classes of younger children. In March 1824 the separate schools run by the three missionaries were combined into one central school at Andohalo, a district of the capital close to the royal palace. This Central School became a kind of teacher training college from which Malagasy teachers were sent to open schools in the villages around Antananarivo. Suspicions understandably aroused by foreigners teaching in a foreign tongue accordingly faded, and the missionaries were soon besieged by demands from village elders for schools to be opened and teachers to be sent out. In September 1824 Griffiths reported that in the previous six months twenty-two schools had been opened in villages within twenty miles (32 km) radius of the capital and that 2,000 children were undergoing instruction.

This rapid expansion aggravated the serious shortage of slates, paper and pencils and lent added urgency to the missionaries' appeals to the LMS to send out a printing press to print the Malagasy lessons and texts which so far had to be copied out laboriously by hand. The LMS provided only minimal financial support and material from Great Britain took ages to arrive. Radama provided his indispensable moral support and land and labour for building houses and schools, but no money apart from pieces of silver as prizes for the best pupils. Money was needed to pay some sort of salary for the Malagasy teachers, to ensure an adequate supply of educational material and provide clothes for the poorer children who would otherwise be ashamed to appear at the schools. In an effort to raise funds, a Madagascar Missionary School Society was formed in November 1825 with Radama as Patron, Jones as Chairman, Hastie as Treasurer and Griffiths as Secretary. The annual subscription for members was four piastres with life membership for 40 piastres. An appeal was made to "the liberality of the Christian world in general" for donations of money or of books for a library which was set up in Antananarivo. In the short term, subscriptions from the European community in Antananarivo (mainly French traders) and a few leading Malagasy eased the financial situation; and later gifts from benefactors in Great Britain enabled the expansion of schools to continue.

Meanwhile the missionaries had made remarkable progress with their task of creating a written language where none existed before.[7] Once Radama had agreed to base the written language on the Roman rather than the Arabic alphabet, the next problem was to decide which letters of the Roman alphabet should represent the various Malagasy sounds. Radama wisely insisted that each sound should always be represented by the same letter, that each letter should always have the same sound and that there should be no unnecessary duplication of letters; as a result Malagasy is an almost perfect phonetic language. But given the great variety of English spelling, the actual choice of the letters to be used gave rise to passionate arguments among the missionaries, into which Hastie and Robin were sometimes drawn. One such argument was a threat by Jeffreys to appeal to Radama if Jones and Griffiths persisted in an earlier proposal to represent the sound "oo" by the letter "w" as in Welsh). To put an end to these disputes Radama ruled that the consonants should be pronounced as in English and the vowels more or less as in French.

The decision on the alphabet made it necessary for Jones and Griffiths to revise the spelling of much of the vocabulary they had collected. Once that had been done, they were able to press on with the preparation of Malagasy texts and lessons for use in the schools and with what was for them the essential task, the translation of the Bible. They tackled the work with dedication and amazing stamina. The average day began at sunrise (around six o'clock) with the arrival of the children for morning school, which continued until half-past eight. After breakfast the rest of the morning was devoted to the translation of the Bible, with the help of some of the more advanced Malagasy pupils. Sometimes there were private lessons for the royal family or secretarial work in English for Radama. Afternoon school lasted from one until five. In the evenings there was more work on the language, the preparation of lessons and catechisms and the composition of Malagasy hymns. On Saturdays sermons had to be prepared in English, Malagasy and French for the services held on Sunday. At first Jones and Griffiths alternated each Sunday, one conducting the service in English and the other in Malagasy, with Jones also holding a service in French. When schools were opened outside the capital one would stay in Antananarivo on Sunday while the other travelled on a horse borrowed from Radama to as many villages as possible to hold services, usually in the open air, and to see how the schools were progressing. And somehow they had to find time for the administration of the Mission and correspondence with their headquarters in London.

By the beginning of 1826, only five years after their arrival, the missionaries had not only created a considerable network of schools in and around the capital, but had completed the translation of the New Testament and substantial chunks of the Old. All this was the achievement, virtually unaided, of David Jones and David Griffiths. Jeffreys and his wife, who had proved to be a discordant element in the mission, left in 1825. It was not until September 1826 that further help arrived in the shape of Reverend David Johns (his real name was Jones but he changed the spelling to avoid confusion with his namesake). Together with Reverend Joseph Freeman who arrived a year later, he was to make a valuable contribution to the work of translating the Bible and to the preparation of the first comprehensive English-Malagasy dictionary. He brought with him the long-awaited printing press and two more artisans, Cummins a cotton spinner and Cameron a carpenter. Their arrival was to give a new impulse to the work of the missionary-artisans, which so far had proved rather disappointing.

It had been the hope of the LMS that the artisans would become self-supporting by selling the work they and their apprentices produced. But of the first group of artisans only the blacksmith, Chick, was able to make progress. In his case raw materials, charcoal and iron-ore, were readily available, although some distance away; while the Merina were already skilled in the production of simple iron tools and utensils. He was able to train hundreds of apprentices in more elaborate techniques of metal working; and in 1825 he signed a contract with Radama for the supply of all the ironwork for the new palace being built at Soanierana, just to the south of the capital. The tanner, Canham, could not find any local source of the lime necessary for the tanning process, and was limited to teaching a few apprentices to work leather imported from Mauritius. Later, some source of lime must have been discovered, and at the end of 1825 he too made an agreement with Radama to set up a tannery and a shoe factory, with Radama providing all the materials and workmen and Canham having the disposal of half the leather produced during the first seven years. The least successful was the weaver, Rowlands. With only local homespun cotton to work with, he could not compete with cloth imported from Mauritius. He soon abandoned his trade to help the missionaries with their teaching. It was to help him that Cummins was sent out with a cotton-spinning machine for the manufacture of cotton yarn. But this also was a commercial failure and Cummins returned home

The missionaries

within two years. Rowlands had meanwhile started an experiment in growing hemp for the making of sails, but death intervened to save him from another probable failure.

By contrast, James Cameron was a success from the start. He was born in the first week of 1800 at Little Dunkeld in Scotland and took up the trade of carpenter. By dint of wide reading he became proficient in several branches of learning – physics, chemistry, mathematics, architecture and astronomy. Before going out to Madagascar he spent a year in Manchester learning about machinery, in particular the spinning machine which was being sent out with Cummins. He had thus equipped himself to practise and teach numerous trades and he was one of those fortunate men who have almost an intuitive knowledge of machinery and how it works.

Cameron was sent out as a replacement for the carpenter who had died soon after his arrival in 1822. But he found more scope for his self-taught skills than for his original trade. A French builder, Louis Gros, who arrived at Antananarivo from Mauritius in 1819, had set up a workshop and trained a number of apprentices in carpentry, joinery and cabinet making. He was responsible for building Radama's palace at Soanierana the design of which, rather French provincial in style, has influenced domestic architecture in Imerina ever since. Cameron thus found plenty of trained carpenters and although he himself gave some instruction to apprentice carpenters his main achievements were in other fields.

His first task was to help Cummins to assemble the cotton-spinning machinery. Towards the end of 1826 the printer, Hovenden, sent out to set up the printing press, died within a few weeks of his arrival. Cameron, with the aid of a handbook found among the machinery, set up the press and after a good deal of trial and error succeeded in making it work. Subsequently he was put in charge of public works and constructed an aqueduct to bring water from a lake to the work-shop area. He introduced the manufacture of bricks, of soap and of sulphur. Like all the artisans he also engaged in evangelistic work among his workmen. As we shall see, it was largely due to his versatility that the stay of the missionaries was prolonged after the death of Radama.

While Radama lived he gave every support to the work of the missionaries in teaching, the development of useful crafts and the dissemination of the written language. But all this activity was for the missionaries subordinate to their main purpose of spreading the Gospel and converting the heathen. In this they received little encouragement from Radama, who gave the impression that he only tolerated the religious teaching as the unavoidable price to pay for the missionaries' useful work in other fields. He himself showed little interest in the Christian doctrine: his main reaction on first hearing the story of the Crucifixion was a practical interest in a novel form of execution. It was not that he was particularly attached to the religion of his ancestors. He told David Jones at an early stage that he did not believe in the superstitions of his people but felt obliged to conform to the customs of the country of which he was king. It would in any case be very difficult to make his people give up polygamy, belief in divination, etc, all at once but he hoped that by a gradual process of enlightenment the picture would be greatly changed after twenty years.[8]

One of the old customs which particularly shocked the missionaries was celebrated on the occasion of Radama's marriage to Rasalimo, the Sakalava princess, in 1823. The scene was described by the French writer Laverdant:[9]

"In the evening, while the crowds besieged the palace, Radama, high on the balcony, gave a sign calling for silence ... , then in the middle of the profound and respectful quiet of the multitude the king dropped one word, a single word. This word was immediately repeated on all lips, with a fearful tumult of laughing and piercing shouts, and at once, on the spot, the most fabulous orgy that could be imagined took place. There were perhaps two hundred thousand people assembled in and around Antananarivo for the royal marriage celebrations. It was a confused, universal mingling, the slaves with the free, the common people with the nobles; no one had the right to protest against the sacred order of the king, and General Brady himself had to endure seeing his wife carried off before his eyes without saying anything. Only the royal wives were excepted."

On the following day Hastie and the missionaries called on the king to protest. Radama, greatly amused by their indignation, explained that the *lapabe* was a custom practised on joyful royal occasions since ancient times. He laughingly promised that no more public orgies would occur. But a little later he forgot his promise in his joy at the birth of Rasalimo's first child, when the scenes of the wedding night were repeated.[10]

To the strait-laced, nonconformist missionaries, the "licentiousness" of the people was both the greatest sin to be stamped out and the most serious obstacle to their progress in the religious field. In the schools they made considerable headway in implanting Christian doctrines in the minds of their pupils, by the use of religious texts for reading and writing and hymns for singing. But for some time they had little success with adults. In 1824, as with the schools, something of a breakthrough occurred as Jones and Griffiths mastered the language sufficiently to hold services and even, with Radama's permission, to preach sermons in Malagasy. Soon they were reporting that their Sunday services were attracting thousands of "hearers" who packed the chapel annexed to the Central School, lining the doors and windows and overflowing into the courtyard. But it is doubtful whether the religion preached was an important attraction. For most of the Malagasy who came, the services were a novel variation of their own *kabary*, at which they could indulge two of their main pleasures, singing and listening to long speeches.

Within a year, the novelty wore thin and congregations fell away both in the capital and in the surrounding villages, partly because of opposition from the idol-keepers and other traditionalists. But the missionaries also found that as soon as they tried to relate their doctrines to the conduct of private life, the people shied away. Listening to colourful sermons and singing hymns was one thing; obeying the Ten Commandments was quite another. The Seventh Commandment in particular encountered opposition, indeed incomprehension: how could they forsake the gratifications of the flesh which constituted the chief pleasure and happiness of man?[11] There seemed no prospect of persuading them of their errors when the royal family set such a bad example. The king's mother and sisters had the privilege of summoning to their beds any man they liked. The king also took to his bed any girl that he fancied, and the family of the girl regarded it as a great honour.[12] Radama was not disposed to alter his personal habits, and he also had a more fundamental objection to the new religion. Like other despots from the Roman emperors onwards, he found the concept of the equality of all men before God incompatible with his own position as the living representative of the ancestral gods. In general, the promise of Heaven and the threat of Hell made less than the usual impact on a people deeply imbued with the idea of survival after death in the family tombs, with the spirits of ancestors presiding over daily life.

Despite their disappointment with his attitude to religion, the missionaries recognised that without Radama they would have achieved nothing. He gave them full support in their work in the schools and with the printing press which together provided their best hopes for the future. He encouraged the scholars by frequent exhortation and visits and by attendance at the annual school examinations where he personally rewarded the better pupils. When school attendance fell off it was to Radama that they looked to revive recruitment. His attitude to Christianity remained a combination of personal indifference and political caution. At one time he warned the missionaries that they were pressing ahead too fast; and he never gave permission for Malagasy to participate in the sacrament of Communion. Otherwise he placed no obstacles in the way of their religious teachings and church services; and he cooperated with their observance of the Sabbath to the extent of ordering his band to play no music on Sundays except "God Save the King", presumably the only "religious" music in their repertoire.[13]

It was accordingly with apprehension that the missionaries observed the steady decline in Radama's health in the first half of 1828. In his later years his increasing fondness for alcohol and nocturnal debauches had weakened his constitution and his resistance to disease. He died on July 27, 1828 at the age of thirty-six.

Radama had no son and never publicly designated a successor. It seems that he originally intended his sister's son Rakotobe to succeed him, but after the birth of his daughter Raketaka he wished her to succeed as queen and to marry Rakotobe.[14] Young Rakotobe had been among David Jones's very first pupils and he could be expected to continue Radama's general policies and to favour Christianity. Traditionalist officers of state therefore moved swiftly to prevent his succession. Radama's death was kept secret, and on July 29 a great *kabary* was held at which the people were called upon to swear loyalty to whomever was chosen to succeed the king. On August 1, leading army officers and other officials were summoned to the palace courtyard in the presence of soldiers to be informed that the idols had chosen Ramavo, Radama's senior wife and cousin, as successor.[15] A few who demurred were instantly speared to death. The new queen was then proclaimed to the multitude as Queen Ranavalona.

Two representatives of the LMS, Mr Tyerman and Mr Bennet, had just arrived in Antananarivo to inspect the Mission. Tyerman, weakened by the journey from the coast, died of apoplexy on July 30. Bennet survived to describe Radama's funeral. The body remained unburied for sixteen days while awaiting an auspicious day and the construction of a tomb. At ceremonies held on August 12, Bennet and the missionaries were overcome by the stench from the unenclosed body and had to retire. They returned next day for the actual entombment. The body was by now encased in a huge coffin of the most valuable hardwood. The tomb constructed within the *rova* was a truncated pyramid of earth faced with granite, 20 feet (6 m) high, 60 feet (18 m) square at the base tapering to 20 feet (6 m) square. On the top of the mound a square well about ten feet (3 m) cube was sunk to receive the silver coffin into which the corpse was finally transferred. Twelve thousand Spanish dollars had been melted for the construction of this coffin. Ten thousand more silver dollars were placed in the coffin for the body to lie on and vast quantities of treasure and personal belongings were deposited in and around the coffin – including eighty costly British uniforms with feathered cocked hats, a golden helmet, epaulettes, sashes, gold spurs, valuable swords, daggers and spears (two of gold), beautiful pistols, muskets, fowling-pieces, watches, brooches and trinkets; his whole superb sideboard of silver plate and gold cup, and great quantities of costly silks, fine cloths and silk lambas. Ten of his favourite bulls and twelve of his finest horses were killed to keep him company in the next life. Twenty thousand oxen were slaughtered to feed the vast crowd assembled for the ceremony. Throughout the day Radama's two military bands, with fifes and drums, alternated to provide an unbroken flow of the music he most delighted in – waltzes, marches and many of the favourite airs of England, Scotland and Ireland.

A proper assessment of Radama's complex character would require a full-length biography. Arrogant, wilful, cruel, childish and self-indulgent – at times he was all these; but he was also warm, impulsive, charming, sensitive, highly intelligent and far-seeing. Europeans whom he met were in general very favourably impressed. But as Prince Coroller[16] shrewdly pointed out, Radama was always at his most charming with European visitors and was very anxious to cut a good figure in their eyes. Hastie soon found that the best way to encourage Radama in a certain course of action was to say how pleased King George would be to learn about it; and conversely the suggestion that the civilised world would be shocked by a certain practice was the surest way to bring about its abolition.

But if ambition and vanity were the mainsprings of his actions this does not diminish the importance of the achievements of his reign. Of undoubted benefit to the whole country were the abolition of the export of slaves, the adoption of a general system of education with the first beginnings of Christian teaching, the establishment of a written language and its diffusion by means of printing, and the creation of new local industries based on the wide range of useful arts taught by the European artisans. Radama's success in modernising his country and opening it up to the outside world is similar in spirit if not in scale to that of Peter the Great of Russia, whom he also resembled in his insatiable curiosity. Opinions may differ as to the value of his other main achievement, the extension of Merina authority over most of the island as a result of the creation of a powerful army on the European model. This was no doubt a necessary step on the way to the unification of the whole island. But the means employed, namely military conquest, caused great suffering and loss of life, and might be contrasted with the more subtle method of diplomacy (backed it is true by force) employed by his father.

The main instrument of Radama's policy was the alliance with Great Britain; and his achievements owed much to the vision of Farquhar, the wise counsels of Hastie and the devoted toil of the small band of missionaries and artisans. But his own role was pre-eminent, as is shown by the sharp reversal of his policies after his death. Hastie, Jones and Griffiths could have achieved nothing without his enthusiasm and energy and his willingess to ride rough-shod over traditionalist opposition. One can only speculate on what he might have achieved if he had lived for another thirty years. It is possible that, like his successor, he might in due course have reacted against the threat to traditional values posed by the rapid spread of Christianity; but it is perhaps more probable that his authority would have ensured a more gradual modernisation of Malagasy society without the violent upheavals of the two subsequent reigns. What is reasonably certain is that the subsequent history of Madagascar would have been very different; and that is a measure of his stature.

Chapter 12

The queen and the martyrs

The short, dumpy woman in early middle age who now succeeded to the throne is an enigmatic figure. Contemporary accounts by missionaries and European travellers presented her to the outside world as a bloodthirsty ogress, a modern Messalina or female Nero. More recently there has been a move to rehabilitate her as a heroine of Malagasy nationalism (a view which will be examined briefly at the end of this chapter) or at least to assess her more sympathetically in the light of the values of the traditional society in which she was raised and the great pressures imposed on that society by the crisis of modernisation. Some writers have tended to regard her as a simple woman, virtuous by traditional standards, a good wife and mother who as queen was a mere puppet manipulated by the forces of reaction. This latter view is difficult to reconcile with contemporary evidence, both European and Malagasy, which shows her as a woman of determination with a mind of her own. The reactionary policies pursued in her name undoubtedly coincided with her own views, whilst the sudden shifts in these policies suggest a royal wilfulness. Letters conveying her views to foreign representatives and governments were usually signed by one of her ministers or secretaries; but we know[1] that she often dictated them herself. She was undoubtedly influenced by her advisers, but there are indications that their influence was at times exerted on the side of moderation and it is possible that but for them her rule might have been even more repressive and bloodthirsty.

Her accession nevertheless marks the end of the system of personal despotic rule by the Merina kings supported by a small group of *andriana*. Henceforward, until the end of the monarchy, the real power was in the hands of an oligarchy drawn mainly from the Hova middle class. The Hova had played a steadily increasing role in previous reigns: for example, leading Hova families had played an important part in supporting Andrianampoinimerina in his rise to power. During Radama's reign they had enriched themselves from the new trading opportunities and had advanced by their merits in the hierarchy of honours created by Radama in the army and civil administration. Although power and the benefits of trading monopolies were still shared with leading *andriana* the Hova now took over the principal posts in army and government. To meet the novel situation of a reigning queen a new appointment was made of a queen's guardian (*mpitaiza andriana*) who was in effect the queen's official lover. Because of its great influence, this post was usually combined with that of commander-in-chief or first minister (terms often used interchangeably as the military system of "honours" also applied to civilian officers). One of the first holders was Andriamihaja, usually described as commander-in-chief, who was almost certainly the father of the queen's only son, born over a year after Radama's death but called nevertheless Rakotond'Radama ("Radama's boy").

The first concern of the new régime was to eliminate in traditional fashion all potential rival claimants to the throne, a task all the more necessary in view of Ranavalona's dubious title. Radama's mother was put to death along with his nephew Rakotobe. Rakotobe's parents (his father was Prince Ratefy who had visited England with the first Malagasy students) were on their way to the capital from Tamatave, where Prince Ratefy occupied the post of governor, when they heard of their son's death. They fled back to the coast where they tried to take passage on a ship leaving for Mauritius; but the ship's captain, not wishing to annoy the new régime, refused to accept them on board. Ratefy was arrested, tried and executed on the charge of leaving his post without instructions; his wife (Radama's sister) died shortly afterwards in provincial exile, possibly from natural causes.[2] Other close relatives and collaborators of Radama were also put to death. Messengers were sent to Majunga to bring back to the capital the governor Ramanetaka, a cousin of Radama, but with secret instructions to kill him on the way. Ramanetaka managed to give them the slip and escape to the island of Moheli in the Comoros where he became a Moslem and imposed himself as ruler. But his exact whereabouts were not known in Antananarivo and for a number of years rumours that he was heading a rebellion and marching on the capital with an army of Sakalava kept alive the hopes of the opponents of the new régime.

Soon after her accession, the queen sent a message to the missionaries assuring them of her protection and promising to act towards them as Radama had done. But the signs were not encouraging for the Europeans. On the pretext of court mourning Mr Bennet, the surviving inspector from the LMS, was refused an audience with the queen; and Dr Robert Lyall, the new British

Agent who had arrived in the capital inopportunely a few days after Radama's death, was likewise not allowed to present his credentials. At the end of November 1828 he was informed that the queen did not regard herself as bound by the treaties with Great Britain and that she would not receive him as Agent of the British government. A further message stated that the queen no longer wished to receive the annual "equivalent" but that she had no intention of reviving the export of slaves. Robin, the French ex-sergeant who had risen to the position of marshal under Radama, was expelled from the country in October 1828.[3] General Brady, who had been naturalised a Malagasy and given noble rank by Radama, underwent a period of uncertainty before being reinstated as commander of the army at the beginning of 1829; but he retired shortly afterwards to his country estate outside the capital.

The court mourning for Radama, which was to last for nearly a year, prescribed the shaving of all heads, abstention from showy dress, riding (whether on horseback or in *filanjana*), music and dancing, and the avoidance of all "licentiousness" among married or unmarried during the day-time. It also included the closure of all the schools and places of public worship. The missionaries, full of foreboding for the future, concentrated on their work of translating and printing the Bible and other religious books. But the tensions of the situation aggravated the internal bickerings inevitable in the claustrophobic atmosphere of the small European community. Lyall, a less sympathetic character than Hastie, appears to have resented the influence acquired by Jones and Griffiths, and accused them of engaging in property deals, money-lending and drinking and smoking bouts with the artisans. He was supported by Freeman, a man of superior class and education who resented being under the orders of the senior missionaries. They for their part regarded Lyall as lacking the sympathetic understanding necessary for dealing with the Malagasy. Lyall was perhaps too conscious of his dignity, but according to his own account he appears to have taken great care in a difficult situation not to offend the queen. But with his medical and scientific knowledge he was seen as a threat to traditional beliefs and the power of the *ombiasy* and the idol-keepers. Their opportunity came when he inadvertently offended against certain *fady* near the village which was the home of the famous idol *kelimalaza*. In punishment for the alleged offence, idol-keepers descended on Lyall's house with sacks of serpents which they scattered around the house and courtyard; and Lyall was compelled to leave immediately on foot for a village some miles to the east pending his expulsion from the island at the end of the wet season.

The schools had meanwhile been allowed to open, but in the absence of positive support from the queen the number of pupils declined. Religious services were also resumed at the end of court mourning. But the revival of practices such as *sikidy* and the *tangena* poison ordeal indicated the queen's attachment to ancient beliefs and customs, and the outlook for religious teaching seemed distinctly gloomy. Freeman, finding the atmosphere within the Mission increasingly uncongenial and worried about reports of an impending French invasion, decided that the days of the Mission were numbered and left with his family in September 1829.

Freeman's pessimism was, however, premature. Almost from the time of his departure things began to improve. The government made some effort to fill up the schools, and no hindrance was put in the way of preaching and the printing and distribution of religious texts. By March 1830 5,000 copies of the New Testament in Malagasy had been distributed along with thousands of copies of tracts and catechisms. Chapel services became so crowded that permission was requested, and granted, for the building of a second chapel in the Ambatonakanga district of Antananarivo. Then in May 1831 the queen went further than Radama had done by granting permission for her subjects to be baptised, to partake of Communion and to be married in the Christian manner.

This astonishing deviation from the queen's traditionalist policies and beliefs requires an explanation.[4] An important contributory factor was the manufacturing skill of the missionary artisans, which acquired a new importance from the government's xenophobic desire to reduce its dependence on foreign supplies. Early in the new reign a message from the queen, while thanking the missionaries for their teaching work, enquired whether they could not teach something more useful such as the making of soap. Cameron asked the messengers to come back a week later, when he produced "two small bars of a tolerably good and white soap" made entirely from local materials. The versatile Cameron was active in seeking out local minerals to be used in manufacture – iron pyrites for sulphur, potash and soda for glassware and pottery. Together with Chick he entered into a contract with the government to carry out various manufactures and public works, including the construction of a watermill and of a reservoir (the present Lac Anosy) and an aqueduct to bring water to it. This contract took some five years to complete, and undoubtedly helped to prolong the missionaries' stay in Imerina.

But the main reason for the queen's temporary change of heart may have been political – the need to maintain good relations with the British at a time when the Merina kingdom faced a serious threat from the French. The death of the "pro-British" Radama and the abrogation of the treaties with Britain encouraged the French to proceed with plans to re-assert their claims to their former establishments on the east coast. In the latter part of 1829 a naval squadron bombarded and occupied Tintingue and Tamatave, but suffered a setback when a careless attack on the Merina fort at Foulpointe was repulsed. With this encouragement, and secure in the protection of "General Hazo ("forest") and General Tazo ("fever")", the queen responded to French demands with a refusal to cede an inch of Malagasy territory. The impasse was resolved by the July Revolution in France, after which the government of Louis-Philippe ordered the evacuation of the mainland of Madagascar. But French rights were not abandoned, and Franco-Merina relations remained embittered.

The missionaries were quick to take advantage of the more favourable atmosphere in Antananarivo. Within weeks of the granting of permission, some forty Malagasy were baptised. Among the more notable was Rafaravavy, a woman of good family who took the name Marie. Another was a *mpisikidy* called Rainitsiheva who was baptised Paul and became known to the missionaries as "Paul the Diviner". The numbers of Christians soon became sufficient to form two Malagasy "societies" based on the chapels at Andohalo and Ambatonakanga. Freeman, who returned to Antananarivo in 1831 with a new missionary Theophilus Atkinson, was astonished at the changed atmosphere, with many converts, large and voluntary attendance at the chapel services, and prayer meetings being held regularly in Malagasy private houses.[5] But this period, marking the height of the missionaries' success in religious teaching, lasted only six months. The number of baptisms alarmed the conservative elements at the royal court, who persuaded the queen that the communion service amounted to an oath of allegiance to the British. At the end of 1831 permission for further baptisms was withdrawn and Malagasy were forbidden to take part in the communion service.

This decision was an indication of the growing strength of the traditionalist party at court. Andriamihaja, although one of the leaders of the conspiracy which put the queen on the throne, had been sympathetic to European ideas and to Christianity. But his youth and his arrogant exercise of the power deriving from his influence with the queen aroused the jealousy and enmity of the traditionalists. A conspiracy was organised against him and he was assassinated, probably in September 1830. His successor as chief minister and the queen's official lover was the handsome Rainiharo,[6] who appears to have shared the queen's amatory favours with his brother Rainimaharo.[6] Their family, which had been prominent in support for Andrianampoinimerina during his rise to power, now became known as the Andafiavaratra ("on the north side") from the location of Rainiharo's house to the north of the queen's palace; they were to dominate the government until the end of the monarchy. Another influential figure, and in due course another lover of the queen, was Rainijohary,[6] head of the other main Hova family to have given early support to Andrianampoinimerina; he was one of the most fanatical traditionalists and, like the Andafiavaratra brothers, a keeper of one of the chief idols. For the time being however the traditionalists were restrained by the need to avoid too obvious a break with Radama's policies or an open breach with Great Britain.

The missionaries were further discouraged when Theophilus Atkinson was ordered to leave after a year on the ground that he could only teach *taratasy* ("paper", i.e. writing). The queen also indicated that Radama's order limiting the stay of Europeans to ten years and a day would be enforced. David Jones, whose health had been broken by recurrent bouts of fever and years of overwork, had already departed with his family in 1830. David Griffiths, whose time was now up, obtained an extension of one year thanks to the influence at court of some of his former pupils. But this extension was far from welcome to the other missionaries and the artisans (apart from Baker the printer) for whom Griffiths had become an intolerable colleague. In response to their letters describing him as "headstrong, ambitious and violent",[7] the directors of the LMS ordered his recall. Griffiths refused to comply, quoting the extension of his stay as proof that the queen wished him to remain. He ignored repeated peremptory orders from the directors to return, and secured further extensions by suggesting that the LMS was usurping the queen's right to decide when he should leave. And when the directors took the extreme step of cutting off financial support he determined to stay on to teach and preach, supporting himself by engaging in trade.

Despite these un-Christian bickerings, the Mission continued to flourish for several more years. The government made greater efforts to fill the schools, although at the same time they made school attendance less attractive by frequent raids on older pupils to serve in the army. Attendance at chapel for services other than communion was not forbidden, and the size of the congregations was most encouraging. Private prayer meetings continued and interest in the Christian doctrine expanded with the printing and distribution of more religious texts. As these were the only printed matter available in the Malagasy language the growth in reading ability – and by now some 10,000 had passed through the schools – was bound to lead to the spread of Christianity.

Inevitably enthusiasm for the new faith produced a fanatical fringe. In a village to the north a keeper of idols began to preach his own fundamentalist version of Christianity – including the return of Christ and the abolition of slavery, war and work – which he managed to combine with respect for the idols as guardians rather than divinities. He acquired some 200 followers and marched with them to the capital to convey his message to the queen. When the queen learned that the message included the equality and common origin of all humanity, she enquired whether this applied to herself and the Mozambique slaves. The affirmative answer brought swift and terrible punishment. The new priest and three of his chief followers were placed head-down in a rice-pit, boiling water was poured on top of them and the pit filled in with earth. Seventeen others were subjected to the *tangena* ordeal, under which eight of them died, and the remainder sold into slavery.

This episode increased the queen's hostility to Christianity, which was fed by frequent reports of the Christians' contempt for the idols and disregard for ancient customs. After one such report involving a high-born lady of the court, who declared that many thousands including even slaves thought the same way, the queen "was so grieved and angry that she wept for about a rice cooking (half an hour) and vowed death against all the Christians".[8]

The blow fell early in 1835. On February 21 the missionaries were assembled to receive a message from the queen.[9] This thanked them for their work in teaching "good dispositions and useful knowledge", assured them that they could continue to practise their own customs but that they must be subject to the laws of the country. It went on: "And I tell you plainly that I will oppose any attempt by my people to change the customs of my ancestors established under the twelve kings up to Andrianampoinimerina and Radama ... and with respect to religious worship, whether on Sunday or any other day, baptisms and societies (i.e. membership of a church), I forbid my people to take part. However, if you have new crafts or knowledge to teach for the good of my people, do that, for it is good."

On March 1 all the people in and around Antananarivo were summoned to a great *kabary*. Thousands of troops were drawn up, and cannon were fired at intervals to emphasise the solemnity of the occasion. The chief judge then read out the queen's proclamation forbidding Christian practices and ordering a strict adherence to ancestral customs. All printed books were to be handed in to the authorities. Those people who had been baptised, had attended public worship or evening prayer meetings, and even those who had voluntarily learned to read, were given one month to come forward and accuse themselves. When some protested that Christian teaching had been encouraged by Radama and even by the queen, the response was to reduce the time limit for confessing to one week, on pain of death.

Under this threat, the great majority of the Christians came forward to confess and recant. Those with "honours", numbering about 400, were downgraded, losing half their honours, e.g. a general (ten honours) became a lieutenant (five honours); some 2,000 ordinary people had to pay a small fine. A few score, including Rafaravavy and Paul the Diviner and his wife, remained faithful despite the risk of being denounced and sold into slavery. The missionaries were not ordered to leave, and the government would have been happy for Cameron and the other artisans to stay. But as they were not allowed to carry out any religious work they saw no point in staying and all except two left in the course of 1835, including Griffiths whose trading venture had not prospered. Before they left, they helped to complete the printing of the Bible, the government having withdrawn the Malagasy apprentices from the printing press. Johns and Baker stayed on to finish the preparation and printing of the English-Malagasy dictionary. After the departure of the other missionaries, their servants were tried by the *tangena* ordeal and several were put to death. The threat of the *tangena* also dissuaded all but the most faithful from visiting the mission. But a handful of Christians continued to meet and pray in secrecy, in the houses of friends they could trust or out in the country at night on the tops of lonely hills. And when Jones and Baker finally departed in 1836 they left quantities of bibles and other religious books to be distributed among the faithful and concealed in caves and holes in the ground.

The departure of the missionaries marked the final break with Radama's policy. But some of the queen's advisers were aware of the dangers of alienating both Britain and France. In 1835 the presence of 21 armed ships in St Augustine's Bay (they were in fact American whalers calling in for provisions) prevented a Merina military expedition from attacking the local people. This incident was a reminder that foreign seapower, which had helped Radama to subdue the coastal areas, could equally well be deployed on the side of the coastal people against the Merina. It was probably a factor in the decision to send a mission of ambassadors to England and France. The object was to try to repair some of the damage caused by the isolationist, anti-Christian policy, and to secure recognition for Ranavalona as queen of Madagascar.

The mission of six ambassadors and two secretaries, led by Andriantsitohaina, arrived in London at the beginning of February 1837. Freeman was attached to them as guide and interpreter (although four of them spoke good English) and they were given an intensive programme of sightseeing, designed to demonstrate the wealth and military power of Great Britain. They saw the Directors of the LMS, who urged them to agree to the resumption of Christian teaching, which was the foundation of Britain's greatness. They were presented to King William IV at a *levée* and invited to Windsor Castle where they had audiences with both the king and Queen Adelaide. In a series of meetings at the Foreign Office, Lord Palmerston proposed a new treaty which would have revived the principal features of the 1817 and 1820 treaties and provided also for free access to Madagascar for British traders and missionaries with the right to buy property, and the exchange of consuls. As the ambassadors had no authority to agree to anything beyond limited access by British traders to coastal ports, no agreement was possible. Their visit to Paris was even less fruitful. The French government showed no interest in serious talks, and the ambassadors were fobbed off with a dinner with King Louis-Philippe.

The ambassadors returned empty-handed to a situation which would soon rule out any possibility of *détente* with the European powers. Already, before the departure of Johns and Baker, Rafaravavy had been denounced by three of her slaves for retaining religious books and continuing to follow Christian practices. At her trial she refused to name any of her fellow-Christians, and the queen ordered her to be put to death, but the sentence was commuted to a fine in consideration of her father's services to the state. With the departure of the last of the missionaries the authorities relaxed their vigilance against the Christians, hoping that the new religion would die away when the foreign source was removed. But the faith not only survived but continued to attract new adherents. The government realised that sterner measures were necessary. In July 1837 Rafaravavy was again arrested along with Paul the Diviner and a dozen other Christians. They were threatened with the death sentence but at the last moment condemned to perpetual slavery and distributed among the households of various dignitaries. While still in confinement however, one of them, a woman called Rasalama, was overheard expressing her unrepentant belief in Christ and willingness to suffer for her faith. She was beaten, cruelly laden with irons and ordered for execution the next morning. She sang hymns all the way as she was led in chains along the narrow street leading to Ambohipotsy. This was the traditional place of execution at the southern end of Antananarivo, from which the condemned criminal's last gaze embraced an extensive view of the hills and rice-plains of Imerina as far as the mountains of Ankaratra, forty miles (64 km) to the southwest. After a final prayer Rasalama was speared to death to become the first Malagasy Christian martyr.

In the following year a man called Rafaralahy was denounced to the authorities for conducting prayer meetings. He refused to name his associates and met the same fate as Rasalama with the same calm dignity. His wife, however, was flogged until she revealed the names, which included most of the Christians enslaved the year before. Paul and some others were arrested and put in irons (some time later Paul successfully passed the *tangena* test and was released). Rafaravavy and a few others were warned in time and took refuge in the Vonizongo district to the northwest of Antananarivo where Christianity had taken especially strong root. For months they were sheltered by friends, moving constantly to evade capture and hiding at times in chimneys, rice-pits and caves while soldiers searched nearby. Eventually they established contact with David Johns, who had returned to Tamatave to try to help Christian refugees. After many narrow escapes, Rafaravavy and a party of ten reached the coast and escaped to Mauritius in October 1838. Six of them accompanied Johns to England where Rafaravavy in particular impressed the LMS by her "intelligence, urbanity, gentleness of demeanour, benevolence and sincerity of character". They returned in 1842 to Mauritius, where they formed a small Malagasy Christian community under the leadership of the saintly Rafaravavy.

The escape of this group led to increased efforts by the authorities to suppress Christianity. In 1838 David Griffiths had returned to Antananarivo to resume his trading activities and give what help he could to the Christians. In May 1840 he helped to organise an escape plan for sixteen Christians, led by Paul and a preacher who had taken the name of Joshua. But they were betrayed by a guide when within a day's journey of the sea, and brought back to the capital in chains. Two escaped, five were sentenced to perpetual slavery and the remaining nine condemned to death. David Jones, the pioneer missionary, arrived in Antananarivo, accompanying Lieutenant Campbell who was on a vain mission from Mauritius intended to improve relations with the queen. Jones was just in time to witness their last hours:

"On the morning of the 9th July there was a tremendous roar of cannon and thousands of soldiers began to march towards the parade ground. ... There was much firing of cannon all day at intervals, the meaning of which was not generally understood. Between three and four o'clock, as Messrs Griffiths and Campbell were standing together on the balcony of Mr Griffiths' house, they saw a number of people coming along the road and they discovered the nine Christians carried quite naked, each being tied under a pole, and the bearers stood for a little time opposite Mr Griffiths' house then carried them by the West side of the town to Ambohipotsy the place of execution; – and, after a short interval, a cannon was fired for a signal and the nine were instantly speared to death and their spirits fled to eternal glory. Paul and his wife, Joshua and his wife, and Flora were of the number of these martyrs ... The head of Paul and that of another man were cut off and fixed on poles. The cannon that was fired for the signal to spear them burst into pieces and the man that fired it was seriously burnt which was considered by many as a bad omen."[10]

Griffiths, whose part in the escape plot became known to the government, was fined £30 and ordered to leave. David Jones also left for Mauritius where he died in the following year, having witnessed the apparent collapse of his life's work (Griffiths lived long enough to see the revival of Christianity in Madagascar). David Johns, who had returned to Mauritius in 1840, spent the next two years in trying vainly to establish a mission on the northwest coast, where French influence among the Sakalava was growing. He died in 1843 on the island of Nosy Be which two years earlier had been taken under French protection at the request of the local chiefs.

Madagascar now entered the darkest period of Ranavalona's reign. The persecution of the Christians continued, but they were not the only nor even the chief sufferers under the savage code of laws. The return to ancestral traditions included the revival of the slaughter of children born on unlucky days and the restoration of the death penalty for certain crimes awarded a lesser punishment under Radama. Slavery and confiscation of goods were the penalty for a wide range of less serious crimes. And the dangerous and capricious *tangena* ordeal was extensively used on the slightest suspicion of guilt. Many people fled from this oppressive régime to the semi-desert regions around Imerina, where they had to support themselves by brigandry. In 1835 Johns had reported the public execution in Antananarivo of nearly 200 of these robbers, about half by spearing, some by burning, others dying from the *tangena* and a few being buried alive. During the whole reign there must have been many thousands who were put to death or perished under the *tangena* ordeal.

This harsh administration of the law bore especially heavily on the inhabitants of Imerina within easy reach of the capital. Other regions of Madagascar suffered at times more severely from Merina military expeditions. With the disappearance from the scene of Hastie, Robin and Brady, the discipline and organisation of the army steadily deteriorated. The tax raised by Radama to equip and feed a professional army was discontinued. Military service became just another branch of unpaid government service or forced labour (*fanompoana*) and soldiers were expected to clothe themselves and live off the country. The army thus reverted to its state in the early days of Radama, a disorderly rabble devastating the country through which it passed.

Some expeditions were undertaken in an attempt, usually vain, to extend the area subdued by Radama. The expedition of 1835, commanded by Rainiharo, traversed the country of the Bara, the Mahafaly and the Masikoro before arriving at St Augustine's Bay; but it proved impossible to maintain any permanent presence in the desolate lands of the southwest. The Sakalava of the Menabe continued to maintain an effective independence by their time-honoured tactic of melting away before advancing Merina armies. Four campaigns from 1829 to 1832 were necessary to secure the submission of the Tanala in the forests of the southeastern escarpment; but a revolt in 1850 threw off the Merina yoke which three subsequent armies were unable to re-establish. In the Boina, the change of monarch in Antananarivo encouraged Andriantsoly to return and raise the flag of rebellion. Several expeditions were needed to drive him again into exile, leaving various chiefs who had supported him to seek refuge in Nosy Be and to appeal successfully for French protection. The harsh exactions of military governors frequently provoked uprisings in other areas which had been under Merina domination for some time. In 1852 a revolt of the Antesaka on the southeast coast was brutally suppressed by an army under Raharo, which slaughtered thousands of men in cold blood and brought back many women and children to be sold into slavery. The acquisition of slaves, cattle and other booty for personal profit seems to have been an important motive for a number of expeditions.

Internal slavery had not, of course, been abolished under Radama, and slave markets for the sale of slaves within Madagascar still flourished. As we have seen Queen Ranavalona's denunciation of the treaties with Britain was accompanied by a statement that the export of slaves would not be resumed. This undertaking appears to have been fulfilled as regards the export of slaves from Imerina and there was no revival of the slave trade from the east coast to Mauritius and Réunion (it would have disappeared anyhow with the abolition of slavery in British territories in 1834 and in French possessions in 1848). In the northwest, however, where

Merina control was more remote, slaves continued to be exported for a time to Réunion and also to the United States and Arabia; and from the same area planters in Mauritius and later Réunion recruited workers under the system of indentured labour which replaced slavery in the plantations. From all causes – the export of slaves and labourers, the savage application of the law and the deaths of countless thousands from starvation, disease and battle during the military expeditions – there was undoubtedly a substantial depopulation of Madagascar during Ranavalona's reign, perhaps by as much as a million.

In some areas however there was progress rather than retrogression. Ranavalona apparently encouraged the collection and recording of traditional poems (*hain-teny*).[11] Although the closure of the missionary schools ended formal education for the ordinary people, education continued for the sons of the leading families at the court. Lessons were given in English and in Malagasy by some of the best pupils of the missionaries and especially by Raombana and Rahaniraka, twin brothers who had been among the first youths sent to be educated in England in 1820. They had returned after nine years to become, as secretaries to the queen, influential officers of the court. (Raombana is also important because of his *History*, *Annals* and *Journal*, written in English,[12] which are a major source of information about this period). This teaching, building on the foundations laid by the missionaries, led to the development of what can be called an Anglo-Malagasy culture in the second half of the nineteenth century. Among the many eminent pupils were the two sons of Rainiharo who were in due course to succeed him as Chief Minister; Raombana's son Razanakombana, future Minister of Justice; and Rainandriamampandry, who was well known as a teacher and preacher before becoming governor of Tamatave and Minister of the Interior.

Ranavalona's reign also saw remarkable progress in the development of local industry, thanks largely to two Frenchmen. The first was Napoléon de Lastelle who just after the death of Radama was put in charge of certain plantations and trading establishments on the east coast owned by the firm of Rontaunay of Réunion. In 1829 he obtained from the new queen a monopoly of the manufacture and sale of *araka* (a local rum), the profits to be shared equally with the queen who provided slaves to carry out the work. He became virtually the import-export agent for the queen and the government, building up an important trade between Madagascar, Réunion and France. He established new plantations of breadfruit, coconut, coffee and sugar, and set up workshops employing Malagasy carpenters and blacksmiths. He also introduced the first steam engines into Madagascar for use in the manufacture of sugar and *araka*. But his most important contribution was to introduce to the queen the second Frenchman, Jean Laborde.

Laborde occupies a special place among all the Frenchmen associated with Madagascar. The son of a blacksmith, he emigrated as a young man to seek his fortune in India. In 1831 he took part in a hare-brained and unsuccessful venture to recover treasure from ships wrecked on the west coast of Madagascar, and on the return journey was himself shipwrecked on the east coast. He was looked after by de Lastelle who sent him in the following year to Antananarivo. He soon attracted the favourable attention of the queen, who set him to work manufacturing muskets and gunpowder to fill the gap left by her rejection of the English "equivalent". With the departure of the British missionary-artisans in 1835 he was called upon to continue and expand the local manufacturing work which they had introduced. He would have been the first to admit his debt to Cameron and the other artisans who had established firm foundations for a local industry, training many hundreds of apprentices in a wide range of crafts and discovering local sources of various chemicals and other raw materials. But Laborde's natural scientific genius was even more inventive than Cameron's and he also had a remarkable talent for organisation.

Laborde's original factory at the village of Ilafy near the capital was too far away from essential raw materials. He accordingly constructed, with 20,000 forced labourers supplied by the queen, a veritable industrial complex at Mantasoa, some fifty miles (80 km) to the east, close to an abundant water supply, wood from the escarpment forest and sources of iron ore. When completed, it comprised living quarters for 1,200 workmen and forges, furnaces and factories producing a vast range of articles and commodities: munitions and arms of all kinds from cannon to swords, bricks, tiles, pottery, glass and porcelain, silk, soap, candles, sealing-wax, lime, cement, charcoal, ink, dyes, sugar, rum, sulphuric acid and lightning conductors. There was an experimental farm where various new crops and animals were introduced and a residential area with country houses where the queen and her courtiers sometimes came to be entertained with dances, bullfights and even fireworks displays. Laborde the architect also constructed a monumental tomb in Antananarivo for Rainiharo. But his most lasting memorial is the great wooden Queen's Palace (subsequently enclosed in stone by Cameron) surmounting the highest point in Antananarivo and visible for many miles in all directions. Its most remarkable feature is the central support consisting of a single tree trunk 130 feet (40 m) high, which required 5,000 slaves to bring it from the eastern forest.

The great weakness of Laborde's work was its reliance on forced labour. The workers at Mantasoa received food and lodging, but no pay, and were under military discipline. Laborde attempted to mitigate the system, for which he was not responsible, by a personal interest in the health and general welfare of the workers; and on occasions, when he received a lump sum payment for a piece of work, e.g. the casting of the first cannon, he distributed it among the men. But industrial labour at Mantasoa remained the most unpopular form of *fanompoana:* the unremitting regularity of work in the factories was alien to the nature of the Malagasy, and left the workers no time to look after their private and family interests. This remarkable achievement therefore contained the seeds of its ultimate destruction.

The industries established by Laborde greatly reduced Imerina's dependence on foreign imports and enabled the queen to take a tougher line against foreign traders on the east coast. Some of these, who had been successful in evading the monopolies established in favour of de Lastelle and members of the queen's entourage, had their goods confiscated and were expelled; and one who resisted was sold into slavery. In May 1845 the European traders in Tamatave, twelve of whom were British and eleven French, were informed that henceforth all provisions of the Malagasy law (including the *tangena* ordeal, forced labour and the penalty of slavery for certain offences) would apply to them. In response to their appeal for protection French and British warships commanded respectively by Commander Romain-Desfossés and Captain Kelly arrived in Tamatave. After an ultimatum had produced no response, the traders were taken on board, whereupon their houses and possessions were immediately looted. The two commanders decided on their own responsibility to bombard the town and attack the fort. The assault was repelled and the warships sailed away with the traders. They left behind a score of dead (16 French, 4 English) whose heads were cut off and impaled on stakes along the beach, where they remained for the next eight years.

When news of these events reached Antananarivo the queen ordered the expulsion of all foreign traders and the cessation of overseas trade, especially the export of beef and rice to Mauritius and Réunion. Preparations were made to resist further attacks from the European powers, but none came. In Paris the government proposed a punitive expedition but the idea was rejected by the Chamber of Deputies. The British were not prepared to take military measures, but pressure from Mauritius led to overtures being made to Antananarivo for the resumption of trade. The queen refused unless a substantial fine was first paid in compensation for the offence committed by Romain-Desfossés and Kelly. The idea of a fine and admission of guilt was anathema to Lord Palmerston, and so the ports of Madagascar remained closed, at least to French and British ships and goods. But the fairly important trade with the United States through Majunga, where an American agent, William Marks worked in close cooperation with American trading interests in Zanzibar, was not affected. For several years the Americans enjoyed a monopoly of foreign trade and Marks became a familiar figure at the Malagasy court.

De Lastelle and Laborde were exempted from the expulsion of foreigners in recognition of their past services. The cessation of foreign trade at first spelled ruin for de Lastelle's ventures but an exception was later made in his favour, and he had made a considerable fortune by the time he died in Tamatave in 1856. Laborde stayed on in Antananarivo, where for some years he was the only European. He continued to enjoy the favour of the queen (there was a widespread belief, unsupported by any real evidence, that he became one of her lovers) and acquired a beneficient influence over her son, Prince Rakoto.

The young heir to the throne seems to have been kindly and compassionate by nature. His education had been entrusted to Raombana and Rahaniraka, the twin brothers who had been to school in England. Their teaching imbued Prince Rakoto with liberal principles and an admiration for England; while the influence of Laborde further broadened his horizons and made him favourably disposed to France. As he grew older he was increasingly appalled by the barbarity of his mother's rule. He became sympathetic to the Christians, attended many meetings and discussions with them and intervened several times with his mother to avert her wrath against them. His cousin Prince Ramonja went further and became a convert, as did a nephew of Rainiharo.

This penetration of the highest families reflected the continuing spread of Christianity throughout Imerina. The willingness of the martyrs to die for their faith and their courage in meeting death made a deep impression and attracted many new adherents. Despite unremitting persecution, reductions to slavery and occasional executions, Christians continued to meet for prayer on the tops of hills at night and in houses behind double walls to deaden the sound of hymn-singing. In 1849, in another major attempt to extirpate the new faith, some two thousand Christians, including Prince Ramonja, were arrested and brought to trial. The great majority were fined, some of them heavily; Prince Ramonja was reduced to the rank of a common soldier and given arduous duties to perform (he was later restored to favour and returned to the royal court); over a hundred were flogged and sentenced to labour in chains for life. The supreme penalty was reserved for eighteen. Fourteen of them, including six women, were hurled to their deaths over the five hundred foot (160 m) precipice below the Queen's Palace (known as Ampamarinana – "the place of the hurling"). The remaining four who were nobles, including a husband and his pregnant wife, were granted the "privilege" of being burnt alive at Faravohitra, the last village at the north end of the rock on which Antananarivo is built. As a culminating horror, it was reported that the woman gave birth at the stake and the new-born infant was thrust back into the flames.

In 1852 Rainiharo died and was succeeded as commander-in-chief by his eldest son Raharo (on the birth of his son, he assumed the name of Rainivoninahitriniony, but for convenience we shall continue to refer to him as Raharo). At the same time a younger son, Rainilaiarivony, was promoted to thirteen honours at the early age of twenty-four and became the queen's private secretary. The two brothers were of the generation who had passed through the missionary schools and were more favourably disposed to European ideas and influences. Power was still shared with the queen's old lover Rainijohary who was usually described as chief minister; he became increasingly identified with the traditionalist party and supported Prince Ramboasalama, the queen's nephew (and elder brother to Prince Ramonja), as a rival to Prince Rakoto for the succession to the throne. For the time being, however, circumstances favoured the modern party.

The cessation of overseas trade had caused great hardship in Mauritius and Réunion and much dissatisfaction among the trading community in Madagascar. The absence of foreign shipping also made it difficult to send supplies to isolated Merina garrisons in places such as Fort Dauphin. The great Hova families, who had made fortunes out of various monopolies, were particularly anxious to see the ports reopened. But the queen remained adamant, advised by Raombana and Rahaniraka, who hoped that her intransigence would compel the great powers to invade and overthrow her government. Her response to a series of petitions from Mauritius and Réunion was to continue to insist on a prior payment of a "fine" of 15,000 piastres. Eventually in 1853 the merchants of Mauritius subscribed the necessary sum (to the disgust of Raombana and Rahaniraka, who regarded the implicit apology for the 1845 incident as a stain on England's honour) and the ban on trade was lifted. The money was taken to Tamatave by the veteran missionary-artisan James Cameron, who had spent the intervening years working in South Africa. Another visitor to Tamatave around this time was the Reverend William Ellis, the former foreign secretary of the LMS who had been sent out by the Society in the hope of re-establishing contact with Antananarivo. But despite the improved atmosphere both Cameron and Ellis were refused permission to visit the capital. Cameron returned to South Africa and Ellis withdrew to Mauritius and, after another unsuccessful attempt to visit Antananarivo in the following year, to England.

One of the first to take advantage of the resumption of trade was a wealthy young French trader and shipowner called Lambert. Arriving at Tamatave in 1855 he won the queen's favour by offering one of his ships to carry supplies to the starving garrison of Fort Dauphin and was granted permission to visit Antananarivo. In the capital his charm and lavish presents won him many friends and he became the confidant of Prince Rakoto. The prince asked him to take a letter to the Emperor Napoleon III, appealing for French protection and armed intervention to overthrow the queen's cruel government.[13] He also signed with Lambert a charter to establish a French company in Madagascar with a monopoly to exploit mines, forests and agriculture over a vast area. Lambert departed after only a month, leaving behind a Jesuit missionary, Père Finaz, disguised as his secretary. A second missionary, Père Webber, reached Antananarivo the following year disguised as an assistant to a surgeon brought from Mauritius to operate on a brother of Rainijohary.

In Paris, Lambert found that the moment was not propitious for his ventures. The Emperor, embroiled in the Crimean War, could not spare any troops and did not wish to annoy his British allies by unilateral action in Madagascar. Lambert was sent to London to propose a joint Anglo-French protectorate. But the British government was not then interested in acquiring any more responsibilities overseas and the foreign secretary Lord Clarendon limited himself to suggesting the formation of an Anglo-French company to take up the charter offered by Prince Rakoto. Ellis, who had meanwhile received permission to visit Antananarivo, decided to return to Madagascar to try to counter-balance the growing French, and therefore Catholic, influence. He was charged with a vague message from Lord Clarendon expressing friendship and giving assurances of non-intervention.

Ellis's visit to Antananarivo, in the late summer of 1856, was less successful than Lambert's. His modest presents and skill as a photographer were insufficient to weaken the French influence sustained by the presence of Laborde. He had a formal audience with the queen, at which the message from Lord Clarendon was received with satisfaction, but nothing of any real substance transpired. He held several long conversations with Prince Rakoto, during which be reproached the prince for plotting with the French against his mother and sowed some doubts in his mind as to the meaning and likely effect of French "protection". He was refused permission to stay longer than a month, and left having achieved little beyond some clandestine contacts with Christians to whom he distributed some bibles.

Ellis was accused by French missionary writers of betraying Prince Rakoto's plans to the queen. But there is no proof of this; and in this period one soon learns not to accept accusations by French Catholics against English Protestants, and *vice versa*, without the firmest independent corroboration. Rumours that Lambert was returning with French troops were current before Ellis's visit and continued after it. They may have helped to strengthen the position of the anti-foreign party under Rainijohary. He now acquired a special ascendancy over the queen and is regarded as largely responsible for the wave of terror which made 1857 the blackest year of the reign. The ordinary administration of the harsh laws resulted in almost daily executions and severe punishments for the most petty crimes. But robberies and petty thefts continued and in March a *kabary* was held at which people guilty of crimes were ordered to come forward and accuse themselves, in which case they would be treated leniently; whereas if they waited to be denounced they would be put to death. Nearly 1,500 accused themselves and others were denounced. Of the latter, thirteen who were accused of sorcery were plunged head-first into boiling water, fourteen others were burnt alive and sixty-five speared to death. Over two hundred who confessed to stealing poultry or sheep were reduced to slavery along with their wives and children and half their goods were confiscated. No less than 1,237 who confessed to cattle-stealing or more serious thefts were condemned to be placed in irons for life; groups of up to six were fettered together with iron collars linked by short iron bars to the collars of the fellow-prisoners and sent to unhealthy districts to die, the survivors carrying the irons of the dead until the last one expired. Hundreds fled to the forests and desert areas to escape the queen's justice and many died of starvation.

It was to this atmosphere, which recalled to the disguised Jesuits the worst days of Robespierre's reign of terror, that Lambert returned at the end of May 1857. He was accompanied on the journey to Antananarivo by Frau Ida Pfeiffer, the celebrated Austrian lady traveller now aged sixty who wrote an enthralling account of the visit, the more valuable because it lacks the distortions of the

French Catholic or English Protestant viewpoint. The visitors were received with honour by the queen and the court and warmly welcomed by Prince Rakoto. Frau Pfeiffer, like Ellis and other European visitors, was most favourably impressed by the heir to the throne:

"Prince Rakoto is a young man 27 years of age. He is short and slim in stature. His features have quite the type of the Moldavian Greeks. His black hair is curly, but not woolly; he has dark eyes, full of life and fire; a well-shaped mouth and handsome teeth. His features wear an expression of such childlike goodness, that one feels drawn towards him from the first moment of seeing him. ... The Prince is honoured and beloved alike by high and low. The son is, in fact, as kind-hearted as the mother is cruel; he is just as averse to the shedding of blood as his mother is addicted to it, and his chief efforts are directed towards mitigating the severe punishments the queen is continually inflicting, and obtaining a reversal of the sentences of death, which she is always too ready to pronounce upon her subjects."[14]

If he could not obtain a pardon, he arranged to pass along the road where the condemned were being led to their fate, and set them free. Because of her love for him the queen never commented on these actions, but tried to limit his opportunities by cutting down the interval between sentence and execution. Prince Rakoto had been driven to desperation by the latest savage persecutions. With Lambert confirming that there was no hope of French intervention, a remedy could only be found by action in Antananarivo. Frau Pfeiffer, staying at Laborde's house along with Lambert and the two disguised priests, found herself in a nightmare atmosphere of plotting and intrigue with the prince visiting his French friends secretly at night, at times disguised as a slave. On June 20 a plan for a *coup d'état* was agreed with a few trusted officials and supporters of Prince Rakoto. At two o'clock next morning the conspirators were to enter the palace, arrest Rainijohary, depose the queen (who was to retain an honoured position as queen mother) and proclaim Rakoto as king.

Raharo, the commander-in-chief, and Rainilaiarivony, his brother, who by now effectively commanded the troops, were essential to the success of the plot. They agreed to arrange that trustworthy guards would be on duty at the palace to open the gates to the conspirators. But during the day Rainilaiarivony reflected on the hazards of the plot and persuaded Raharo that the risks were too great.[15] They sent a message saying that they could not be sure of the support of all the guards in the palace and advising that the *coup* be postponed. This news threw the plotters into consternation, since the delay made it almost certain that they would be betrayed. And so it proved. Within two days one of the conspirators, fearful for his own life, revealed the plot to Rainijohary who immediately told the queen.

Because of Prince Rakoto's involvement, the plot was not publicly denounced, but eight high-ranking officers suspected of involvement were put to the *tangena* test. Fortunately for them, whoever administered the test could influence the outcome by varying the amount of poison. In this case he was no doubt bribed, as all eight were declared innocent. However, many humbler persons not involved suffered because of the plot, which Rainijohary seized on as an excuse to strike another blow at the Christians.[16] On July 3 a summons to another *kabary* aroused terror among the population of Antananarivo, with "a general howling and wailing, a rushing and running through the streets, as if the town had been attacked by a hostile army".[17] At the *kabary* the Christians were again ordered to come forward and accuse themselves, within fifteen days, or face a terrible death. As few came forward, orders were given for a most intensive search in the capital and surrounding villages. Christians were dragged out of rice-pits and other hiding-places, and sometimes the whole population of a village was arrested for helping to conceal them. Many fled in terror to the forests and desert areas. The hundreds who were arrested suffered a variety of grim fates. The *tangena* took its customary toll. About twenty suffered a novel form of execution, being stoned almost to death, before having their heads cut off. Ida Pfeiffer mentions an old woman who was denounced and dragged to the market place, where "her backbone was sawn asunder".[18] Several more were condemned to irons and sent to unhealthy spots to await a lingering death from sickness.

Meanwhile the Europeans were confined strictly to their houses while their fate was being considered in protracted discussions at the palace. The traditionalists demanded their death for conspiring against the queen, or at least their subjection to the *tangena* ordeal; while the more cautious advisers pointed out the danger of provoking France too far. According to Frau Pfeiffer it was Prince Rakoto himself who persuaded his mother against killing the Europeans. As a compromise the *tangena* was administered to five chickens representing each of the Europeans. This time Rainijohary made sure of a verdict of guilty by the death of the chickens, except for the one representing Père Webber, whom he wished to spare because of his services to his brother. The four "guilty" were sentenced to immediate banishment (Webber in fact followed them a week later).

Because of his past services Laborde was allowed twenty-four hours to gather some of his possessions together, and was conducted to the coast by the quickest route. His son Clément, being half Malagasy, was not compelled to leave, but decided to go with his father. Lambert and Ida Pfeiffer, both of them suffering from fever, had to leave at a moment's notice along with Père Finaz They were given an escort with instructions to delay them as long as possible in the unhealthiest spots in the hope that they would die. The journey to the coast, normally eight days, was prolonged to fifty-three days, during which Frau Pfeiffer never changed her clothes as the commander of the escort never allowed her any privacy. Despite fearful suffering and days of unconsciousness and delirium she survived to write her account, but her health was broken and she died a year later.

After Laborde's departure the forced labourers of Mantasoa rose up and destroyed the instruments of their oppression, machinery, workshops and factories. On his return Laborde never attempted to rebuild the complex, and all that remains today is a furnace and a huge hydraulic wheel. But although this was the end of large scale industry in Madagascar for a century, the skills taught by Laborde were used in numerous small businesses where a high standard of craftsmanship was maintained.

The last few years of Ranavalona's reign were relatively peaceful. The old queen amused herself with her favourite sport of bullfighting (i.e. fighting between bulls) and with leisurely journeyings through the countryside (an apparently harmless occupation; but in 1845 an ambitious journey with a huge entourage, which the people of the villages through which she passed were compelled to join, had caused thousands of deaths from starvation and disease). As death approached she repeatedly affirmed her wish that the crown should pass to her son Rakoto rather than her nephew Ramboasalama, whom she had originally named as her heir before the birth of Rakoto. She died on August 16, 1861 and was buried with great pomp at Ambohimanga, the most sacred of the twelve sacred villages of Imerina. On the twelve-mile (20 km) journey from the capital, the royal coffin was carried over the corpses of the queen's fighting bulls and of 25,000 other cattle slaughtered to accompany her into the next world. At her funeral several gunners were killed in blowing up two cannons, likewise destined to accompany the queen beyond the grave; and a powder magazine accidentally exploded, causing 80 deaths. A fitting conclusion to a life so stained with blood.

For Europeans and Malagasy Christians the predominant impression left of Ranavalona's reign is of bloodstained terror and re-

The queen and the martyrs

pression. Yet there were some exceptions to the general reversion to barbarism. The industry created by Laborde was more extensive than anything developed during the next hundred years, including the colonial period.[19] The value of reading and writing was acknowledged; and a written code of laws was produced for the first time during her reign. European dress and furniture at the queen's court gave a superficial impression of sophistication and at times of some splendour, as when on special occasions interminable banquets were served on fine china to the officers of the court in brilliant uniforms and their ladies in elegant dresses from Paris. During the French colonial occupation, Malagasy nationalists looked back with nostalgia to the days of the old queen who re-asserted traditional values against the seductions of European culture and successfully defied the might of Great Britain and France. But such reflections made at a safe distance in time would have been small consolation to the great numbers of the population who suffered persecution and repression under her government. Such benefits as the country derived from her fiercely independent and anti-European policies were shared among the small group of oligarchs who enjoyed her favour. For the people of Madagascar as a whole, her reign must be counted a disaster.

Chapter 13

The tragedy of the prince and the playboys

As the old queen lay dying there was a real danger of a bloody struggle for the succession between the traditionalists, led by Rainijohary and supporting the queen's nephew Prince Ramboasalama, and the modernists who favoured her son Prince Rakoto. But Rainijohary's position had declined owing to idleness and dissipation and he allowed himself to be out-manoeuvred by Raharo and Rainilaiarivony. As the end approached they placed loyal troops in key positions and strengthened the palace guard; and when the queen's death was announced they immediately proclaimed Rakoto king as Radama II. The guards clamoured for orders to kill Ramboasalama, Rainijohary and their supporters in accordance with tradition; but they were restrained by Rainilaiarivony, who favoured a policy of conciliation, and by the young king who abhorred all bloodshed. Ramboasalama was summoned to make his submission and was then allowed to retire to his country estate where he died within a year. Rainijohary was relegated to the honorific but powerless post of guardian of the old queen's tomb at Ambohimanga. Raharo was confirmed as chief minister, with Rainilaiarivony as commander-in-chief. Their family, the Andafiavaratra, thus established a firm grip on the government which they were not to relinquish for the duration of the monarchy.

The joy with which the people greeted the new reign soon proved to be justified. The new king announced that no one would be put to death during his reign and that the *tangena* ordeal was abolished. The frequency of military exercises was reduced from once a fortnight to once every two months. A limit was placed on the number of days of forced labour each citizen was required to perform, and the king set an example by paying the workers he employed on building. An amnesty was declared for all those condemned for their adherence to Christianity, followed by an amnesty for political and common law crimes. The prisoners who

The tragedy of the prince and the playboys

had survived the harsh regime of fetters returned enfeebled and emaciated to their homes along with Christians and others who had fled to Mauritius or remote parts of Madagascar.

The amnesty was extended to captives from the Sakalava and other coastal peoples brought to the capital after military expeditions. They included three Sakalava chiefs who had been captured many years before by Radama I and who were now sent home with rich presents. More important, they were allowed to take with them, for burial in family tombs, the bones of other chiefs who had been executed or had died in captivity. This gesture, together with a declaration that war would no longer be waged against the coastal peoples, made a most favourable impression. A Sakalava chief reciprocated by returning Merina captives taken in border raids, and many tribal leaders came to Antananarivo to express their allegiance to King Radama II. A new era of internal peace seemed to have dawned.

For Europeans too the new régime appeared to usher in a golden age. The ports were opened up to European traders and the 10 per cent duty on imports and exports was abolished. The king wrote to the governors of Mauritius and Réunion to inform them of his accession, his desire for good relations and the establishment of complete freedom of trade. The governor of Mauritius responded immediately by sending a mission under Colonel Middleton to congratulate the king, an action which was well received and contrasted with the failure of the governor of Réunion to respond pending instructions from Paris. The French government subsequently, however, sent an official mission under Baron Brossard de Corbigny who arrived in Antananarivo in February 1862 bearing the good wishes of the French Emperor.

One of Radama's first acts had been to proclaim freedom of religion and to invite missionaries of all persuasions to come and teach in Madagascar. First on the scene on a brief visit from Mauritius to encourage the Malagasy Christians was the Reverend John Le Brun, whose father, still active in Mauritius, had first come out as an LMS missionary nearly fifty years earlier. Next was the Jesuit Père Webber who arrived in Antananarivo in September 1861, followed a few weeks later by Père Jouen, accompanied by Laborde and Lambert. They were greeted with joy by Radama, who created Lambert Duke of Imerina and, despite some opposition from his ministers, confirmed the Charter which he had promised Lambert in 1855. Back in London the LMS, recalling the young king's close friendship with the Frenchmen, urged the foreign secretary to do his utmost to prevent the establishment of a French protectorate in the island. They were somewhat reassured when Mr Ellis received a letter signed "your friend Radama" promising protection for Protestant missionaries; and it was decided that Mr Ellis should proceed at once to Madagascar.

Ellis, now in his late sixties, arrived in Mauritius at the end of 1861, and, as the season was unfavourable for travelling in Madagascar, stayed there for several months. His first concern was to put in train his imaginative idea of building memorial churches on the sites where Malagasy martyrs had died for their faith, using funds to be collected by the missionary organisations in Britain. He wrote to Radama II asking that the sites should be reserved for this purpose, to which the king readily agreed. Ellis was also encouraged to receive from Antananarivo a 300-page English-Malagasy vocabulary compiled by three Malagasy officers who had been taught English by Rahaniraka; and he was glad to send it to London to be printed. The wet season having ended, Ellis landed at Tamatave in May 1862. He was concerned and depressed to witness two unsought results of the lifting of all restrictions on trade. Huge quantities of alcohol were being imported and drunkenness was rife, with one hut in four in Tamatave serving as a rum shop; and the greater number of foreign seamen in the port had brought the inevitable increase in "licentiousness". But to balance this, he was delighted to see substantial numbers of Christians, both in Tamatave and on the way to the capital, availing themselves of the new freedom to worship.

Ellis's reception in Antananarivo left nothing to be desired. He was greeted on his arrival by Rahaniraka who had been appointed Foreign Minister. On the next day he had an audience with King Radama II and Queen Rabodo. He conveyed to them messages of goodwill from Queen Victoria, Earl Russell and the governor of Mauritius and announced that the LMS were sending six missionaries, including a doctor and a printer with printing machinery. On his first Sunday Ellis, although suffering from fever, was taken in a litter to attend a service at one of the three buildings allocated by the king to the Christians as temporary chapels. His genuine emotion at seeing the chapel packed to overflowing shines through his stately Victorian prose: "When I looked round on the large assembly as they stood up and poured forth their loud and joyous hymn of praise, and recalled the time when we could only meet, a few together, under the darkness of the night, and even then with closed doors and persons to watch the gates, and could only sing in an undertone or sort of whisper; when I further contrasted the air of joyous freedom and conscious security beaming almost in every countenance, with the sorrow occasioned by some mournful loss, or the trembling anxiety and keenly sensitive apprehension of those who were themselves at that former time proscribed, and had their lives given them for a prey, I was filled with wonder and delight; and was not surprised that in the letters I had received from some of them, when describing their present state they had said, 'We are like them that dream.' "[1]

Ellis's arrival ushered in a period of intense Anglo-French rivalry, manifested partly in political matters but more strongly in religion. In French writings of the period Ellis is again cast as the villain of the piece – a secret agent of the British government, whose success in spreading the Protestant religion and furthering the British cause was attributed to large-scale bribery. It was suggested that some of the money subscribed for the building of the memorial churches was used for bribery and that in addition Ellis had available a secret government fund of £50,000.[2] The idea that the British government would allocate such a large sum (equivalent to several million pounds today) for secret purposes in a remote country in which they had never shown much interest and that they would entrust this fund to a missionary, is too absurd to bear scrutiny. Ellis had from the outset made it clear that he was not in any way an agent of the government and that his sole purpose was to promote Christianity. He was, as we shall see, on bad terms with the British Consul, Thomas Pakenham, who arrived in Antananarivo shortly after Ellis. But in promoting his version of Christianity Ellis felt it his duty to oppose the rival Roman Catholic version as expounded by the French Jesuits. In so doing he felt obliged to do what he could to frustrate French policies in other fields. And in some matters at least, as when he advised against the granting of huge commercial concessions to Lambert and of excessive privileges to French citizens, he was certainly acting in the best interests of Radama and of Madagascar.

The Jesuit accusations against Ellis were designed partly to explain why Protestant places of worship were filled to overflowing while the Catholics had great difficulty in attracting pupils and congregations. But the explanation lies elsewhere. Ellis and the other British missionaries were reaping the fruits of the labours of Jones, Griffiths and their colleagues thirty years earlier. The persecution, as so often happened, had strengthened the Christian movement. Moreover the blood of Malagasy martyrs had consecrated the new religion, converting it from a foreign import into something which belonged to the Malagasy. It was entirely natural, when Christian practices were again permitted, that the Malagasy should favour the Protestant version with which they were already familiar and for which so many of their friends and relatives had given their lives. This is sufficient to explain the Catholics' lack of success in the plateau region prior to the French annexation; but they were also severely handicapped by the local hostility aroused by the French government's aggressive policy towards Madagascar.

At first the Jesuits had great hopes from Radama II's apparent pro-French feelings expressed in his close relations with Laborde and Lambert. But the young king and, at this stage, his chief ministers were favourably disposed to both the French and the British,[3] regarding both as sources of civilisation and aid. The king frequently received the Jesuit priests, to whom he sometimes spoke unflatteringly about Ellis. But he asked Ellis to spend some time with him nearly every day reading the Bible in order to improve his English; and also invited him to hold a religious service every Sunday in his palace attended by high officials and the king himself

Radama never actually became a Christian, despite strenuous efforts by the Jesuits and Ellis to convert him to their way of thinking. In pursuit of this aim Ellis even became friendly with Radama's favourite concubine, Mary Rasoamieja, an intelligent woman who was sympathetic to Christianity and appears to have become a Christian in February 1863.[4] Ellis had frequent talks with her, went to dinner at her house with Radama and held services there. This association was somewhat surprising for a Victorian nonconformist minister for whom sexual licence was the greatest sin. But his purpose was to exploit Mary's influence for good over the king and also to make her a better Christian; he succeeded in persuading her that being a Christian was incompatible with sleeping with another woman's husband, a success which was not calculated to endear him to the king. At the same time Ellis's relationship with Mary was inevitably resented by Queen Rabodo and was probably the reason why she withdrew her adopted son from the teaching of Ellis and entrusted him to the Jesuits. It was also strongly criticised by the British Consul, Thomas Pakenham, as "not moral, and calculated to outrage the feelings and to give the natives an unfavourable impression of the English generally"[5] Conflict between Ellis and Pakenham was perhaps inevitable. As official representative of his country Pakenham was understandably jealous of Ellis's ready access to and great influence with the king and his ministers (Lyall had a similar problem with Jones and Griffiths in 1828). And his resentment was probably increased by lack of self-confidence: he had been lucky to get the job having previously been a very humble official in the Mauritian government, and his letter of appointment from London had crossed a letter from the governor describing him as quite unsuitable for the post. Whatever the reason, he soon allied himself with Laborde, who had been appointed French consul, in criticising Ellis's interference in political affairs. And in presenting his credentials to the king he spoke in French with Laborde interpreting, when it would have been more natural for him to speak in English, which Radama understood better than French,[6] with Ellis acting as interpreter.

These petty squabbles were soon overshadowed by more important events which took place amid the preparations for the coronation. A special British mission had arrived, led by General Johnstone, commander-in-chief of the troops in Mauritius, and including the Bishop of Mauritius, a leading trader called Caldwell, and a young ADC Lieutenant S Pasfield Oliver who was later to become an authority on Madagascar. It was preceded by a French embassy, led by Captain Dupré, who was empowered to conclude a treaty with the Malagasy government. The vast concessions of the Lambert Charter opened up great opportunities for the French, and a *Compagnie de Madagascar* had been founded to exploit them. A treaty was necessary to regulate the status of French citizens operating in Madagascar. The document which was signed on September 12, 1862, despite strong opposition from the chief ministers supported by Ellis, granted French citizens wide privileges including the right to trade without restriction and to own property (contrary to a fundamental Malagasy law against the alienation of any of the land of Madagascar). One gain for the Malagasy was French recognition for Radama as king of Madagascar, and the treaty made no mention of "the rights of France".[7] The Malagasy ministers also succeeded in delaying the application of the treaty by making it subject to ratification in a year's time. The English trader Caldwell had meanwhile obtained a concession similar to Lambert's, though on a smaller scale; and a treaty with Britain, giving British subjects the same rights as those accorded to the French, was signed towards the end of the year.

Radama's coronation took place on September 23 before a vast crowd on the plain of Mahamasina at the foot of the "place of the hurling". Ellis took photographs of the scene and later of the king in his coronation dress which was a British field-marshal's uniform, one of the presents brought by the English mission (the queen wore a splendid Paris creation, one of the gifts of the emperor). The coronation procession gave Ellis a rare opportunity to see the assembled *sampy* or idols which exercised such a strong sway over the traditionalist Malagasy:

"These idols, or objects of worship, thirteen in number, were carried on tall slender rods or poles, from eight to ten feet high. There was not much in any of them to inspire respect, much less veneration or worship. Dirty pieces of silver chain, silver balls varying in size from a pistol bullet to a hen's egg, pieces of coral, and what seemed like bone and silver ornaments intended to represent crocodiles' teeth, and with these narrow strips of scarlet cloth, from a foot to a yard or more in length, some of them underneath what looked like a red woollen cap, resembling a cap of liberty; others invisible, consisting of something tied up in a small bag of native cloth or rush basket; such were the objects of worship, or the representatives of such, on which the safety and welfare of the nation were supposed to depend, and for refusing to worship which, many of the most intelligent and worthy among the people had been subjected to banishment, slavery, torture and death."[8]

The splendour of Radama's coronation, in the presence of high-ranking foreign missions and representatives of most of the peoples of the island, marked the high spot of his brief reign. The people rejoiced in their freedom from the oppressive laws of the previous reign, and many of them flocked to the temporary chapels opened for Christian worship. The first reinforcements for Ellis sent out by the LMS arrived shortly before the coronation. They included Dr Andrew Davidson, who was to lay the foundation of all medical work on the plateau; Mr Parrett, a printer who set up a new press to print not only religious publications but, in the early days, government documents; and Rev W E Cousins, who was to stay for forty years in Madagascar and to preside over a monumental revision of the Malagasy Bible. The new arrivals were astonished to see how Christianity had spread under the persecution. The strength of the indigenous roots put down by the foreign religion is shown by the way in which, even before Ellis's arrival, local Christian leaders had set up churches and organised well-attended services. Although the more perceptive missionaries realised that as yet Christianity had only scratched the surface of the Malagasy way of life, the prospects for evangelisation were clearly excellent.

The king continued to give general encouragement to Christianity while maintaining his impartiality by attending both Catholic and Protestant services. But he showed no signs of giving up what Ellis described as his "sinful habits" – drunkenness and debauchery with the companions of his youth, the *menamaso* (literally "red eyes"). When Radama was heir to the throne, these young men had acted as his aides in attempting to protect the Christians from persecution and in other good works, including even the building of bridges around the capital. But after his accession they abused their position as the king's intimates to acquire prerogatives and wealth and to engage in frequent debauches in which they involved the weak young king.

Weakness of character was the main cause of Radama's downfall. His natural goodness, undoubted intelligence and excellent intentions were not matched by self-discipline, powers of application or good judgement; and he proved unable to cope with the opposition aroused in various quarters by his sharp reversal of nearly all his mother's policies. It was to be expected that the traditionalists would resent the influx of Christian missionaries and other Europeans; this group was particularly outraged when Ellis, albeit with Radama's permission, tactlessly preached in the sacred village of Ambohimanga. But even the "modernist" group of senior ministers who were responsible for ensuring Radama's accession were gradually alienated by his trade and foreign policies and the favours granted to foreigners and the *menamaso*. Complete freedom of trade was splendid in principle. But the abolition of customs duties deprived the government of the principal source of its pitiably small revenue and senior officers of their only income; whilst the lifting of all restrictions meant the disappearance of lucrative monopolies enjoyed by the leading families. The ruling classes were also unhappy about the reduction of the forced labour which gave them a free source of manpower. The older ministers resented the increasing influence of the *menamaso*: the appointment of one of them, Rainiketaka (in fact a capable man and a leading Christian), as Minister of Justice early in 1863 hardened the opposition to the king. Ministers were also worried about the extent to which Radama relied on foreign advisers (Laborde, Ellis and the Jesuits) and his appointment of non-Malagasy to official positions. The latter included the appointment as joint Ministers for Foreign Affairs, after the death of Rahaniraka, of Laborde's son Clément (to the embarrassment of the Quai d'Orsay) and the American trader William Marks, described by Ellis as "an ignorant, profligate, drunken American".[9] And all classes and parties were shocked by the vast concessions of the Lambert Charter and the privileges granted to foreigners in the treaties, especially the right to own property.

Early in 1863, traditionalist opposition to the king's policies manifested itself in an extraordinary outbreak of *imanenjana* or dancing mania, a kind of collective St Vitus's dance which affected considerable numbers at first in country villages and later in the capital. The victims danced and leapt about in a stiff jerky manner until they fell exhausted, and often acted as if they were carrying an invisible heavy load. They were said to be possessed by the spirits of ancestors and some claimed that the spirit of the old queen had commanded them to protest against the abandoning of the old customs. A medical explanation is possible[10] but more probably it was a case of mass hysteria or suggestibility inspired by the idol-keepers. Pakenham reported to the Foreign Office his view that the whole epidemic was simulated as part of a campaign against the Christians, provoked by Ellis's indiscreet behaviour.[11] Whatever the cause, the dancing mania made a deep impression on the people of the capital and helped to weaken the young king's position. Ellis recorded a dramatic scene at the palace when a group of the crazed dancers burst in and he and the king with the king's concubine Mary had to take refuge in a totally dark room and wait in fear of their lives until the intruders were persuaded to disperse.[12]

The immediate cause of the final breach appears to have been a row at the palace at which the choleric chief minister Raharo and one of the *menamaso* came to blows. Radama, who had heard that duelling was fashionable in some European countries, suggested that the quarrel should be resolved by a duel. He went on to announce his intention of issuing a decree ordering that disputes between individuals, families and even villages should be settled by combat. This extraordinary proposal united all members of the government in opposition. Early on the cold, grey, misty morning of May 8, 1863 Ellis saw a long procession of them, led by Raharo and his brother, on their way to ask the king to withdraw the proposal. "All wore native broad-brimmed straw hats, and large thick plain white lambas, reaching to their ankles, and drawn up over their mouths to protect them from the cold foggy morning. Two or three abreast they walked slowly and silently along."[13] But their mission was unsuccessful. Radama, with an extraordinary stubbornness which suggested to some that he had taken leave of his senses, refused to budge and so the die was cast.

Next day the capital was filled with troops and the *menamaso* were hunted down and slaughtered on the spot. Some managed to take refuge with the king who bravely protected them for two days while he tried to bargain with Raharo for their lives. He eventually yielded them up on a promise that they would be exiled in chains instead of being killed; but they were speared to death the same evening. It is not known at what stage it was decided to kill Radama as well; but presumably Raharo realised that he could not expect to remain as chief minister to a king whose friends and intimates he had massacred. So on May 12 a band of assassins was sent to the palace. In the presence of his terrified queen, Radama was thrown to the ground, brutally kicked and trampled on; according to tradition he was finally despatched by strangling with a silken sash so as to avoid the shedding of royal blood. The same night he was hastily buried without ceremony in the village of Ilafy, a few miles to the northeast. A tragic end for a prince of such good intentions, who (until his final aberration over duelling) had always been opposed to violence and bloodshed. Ellis, summing up Radama's virtues and weaknesses, concluded: "I have never said that Radama was an able ruler, or a man of large views, for these he was not; but a more humane ruler never wore a crown."[14]

The reader will not now be surprised to learn that Ellis was accused by French writers of the time of responsibility for the overthrow and death of Radama. This has been disproved by a modern Jesuit author[15] who suggests plausibly that the accusation originated with the jealous Pakenham! There can be no doubt that the *coup* was inspired by internal reasons. While the immediate cause was Radama's duelling proposal the main motive of the ministers was probably fear of losing their power to the younger *menamaso*.

Following the precedent set on the death of Radama I, Raharo decided to put the king's widow Rabodo on the throne and marry her himself. The choice of Rabodo was justified by an alleged but implausible edict of Andrianampoinimerina that after Radama I the succession should pass through the female line. Rabodo was Radama II's first cousin, being the daughter of the elder of Ranavalona I's two sisters. Radama II had in fact earlier married another first cousin, Ramoma, daughter of Ranavalona's younger sister, but she had been relegated to the status of second wife after his marriage to Rabodo.

On the day after Radama's death, which was announced as a suicide, Rabodo was proclaimed queen with the new name of Rasoherina, meaning "chrysalis". At the same time it was announced that freedom of religion would continue and that the *tangena* ordeal would remain abolished; but that the death penalty would be reintroduced for wilful murder and various forms of treason against the Crown. However, for the first time limitations were placed on the hitherto absolute power of the monarch. The death penalty could not be imposed on the word of the sovereign alone but required the consent of her council of ministers and the chiefs of the people. Similarly, the queen could alter laws only with the agreement of her ministers and chiefs. The queen also had to agree not to drink alcohol and not to disband the army. Thus most of the worthwhile reforms of Radama's reign were preserved in the framework of a major new innovation – a constitutional monarchy accountable to the leaders of the people (although in practice it turned out to be a cover for a dictatorship by the prime minister).

In the external field, satisfactory assurances were given regarding continued freedom to trade, subject to the reimposition of a tax of 10 per cent on imports and exports. But the government indicated that the treaties with France and Britain, which were not yet ratified, would have to be modified, and that the concessions granted by Radama II to Lambert and Caldwell were no longer valid. The British government accepted the situation and the foreign secretary Lord John Russell gave no support to Caldwell. But the French, whose prestige was much more deeply involved (the Emperor had ratified the treaty and was patron of the new *Compagnie de Madagascar*) were most reluctant to acquiesce. Captain Dupré, who had returned to Madagascar to watch over the application of the treaty, refused even to discuss any modifications and broke off official relations. The Malagasy government sent ambassadors to Europe to try to win British support and to negotiate an acceptable settlement with France. Their reception in London was sympathetic (they were received by Queen Victoria and Lord Palmerston, now prime minister, as well as Lord John Russell) and good progress was made in drafting an acceptable revised treaty; but there was no question of any positive support against the French. In Paris the French government was under pressure from the interested parties to insist on the application of the treaty and of the Lambert Charter. However Napoleon III was not prepared to impose the French view by means of a military expedition. He proposed as a compromise that the Malagasy should pay an indemnity of 1,200,000 francs to compensate Lambert and the *Compagnie de Madagascar* for the expenses they had undertaken. The ambassadors had no authority to agree to such a payment – a huge sum for Madagascar – and they returned with the matter unresolved.

Meanwhile Raharo was experiencing difficulties at home. Radama had been a popular ruler and news of his murder caused great discontent both in Imerina and among the coastal peoples who had welcomed Radama's peaceful policies. Opposition to the new regime was stimulated by rumours that Radama had not been killed. It was said that the strangling had not been fully effective, that he had recovered consciousness on the road to Ilafy, his escort had released him and he was now at large to the west of the capital.[16] Several uprisings in this area, supposedly organised by Radama, were put down by military expeditions, but the rumours persisted despite the threat of severe punishment to those spreading them. Both Ellis and Laborde became convinced that the king was alive, and made several unsuccessful attempts to arrange a meeting with him. They reported a series of plots by Radama's supporters to seize Antananarivo while the court was away, but these all failed in the face of Raharo's energetic counter-measures. After a particularly serious plot in May 1864 had been foiled at the last minute, seventy-nine people were arrested for spreading rumours of the king's survival. Disagreement about their fate brought to a head growing opposition to Raharo within the government itself.

The acquisition of supreme power had gone to Raharo's head

and he alienated even his own family by his arrogance, violence and drunkenness. On one occasion, reported by Laborde, he forced the queen to drink alcohol (contrary to the new constitution) and menaced his brother and others with his spear. He felt himself particularly threatened by the rumours about Radama and at a meeting at Ambohimanga he demanded that the seventy-nine rumour-mongers be put to death without delay. When the queen, his brother Rainilaiarivony and most of the other ministers opposed him he became violent, struck old Rainijohary and threatened the others with his sword. Some sort of peace was patched up and the seventy-nine accused were referred to an assembly of chiefs who recommended the death penalty for sixteen who continued to maintain that they had seen Radama (perhaps the most impressive evidence that Radama may indeed have survived), exile in chains for ten and release for the remainder.

But Raharo's intemperate behaviour continued to cause alarm and eventually the other members of the Andafiavaratra family combined against him. They had little difficulty in persuading the queen and other officials that he should be deposed and replaced by Rainilaiarivony, and this was decided at a meeting at the queen's palace in July 1864. The queen sent a message to Raharo to the effect that in accordance with his wishes and because of his poor health she was retiring him. Raharo accepted his dismissal with dignity, made his submission to the queen, and withdrew to his country estate.

As for Radama, some unrest to the south a few months later and another plot against the new régime in February 1865 were attributed to him or to his supporters; but after September 1864 there were no further reports of his having been seen. According to his biographer Delval, he must now have despaired of recovering his throne and retreated to the inaccessible and barren country some 200 miles (320 km) to the west of the capital where eighty years later Delval found his alleged tomb and traces of his descendants. Whether or not he survived his assassination (and *pace* Delval a strong element of doubt must remain) he disappears from the pages of history leaving an intriguing enigma to add to the fascination of his flawed personality and the drama of his short, tragic reign.

PART 4   THE KINGDOM IN DANGER

Chapter 14

The prime minister and the Christian monarchy

Rainilaiarivony, who now took the centre of the stage, ranks with Andrianampoinimerina and Radama I as one of the three major figures in the history of Imerina. Though lacking the heroic attributes of the two great Merina kings, he was in some respects the most remarkable of the three. Whereas they were born to the purple he was very largely self-made. It is true that his father Rainiharo was the powerful chief minister of Queen Ranavalona I. But he had been born on a day (January 30, 1828) which the *mpisikidy* deemed unlucky, and but for the reform instigated a few years earlier by Hastie he would have been left in a cattle pen to be trampled to death. As it was his parents rejected him, having cut off the top joint of the first two fingers of his left hand, and named him Tsimanosika, meaning "the degraded one." He was brought up by sympathetic relatives who in 1834 sent him to Griffiths's school. He showed great promise and after the missionaries left he continued lessons with Raombona and Rahaniraka. At the age of ten he was given a small sum of money to start him off earning his own living by trade, which he did very successfully. An admiring English trader called him "he who deals fair"; he accordingly became known as Radilifera, a name which he retained until on the birth of his first son he changed it to Rainilaiarivony ("father of Ralaiarivony"). His success and intelligence became known and Queen Ranavalona I appointed him an officer of the palace when he was only fourteen. His father now had to recognise him and receive him back in the family. In the palace his quick intelligence and capacity for work soon made him indispensable and his youthful charm won the favour of the queen. His rise was rapid and unprecedented – seven honours at the age of sixteen, nine honours at twenty; then after the death of his father rapid promotion to 12 honours and to the then highest rank of 13 honours by the age of twenty-four. As commander of the army he supported his brother Raharo during the difficult last years of Ranavalona I and the short, troubled reign of Radama II. His caution and shrewdness acted as a valuable counter-weight to Raharo's forceful but at times rash leadership. He remained largely in the background but was probably responsible for most of the more sensible government measures, including the major innovation of the constitutional monarchy. When Raharo's conduct became unbearable, he was the obvious choice for the highest position.

His portrait shows a small, neat, dapper man, good-looking with a fine head of hair and a moustache which grew longer with the years, reaching Clemenceau-like proportions in his old age. He was something of a dandy, accumulating a vast wardrobe of military uniforms and court dress with knee-breeches and embroidered waistcoats. His long subsequent years of power fed his vanity – he was sometimes referred to in speeches and documents as "Rainilaiarivony, prime minister and commander-in-chief, supreme director of all officials, grand master of the army and president of the council". The undoubted decline of his latter years and the final collapse of his régime when the French invaded have led some writers to underestimate him and even to dismiss him as a vain popinjay. But for a quarter of a century he governed the country with energy, intelligence and immense hard work. By skilful diplomacy he kept the French at bay for a number of years; and if in the end he must be held partly responsible for the failure to preserve his country's independence it is not easy to see how anyone else could have succeeded in the face of the French determination to take over the island.

A few months after Raharo's downfall Rainilaiarivony followed the now established tradition by becoming the queen's lover or husband, although she was his elder by some fifteen years and already past fifty. He was the first to combine the posts of prime minister and commander-in-chief (the English titles were used in his official seal), but in the early years his situation was far from secure. His rapid rise had aroused jealousy which was strengthened by the grandiose palace which he constructed for himself near to the queen's palace; and as he had preferred to work in the background, in the shadow of Raharo, his abilities were little known outside a small circle. For some time there were rumours of plots to restore Raharo, until in February 1865 Raharo was exiled to a small estate near Antsirabe, 80 miles (130 km) to the south.

With Raharo out of the way, the new prime minister could

breathe more easily. But the problem of the foreign treaties and the Lambert Charter remained unresolved. Progress was possible on the British treaty on the basis of the draft brought back by the ambassadors, and a new treaty was signed on June 27, 1865. The text enshrined some of the features of the new Malagasy constitution, including the abolition of the *tangena* and freedom of religion, except in Ambohimanga and two other sacred villages which remained forbidden to Europeans. The prohibition of the slave trade was renewed and strengthened, with British ships empowered to seize slave-trading ships around Madagascar. British subjects were authorised to trade freely in areas where Merina officials operated. The missionaries were allowed to build churches but these were to remain the property of the queen. The general right to own property was granted on a most-favoured nation basis and in accordance with the law of the land; but since no other nation had the right, and it was a fundamental Malagasy law that all land belonged to the queen, nothing was in fact conceded by this article.

Rainilaiarivony (for convenience we shall henceforth refer to him as the prime minister) was content with this treaty and hoped for a similar agreement with the French. But the French insisted on prior payment of the indemnity in respect of the Lambert Charter. A personal appeal from the queen to the emperor was discourteously left unanswered, except by instructions to Laborde to press for payment. In the absence of any support from the British the prime minister decided that the 1,200,000 francs would have to be paid. The queen declared that the people should not suffer and offered to pay the whole indemnity from her own treasure; but when this was announced at a *kabary* the leaders of the people insisted on paying a share. The huge sum was collected in silver dollars (it was necessary to retrieve some from the royal tombs to make up the amount), packed in five hundred cases and conveyed by two thousand porters and guards to Tamatave. Here there was a moment of comedy when the Malagasy governor insisted on being given the Charter before handing over the money and the French representative had to admit that he did not have the document. There was a delay of several months while it was fetched from Paris to be publicly burned on the beach.

The payment of the indemnity naturally aroused hostility against the French, which was extended for a time to Europeans in general and to the Christian religion. Resentment against the French was further increased by the behaviour of Count de Louvières who was sent out in 1866 to renegotiate the treaty with France, with instructions to insist on the retention of the right of

Frenchmen to own property. His arrogance and insolence caused great offence (about this time Queen Rasoherina, who had been well-disposed to the French, removed her adopted children from the Catholic school); and when he died suddenly of dysentery at the beginning of 1867 there was a rumour that he had been poisoned. By the time his successor, Garnier, had arrived the position of the Malagasy government had been strengthened by the arrival of a United States commercial agent, Major John P Finkelmeier, who negotiated a treaty of commerce and friendship. They therefore showed no disposition to hasten the conclusion of the French treaty. Laborde, who throughout seems to have played a conciliatory role, advised that it was unrealistic to expect greater concessions than those agreed with the British, and Garnier finally had to accept this. After further delays, caused partly by the illness and death of Queen Rasoherina, a treaty was signed in August 1868 on substantially the same lines as the British treaty, with a similar ambiguous clause on the right of property which was to cause trouble later.

The other main feature of the prime minister's early years of power was the rapid growth of activity by missionaries from various sources. The LMS exploited their advantage on the plateau by sending out more missionaries for teaching and evangelising work in and around the capital. At the same time they pressed on with the project of building stone churches to commemorate the martyrs. The estimated cost of four churches – £10,000 – was quickly subscribed by congregations in Great Britain. Versatile old James Cameron was sent from South Africa in 1863 to act as superintendent of the building operations. A young architect called James Sibree was appointed in the same year on a three-year contract to design the churches; and in 1865 William Pool was sent out as builder to work in cooperation with Sibree. All three were destined to leave their mark with buildings which still dominate Antananarivo. Apart from the various churches which they constructed jointly or separately, Cameron was responsible for the imposing stone exterior of the wooden Queen's Palace (Manjakamiadana) built by Laborde and for the charming small wooden palace (Manampisoa) built within the royal *rova* for Queen Rasoherina in 1866. Pool's main monument is the curious pink and white wedding-cake structure of the prime minister's palace with its four mushroom-capped corner towers and a large central room surmounted by a glass dome; he also built the fine palace church within the *rova* in the classical style of Wren. Sibree, who devoted the rest of his long life to Madagascar, was to construct altogether more than a hundred buildings, including some fifty churches; but he is perhaps better known as one of the best and certainly the most prolific of writers in English on Madagascar, and an authority on its history, geography, ethnography and natural history.

At the outset there were considerable difficulties to be overcome. Cameron, who was under the impression that he was to design as well as build the churches, was offended by the appointment of Sibree and at first refused to cooperate with him. No stone buildings of the size proposed (each church was to hold at least a thousand worshippers) had ever been built in Madagascar and Sibree had to train and supervise the workmen in the precise skills required. The workmen were not used to the discipline of regular working hours and tended to disappear when they had earned enough money for their immediate needs; and at other times they were requisitioned by the government for public works or for building private houses for the great chiefs. The first church was built at Ambatonakanga, the site of the early chapel and the place where many martyrs had been imprisoned prior to execution; but its situation on the side of the hill meant that an immense effort was necessary to level and clear the site. The foundation stone was laid in January 1864 by Raharo a few weeks before his downfall. The building, a plain adaptation of the Norman style with a corner belfry-tower surmounted by a small broach spire, rose slowly to the wonder of the crowds in the nearby market-place and the alarm of the workers' wives fearful for their husbands' safety. It was completed after three years and opened for worship in January 1867.

Meanwhile work had begun on the second church at Ambohipotsy, where the first martyr Rasalama and many others had been speared to death. The magnificent site justified a more impressive building and Sibree designed a fine Early English church with a tall, elegant spire. Built under the direction of Pool, it was opened for worship in November 1868. Sibree had left the previous year on the expiry of his contract. The LMS, alarmed at the way the money was running out, did not renew his contract. They set aside his plans for the remaining churches and employed Cameron to construct them with plans prepared by London architects. The church at Faravohitra, the site of the burning of the noble martyrs in 1849, was completed in 1870; it was financed by contributions from children in Sunday schools throughout Britain, in special memory of the child born in the flames, and was sometimes known as the children's memorial church. The fourth church on the edge of the cliff at Ampamarinana ("the place of the hurling") was opened in 1874. Later a smaller memorial church was built at Fiadanana, where martyrs had been stoned to death in 1857. William Ellis, who had conceived the plan for the memorial churches, had left Madagascar in 1865. The churches, which are still important landmarks in

Antananarivo and active centres of worship, remain as a tribute to his vision as well as to the steadfastness of the Malagasy Christians under persecution. But they were only the most spectacular of the many churches and chapels being built in this period, most of them of local sun-dried brick, the remainder of mud. By 1870 the LMS had under its direction no less than 261 country churches, with a total of over 20,000 "members", i.e. communicants and over 130,000 "adherents" or regular churchgoers. For reasons we have discussed the progress of the Jesuits was much slower: by 1870 they had only 38 churches outside Antananarivo. But they were laying the foundations for a steady expansion in the future and as always their missionaries included a number of dedicated and able men, notably Callet, who collected the *Tantaran' ny Andriana*, and Malzac, author of the standard French-Malagasy dictionary and of a substantial historical work, his *Histoire du Royaume Hova*.

Rivalry between the LMS and the Jesuits was unavoidable. But the LMS had hoped to avoid competition from other Protestant missionary organisations, which they feared would confuse the Malagasy Christians who already found the differences between Protestant and Catholic difficult to comprehend. In 1862 Ellis had made an oral agreement with the Bishop of Mauritius that the LMS should continue to concentrate on the plateau; while Church of England missions should confine themselves to the north and east coasts under the direction of the Bishop of Mauritius. In the event the Church Missionary Society (CMS) honoured this agreement but the other Anglican group, the Society for the Propagation of the Gospel (SPG), accepted it only under protest and began to agitate for the appointment of a Bishop of Madagascar resident in Antananarivo. This led to a major row in England, with the traditional hostility between Nonconformity and the Established Church complicated by the inter-Anglican disagreement between the SPG and the CMS. The Archbishop of Canterbury eventually advised as a compromise the appointment of a bishop, not from the Anglican Church but from the Episcopal Church of Scotland. The CMS in protest withdrew from Madagascar. But in practice relations between the new bishop and the LMS missionaries in Antananarivo were harmonious, and the SPG never competed on any serious scale with the LMS.

Norwegian Lutherans sent their first missionaries in 1866, and at first there was some conflict with the LMS. The latter had hoped that the Lutherans would confine themselves to Betsileo and the south, but the Lutherans insisted on establishing a mission in Antananarivo and themselves complained about LMS activity in

Betsileo. The differences were amicably resolved with a region of Betsileo being reserved for Lutheran activity, and thereafter cooperation was good. The first American Lutheran missionaries (in fact from the Norwegian-American community of Minnesota) arrived in 1888 to work in the far south, starting with a small mission in Fort Dauphin, where they had no competition from other Protestant missions.

There was never any difficulty with the Society of Friends who entered the field in 1867. There were no important doctrinal differences between the Quakers and the Congregationalists of the LMS, and Ellis had in fact invited the Friends to send out missionaries. There were also family connections: the first Quaker missionary, Joseph Sewell, was a nephew of Ellis's second wife. From the beginning the Quakers and LMS worked side by side in teaching and medical work in Antananarivo, and later the Quakers were allocated an area to the west and southwest of the capital.

During the reign of Queen Rasoherina, Christianity was tolerated rather than actively encouraged by the government. The queen, who had been the favourite niece of Ranavalona I, remained attached to the old customs; and the cautious prime minister, while welcoming the teaching work of the missionaries, had never shown much inclination to adopt their religion. When, therefore, early in 1868 the queen became very ill, the missionaries were hopeful that she would be succeeded by a Christian cousin, Prince Rasata. This hope was shared by the Malagasy Christians, led by two cousins of the prime minister, Rainimaharavo (the foreign secretary who was married to a sister of the prime minister) and his brother Rainandriantsilavo. They saw the impending change of monarch as an opportunity to supplant their cousin and plotted a palace revolution which would put Rasata on the throne with either Raharo or Rainimaharavo as head of the government. But a false report of the queen's death led them to reveal their plans too soon and the prime minister nipped the plot in the bud by showing the queen to the people. When the queen died a few days later he was able to proclaim the succession of her cousin Princess Ramoma (Radama II's first wife) with the title of Queen Ranavalona II. Once again Andrianampoinimerina's alleged preference for the female line was invoked, but there can be little doubt that the main reason for choosing a queen rather than a king was to preserve the power of the prime minister, which was consolidated when in due course he married her.

The prime minister's cousins were allowed to make their peace by swearing loyalty to him. A few plotters were executed, others including Prince Rasata were exiled. Raharo, whose degree of involvement in the plot is uncertain, was sent into more distant exile in Betsileo; and the opportunity was also taken to exile old Rainijohary, who as leader of the traditionalists still had important influence and potential as a trouble-maker. Both the former chief ministers died in exile shortly afterwards.

Despite its failure, the "Christian" plot indirectly achieved its purpose of putting a Christian monarch on the throne. It opened the prime minister's eyes to the growing strength of the Christian movement to which most of the able and educated younger people now belonged (Rainimaharavo himself was generally regarded as the most able member of the government). Short of an unthinkable reversal of policy, involving expulsion of the missionaries and suppression and persecution of the converts, Christianity was likely to continue its expansion. On the principle "if you can't beat them, join them", the prime minister decided to throw in his lot with the Christians and take over the leadership of what was coming to be called the Protestant party. He was undoubtedly pushed in that direction by the queen who, as might be expected from a sister of Prince Ramonja, was strongly attracted to Christianity. The plump and placid Ranavalona II probably had more strength of character than she is generally credited with. Shortly after her accession she gave orders that Sunday should be observed as a sabbath day with no work and no markets. She also ordered the palace idols to be removed and subsequently banned them from her coronation ceremony, where a large Bible was given a place of honour and Biblical texts were embroidered on the frieze of the canopy over her throne.

The extent to which the Protestant faith had been accepted as a Malagasy religion, with Malagasy martyrs, preachers and even a number of ordained pastors[1] made the prime minister's decision easier. When the queen and he received Christian instruction to prepare them for entering the Church, it was at the hands of a famous Malagasy pastor, Andriambelo, who had narrowly escaped death during the persecution; and at the baptism ceremony on February 21, 1869 no Europeans were present.

Shortly afterwards the queen and the prime minister were married in accordance with the rites of the Christian church. Before this event could take place the prime minister had to renounce his wife Rasoanalina, by whom he had had sixteen children. This first marriage was obviously a happy one. By the standards of the time Rainilaiarivony had been a faithful husband (he was known to have only one mistress who gave him several more children whom he recognised). The decision to divorce the mother of his children, to whom he remained devoted, must have been a painful one; and the break-up of the marriage was to have disastrous consequences on the character and behaviour of the children.[2] It is perhaps significant that this prolific father had no children by any of the three queens he married.

The queen's conversion to Christianity and the setting aside of the idols was a severe blow to the idol-keepers, who had hitherto enjoyed important privileges. The keepers of the most important idol, *kelimalaza*, had been treated almost like members of the royal family with the right to bear the red parasol which was the symbol of royalty. After enduring in silence for some time their loss of status and privileges they finally, in September 1869, marched to the capital to demand their restoration. The queen's reaction was to send officers on horse-back to burn the idol, which was nothing more than "a small piece of wood resembling an insect, wrapped in scarlet cloth, and decorated with silver chains".[3] This was followed by the burning of the other royal idols and an order to the people to burn their own idols. The decision appears to have been the queen's own, with the prime minister advising against it. He and the missionaries feared that such a frontal attack on the old beliefs might provoke a popular uprising. The discarding of the symbols of the ancestral religion undoubtedly caused a profound shock to the people as a whole, but in the event it all passed off calmly and without overt opposition.

The conversion of the queen and the prime minister gave a great impetus to Christianity, which was further strengthened when the destruction of the idols was not followed by the failure of crops or other disasters predicted by the idol-keepers. Large numbers of people now flocked to the churches, partly through their own natural wish to please the queen, partly through coercion by sycophantic local governors. The missionaries were overwhelmed with demands for assistance in preaching, teaching and building new chapels or churches. The LMS responded by sending out sixteen new missionaries, including two medical missionaries and two schoolmasters. Among them were James Richardson, who directed the Normal School in Antananarivo for over a quarter of a century and was the author of a Malagasy-English dictionary which is still regarded as the best available dictionary of the Malagasy language; James Sibree, who now returned as an ordained missionary; T T Mathews, subsequent author of *Thirty Years in Madagascar*; P G Peake, who twenty years later was to found the leper hospital at Manakavaly; and William C Pickersgill, who became too involved in politics for the liking of the LMS and was to make the unusual transition from missionary to vice-consul. But even with these reinforcements the missionaries were too few to do more than supervise in a very general way the hundreds of chapels which were springing up in the country districts. Some of these new congregations were fortunate enough to have the services of a trained and ordained Malagasy pastor, but the remainder were looked after by largely untrained, though frequently eloquent, local preachers.

The conversion of the queen and the prime minister facilitated the work of all groups of missionaries, including the Catholics, the Lutherans and other Protestant sects, but the LMS were inevitably, and no doubt deservedly, the main beneficiaries. The Jesuits fulminated against the success of their heretical rivals in having Protestantism established as the state religion; but the LMS missionaries viewed the matter rather differently. They were unhappy about the motives of the many thousands who now rushed to join their congregations and would have much preferred a slower process of conversion by persuasion. Moreover, as good nonconformists the idea of a state religion was anathema to them. It was largely due to their advice that the prime minister did not follow his own centralising instincts and proclaim a state religion. In fact, although coercion was certainly used in favour of Protestantism by over-zealous local governors, official government policy remained complete religious toleration. This applied even within the prime minister's own family. Several of his children became Catholics including his eldest son Radriaka[4] who married a devout Catholic known as Madame Victoire who a century later was canonised for her piety and good works.

Nevertheless there was substance to the LMS fears of a quasi-state religion interfering in their affairs. Their own highly democratic system of church government was in sharp contrast to the prime minister's strongly centralised and authoritarian method of ruling the country, and some conflict was inevitable. The regulation of Protestant affairs in Imerina was in the hands of a Congregational Union set up in 1868 and consisting of missionaries sitting on a basis of equality with Malagasy pastors representing different groups of churches. The palace church, established in the *rova* for worship by the queen and her court under Malagasy pastors, remained to a large extent a separate organisation, supporting a large number of churches in the countryside; and there was an inevitable tendency for the Malagasy, accustomed to authoritarian rule, to look for guidance and leadership to the palace church rather than to the Congregational Union. There were also some personal clashes when the prime minister felt that his authority was threatened by individual missionaries. In 1875 Dr Davidson caused offence when he made two relatives of the prime minister wait their turn at his surgery and then issued an announcement,

The kingdom in danger

without consulting the prime minister, that in future only the poor would receive free treatment. In retaliation the prime minister took away Davidson's helpers at the hospital, forbade people to go to him for treatment and sabotaged a plan for a new hospital at Faravohitra. Dr Davidson had no alternative but to leave the country in 1876. Sibree had to leave in 1877 after a similar brush with the prime minister, but was allowed to return in 1883 because of his services to the Malagasy embassy which visited London at that time. The prime minister also interfered in other ways, taking away for government service young men also trained as pastors and on one occasion in 1875 encouraging a strike by students at the LMS College.

These various incidents are sufficient proof that the prime minister was anything but subservient to the British missionaries as alleged in some French writings. But they were only ripples on the surface of the broad flow of Christian progress during his long rule. This is perhaps a convenient point at which to review the achievements of the missionaries up to the time of the French conquest.

In the words of the historian of the London Missionary Society[5] "Madagascar, during the last twenty-five years of the century, was in number of churches, converts, adherents and proportion of Christians to the heathen population, the most successful mission conducted by the Society." This would appear to be an understatement: in terms of "adherents" the Madagascar Mission could count more than twice as many as all other LMS missions put together.[6] In 1890 the statistics were: 1,223 churches, 59,615 members and 248,108 adherents. Most of these were concentrated in Imerina, but small missions had also been opened among the Betsileo in the southern plateau, in the Sihanaka country around Lake Alaotra, among the Betsimisaraka around Tamatave, at Farafangana in the southeast and, for a short time, at Majunga in the northwest.

By 1895 Malagasy Christians of all denominations probably numbered over half a million. The LMS and the Quakers accounted for more than half of these; the Catholics, divided roughly equally between the plateau and the coast, for about a fifth; the Lutherans, mainly in Betsileo and the south, for another fifth; the remainder being mainly the responsibility of the SPG operating in Antananarivo and on the east coast. As a result of the concentration of missionary activity in Imerina, most of the adult population of that region were regular churchgoers by the end of the century; but many other areas, notably the Sakalava and the south, where the government's writ applied only fitfully or not at all, were as yet untouched by Christianity. And even in Imerina, especially in the country districts, adherence to Christianity was often only nominal and accompanied by a continuation of traditional beliefs and practices and only a marginal improvement in moral and social behaviour. Nevertheless the total achievement in so short a time was remarkable and has proved to be lasting. In terms of the proportion of population regularly attending church, Madagascar must rank high among the Christian nations of the world at the present day.

Closely associated with the evangelisation was the educational work of the Christian missions. Primary education in the villages was largely an adjunct of the local church or chapel, with the native preacher frequently doubling as teacher, especially in the early days. Later separate schools were built and many supplied with Malagasy teachers trained at central teacher training establishments. In 1880, when there were already over 40,000 pupils in the schools, the prime minister decreed that all children over the age of seven must attend school – only ten years after compulsory elementary education had been introduced in Britain and two years before it was decreed in France. But the State continued to rely entirely on the missions for the financing and organisation of the schools, the training of teachers and the holding of annual examinations in reading, writing and arithmetic. By 1894 there were 137,000 pupils in the schools of the various Protestant missions, with the LMS accounting for a substantial majority. The schools of the Catholic missions, handicapped as in their religious work by the resentment caused by the French government's aggressive policies, accounted for another 27,000 pupils. The great bulk of the schools, like the churches, were in the central plateau area; lack of communications and the sparseness of population militated against the establishment of schools elsewhere, especially in the south and west. But within the plateau, by the end of the century the bulk of the population had had at least some grounding in basic education.

Secondary education was inevitably concentrated in the main towns, especially Antananarivo. The principal LMS establishments were the Normal School for training teachers, directed for many years by Rev James Richardson; and the LMS College for training pastors, of which James Sibree assumed charge after his return in 1883. The Lutherans and the SPG also established colleges for training ministers. The Roman Catholics opened an *Ecole apostolique* in 1873 but, with their stricter standards for the priesthood it was not until long after the other missions had native pastors that the first Malagasy Catholic priest appeared. As with primary education, secondary education was open to both sexes, and missions of all denominations supported their own separate high schools for boys and girls. However the precocious nubility of Malagasy girls posed special problems. Pregnancies among early teenagers and even twelve-year-olds caused frequent interruptions, while many girls left at twelve or thirteen to get married. European women teachers were brought in to teach at the girls' schools. As usual the LMS were first in the field, with Mrs Margaret Irvine (a widow) and Miss Margaret Milne who arrived in July 1865. Within four months both were married, the first to the widowed Rev J Pearse and the second to the missionary printer Mr Parrett. But like most other women who came out and married missionaries, and some who arrived already married, they continued their teaching work after marriage.

The great expansion of education was facilitated by the large output of the printing presses set up by the missions, with the LMS again leading the way. Their publications, mainly in the Malagasy language, covered a wide range of religious works, hymn books, dictionaries and school textbooks. (The splendid revised version of the Malagasy Bible, completed in 1886, was however printed in England.) The LMS press also produced in 1866 the first periodicals to appear in Madagascar, a monthly *Teny Soa* followed later by a quarterly *Mpanolo Tsaina*. Several newspapers also emerged during this period, including the *Madagascar Times*, in English and Malagasy (1882), the government newspaper *Ny Gazety Malagasy* (1883) and the *Madagascar News*, replacing the *Madagascar Times*, in English (1890). Among the more valuable publications was the *Antananarivo Annual* containing scholarly articles in English on many aspects of life in Madagascar, and edited by the omnipresent James Sibree and another missionary scholar, the Rev Richard Baron who became the chief authority on Madagascar's botany and geology.

Apart from printing, where Malagasy apprentices gradually assumed more responsible roles, technical training was no longer an important feature of mission work, and no new artisan-missionaries were sent out. The LMS did not regard technical training as part of their normal work, and had engaged in it originally only in order to gain a foothold in Imerina. Now that the skills imparted by the early artisans and by Laborde were fairly widespread they preferred to concentrate their resources on evangelistic or educational work. However, the construction of the memorial churches required the teaching of new techniques in stone-working, woodcarving, tiling and glazing. Cameron, the sole survivor of the early missionary-artisans, continued working actively on various public works projects which involved the training of workers and apprentices, until his death in 1875.

Another major achievement of the missions was the establishment of medical services and the training of Malagasy doctors. The pioneer was Dr Andrew Davidson of the LMS who opened a dispensary shortly after his arrival in 1862 and three years later a hospital, constructed by Cameron at Analakely in the centre of Antananarivo. The hospital flourished, especially after 1867, when a group of Scottish benefactors assumed financial responsibility for the hospital. Unfortunately this support was withdrawn in 1876, the year of Dr Davidson's enforced departure following his row with the prime minister, and the hospital was closed for several years. It was reopened in 1881 by Dr Tregelles Fox of the Quaker mission, and thereafter the Quakers became primarily responsible for the medical mission, with some help from the LMS. In 1891 the hospital was moved to fine new premises just outside Antananarivo where it remains to the present day, expanded and modernised, the principal hospital on the island. The Norwegian Lutherans included doctors among their very first missionaries as did the French Jesuits at a later stage. In accordance with their splendid traditions in other parts of the world, the Catholic missionaries pioneered the work of caring for lepers; although it was a LMS non-medical missionary Rev P G Peake who founded in 1892 the leper settlement at Manankavaly, to the east of the capital.

In 1875 the Malagasy government set up its own medical service the personnel of which, unlike those in most forms of government service, received a salary. At first it employed LMS medical missionaries supported by Malagasy assistants, but later it was able to rely on fully qualified Malagasy doctors. In line with the other missionaries engaged in preaching and teaching, it was the aim of the medical missionaries to train Malagasy counterparts who would eventually make expatriates unnecessary. From the outset Dr Davidson had selected young Malagasy students for basic medical training and a few of the most promising had been sent to Edinburgh to acquire a medical degree. The first of these, Dr Andrianaly and Dr Rajaonah (a son-in-law of the prime minister) returned in 1880 and were assigned to the government medical service. In 1887 another Edinburgh graduate, Dr Ralarosy, took charge of the Mission Hospital for a year when no missionary doctors were available. Meanwhile in 1880 the three Protestant missions had combined to organise pre-medical instruction in physics, chemistry and biology, leading to the establishment in 1886 of a Medical Missionary Academy. This provided a five-year course and successful students were given the title of Member of the Academy (MMMA) which authorised them to practise medicine. In 1895 the staff of the Academy consisted of four doctors, two British, one Norwegian and one Malagasy (Dr Ralarosy) and no less than forty-five students were receiving medical training at the Academy and the closely-associated Norwegian medical school. Dr Ralarosy had set up in 1891 a Malagasy Medical Mission with the main purpose of organising dispensaries in the country villages. The training of nurses, begun in 1880 by two British nursing sisters, encountered a lot of difficulties in the early stages, but by 1892 there were thirty-one trained Malagasy nurses.

The work of the missionaries in all these fields gradually altered the social climate and had an indirect influence on various administrative reforms carried out by the prime minister. The severity of the harsh penal system was gradually alleviated. In 1868 a new legal code of 101 articles, which for the first time was printed (on the LMS presses), reduced the number of offences punishable by death from eighteen to thirteen, one of which was wilful murder and the other twelve being various forms of revolt against the state. A major improvement was the abolition of the concept of family responsibility, under which wives and children were punished for a man's crimes. But otherwise the code was still severe, with relatively minor offences punishable by exile in irons to the provinces for long periods or even for life.

The prime minister also attempted to reform the administration of justice. Previously there had been one central court of justice in Antananarivo, with local justice administered since the days of Radama I by local lords, known as *andriambaventy*, who were usually open to bribery. In 1878 the single court was replaced by three courts for different types of cases, each with thirteen judges, eleven of whom were officers of the palace and only two local lords. The functions of the *andriambaventy* in the country villages were largely taken over by a new class of officers known as *sakaizam-bohitra* ("friends of the village") and recruited from the ranks of old soldiers. These were intended to act as guardians of civil rights and intermediaries between the government and the people. They were responsible for the registration of births, marriages and deaths and for the application of the law. When disputes arose, however, they had no power of adjudication but were simply required to report to the prime minister with the aid of secretaries who were usually the best scholars from the village schools. Even the courts of justice were restricted to examining witnesses and presenting a report to the prime minister in whose hands the final decision lay.

This centralisation ensured a more even dispensation of justice, reduced the opportunities for corruption and improved the government's knowledge of what was going on outside Antananarivo. But it imposed an intolerable burden on the prime minister, which he soon sought to alleviate by devolving responsibility on ministers. In 1881 eight ministries were set up – of the Interior, Foreign Affairs, War, Justice, Legislation, Commerce and Industry, Finance and Education. The new ministers, though many of them able men, proved to be a disappointment. The absolutist tradition of the Merina monarchy, which was continued under the personal rule of the prime minister, required officials to be merely the servile instruments of the monarch's will, and the assumption of the title of minister was not sufficient to induce any real change. The ministers remained fearful of responsibility and reluctant to take any decision without knowing what the prime minister's wishes were. Frequent exhortations to ministers to assume their responsibility had little effect – the prime minister's autocratic temper was no doubt partly to blame – and the continuing excessive centralisation undoubtedly contributed to the decline of the government's authority in the prime minister's later years.

The setting up of the ministries had been announced at a great *kabary* on March 29, 1881 at which a new and more comprehensive legal code of 305 articles was also promulgated. This new code was more of a success than the creation of ministries, and was taken by Gallieni as the basis of the legal system administered under the French occupation. It marked a further advance towards a more humane system, although many punishments remained harsh and the code retained its essentially Malagasy character. Capital crimes were reduced from thirteen to twelve, one of them being the casting or use of spells to kill the queen. The casting of any kind of spell was punishable by twenty years in irons, whilst the penalty for violating tombs or buying gunpowder without the prime minister's permission was ten years in irons. The missionary influence is shown in the penalties against polygamy (a fine of ten cows and ten piastres),[7] adultery (a fine of a hundred piastres, one third to be paid by the woman and two thirds by the man) and the writing or printing of pornography (three months' imprisonment); and in measures to make divorce more difficult. The Code repeated a provision of the 1868 Code prohibiting the importing of slaves, the penalty for infringement being irons for life. But the most effective measure against the external slave trade had already been taken several years earlier, namely the freeing of African slaves, or "Mozambiques", for which the credit belongs largely to the missionaries and the British government.

The early slave-trade treaties with Britain had prohibited only the export of slaves from Madagascar. As we have seen this prohibition was generally effective on the east coast but less so in the northwest; and even here the export trade gradually dried up with the freeing of slaves in Réunion and later in the United States.

However around the middle of the century the importing of slaves into Madagascar from Africa assumed a greater importance. In August 1862 Ellis received a letter on the subject from his "old and valued friend" Dr David Livingstone, who was passing through the Comoros after spending some time in Mozambique. Dr Livingstone wrote: "A great deal of slave-trading goes on from the coast of Africa to Majama Bay (Mahajamba Bay?) near Cape St Andrew. The people here name the principal slave-port Menabay (presumably the southern Sakalava region of Menabe). It is carried chiefly by Arab dhows; and if Radama II knew half the misery inflicted on Africa by those who carry on the traffic, he would not hesitate to imitate Radama I in stopping the export trade, by at once forbidding their import into his dominions."[8]

Armed with this letter, Ellis persuaded the young king to reinforce instructions which Radama said already existed to prevent the import of slaves, but it is doubtful if this was effective. LMS influence may have been largely responsible for the inclusion in the Anglo-Malagasy Treaty of 1865 of clauses forbidding the importing of slaves and empowering the Royal Navy to intervene to prevent it. Similar provisions were included in the Franco-Malagasy Treaty of 1868. But these measures seem to have had little effect. There was a continuing demand for African slaves among the Malagasy, presumably because the rarity of conquering or punitive expeditions within Madagascar meant that fewer Malagasy slaves were available; and this demand was satisfied by the importation of substantial numbers of slaves every year from Mozambique via the west coast. It became apparent that the only way to stop the trade was to destroy the market by ensuring the liberation of the African slaves, and missionary efforts were now bent in this direction. Not wishing to be accused of intervention in internal affairs, their main action was to persuade the Foreign Office, through LMS headquarters in London, to apply pressure on the Malagasy government. The instrument of this pressure was the British consul, Thomas Pakenham.

Pakenham emerges from contemporary documents as an unattractive figure, for whom very few people had a kind word. His hostile attitude to the missionaries seems to have been based on a petty jealousy of the influence of Ellis and the others, encouraged no doubt by his Roman Catholic wife, a French creole from Réunion. In his dealings with the Malagasy government he often showed insensitivity, a concern for his own dignity and a lack of tact, and the prime minister tried several times to get him recalled. But his very insensitivity, allied to a certain dogged persistence, enabled him to nag away at the authorities until in the end his object was achieved. Some two years after the conclusion of the 1865 treaty he began complaining that the Malagasy authorities on the coast were not implementing the treaty and in particular were conniving at the importing of slaves. He kept up the campaign for years and was eventually rewarded in October 1874 by a government decree announcing the liberation of all Mozambique slaves introduced after the date of the treaty, the slaves being given the option of either returning home or staying as free men and women in Madagascar. But Pakenham was soon complaining that the decree was being ignored, and he named the foreign secretary Rainimaharavo as the main culprit. Owners of slaves did their best to evade the law by claiming that their slaves had been imported before 1865. Clearly the only satisfactory solution was to free all the Mozambique slaves; and after continuing pressure from Pakenham emancipation was proclaimed on June 20, 1877. This measure virtually ended the external slave trade, apart from a few isolated clandestine incidents, and Pakenham deserves much of the credit. But internal slavery involving indigenous Malagasy slaves was to continue until the French occupation.

One area of government which had been sadly neglected was the organisation of the army. As we have seen the useful reforms of Radama I were discarded under Queen Ranavolona I and the army reverted to being an unpaid, undisciplined rabble. By reducing the frequency of regular training, Radama II further weakened its effectiveness. In 1866 an assembly of all old soldiers who had served under the two previous reigns produced a sorry collection with a high proportion of cripples and invalids. Fortnightly military training was resumed for the few thousand able-bodied men with their ancient muskets. But in the absence of proper instructors they made little progress.

In 1872 the prime minister reverted to the policy of Radama I and obtained a British instructor, Sergeant Lovett, from Mauritius. The sergeant, a tall, handsome figure, was made a general and received with every honour and attention. For a time all went well and the drill and bearing of the troops showed a marked improvement. But the many favours he received went to the sergeant's head. He became increasingly arrogant and demanding, treating his servants and troops with brutality and pestering the prime minister with constant petty requests. He was finally dismissed after he had called a minister an "old nigger" and threatened to throw him down a flight of stairs. He was succeeded by another British sergeant who was however a small unimpressive man who made himself ridiculous by his favourite sport of riding bare-back on bullocks. The prime minister then took up an offer by Laborde to supply a French instructor, who appeared to give satisfaction until the deteriorating relations with France made it inappropriate to employ a Frenchman in this position. But it was hardly an ideal arrangement to have part of the army trained in the British style and part in the French.

Improving the armament was more difficult. Since the destruction of Mantasoa there were no local facilities for manufacturing modern weapons and they had to be bought from abroad. In 1872 an Armstrong field cannon and 250 Sneider rifles were ordered from England. But these were expensive (the cost of the cannon and its transport was over 2,400 piastres) for a government with very few sources of regular income, and at a later stage some local manufacture was resumed.

Meanwhile some very useful reforms were introduced. From 1876 soldiers received an annual medical examination carried out by missionary doctors. The purchase of "honours" and of release from military service was prohibited and an end was made to the abuse of the system of ADCs. Senior officers had accumulated large numbers of personal ADCs. The secretary of state Rainimaharavo, for example, had over 1,200 which, together with their ADCs, made a total of 3,000 attached to him alone. Apart from the loss of effective manpower (ADCs were exempt from the *fanompoana* and from active military service) these substantial private armies were a potential danger to the prime minister. In July 1876, following a *kabary* at which the abuse was denounced, the number of ADCs was drastically reduced. Rainimaharavo was permitted 30, with smaller numbers for lesser-ranking officers, and the many thousands thus released reverted to being ordinary soldiers. Finally in 1879 the whole basis of military service was changed. From the time of Radama I the army had been composed of volunteers who remained soldiers, largely on a part-time basis, for the rest of their active lives. The prime minister now introduced compulsory service (with numerous classes of exemption) for a period of five years and called upon each of the six provinces of Imerina to produce 5,000 troops. In fact the provincial levy fell short of the required numbers but volunteers were forthcoming to make up the total of 30,000 troops, a substantial force for the size of the population.

In the early years of his rule the prime minister was mainly concerned to build up an effective force to support his authority against potential rivals. There was also the occasional need to assert the central government's authority over distant provinces. During this period the major military venture was a two-pronged expedition in 1873 to suppress rebellion among the Sakalava of Menabe and the Bara in the southern central area. In Menabe Prince Itoera, grandson of Radama I's adversary Ramitraho, had followed ancestral tradition and expelled the Merina garrison. Rainimaharavo was sent against him with 3,000 troops but ran into the usual difficulties from Sakalava guerrilla tactics. Although Itoera had to flee into inaccessible country, the Merina troops suffered heavily from ambush and from starvation. The column sent against the Bara was commanded by Ravoninahitriniarivo, Rainimaharavo's son and eventual successor as foreign secretary. He was rather more successful, mainly by using peaceful methods of persuasion, including the release of prisoners and generous payment for supplies, and many Bara made their submission. Merina authority was therefore somewhat enhanced in the Bara region but elsewhere in the south and west it remained as tenuous as ever.

However, by the time of the military reforms of 1879 it was becoming clear that the main role of the army in the future would no longer be the maintenance of internal authority. An adversary far more formidable than the Sakalava and Bara warrior chiefs now loomed over the horizon. Henceforward the prime minister's major preoccupations were to be the defence of his country and the preservation of its independence against the might of France.

Chapter 15

War and diplomacy

Rainilaiarivony was well aware that the policy of opening up the island to the great European powers carried with it the risk that one of the powers might seek to take over the country or at least establish a protectorate. But he hoped to contain this risk by balancing the two most important powers, Great Britain and France, against each other. This policy could well have worked if both countries had been equally interested in Madagascar. But, apart from Farquhar's short-lived attempt to annex Madagascar as a dependency of Mauritius, the British never showed any interest in establishing a special political position in Madagascar. They had of course sought to promote British trade and to extend British cultural influence by support of the missionaries; but there was never any question of imposing British influence by force (again with one exception, Captain Kelly's unauthorised bombardment of Tamatave in 1845) or of establishing an exclusive sphere of influence by means of a protectorate. The French on the other hand had maintained sporadically over a number of years claims to special "rights" and even at times to sovereignty over part or the whole of the island; and they had secured acceptance of their sovereignty over the off-shore islands of Ste Marie and Nosy Be. So in order to maintain some sort of balance in the face of increasing French demands the prime minister had to lean more and more on the British side, thereby of course provoking complaints from the French that they were being unfairly treated.

Even so the policy of balance had a very good chance of succeeding so long as the sea route to India passed by the shores of Madagascar. In the latter half of the nineteenth century the Indian Empire dominated the strategic thinking of the British Foreign Office; and it is almost inconceivable that Britain would have permitted the country which she still regarded as her most likely enemy in war to acquire control of the great island which dominated the route around the Cape. The opening of the Suez Canal in 1873 changed all that and, although its significance was not perceived for some time, in effect sounded the death-knell of

Madagascar's independence.

France's defeat in the Franco-Prussian War lowered French prestige and for a time took the heat off Madagascar. Garnier, the French *résident* who negotiated the 1868 treaty, was not replaced when he left in 1871, and affairs were left in the sympathetic hands of the Consul, Jean Laborde. But the French recovery was remarkably rapid. And in the long run the Prussian victory increased the pressure on Madagascar as the French sought compensation overseas for their humiliation in Europe. The death of Laborde in 1878 marked the end of a period of *détente* in Franco-Malagasy relations; not least because a dispute over the inheritance of his property was the occasion of a major row between the two governments.

During his long stay in Madagascar, Jean Laborde had accumulated substantial property, some of it a gift from Queen Ranavalona I as a reward for his many services to her. The succession to these properties was claimed by his heirs – two nephews, Edward Laborde and a Monsieur Campan, who took over temporarily as acting consul. They were supported by Eugène Cassas, who arrived in 1879 as French *commissaire* in Madagascar. But the Malagasy riposted that all land belonged to the queen: foreigners could hold property during their lifetime, but on their death or departure it reverted to the Crown, as had happened with, for example, Hastie and Cameron. They also questioned the validity of the title deeds produced (one document allegedly signed by Radama II was dated a year after his death) and suggested they had been forged by Laborde's son Clément, who as one of the secretaries of state had charge of the royal seal for some time. Veiled threats by Cassas produced no effect and after eight months he asked to be recalled.

Cassas was not replaced for over a year, during which time the French government appeared to have lost interest in Madagascar. A new commissioner, Meyer, arrived in 1881, and although his manner and his intentions seemed friendly he soon became embroiled in the question of the Laborde inheritance. The new code of laws promulgated just before his arrival contained in its Article 85 the first written statement of the customary law that Malagasy land could not be sold to foreigners. The French chose to regard this as a breach of their treaty and as a device to legalise the "expropriation" of the Laborde property. Mayer was instructed to demand an indemnity of 450,000 francs, and he refused a counter-offer by the prime minister of 250,000 francs.

A second difficulty arose over what became known as the *Toualé* incident. The *Toualé* was a dhow owned by a French *colon* with a crew of Arabs from the Comoros which were now a French possession. In a shooting affray at Marambitsy on the northwest coast in May 1881 several of the Arab crew were killed. Meyer demanded the execution of the Malagasy responsible for the killing of these French subjects, together with an indemnity of 6,000 francs. The Malagasy government set up an enquiry which showed that the dhow had been engaged in the illegal sale of arms to local Sakalava (*inter alia* this was contrary to the Franco-Malagasy treaty of 1868); and that its crew had fired first, with fatal effect, on the Malagasy troops sent to stop them. At this stage Meyer was suddenly recalled and replaced by Baudais who took a much more aggressive line. After much hesitation, the prime minister agreed to pay, partly because the French demand that the Malagasy government accept responsibility for the incident was tantamount to recognition of Malagasy sovereignty over the area in question. Baudais also reverted to the question of the Laborde inheritance, only to be politely referred to Article 85 of the new code of laws. Much more serious was his demand that the Malagasy government recognise French sovereignty over the north-west coast of Madagascar based on treaties obtained by French naval officers from local chiefs between 1840 and 1842.

No complex legal arguments are necessary to prove the flimsy nature of the French claim. The original validity of the treaties in question was dubious, as they were negotiated with Sakalava chiefs, notably Andriantsoly, who had been driven into exile after unsuccessful rebellion against Merina authority. They had not been followed up by effective occupation, except in the case of Nosy Be. They had been implicitly repudiated by the Franco-Malagasy treaty of 1868 which recognised the queen as sovereign of the whole island. The acceptance of the *Toualé* indemnity was also a clear recognition of Merina authority in the northwest, as was explicitly stated in Meyer's original demand for compensation.[1]

The conclusion is inescapable that the French government did not seriously believe in the legality of their claim, but were casting around for any plausible pretext to further their ultimate aim of establishing a protectorate over Madagascar. A major motive of the unstable governments of the Third Republic was to distract attention from internal troubles by pursuing an aggressive policy overseas. They were also under pressure from the *colons* of the over-populated and impoverished island of Réunion who saw the great island under French protection as a natural outlet for their surplus population and energies; and from French traders in Madagascar itself who chafed at the restrictions on trade imposed by the Merina government. In these circumstances, concern for international law was a minor consideration, although there was some regard for appearances. French tactics were far from clear-cut or consistent. But the series of humiliating demands they made on the Malagasy, which were bound to be rejected, seemed designed to provide a pretext for armed intervention. In fact the excuse for military action arose from an episode in which two LMS missionaries were involved.

The British missionaries had watched the developing situation with growing anxiety. They were concerned that an increase in French influence was likely to favour the Catholic religion at the expense of their own; and because of their close relations with the Merina court they naturally tended to favour the Malagasy side in the dispute. They were encouraged by a visit to Antananarivo in May 1881 by Rear-Admiral Gore Jones, British commander-in-chief of the East India Station. The admiral was most impressed by the prime minister and by the advanced state of education and civilisation on the plateau. In his official report he commented that the Malagasy had become "a race fit to govern their native land: and the fact obviates the necessity for the intervention of any outside nation".[2] He proposed to the British government that some naval assistance be given to help the prime minister strengthen his control over the western coastal districts, thereby improving security for trade and stamping out the residual slave trade. This proposal was not in fact followed up, but it encouraged the prime minister to become more assertive on the west coast, in the hope that he would receive British support.

Shortly after the admiral's visit, the prime minister sent two members of the LMS on a mission to the northwest. They were the printer Parrett, who had become a close friend and adviser of the prime minister; and William Pickersgill who had spent five years at the small mission which the LMS had opened in Majunga. The ostensible object of the mission was to prospect for coal and other minerals in the area. But the real purpose may have been to rally local Sakalava chiefs to the Merina crown and to investigate Sakalava complaints against abuse of authority by Merina officials. If so the mission was entirely successful. They were well received by the Sakalava who confirmed their allegiance to Queen Ranavalona II and sent a high-ranking delegation to accompany the missionaries back to Antananarivo. The delegation obtained satisfaction of their complaints from the queen and returned to the northwest with several of the queen's flags, two of which were hoisted in important villages on the coast. This act was regarded by the French as a serious provocation at a time when they were asserting a claim to sovereignty over the area in question. When a protest by Baudais produced no result he withdrew to Tamatave in May 1882 and called upon his government to send a warship.

In response a French frigate was sent in the following month to remove the offending flags.

The two parties were now set on a collision course, but Rainilaiarivony still hoped to avoid either war or capitulation to French demands. He decided to appeal directly to the French government and to the other great powers by means of an embassy to Europe and the United States. The embassy consisted of the foreign minister Ravoninahitriniaiarivo (who had succeeded his father Rainimaharavo in 1878), one of the queen's councillors Ramaniraka (a son of the former foreign secretary Rahaniraka) and two interpreters. The secretary of the embassy was Anthony Tacchi, editor and proprietor of the *Madagascar Times*. The American consul, Colonel William Robinson, who had acquired considerable personal influence with the Malagasy government, also travelled with the embassy as a "friendly adviser and guide".[3] The embassy went first to Paris where discussions were held with a French delegation in October 1882. The French, while threatening hostilities if their demands were not met, offered a face-saving compromise by which the French would establish a "temporary" occupation of the northwest coast until the Malagasy government was strong enough to maintain order. This was more than the Malagasy envoys dared agree to, but their position was weak and the timing of their visit proved to be most unfortunate. French public opinion was smarting over the British occupation of Egypt and demanding that the government take a firm line over Madagascar. The British government was not disposed to quarrel with the French over an area which was now peripheral to Britain's major interests. The embassy's friends advised them that it would be prudent to make concessions. They consequently proposed the neutralisation of the territory in question: the Malagasy to withdraw their flags and custom posts in return for the French dropping their claim to a protectorate over the area. But the French response to this concession was to press further demands, including the right of French citizens to acquire land on renewable ninety-nine year leases. When the Malagasy refused to agree they were brusquely informed on November 28, 1882 that they were no longer the guests of the French government and the Malagasy flag was removed from their hotel.

The embassy left the same day for London where they still hoped for support. There was certainly no lack of sympathy. A Madagascar Committee had recently been formed, inspired largely by the LMS, and consisting of MPs and other influential people whose aim was to persuade the government to support the Malagasy cause. Members of the committee, briefed by the embassy, raised questions in Parliament about the Madagascar affair and wrote to the Foreign Office urging British intervention. Queen Victoria gave the embassy luncheon at Windsor Castle. Lord Granville, the foreign secretary, also received them sympathetically, and at his request they submitted a memorandum setting out ably and at length their side of the affair. The Foreign Office were impressed, and the under-secretary responsible minuted perceptively: "the Malagasy business does not look from this statement as if it could be peacefully settled except by arbitration, and I fancy the French case is too bad to make that solution possible."[4] And so it proved. An offer of mediation by Lord Granville was firmly, even indignantly, rejected by the French government. The Foreign Office regretfully decided that it could do no more. As the permanent under-secretary had explained frankly to Samuel Procter, the Malagasy consul in London: "important negotiations are proceeding between France and England relative to the re-establishment of authority in Egypt, and England is most anxious, while the Egyptian question is under discussion, not to irritate France by offering any remonstrance on the Malagasy case."[5] As a modest consolation prize, the embassy obtained a minor modification of the ambiguous clause on property in the 1865 treaty, to replace the reference to "sale" of property by "long lease".

The embassy then proceeded to the United States. They were received by the president and the secretary of state and again encountered much sympathy, but there was never any question of official American intervention. All that the ambassadors achieved was the ratification of the 1881 treaty which recognised Queen Ranavalona II as ruler of the whole island. They then went to Berlin where the story was repeated: an audience with the emperor, a treaty of friendship and commerce recognising the queen's sovereignty over the whole of Madagascar, but no disposition to intervene with the French. Before leaving for home in July 1883 they negotiated a similar treaty with Italy. But paper recognitions of sovereignty counted for little when the news from Madagascar was that hostilities had broken out. Reporting to the prime minister on the failure of their diplomacy they concluded "God alone can help us".

In a change of government in Paris early in 1883, a Deputy from Réunion, François de Mahy, became for a short period Minister of the Navy. He was an ardent advocate of the annexation of Madagascar, and he seized his brief moment of power to order aggressive action. Admiral Pierre, the commander-in-chief of the French Naval Division in the Indian Ocean, was instructed to destroy any Malagasy government stations in the northwestern area claimed by the French, and to occupy Majunga and Tamatave. On May 7, 1883, he bombarded two posts on the coast near Nosy Be. On May 16 he appeared off Majunga and called upon the governor to evacuate the port within an hour. When the governor refused, the squadron bombarded the town, killing many people and forcing the withdrawal of the Malagasy troops. After leaving a garrison in charge of the port the admiral sailed for Tamatave where on June 1 he and Baudais addressed an ultimatum to Queen Ranavalona II. They demanded recognition of a French protectorate over Madagascar north of latitude 16°S; the repeal of Article 85 of the 1881 code, prohibiting the sale of land to foreigners; and an indemnity of one million francs for the claims of French nationals, including the heirs of Laborde. Unless acceptance was received within eight days (three days for the message to reach the capital, two days for reflection and three days for the return journey) Tamatave would be occupied.

Antananarivo was already in a ferment with the news of the bombardments in the northwest. All French residents, including missionaries, had been ordered to leave, although the prime minister insisted that this should be done in a "civilised" manner (five days to pack, assistance with porters) to point the contrast with French behaviour. There was never any question of accepting the ultimatum. At a great *kabary* speeches by the queen and prime minister set out the justice of the Malagasy cause and called upon the people to defend the ancestral lands. The ageing queen's speech carried echoes of Queen Elizabeth I's famous address to her soldiers at Tilbury as the Armada approached:

"If this land which God has given to me, and where my ancestors rest, and where the bones of your ancestors lie buried, is claimed by others, then I stand up for the defence of the benefits which God has conferred. God made me a woman, still, when anyone attempts to seize that which He has given me, and the country which my ancestors conquered is threatened, then I feel strong to go forth as your leader, for I should feel ashamed ... if I did not protect what God had entrusted to me."[7]

Rejection of the ultimatum was received on June 9 and on the following day Admiral Pierre bombarded and occupied Tamatave. The Malagasy governor, Rainandriamampandry, had been instructed not to resist but to withdraw to an entrenched position at Farafaty a few miles inland from which he could harass the French troops. The occupation was accompanied by high-handed behaviour towards European, and especially British, residents which for a time threatened a serious breach between Britain and France. Foreign consuls were given twenty-four hours to leave, as they were not accredited to the French authorities. Pakenham, who was gravely ill, died during the twenty-four hours and it was believed in London, probably wrongly, that the ultimatum hastened his death. More seriously a British missionary, George Shaw, was arrested on a charge of attempting to poison French troops, incarcerated in a French warship in conditions of considerable hardship and threatened with execution if the charge was proved true.

What had happened was that during the bombardment Shaw's house had been looted by some Malagasy who scattered in the garden the contents of his medicine chest, including bottles of laudanum and pure alcohol. These were found and drunk by marauding French soldiers who naturally were violently sick. But it was fifty-four days before Shaw's innocence was established and he was allowed to go, and meanwhile British public opinion became highly incensed and the Foreign Office addressed strong protests to Paris. The French government eventually made amends with a grant of the then substantial sum of £1,000 to Shaw and an unreserved apology: "It has to be admitted that an innocent man, the subject of a friendly power, has been deprived of his liberty during fifty-four days, and this under painful conditions, and to the prejudice of his interests, and under the weight of an accusation which has proved not to be justified."[8]

In Madagascar meanwhile Queen Ranavalona II had died on July 13, 1883. To succeed her the prime minister chose, and in due course married, a 22-year old Princess Razafindrahety, who took the name of Queen Ranavalona III. She was an intelligent girl, recently widowed, who had received a good education at Protestant schools. Her photographs show her as small, pretty and fragile with an ineffably sad expression as if she never became reconciled to her royal duties and her marriage to the now elderly prime minister. But she fulfilled her role dutifully, and at her coronation four months later the speeches which she and the prime minister made, affirming their determination not to yield an inch of soil to the invader, roused the people to wild enthusiasm: "cannon, swords, spears, shields, rifles, hats, handkerchiefs and hundreds of thousands of throats gave forth the wild assent."[9]

The "war" however had already settled down into stalemate. The Malagasy were not strong enough to dislodge the French from Tamatave or Majunga. But the French forces were too small to make any significant advance into the interior or even to dislodge the Malagasy from their stronghold near Tamatave where Rainandriamampandry proved to be a capable military commander. The French, who had hoped that the occupation of the main ports would compel the Malagasy to accede to their demands, were somewhat nonplussed by the stubbornness of the government in Antananarivo. The high-handed Admiral Pierre soon left his post because of illness and died on the way home, thereby escaping a reprimand for his treatment of Shaw and the consuls in Tamatave. He was succeeded by Admiral Galiber, who arrived at Tamatave in October 1883 with instructions to pursue negotiations and to adopt a rather more conciliatory line. But during several months of talks in Tamatave the Malagasy delegation under Rainandriamampandry refused to contemplate the surrender of any part of the mainland, though they offered to give up two offshore islands and to pay an indemnity of one million francs. A French compromise proposal to "neutralise" the disputed territory in the north west was also rejected as implying a recognition of either a French protectorate or Sakalava independence. Galiber left in March 1884 and was succeeded by Admiral Miot who adopted a tougher line, including a demand for an indemnity of 3 million francs. This led to a breakdown of the negotiations and a resumption of hostilities.

However the French government was still not in a position to organise a full-scale invasion of Madagascar, and Miot's sphere of action remained limited to the coasts. He bombarded and occupied several more ports and in December 1884 he seized the splendid natural harbour of Diego Suarez at the northern tip of the island. But the need to leave garrisons in these places further reduced the number of troops available to Miot for attacks on the main Malagasy positions. The occupation of the ports, while seriously disrupting Madagascar's external trade, posed no immediate threat to the government in Antananarivo and served only to stimulate their determination to resist French demands. The prime minister, at the height of his powers, showed great energy in maintaining the people's enthusiasm by rousing patriotic speeches and in organising the recruitment of troops and the purchase or manufacture of weapons. Laborde's former employees were put to work to manufacture spears and muskets, and one of them even succeeded in making a kind of machine gun. Nor was the propaganda war neglected: in response to a series of French government "Yellow Books" (in the style of a British "Blue Book") the Malagasy government published a "Red Book" containing the text of letters exchanged with French representatives and summary records of the negotiations in Tamatave, which effectively presented the Malagasy case in a reasonable light.[10]

The Malagasy also secured the services of Colonel Digby Willoughby, a British officer who had fought in the Zulu Wars. In August 1884 he was appointed adjutant-general of the Malagasy army and principal military adviser to the prime minister. The latter was not an easy task as the prime minister did not always accept Willoughby's advice. In particular, whereas Willoughby favoured withdrawal from some defensive positions in order to concentrate forces for an attack on one of the French positions, the prime minister refused to abandon any territory unless forced to. But Willoughby improved the training of the Malagasy troops and further strengthened the entrenched position at Farafaty so that it became impregnable to any forces that the French could deploy at that time.

The military stalemate thus dragged on into 1885. In Paris enthusiasm for colonial adventures was temporarily dampened by difficulties in Tonkin, which led to the downfall of the Jules Ferry government in March 1885. Protestant elements in France organised opposition to the government's aggressive policy in Madagascar and circulated to members of the National Assembly copies of a book by Saillens entitled *Nos droits sur Madagascar et nos griefs contre les Hova, examinés impartialement* which concluded: "Our centuries-old rights in Madagascar have been abrogated – Our modern rights have never existed."[11] This did not prevent the Assembly from voting new credits for the Madagascar campaign in July 1885, but over a hundred deputies voted against. The ravages of disease among the French troops, severe damage caused to naval ships by cyclones, and the repulse in September 1885 of another French attack on the entrenchments at Farafaty, all strengthened the view that French objectives in Madagascar could not be achieved by the forces then likely to be made available.

In Antananarivo too the war was becoming more unpopular. The cost was enormous for a country with so few sources of revenue. The disruption of external trade caused considerable loss to the government and to the influential trading class. And compulsory military service on the coasts was highly unpopular among the Merina who, accustomed to the agreeable climate of the plateau, found the steamy heat of the coasts just as unbearable as the French did.

Towards the end of 1885, both sides were ready for peace. In August the LMS missionary Parrett, accompanied by Samuel Procter the Malagasy Consul in London, presented to the French government proposals by the prime minister (cession of Diego Suarez, withdrawal of Merina posts from the northwest, and an indemnity of 2.5 million francs) which offered the basis of a compromise. The dismissal of Baudais in October removed an obstacle to successful negotiations as he was regarded in Antananarivo as being particularly hostile to Madagascar. His successor Patrimonio joined Admiral Miot to conduct peace negotiations which opened at

Tamatave on December 15, 1885. The Malagasy negotiating team comprised one of the prime minister's sons Rainizanamanga, his private secretary and rather surprisingly General Willoughby.

The negotiations were completed in only two days. This astonishing speed was due largely to Willoughby who, contrary to expectations, showed himself remarkably accommodating to French demands. As Patrimonio reported to his foreign minister, Willoughby "served us well in this affair; he offered his service to us without any remuneration; and it appears that he was inspired only by the glory of affixing his signature by the side of the representatives of a great nation like France."[12] The outcome was a treaty in which both sides could take some satisfaction but which undoubtedly favoured the French. They obtained the right to occupy the harbour of Diego Suarez, a huge indemnity of ten million francs, the right of French citizens to lease property on renewable leases of indefinite duration, and the appointment of a French Resident in Antananarivo responsible for the conduct of Madagascar's foreign relations. For their part the Malagasy had avoided any specific mention of a protectorate or any cession of territory in the north (apart from Diego Suarez) in return for a promise to treat the Sakalava well; indeed they secured a recognition of the queen's internal sovereignty over the whole island.

In Antananarivo, however, there was much dismay among the queen's councillors, especially over the powers of the Resident and the loss of Diego Suarez. To appease this the prime minister sought and obtained from the French negotiators certain clarifications of the treaty, which were conveyed in a letter of January 9, 1886. According to this letter the Resident's role would be limited to political aspects of foreign relations, and the Malagasy government could continue to negotiate treaties of commerce with other nations; the territory which the French would occupy along with the harbour of Diego Suarez was limited to a few miles around the harbour; and there were other clarifications including the "limitation" of leases of property to foreigners to ninety-nine years renewable. The Malagasy government then ratified the treaty, of which they regarded the explanatory letter an integral part. But the French government refused to recognise the letter, despite the fact that it was signed by their plenipotentiaries, and it was not submitted along with the treaty for ratification by the National Assembly.[13] There was thus plenty of scope for discord when the first French Resident-General, Le Myre de Vilers, arrived in Antananarivo in May 1886.

Article 9 of the treaty provided that French troops would occupy Tamatave until the indemnity of ten million francs was paid.

Anxious to get rid of these troops as soon as possible, the prime minister sent Willoughby to London in May 1886 to negotiate a loan of four million dollars (20 million francs) of which half would be used to pay off the loan and the remainder mainly to purchase a warship, various armaments and machinery for manufacturing arms. Willoughby appears to have crossed a mission in the opposite direction representing a syndicate of London bankers, notably the New Oriental Bank, which wished to establish a bank in Madagascar. The syndicate's emissary was Abraham Kingdon, a former Quaker missionary. He obtained the prime minister's agreement to the establishment of a Royal Bank of Madagascar which would advance a loan of four million dollars at 7 per cent, the loan to be secured on customs duties in the collection of which representatives of the Bank would participate. A formal agreement to this effect was signed in London on June 23, 1886 by Willoughby, on behalf of the Malagasy government, and the syndicate.

The French reacted strongly, realising that the agreement, and in particular the role of British officers in collecting customs, would seriously weaken the pre-eminent position they had obtained under the treaty. They refused to admit Madagascar's right, implicit in the "interpretative letter" of January 9, 1886, to deal directly with foreign countries on economic or commercial matters; and eventually announced that they could not accept payment of the indemnity based on a British loan. The British financiers appealed to their government but the Foreign Office refused to support them and the "Kingdon contract" collapsed. Willoughby, who had meanwhile set himself up at 12 Pall Mall as Ambassador of Madagascar in London, was recalled at the end of 1886. Subsequently accused and convicted of misuse of public funds and extravagance, including the purchase of a uniform costing £300, he was expelled from Madagascar in September 1888.

As an alternative to the British loan, the French offered a loan of 15 million francs from the *Comptoir d'Escompte de Paris*. The prime minister had to accept this as the only way of getting rid of the French troops in Tamatave, and they accordingly left at the beginning of 1887. France thus received not only the indemnity but the interest on the loan, together with the commercial and political benefits arising from the establishment of branches of the *Comptoir* in Antananarivo and Tamatave and the bank's involvement in the collection of customs duties. Moreover the Malagasy government were inhibited from using the loan money to buy arms which, it was becoming increasingly apparent, were most likely to be used against the French.

Le Myre de Viler's triumph over the loan was not however repeated in the next important trial of strength, which arose over the apparently trivial matter of the granting of *exequaturs* to foreign consuls. The underlying issue was of course control of foreign affairs. The French argued that, as a consequence of their Resident's right under Articles 1 and 2 of the treaty to deal with "all external relations of Madagascar", the Malagasy foreign ministry and consulates abroad should cease to exist. The Malagasy, basing themselves on the interpretative letter maintained that they were still responsible for non-political external affairs, including the granting of *exequaturs*. Their position was strengthened when Captain Haggard, the new British consul who arrived in Tamatave in November 1886, sought and obtained his *exequatur* direct from the Malagasy Foreign Minister, neither party informing the French Resident-General. This example was followed by the Italian consul-general and the American consul. When the protests of the French Resident-General produced no response, the French government urged the three foreign governments to re-apply for *exequaturs* through the Resident. Lord Salisbury agreed to do so, but only when the consuls of the other powers had followed this procedure. In May 1887 the American consul, John P. Campbell[14] was in fact instructed to re-apply through the Resident-General. Le Myre de Vilers forwarded the application to the prime minister, who promptly rejected it, withdrew recognition from the American consul and announced that he would not recognise any consul who endeavoured to obtain his *exequatur* through the Resident-General. Le Myre de Vilers angrily hauled down his flag and retreated to Tamatave, urging his government to apply military coercion. But the French government were not yet ready to resume war and Le Myre de Vilers eventually returned to Antananarivo and accepted a face-saving compromise which in fact represented a victory for the Malagasy: consuls were to apply direct to the Malagasy foreign ministry, but the *exequatur* would include a reference to the Resident-General's responsibility for foreign affairs "having a political character". This latter restriction was a further victory for the Malagasy, as it implied acceptance of part of the interpretative letter.

For Le Myre de Vilers it was a question of *"reculer pour mieux sauter"*. He accepted his defeat over the *exequaturs* with a good grace and set to work quietly to strengthen the French position by diplomatic methods. Other disputes had arisen over the interpretation of the treaty, concerning the delimitation of the French base at Diego Suarez and the status of two small islands off the north-west coast, Nosy Faly and Nosy Mitsio (occupied finally by the French in 1889). But they were not allowed to develop into a major confrontation with the Malagasy government. Subordinate French Residents were established in five provincial towns. A telegraph service between Tamatave and the capital, established and operated by French technicians, was inaugurated in 1887. A dozen young Malagasy were sent on courses to military and technical schools in France and French military instructors were attached to the Malagasy army. The prime minister's favourite son Rainiharovony (also known as Mariavelo) was sent on a diplomatic mission to France and received with flattering marks of attention. Le Myre de Vilers also succeeded in establishing relations of mutual respect with the prime minister, and of warm friendship with the young queen and other personalities of the court. His departure for France in 1889 was accompanied by many expressions of genuine regret. The next Resident-General, Bompard, continued the policy of quiet diplomacy to strengthen French influence at the expense of the British. Concessions for mineral and other exploitation were obtained for Frenchmen to balance those awarded to Englishmen, notably Kingdon. And in January 1890 French warships transported to Tulear a Malagasy expedition, led by the popular Prince Ramahatra, to put down a rebellion in the southwest.

These various signs of surface cordiality may have deluded the prime minister into believing that he could stave off the French threat indefinitely. But the aims of the French government had not changed, only their methods. They appear to have appreciated that direct confrontation with the Merina government would not succeed so long as the latter could rely to some degree on the support, however half-hearted or ambiguous, of the British. It was therefore necessary to obtain formal British endorsement of French pretensions. The opportunity came with the development of British policy in East Africa.

Having secured the Suez Canal, the Foreign Office shifted its gaze to the headwaters of the Nile, fearing that an enemy power established there could threaten British control of Egypt. As a first step to the penetration of Uganda, they wished to secure control of Zanzibar. Germany, the most active power in the area, was bought off with a treaty of July 1, 1890 under which the island of Heligoland was ceded to Germany in return for German recognition of a British protectorate over Zanzibar. The French seized their chance and pointed in pained surprise to the Anglo-German Convention of 1862, guaranteeing the independence of the Sultan of Zanzibar. France's subsequent adherence to this Convention gave them a clear right to be consulted on any change in Zanzibar's status. The embarrassed Lord Salisbury, who admitted that he had forgotten the 1862 Convention, felt obliged to concede that France should be compensated in Madagascar. Accordingly, in a treaty signed in London on August 5, 1890, Britain recognised a French protectorate over Madagascar in return for French acquiescence in the British protectorate over Zanzibar.

In Antananarivo, news of the "British betrayal" came as a great shock to the court and government. The loss of the British prop, on which he had based his whole policy, momentarily shook the self-confidence even of the prime minister. The jubilance of the French community was matched by the dismay of the British, and especially the missionaries who sent a petition to Queen Victoria. But this was fobbed off with a polite rejection through the British consul; and a similar petition from British traders on the island was simply ignored. In London the LMS organised a series of protests and questions in the House of Commons. In the debate on the Foreign Office estimates on August 9 and 11 several MPs forthrightly criticised the government's action. But their arguments were of no avail against considerations of global strategy. In his reply to the debate the Parliamentary under-secretary of the Foreign Office confined himself to stating that the government had done nothing more than recognise the French protectorate which had been accepted by the Malagasy government in 1886. The "betrayal", perhaps the most shameful episode in the history of Anglo-Malagasy relations, was thus disposed of in a few sentences. With the grouse-shooting season opening next day, Parliament dispersed for its long summer recess. No international obstacle now remained to block French ambitions in Madagascar.

Chapter 16

The French conquest

During the last few years of its existence, the Merina monarchy of Madagascar presented an exotic picture of striking contrasts. The capital, Antananarivo, still a dramatic and beautiful city, was then even more picturesque, with the jumble of characteristic red brick or mud houses clinging to the steep hillsides offset by the dignity of the great stone palaces of the queen and the prime minister and the spires and towers of churches on the skyline. Mr E F Knight, special correspondent of *The Times* sent to cover the war in 1895, had his first glimpse of the capital in the distance, "appearing as a far blue peak crowned with the towers and domes of palaces and churches. There were many signs that I was approaching a great centre of population. The villages became more frequent and the landscape was studded with the country villas of the Hova nobles; well-built houses of red brick of a uniform style of architecture, and generally surrounded with shrubberies, suggesting reminiscences of the genteel but cheap suburbs of some of our own large towns"[1]

The royal court was relatively sophisticated, achieving at times a certain elegance, and might reasonably be compared with the court of a minor Balkan country of the same period. The queen and her ladies wore European dress only a year or two behind the latest fashion; while the gentlemen of the court wore top hats and frock-coats or dazzling military uniforms. The palaces and better houses were furnished with European-style furniture, either imported or copied by local craftsmen. The court calendar included banquets and balls, tennis parties with European friends and trips to the countryside to enjoy the simple rural life at places like Ambohimanga where the queen had a modest little chalet. The European community in and around the capital – missionaries, traders, and the small consular corps – found life comfortable in the agreeable climate; and with many European goods available in the shops they suffered few deprivations. The English-language *Madagascar News* carried advertisements for familiar products such as tinned Oxford sausages, Cheddar and Cheshire cheese, Suffolk kippers, Bartlett pears and Keating's insect powder. Also on offer were white

Manchester shirtings, with Oxford shirtings "suitable for servants", and English boots and shoes "for the Ladies, Lads, Lassies and Little Tots".

The government was also, at least in structure, relatively sophisticated. Although the prime minister's power was in practice absolute, government business was carried out, and proclamations issued, in the name of the queen. Work was distributed among various government departments headed by ministers or in some cases, following the British-style, secretaries of state. Control of the provinces was entrusted to governors, and official correspondence was conducted with these and with the lower echelons of government in the Malagasy language. Quasi-diplomatic relations were maintained with European powers and the United States through the small consular corps in Madagascar and a few Malagasy consuls abroad; and a voluminous diplomatic correspondence was carried on in both English and French.

This degree of sophistication, and in particular the widespread literacy on which it depended, was largely the result of the work of the missionaries which has already been described. The rapid spread, at least in the plateau area, of primary education, Christianity and medical services in a period of only thirty years was in itself a sufficiently noteworthy achievement. What was even more remarkable was the extent to which the schools, churches and medical services were in the hands of Malagasy teachers, pastors and doctors, graduates of training establishments which themselves had Malagasy among the teaching staff. In all these respects, Madagascar in 1895 was considerably more advanced than most of the black African countries when they achieved their independence from colonial rule sixty or seventy years later. The usual justification for the imposition of European rule – "*la mission civilisatrice*" – was thus not easy to find. On the contrary the experience of Madagascar seemed to show that a primitive pagan nation could, with disinterested European help, aspire to a degree of Christian civilisation without needing a framework of colonial administration.

Beneath the surface, however, there were grave weaknesses. As most of the missionaries realised, Christianity was still for most Malagasy a matter of outward conformity and church-going which had yet little effect on their traditional way of life. Although the worst cruelties of the law had been abolished there was still much inhumanity. Domestic slavery continued and a slave market was a feature of the great Zoma market of Antananarivo until 1895. But the yoke of slavery, which was little more than tied domestic service, was light compared with the exactions of the government; and some free men offered themselves as slaves in order to avoid military service and especially *fanampoana*, the system of compulsory unpaid labour which imposed a heavy and unequal burden on the ordinary citizen.[2]

The burden had greatly increased in recent years. To help pay off the huge indemnity to the French, a new gold *corvée* was introduced to increase production from the small gold mines. Foreigners granted concessions for exploiting forests, mines, etc, obtained forced labour on contracts for which they paid the prime minister substantial sums, none of which accrued to the labourers. The better-off could buy exemption by bribing officials, thus further increasing the burden on the poor, who at times were required to labour without pay for six or more months in the year. They were thus prevented from growing enough to feed themselves and their families or to pay the new capitation tax which was levied in 1891 to supplement the inadequate gold production. Destitute and starving, many peasants fled from their villages to form robber bands which contributed greatly to the decline of law and order.

A central weakness was that government service was for the most part unpaid. Government officials were thus bound to resort to various exactions, bribery and abuse of *fanompoana* in order to survive. Favouritism and corruption compounded the inefficiency of the government machine which was excessively centralised in the person of the prime minister.

Now well over sixty, Rainilaiarivony had lost little of his energy and capacity for work. An English observer[3] gave the following description of the "Grand Old Man" in 1892:

"He really is a wonderful old man, physically as well as mentally. To see him at a Public reception, with his little dapper, well-made-up figure, and admirably tinted coiffure, skipping about and posturing, one would be much more inclined to place his age at 40 years, than at the nearly seventy to which he owns. May he live forty more and may the writer live to see them! As for his intelligence, no doubt it has been largely exaggerated, and his ultra-conservatism would make even the First Charles blush if he were alive. But he knows his own country thoroughly, and, above all, his own countrymen."

His resilience was all the more remarkable because of the constant family problems which added to the great burdens of his office. His apparently enviable family of eleven sons and five daughters caused him much more pain than joy. It was his great hope that one of his sons would succeed to his power, but they either died young or succumbed to drink and debauchery. Elementary psychology would suggest that their unsatisfactory behaviour was the result of the repudiation of their mother when the prime minister married Queen Ranavolona II. Whether or not because of his feelings of guilt, the prime minister spoiled them outrageously and would not listen to accounts of their misdeeds and failings. The resentment aroused by his nepotism was an important cause of the decline of his authority.

The prime minister's eldest son, Ralaiarivony, was the first favourite and probable successor, but he was shot in a hunting accident by a younger brother (and perhaps it wasn't an accident). Hopes were then centred on another son Mariavelo, despite the fact that he was notorious for his drunken and lawless behaviour. His despatch on an embassy to Paris in 1887 was intended primarily to enhance his status as future prime minister, and on his return he was raised to sixteen honours and made commander-in-chief. This outrageous favouritism provoked the able foreign minister, Ravoninahitriniarivo, into plotting the overthrow of the prime minister; but the plot was exposed and the foreign minister sent into exile.

The prime minister continued to ignore the vices and weaknesses of Mariavelo, and was inconsolable when Mariavelo died in 1891. It was from this time that some observers[4] dated the beginnings of the prime minister's decline, shown in loss of memory and uncharacteristic lack of decision. With only three sons left alive, each of them unsatisfactory in one way or another, he now chose as his successor a bright young grandson Ratelifera, son of his eldest daughter. This choice inevitably aroused jealousy among those passed over. In 1893, one of the discarded sons Rajoelina, intrigued with a son-in-law, Dr Rajaonah,[5] to obtain the succession for himself and secured the support of Abraham Kingdon in return for the promise of further concessions. The plot was again exposed and the prime minister expelled Kingdon and exiled to distant parts his son and son-in-law. It was a lonely and embittered old man who penned a last will and testament disinheriting most of his remaining children and leaving the bulk of his property to Ratelifera.[6]

The decline in the old man's authority no doubt contributed to the serious increase in crime and disorder which was a feature of the last years of the monarchy. The Merina government had never been able to subdue the thorny desert regions of the far south, and its control of the Sakalava regions of the west was at best tenuous. Sporadic raiding across the unpopulated no-man's-land which separated Imerina from the Sakalava country had been an accepted feature of life for many years. But from around the end of the first war with France in 1885 this kind of raiding became more frequent, with Sakalava bands attacking frontier Merina villages with impunity and carrying off the inhabitants as slaves. Later, disorder spread to other parts of the country and even to the centre of Imerina, with armed bandits known as *fahavalo* pillaging and robbing and even attacking Europeans.[7] This state of affairs seemed to present the French with the excuse they were seeking to intervene – "to restore law and order". By 1894 even some British missionaries were expressing the view that French intervention was the only hope for the country.

It has been argued with some plausibility[8] that the serious decline in law and order was the direct result of France's aggressive policy; and in particular that the further decline after 1890 and the attacks on Europeans were caused by widespread resentment of the 1890 Convention by which the Great Powers disposed of Madagascar's independence. In fact, as mentioned above, disorder had already reached serious proportions before 1890; and even in the days of the prime minister's maximum power banditry on the borders of Imerina was a serious problem. But there can be little doubt that the government's ability to cope with its internal problems had been eroded by the great efforts deployed in the war against the French; its resources had been further depleted by the huge indemnity imposed at the end of that war; and thereafter the diplomatic struggle with successive French Residents used up too much of the energies of the ageing prime minister. Moreover after 1890 the activities of various sectors of the French community contributed to the decline of the government's authority.[9] The resident-general's military escort frequently behaved in an arrogant and brutal manner towards Malagasy citizens. The French bank which had acquired a privileged position by advancing the loan to pay the indemnity acted illegally in arresting and maltreating defaulting debtors; and its agents who were concerned with the collection of customs duties arbitrarily granted exemptions so that the sums accruing to the government diminished. French representatives in the capital helped to foment palace intrigues against the prime minister; and a Malagasy newspaper published in the French Residence openly attacked members of the court and even the prime minister and the queen.

The old prime minister, fighting a hopelessly unequal battle, made things more difficult for himself by his autocratic egoism and his neurotic suspicions of possible rivals. But one cannot help admiring his stubborn refusal to submit to the loss of his country's independence. He refused to take cognisance of the Anglo-French Convention of 1890; and when the French Resident communicated the text to him he replied that it was an affair between *vazaha* ("foreigners") which did not concern him. In the convention the

British had recognised the French protectorate over Madagascar "with its consequences, especially as regards the *exequaturs* of British consuls and agents, which must be applied for through the intermediary of the French Resident-General". But when newly-appointed German and British consuls applied through the Resident-General for their *exequaturs*, the prime minister refused to authorise them (although he in fact permitted the consuls to exercise their functions in the normal way). There was nothing he could do when the British Government, under French pressure, withdrew the *exequaturs* of the consuls of Madagascar in London and Mauritius. But he continued to correspond direct with foreign governments and their representatives in Madagascar – thus denying to the French Resident-General an effective control over the country's foreign relations.

In the north of the country the prime minister continued to resist French encroachments to the south of Diego Suarez beyond the narrow limits set out in the "interpretative" letter of January 1886. There were several confrontations between French troops and the nearest Merina garrison, as well as numerous disputes arising when slaves escaping from Malagasy territory claimed their freedom in French territory or when criminals from either side took refuge in the territory of the other. In 1892 Malagasy troops attempting to re-occupy some villages taken over by the French were dislodged by the superior French garrison. Over the next two years the prime minister built up the strength of the Merina forces in the area, including the recruitment of British and German mercenary officers, so that in July 1894 they were able to re-occupy much of the disputed territory with impunity.

There was also a continuing dispute over the importation of arms. Through his British friends the prime minister ordered a substantial number of Winchester and Martini repeating rifles. The Hamburg firm of O'Swald and Company were asked to supply more Winchesters and a large quantity of gunpowder. When the French Resident-General protested that the armaments were not necessary since France would protect Madagascar against any outside attack, the prime minister blandly replied that the arms were needed for internal policing. There was a certain inconsistency in the French complaining about the break-down of law and order while opposing the supply of the means to make the Malagasy army more effective. The Resident-General argued that any necessary arms should be bought from France; but the French would not of course have acquiesced in the supply of weapons which would have been useful against an invading French force. The enormous length of the Madagascar coastline made it impossible for the French Navy to intercept the arms shipments. The prime minister thus ensured that his army was not lacking in modern weapons for the conflict which was now inevitable.

The stubborn refusal of the prime minister to accept a protectorate left the French government with no alternative but a military expedition to impose their wishes. Support for a military solution was whipped up by alarming reports from French residents, official and private, about the widespread disorder and violence in the island. In January 1894 the National Assembly unanimously adopted a resolution which gave the government full support in any measures taken to uphold French "rights" in Madagascar, protect French nationals and restore order. By the second half of 1894 the government was ready to back its diplomacy by force of arms. In a final attempt to secure a peaceful surrender, Le Myre de Vilers was despatched on a special mission to Antananarivo.

Le Myre de Vilers arrived in the Malagasy capital on October 14, 1894. At an audience with the prime minister three days later he stated that his government could no longer tolerate the Malagasy refusal to carry out the treaty of 1885. He accordingly presented a new draft treaty designed, he said, to ensure the execution of the 1885 treaty but in fact going very much further and imposing virtually complete French control over internal as well as external affairs. Under the draft the Malagasy government would be forbidden to carry on any relations with foreign countries except through the French Resident-General; all concessions to foreigners would have to be approved by him; the French would be empowered to bring in as many troops as they thought necessary to protect their nationals; and the French government would be authorised to carry out all kinds of public works and levy taxes for this purpose.

There was never any possibility that the prime minister would accept such terms. But when he tried to resort to his usual delaying tactics, Le Myre de Vilers issued an ultimatum demanding acceptance of the treaty by October 26, otherwise he would withdraw to the coast with the military escort and all French residents. At a further meeting on October 22 the prime minister handed over a long letter complaining about French behaviour on the island, together with a refutation of the new French draft treaty and a counter-draft based on his own interpretation of the 1885 Treaty. Le Myre de Vilers replied that the new text was not open to negotiation and that it must be accepted or rejected as it stood by October 26. When the day came and went with no clear answer from the prime minister, the French emissary carried out his threat and withdrew with the French community to the coast, an act tantamount to a declaration of war.

Le Myre de Vilers, a man of some sensitivity and with a genuine affection for Madagascar, clearly found his task distasteful. In a letter to a friend in France,[10] he reported the failure of his mission, "for it is a failure for diplomacy, concerned with preserving peace, to hand over to the military when neither the essential interests of the country nor the national honour are at stake". In this letter and a separate letter to another friend[11] he put the blame for the situation squarely on the Residents who had succeeded him since 1889: "As in all conflicts, there are faults on both sides, but in terms of incorrect behaviour we take the cake (*le pompon nous appartient*)". He concluded: "I accept the inevitable, while regretting that my name is attached to such a bad business".

As both sides prepared for the inevitable war, British friends of Madagascar made a final attempt to persuade the British government to intervene. In February 1895 a letter to the new Liberal prime minister, Lord Rosebery, urged him "to pause before you irrevocably confirm the wicked act of your predecessor in office, Lord Salisbury, in delivering over a true and Christian nation to France, in exchange for an extension of British rights in Zanzibar".[12] But these appeals fell on deaf ears and the French were left undisturbed to continue with their preparations.

At the end of November 1894 the French National Assembly voted (in the face of some opposition from the anti-colonial party, who mustered 135 votes in the Chamber of Deputies against the majority vote of 372) a special credit of 65 million francs for an expedition to Madagascar. General Duchesne was appointed commander-in-chief of the expeditionary force, which was to consist of thirteen battalions of infantry, one cavalry squadron, two batteries of artillery and four companies of engineers plus administrative troops – a total of 658 officers and 14,773 men. The latter figure included 3,800 "native" troops from West Africa and a battalion of Sakalava raised and trained in what was now the French territory of Diego Suarez; but French hopes that the Sakalava in the northwest of Madagascar would rise in support of the invasion force were not fulfilled. The expedition was supported by over 7,000 porters (mainly from North Africa), almost the same number of mules and 5,000 "Lefebvre waggons", mule-drawn carts which indirectly were to prove far more murderous to the French soldiers than Malagasy bullets. The French Navy provided a flotilla of 12 gunboats and 48 barges for river operations, with a supporting naval division of two cruisers, two sloops, three gunboats and three transport ships.

This amounted to a formidable fighting force; and the subsequent ease of the French advance might give the impression that the contest was from the beginning hopelessly unequal. But the forces at the disposal of the Malagasy government were far from negligible.

After general mobilisation had been decreed, it was estimated that the prime minister could dispose of some 45,000 troops. All of these had received at least some training mainly at the hands of British sergeants recruited from Mauritius and British mercenary officers who had had experience in the Zulu wars. Two of the latter, Colonel Shervinton and Major Graves, were re-engaged in 1894 by the prime minister along with a Major Giles. The three officers arrived at Antananarivo in October 1894 and began further intensive training. Early in the following year the missionary Sibree attended a military review and was "astonished to see the perfect order and precision with which the Malagasy executed all the manoeuvres, and the excellent discipline of the large body of men encamped there".[13] As we have seen the prime minister had in recent years purchased substantial quantities of weapons, including repeating rifles and modern artillery; and there was no shortage of ammunition, some of it manufactured locally, using Cameron's old powder factory and a modern cartridge factory with British machinery imported around 1892.[14]

The French expedition was in fact a hazardous affair which in different circumstances might have ended in disaster. The French troops had to advance across some three hundred miles (480 km) of difficult, trackless, unfamiliar[15] and fever-ridden country in the face of well-armed and more numerous Malagasy troops. The individual quality and discipline of the French troops was certainly superior. But the fierce and at times successful resistance put up against European troops in recent years by Matabele and Zulu *impis* armed only with spears showed the danger of underestimating "native" forces; and only a year later an Abyssinian army was to inflict a decisive defeat on the Italians at Adowa.

However the Merina army was much more impressive on paper than in reality. Their weapons were poorly maintained and their organisation and administration incompetent. Their impressive parade-ground technique was not matched by comparable battle training and they had no experience of facing the fire-power of modern rifles and artillery. These weaknesses might have been overcome if the troops had been sustained by high morale and active leadership; but these two essential ingredients of a fighting force were conspicuously lacking. Normal patriotic feelings were eroded by the harsh exactions of the government and the corruption, self-seeking and nepotism of the ruling oligarchy. There could be no spirit of common sacrifice when the better-off could purchase exemption from military service or send slaves in their place; or when a bloody reverse in the field was followed by news that one of the prime minister's grandsons, safe in the capital, had been promoted to 15 honours.

The Malagasy might well have given a much better account of themselves if an experienced officer like Shervinton had been placed in command and given a free hand. But the prime minister was fearful of allowing control to slip from his own hands, and the oligarchy were strongly opposed to the idea of a foreigner winning the glory and the spoils of battle. Finding his advice constantly ignored, Shervinton resigned in despair and left the country with Giles in April 1895 (Graves stayed on for several more months). Competent Malagasy military commanders did exist. There was Rainandriamampandry, the redoubtable defender of Farafaty in the 1883-1885 War; and Prince Ramahatra the hero of the campaign in the southwest in 1889-90. But their very qualities made them suspect to the prime minister who was pathologically jealous of any possible rivals. And so Rainandriamampandry remained inactive at Farafaty; while Prince Ramahatra, although appointed minister of war, was allowed no effective power and pleaded in vain for a command in the field. Instead the prime minister appointed a series of incompetent and for the most part cowardly commanders who owed their positions to court intrigue or bribery. The commanders were further handicapped by the prime minister's parsimony in despatching troops to the front in small batches instead of concentrating all available forces for a major action; and even towards the end of the campaign he was still hoarding modern rifles in Antananarivo and sending troops into battle with "rusty old flintlocks".[16] With such leadership the Malagasy never had a chance.

The campaign began with the bombardment and occupation of Tamatave on December 12, 1894. The defending garrison under Rainandriamampandry withdrew to their defensive position at Farafaty, but after one initial assault which they repelled they were not put under serious pressure. The French had decided wisely not to invade via the usual route to the capital from Tamatave up the steep, thickly-forested escarpment which would have presented a formidable and easily-defended obstacle. Instead they chose the route from the north west where the ascent was more gradual and the open country provided less cover for the defenders. After leaving a garrison at Tamatave the French Admiral Bien-Aimé sailed to Majunga which was occupied on January 14, 1895. The advance guard of the expedition under General Metzinger landed on February 25. With the advance guard he pushed a little way up the Betsiboka river, meeting little resistance from the Merina forward troops, who fled at the first shots. But heavy rain and losses from fever persuaded Metzinger to wait for the end of the rainy season and the arrival of more troops.

At the end of April the advance was resumed towards Marovoay where the Malagasy governor-general, Ramasombazaha, had assembled his main force. The Malagasy troops, attacked both from the land and by gunboats on the Betsiboka, put up some resistance before fleeing, leaving a number of dead and wounded on the field, together with 25 cannon and large quantities of ammunition and supplies. Rajestera, a middle-ranking officer (10 honours) who kept a diary of the campaign, alleged that Ramasombazaha and other Merina officers fled in civilian clothes.[17] After the battle, Marovoay ("many crocodiles") lived up to its name when hundreds of crocodiles appeared on the battlefield to drag corpses and wounded men into the river. Shortly afterwards 2,000 Malagasy reinforcements sent from Antananarivo under the command of Andriantavy made a courageous attack on the advancing French troops but retreated after losing 60 dead. They joined up with the remnants of Ramasombazaha's force, but the troops were so demoralised that the clatter of a metal bucket dropped by a servant-girl in the middle of the night caused them to flee in all directions.[18] They reassembled at Maevatanana, where a fortress on a strong, natural position dominated the small town of Suberbieville on the Ikopa river. The French appeared on June 9 and opened fire with their artillery. The Malagasy artillery replied, but a direct hit on one of their guns caused a general panic and abandonment of the fort with five cannons and much baggage and ammunition.

So far the French had suffered few battle casualties, and such Malagasy resistance as they had encountered had not seriously delayed them. But already their strength had been seriously depleted by deaths and sickness from malaria and dysentery. And their advance was delayed by problems of supply as they progressed inland across trackless, fever-ridden and barren regions which offered no shade and no possibility of living off the country. The decision to use Lefebvre waggons rather than pack-mules or human porters meant that a road had to be built. The consequent hard labour under the hot sun greatly increased the suffering, sickness and mortality and seriously held up the advance.

The French commander-in-chief General Duchesne, who had arrived in Majunga early in May, now set up his headquarters at Suberbieville and began organising his transport and supplies for a further advance as the arduous road-building slowly proceeded. Meanwhile, reports of the incompetence and cowardice of Ramasombazaha had already decided the prime minister to replace him. The new commander, Rainianjalahy, arrived at the front on June 13 with 5,000 reinforcements. He was capable and energetic, though lacking in military experience[19] and two weeks later he directed the most serious counter-attack of the whole campaign. A French advance guard of 200 soldiers entrenched at Tsarasaotra was attacked three times on June 28 and 29 by some 5,000 Malagasy soldiers; but the fire-power of repeating rifles from entrenched positions together with some well-timed bayonet charges drove the Malagasy back and they finally retreated leaving 200 dead on the field. An artillery attack the next day completed the Malagasy rout. This was perhaps the decisive battle of the campaign which shattered Malagasy morale by showing that even when relatively well-led and in greatly superior numbers they could not withstand the disciplined fire-power of the French troops.

Rainianjalahy retreated to Andriba, only 100 miles (160 km) north of the capital, where the route of the French advance was barred by a mountain rising nearly 3,000 feet (900 m) from the plain and flanked by lesser hills. Major Graves, who had been training artillery cadets at Antananarivo, was promoted colonel and sent forward to organise the fortification of this immensely strong position and to take personal command of the artillery. On the steep slopes overlooking the approach route, which was devoid of any cover, he constructed a series of inter-locking entrenched forts supported by twenty pieces of artillery, more than half of them modern Hotchkiss guns with a range of two miles (3 km). This position should have been impregnable against a much stronger force than Duchesne's, now greatly reduced and enfeebled by sickness. When the French finally appeared on August 21, their initial infantry attack was checked. Artillery was then brought up and an artillery duel continued for several hours in the late afternoon. Next morning when the French troops again advanced they were astonished to find all the forts abandoned. Demoralised by the shrapnel and melinite shells, the defenders of one fort after another had fled until a general panic set in.

The road to the capital was now open. General Duchesne had already decided that his previous rate of advance, at the pace of the road-building, would not get him to the capital before the onset of the rains. He accordingly constituted a small flying column to carry out the final assault on Antananarivo, consisting of those troops still reasonably fit – some 4,000 – with 12 mountain howitzers and 22 days' supplies carried by porters and mules. They set off on September 14 to cover the last 100 miles (160 km) from Andriba. At first sight this was a highly risky operation in the face of a vastly more numerous enemy, whose resistance could be expected to stiffen as the capital was approached. But with the low state of Malagasy morale confirmed by the abandoning of Andriba, Duchesne correctly judged that the gamble was justified.

The French conquest

The last stages of the campaign and the assault on Antananarivo are better documented than most similar colonial operations, owing to the presence in the capital of many British missionaries as well as Knight of *The Times* and Bennet Burleigh of *The Daily Telegraph* (the two journalists had been refused permission to visit the front). In their reports to their newspapers and in their subsequent books, the journalists recorded the gradual crumbling of the old prime minister's authority and the growing despair of the queen as the army's inability to stop the French slowly became clear. As early as May, placards had been put up by the pro-French party calling on the people to put the queen, the prime minister and their families to death. Robberies increased in the countryside and in the capital. As the French steadily advanced there were outbursts of anti-European feeling. The "perfidious English", and especially the missionaries, were accused of having promised assistance and encouraged the Malagasy to resist the French and then left them in the lurch. Knight was critical of the missionaries for endangering the lives of their families by insisting on staying on to continue their work. He was also critical of the editor of the *Madagascar News* who was violently anti-French and who encouraged the Malagasy in what Knight regarded as a futile resistance by publishing wildly exaggerated reports of Malagasy victories.

The mood in Antananarivo alternated between panic and confidence. Panic followed the news that the impregnable fortress of Andriba had been abandoned. But the French pause of three weeks restored confidence, since at the previous rate of advance there seemed no prospect of their reaching the capital before the rains. Then news came that the advance had been resumed and on September 21 fugitive peasants announced that the French were only 30 miles (48 km) away. Preparations for the defence of the capital, including plans to flood the rice-fields, were intensified, and large numbers of rifles distributed. A few Europeans, including the editor of the *Madagascar News*, left for the coasts, and the missionaries and their families took refuge in the mission hospital to the northeast of the city. After a further French advance the queen addressed the assembled people on September 25, concluding: "Are there no men among you who will fight? As for me, I am but a woman; but I would far rather die in my palace than yield to the French." And the great crowd shouted with one voice: "We will fight for our queen and our country until we are all killed."[20] The next morning the booming of cannon was heard for the first time. Around midday, rumours of a Malagasy victory produced an extraordinary commotion, vividly described by Knight: [21]

"Thousands of men of all ages – Hovas, Betsileo, and savage

tribesmen from remote portions of the island – armed with guns, spears, swords and knives, frantically excited, waving their weapons, shrieking, fantastically dancing and gesticulating, rushed up the street in a continuous stream towards the palace. On looking beyond the city I saw that every track leading from the country was crowded with people, sinuous white streams of lamba-clad peasants pouring in from all directions. Then in every quarter of the city there rose above the shouting of the men a huge volume of sound – the *mirary* war-song, sung with fierce energy by many hundreds of groups of women ... And now once more we heard the booming of cannon in the west, and all the people howled in derision at the sound ... The excitement and noise of triumphant song and shouting continued until nearly dusk, when a sudden stillness fell upon the city."

The truth had leaked out. There was no victory, in fact the French had advanced all day and were now at the sacred village of Ambohidratrimo only ten miles (16 km) away.

On Sunday September 27, while the French column rested, Malagasy troops were busy posting cannon and throwing up barricades on the approaches to the city. Women and children and slaves carrying their masters' property streamed out in panic to the south and east. Colonel Graves, finding his offers of assistance ignored by the prime minister, left for the coast to return to England. The next day the French turned off the direct road, which would have led them across the rice-fields, and moved east to camp near Ambohimanga. On September 29 they advanced steadily southwards to within a few miles of the capital, despite increasingly stubborn resistance, especially from the artillery cadets, and attacks on their baggage-train in the rear by a large Malagasy force coming from the north.

The final assault took place on September 30, witnessed by the missionaries from the hospital and by the journalists and other British residents from the British consulate on the hill of Faravohitra which gave them a panoramic view of the battlefield. They saw the French troops lined up on a ridge three miles (5 km) to the north, with a nearer range covered with Malagasy troops, perhaps 10,000 with several guns. The northern slopes of the town itself and the hills for miles around were white with *lambas*; altogether, including carriers and non-combatants, 100,000 must have been visible to the small French force. After exchanging fire at a distance for some time the French advanced in skirmishing order on the nearer ridge. There was a great deal of firing and the French seemed on the point of taking the ridge when their firing ceased. The Malagasy shouted joyously, thinking that they had won a victory, when suddenly firing broke out to the east of the city. The frontal assault had been merely a cover for a main flanking attack which seized the Observatory hill less than a mile to the east of the queen's palace. The remaining heights to the north and east were soon occupied so that only the ring of rice-fields stood between the French and the great rock of Antananarivo. A few accurate shells falling in the palace courtyard, killing many of the soldiers who were congregated there, caused the queen to order the white flag to be hoisted over the palace. Three emissaries under a white flag conveyed the formal surrender to General Duchesne, and French troops occupied the city before nightfall. The military casualties of the whole French campaign were surprisingly slight – only 20 dead and 100 wounded. But the deaths from disease, nearly 6,000, or almost one in three, made it the most costly of all French colonial campaigns. "General Tazo" had indeed proved Madagascar's best defender, but he was greatly helped by the French General Staff's insistence on the use of the Lefebvre waggons, which were inevitably dubbed *"les wagons la fièvre"*.

On October 1, 1895 General Duchesne made his formal entry into Antananarivo and signed with the queen's representatives a treaty imposing a French protectorate. Under the treaty the French Resident-General was to control internal as well as external affairs and the French had the right to station in Madagascar whatever forces they deemed necessary. The queen remained on the throne, and the first intention was to rule indirectly through Malagasy ministers. But Rainilaiarivony was dismissed as prime minister and confined under house arrest in his country home just outside the capital (shortly afterwards he was exiled to Algiers, where he died in July 1896). He was replaced by an elderly, stout official, Rainitsimbazafy (the son of Rainijohary, the last of Queen Ranavalona I's lovers) who had been in charge of the Foreign Ministry. The queen enquired anxiously whether she would have to marry him and was greatly relieved when General Duchesne told her that she was free to marry whom she pleased. Rainandriamampandry, the respected defender of Farafaty, was made Minister of the Interior. The British missionaries, who were understandably anxious about their future, were received courteously by General Duchesne and told they could continue their work; and chapels and schools were able to re-open after only one week's interruption. But the teaching of English was to be prohibited and the missionaries had to learn to teach French.

A brief period of calm ensued, with the population seemingly stunned by the shock of their defeat by such a small force. But the French soon faced serious difficulties from uprisings in various parts of the country. On November 22, 1895, a large band of rebels attacked Arivonimamo, 25 miles (40 km) west of the capital, and killed the Merina district governor and a Quaker missionary William Johnson together with his wife and daughter. Their motives were xenophobic and anti-Christian coupled with a desire to return to ancestral traditions. Believing themselves protected by sorcerers' charms they resisted fiercely the French troops sent against them and were dispersed only after losing 150 dead. On the east coast the people seized the opportunity to rebel against Merina rule, and many Merina officials and their families were killed before the French were able to restore order. By deciding to rule indirectly through the existing Merina administration the French had placed themselves in the impossible situation of supporting a régime which, outside Imerina, was highly unpopular.

With order apparently restored the French proceeded to recall the Military Governor Duchesne and to appoint a civilian Resident-General, Laroche, who arrived in January 1896. Laroche appears to have been honest and well-meaning, but he had no previous colonial experience and proved incapable of dealing with the grave situation which soon faced him. For a short time the rains inhibited hostile activity. But when the rains ended at the end of March, rebellion broke out on the northern and southern frontiers of Imerina. For a time Laroche tried to maintain that the disorder was merely an upsurge of *fahavalo* banditry without political significance. But it soon became apparent that he was faced with a major nationalist uprising aimed at driving out the foreign invader, destroying the foreigners' religion and restoring Malagasy rule and ancient practices. Its leaders were two district governors, Rabezavana in the north, Rabozaka in the northeast and a farmer turned outlaw, Rainibetsimisaraka, in the south of Imerina; and they may well have received some encouragement and support from high-ranking Merina officials in the capital, though this was never conclusively proved. The rebels acquired the name *menalamba* ("red *lamba*" or toga) from their distinctive dress.[22] Repressive measures by the French occupation force, including burning of villages and destruction of rice-fields, merely swelled the ranks of the rebels with those who had lost their homes and crops. By the middle of 1896 they controlled most of the central province. Antananarivo was a besieged city where night after night the horizon was ablaze with the flames of burning villages and churches.

As the rebellion grew, its character changed in response to the severity of French oppressive measures and the attempts of Jesuit missionaries and Malagasy Catholics to exploit the French invasion by taking over Protestant churches. From being generally xeno-

The French conquest

phobic and anti-Christian it acquired a more normal nationalist and anti-French character, with Malagasy Catholics seen increasingly as pro-French and the British-trained Protestants, instead of being one of the main targets, becoming in some cases the allies of the *menalamba* against the French. All this widened and exacerbated existing divisions between Catholics and Protestants which were to continue throughout the colonial period, with the Merina Protestants providing the main nationalist opposition to the French.

In Paris the rebellion strengthened the hand of those who thought that the protectorate treaty provided inadequate control and who advocated full annexation. On August 6, 1896 the French Parliament (with 77 dissenting votes) formally declared the annexation of Madagascar as a French colony. As a logical consequence of this formal incorporation of Madagascar as a French colony, the Parliament went on to decree the abolition of slavery in Madagascar. The promulgation of this decree was almost the last act of Laroche in Antananarivo, and it was left to his successor to deal with the considerable social upheaval which resulted.

At the end of September Laroche was replaced by a "strong man", General Gallieni, who assumed both military and civil powers. In the English-speaking world Gallieni is remembered for his decisive intervention in the Battle of the Marne when, as military governor of Paris, he put all available troops in the capital into taxicabs and deployed them on the unprotected right flank of the advancing Germans. But in France his fame rests on his achievements as perhaps the ablest of all French colonial administrators. After earning a high reputation in French Sudan and Tonkin, he was to leave an indelible mark on Madagascar during nine years' rule.

Gallieni's task was to crush the rebellion and then to make Madagascar French (*"franciser Madagascar"*). Two subsidiary but related aims were to humble Merina pride and power and to undermine the influence of the British. [23] The desperate military situation called for immediate stern measures. On October 10, the day after Laroche's departure, the Minister of the Interior, Rainandriamampandry, and an uncle of the queen, Prince Ratsimamanga, were arrested on a charge of complicity with the rebels. After a summary military trial conducted in French which the accused did not understand, and with the defence entrusted to the French intelligence officer who had produced the "evidence", they were condemned to death. An appeal was rejected in equally summary fashion and they were executed by firing squad early on the following morning, October 15. Even at the time the evidence looked flimsy and the manner of the trial aroused criticism in France. It has subsequently been established beyond doubt that the executions were a political act *"pour décourager les autres"*, decided on by Gallieni even before his arrival in Madagascar.[24] A Protestant and allegedly Francophobe aunt of the queen was exiled and Rainitsimbazafy replaced as prime minister by Rasanjy, an enemy of the queen and leader of the pro-French group.[25]

The humbling of the Merina had already been carried a stage further by the act of annexation which in effect deprived the queen of her position as queen of Madagascar and reduced her to the status of queen of the Merina with not even formal authority over the rest of the country. Gallieni rubbed home the point that she was now a subject of France by insisting that she should pay the first formal call on him rather than *vice versa*. But for the time being he thought that his purposes would best be served by keeping her on the throne and making use of her prestige to weaken the rebellion. And so while French authority was gradually extended through an expanding ring of military posts, the queen dutifully made speeches calling on the people to lay down their arms and accept French rule. But these appeals had little effect and the rebellion continued to rage outside areas under the immediate control of French troops. Gallieni concluded that as long as the monarchy existed it would serve as a rallying-point for opposition to the French. On February 28, 1897 the people of Imerina were informed that the monarchy was abolished and that Queen Ranavalona III was already on her way to exile in Réunion.[26] At the same time the abolition of the post of prime minister (Rasanjy becoming governor-general of Imerina) made it clear that the policy of indirect rule was at an end. Gallieni assumed full powers as governor-general of Madagascar.

As Gallieni had foreseen, the disappearance of the monarchy took the heart out of the rebellion in Imerina, assisted by Gallieni's prohibition of punitive measures against villages. The gradual imposition of an orderly administration also had its effect. Within a few months two of the rebel leaders, Rabezavana and Rainibetsimisaraka, had surrendered; Rabozaka held out until early 1898. In the outer provinces the destruction of Merina authority assisted the collapse of the rebellion. By the end of 1897 Gallieni, backed by a mere 7,000 troops, only 1500 of them European, was master of virtually all those parts of the island which had formerly been controlled by the Merina government.

Rather surprisingly the rebel leaders were not executed or even imprisoned, merely exiled and later amnestied.[27] There was advantage to Gallieni in appearing magnanimous once the back of the rebellion was broken. But we also know that the leaders were promised lenient treatment if they provided faked evidence that they had acted under orders from Rainandriamampandry and

The French conquest

Prince Ratsimamanga.[28] This retrospective "proof" that the executed men had been the real leaders of the rebellion was designed to counter criticism in Paris of their trial. One effect was to elevate the status of Rainandriamampandry in particular as a martyr of Malagasy nationalism, and his memory was to be one of the inspirations of later anti-colonial movements. It was perhaps poetic justice when in the 1970s the name of Rue Gallieni in Antananarivo was changed to Lalana Rainandriamampandry.

Other rebels who surrendered were similarly persuaded to provide "evidence" of British involvement in the rebellion. The idea that the British, and especially their missionaries, might be encouraging an anti-European and anti-Christian revolt whose first victims were British missionaries can now be seen as absurd. But it did not seem so to the French government at a time of intense colonial rivalry with the British, culminating in the confrontation between Marchand and Kitchener at Fashoda in 1898. It was also easy for the French in Antananarivo to accept, as they believed that the LMS missionaries continued to exert a malign political influence in support of the Merina and against the French. The extent to which the missionaries consciously sought to exercise political influence is difficult to establish, but was certainly exaggerated by the French. Knight, who confessed to a prejudice against Nonconformist missionaries, grudgingly admitted that, at least during his stay in the capital, they all "scrupulously avoided any meddling in political matters".[29] Although this may not have been so in earlier years, by 1895 most of the missionaries were reconciled to a French protectorate and were anxious to adjust to the new situation. But inevitably their personal sympathies lay with their friends in the Merina court and government and they were apprehensive that the French occupation would lead to their eclipse by Catholic missions. Gallieni soon came to accept that the attitude of the missionaries, at least in the capital, was "correct"; the trouble was that the rebels themselves continued to believe that they could count on British support, and they were encouraged in this belief by Malagasy pastors. Moreover, as long as most of the schools and churches were in the hands of the British, the Merina would tend to believe that the French occupation was only temporary.

Laroche, a Protestant, had been well-disposed to the LMS, and during his time as Resident, some French Protestant missionaries arrived with a view to working with rather than replacing the British. But Gallieni immediately adopted a hostile attitude. One of his first acts was to expropriate the Mission hospital for use as a military hospital. A few months later he took over the LMS College to be used as law courts,[30] and the Boys' High School for government offices. Compensation was in due course paid, but only to the amount of half the value of the buildings and the land. Gallieni no doubt hoped that the loss of their main buildings would persuade the LMS to pack up and go. A number of individual missionaries did decide to leave; and in March 1897 the LMS concluded an agreement with the leading French Protestant mission, the Paris Missionary Society, handing over to the latter control of all LMS elementary schools.[31] At the end of that year the LMS agreed to hand over to the Paris Society two large churches in the capital and 500 village congregations. But this still left the LMS with 700 congregations to supervise, and Sibree and other missionaries stayed on, retaining control *inter alia* of the Martyr Memorial Churches.[32] And after a few years they were able to erect new buildings for a college to train pastors and a boys' high school.

While Gallieni was engaged in putting down the rebellion, some Jesuit missionaries, supported and often instigated by Malagasy Catholics seeking to strengthen their own position, seized the opportunity to try to crush Protestantism. They went around the villages telling the people that as Roman Catholicism was the French religion, all Malagasy who wished to be considered loyal to France must become Roman Catholic. In many places, and especially in Betsileo, they accused the pastor and leading Protestants of disloyalty and had them arrested and in some cases shot. They also seized many Protestant churches. However the arrival of French Protestant missionaries exposed the Jesuit deception. And when Gallieni, a staunch anti-clerical, heard about the Jesuit activities, he ordered the churches to be restored to the Protestants and made it clear that the Malagasy were entirely free to choose between the different versions of the Christian religion. In due course Gallieni came to appreciate the achievements of the LMS and spoke warmly of their educational and medical work. He became friendly with a number of the missionaries, two of whom, Sibree and Baron, were nominated among the first members of the *Académie Malgache* which he founded in 1902; and when he finally left, the missionaries sincerely regretted his departure.

Having established French authority in the areas formerly under the control of the Merina monarchy, Gallieni was faced with the task of subduing the substantial regions where the Merina writ had never run – parts of the southeast, nearly all the south, and large parts of the Sakalava regions in the west. The difficulties of the terrain, the fierce independence of the inhabitants and the barrenness of many areas were formidable obstacles which it took a number of years to overcome. Gallieni favoured a policy of peaceful penetration – *"la tache d'huile"* by which a nucleus of orderly administration represented by a military post was gradually extended into the surrounding countryside. Colonel Lyautey, the future Resident-General of Morocco, was Gallieni's main instrument in bringing this about in the south. But in many places there was initial armed resistance and subsequent rebellion causing the loss of many lives before "pacification" was finally completed.

The southern Sakalava region of Menabe, which had proved so resistant to Merina conquest, was the scene of some fierce fighting and of one appalling incident when a column of French troops massacred the whole population of the large village of Ambiki which had apparently been preparing to welcome them.[33] Most of the chiefs in the area had made their submission by 1900, but one chief held out until 1904. The Bara region was also subdued by 1900. The thorny scrub regions of the Antandroy and the Mahafaly in the extreme south were penetrated more slowly, usually by relatively peaceful means. One effective method was to occupy water-holes, thus compelling the submission of the cattle-owning tribesmen. An uprising took place in 1903 and a particularly widespread revolt in 1904 but thereafter French authority was uncontested (although inter-tribal fighting continued sporadically for several decades). The forested escarpment area in the southeast was especially favourable to guerrilla resistance and was the scene of a serious revolt in 1904 which took a year to subdue. When Gallieni left in 1905 the "pacification" was complete and he had united the island under one administration for the first time in its history; but at a cost of many Malagasy lives.[34]

During his nine years' rule Gallieni established the framework of the colonial administration, dividing the country into provinces (to the number of twenty), districts and cantons. He retained the hierarchy of Malagasy officials established under the monarchy, headed by governors and deputy governors, but with French officials placed above the Malagasy at the higher levels; the French *chef de district* was to become the key element in the administration. Within Imerina an attempt was made to revitalise the *fokonolona* as the basic unit, corresponding to the clans elsewhere, but with reduced legal powers their importance continued to decline. For the administration of the other provinces, Gallieni adopted "*la politique des races*", under which each ethnic group was administered separately and through its own chiefs. As far as possible the administrative divisions were made to correspond with ethnic groups, usually one province for each group; the larger groups such as the Merina and Sakalava were divided into several provinces while smaller groups, principally in the south east, were included in one province, within which the districts were made to correspond with ethnic boundaries. This policy had some obvious good points and was no doubt preferred by the local people to the alternative of administration through Merina officials. For the French it had the political advantage of dissociating them from the unpopular Merina administration. But there was also a strong element of "divide and rule" in more or less conscious imitation of the successful British policy in India and elsewhere.

To meet the serious problem of the shortage of educated *côtiers* to fill the provincial administrative posts Gallieni set up "administrative sections" in the three regional schools, respectively for the plateau (*l'école Le Myre de Vilers*), the east coast and the west coast. As we shall see, the coastal schools were later closed for economy reasons and the administration had once more to rely mainly on Merina officials. Gallieni himself, after his initial hostility to the Merina, came to appreciate their qualities; and he contributed to their continuing predominance by adopting the Merina dialect as the official language of the administration alongside French.

Following a policy of evolution, Gallieni decided that Malagasy law based on the 1881 Code (with some of its severity diminished) should continue to apply to the Malagasy; but a separate system of justice, based on the French penal code, was introduced for Europeans. The medical services operated by the missionaries on the plateau were greatly expanded by the French authorities and extended to other parts of the country. State schools were also set up, but Church schools continued to provide the great bulk of the available education, especially at the primary level. Education was given a strong practical bias, with gardens and workshops at the primary schools to train farmers and mechanics; and secondary education was limited to what was necessary to train officials and doctors. A School of Medicine set up in Antananarivo in 1896 attracted many of the brighter young Merina as offering the best hope of a career under the colonial régime, although the diplomas qualified them only as medical assistants, subordinate to doctors with metropolitan degrees.

The establishment of law and order throughout the country and the extension of medical services and education were of undoubted benefit to the whole people. Less welcome, and of more dubious benefit to the country, was the setting up of a colonialist economy, by which imports were virtually reserved to France and cheaper goods from other sources were excluded by high tariffs. Before the conquest most imported goods came from Britain or America (British exports to Madagascar were of the order of £1 million a year, in real value about ten times as much as British exports in the 1980s); many of these, and especially textiles which were the most important item, were much cheaper than the French alternative. The resultant higher prices for imports, at a time when lower prices were being paid for local products, caused hardship among those Malagasy engaged in the monetary economy. Also unpopular were the substantial grants of farming land to French *colons*, originally demobilised soldiers, later mainly immigrants from Réunion. Very large concessions were also granted to major French companies, in the hope of encouraging substantial investment to develop the country's economy. Private investment was to prove disappointing, and some of the larger concessions were later revoked or reduced. But public investment under Gallieni developed modern port facilities, extended the telegraphic services, initiated a postal service, built roads, especially a road from Antananarivo to Tamatave, and started work on the first railway which was also to link the capital with the main port.

All these public works and the running of the administration required a substantial budget, but unfortunately a French parliamentary decree in 1900 insisting that the colonies should be self-sufficient led to the tailing-off of subsidies from the metropolis. Gallieni raised loans in France for the railway but otherwise had to rely on the island's resources. Receipts from customs duties, which had been the main revenue source under the monarchy, declined sharply with the customs union between France and Madagascar and the near monopoly of import and export trade by France. In the early years taxation in kind in the form of *prestations* or compulsory labour for all male Malagasy aged between 16 and 60 was used to minimise the cost of construction works. However the unfairness of the system under which exemptions could be bought and the abuse of exemptions granted to those working for French settlers led to the abolition of *prestations* in 1901 and thereafter the government had to resort to increased monetary taxation. Taxes were levied on rice-fields, livestock and markets but the principal source of revenue was the personal tax. Although this varied according to the resources of the different regions and the average amount levied was small in European terms (about 25 Francs a year) it was nevertheless a considerable burden on the many people who lived virtually outside the monetary economy. Like other colonial administrators, Gallieni defended the personal tax as a motivating force for modernising the economy by persuading subsistence farmers to take up salaried employment or develop crops for marketing or export. It was certainly an element in later migrations of workers to the towns and to the French-owned plantations and in increasing Malagasy involvement in growing cash crops. And it was in Gallieni's time that French companies and planters introduced or developed most of the crops, such as robusta coffee (after the failure of arabica), vanilla and cloves, which were to be the staple of the future export industry.

Gallieni thus occupies an important place in Malagasy history. By unifying the whole island for the first time, and by establishing the administrative and economic framework of a modern state, he laid the foundations not only of the French colony but also of the Malagasy Republic which gained, or rather recovered, its independence in 1960. But it is not forgotten in Madagascar that his *"politique des races"* was designed partly to perpetuate ethnic divisions and to hinder the growth of a sense of Malagasy nationality. Certain of his actions in crushing the *menalamba* rebellion and imposing "pacification" on the whole country aroused criticism in France, as did his enthusiasm for large-scale public works carried out in the initial years by forced labour, and he left Madagascar under something of a cloud.[35] But judging him in the context of his times and in the perspective of history, his total achievement was remarkable.

A Malagasy people, united by language and a common culture, had existed for many centuries. Gallieni was the first to establish a unified Malagasy state. But it was opposition to French colonial rule which was to create a Malagasy nation.

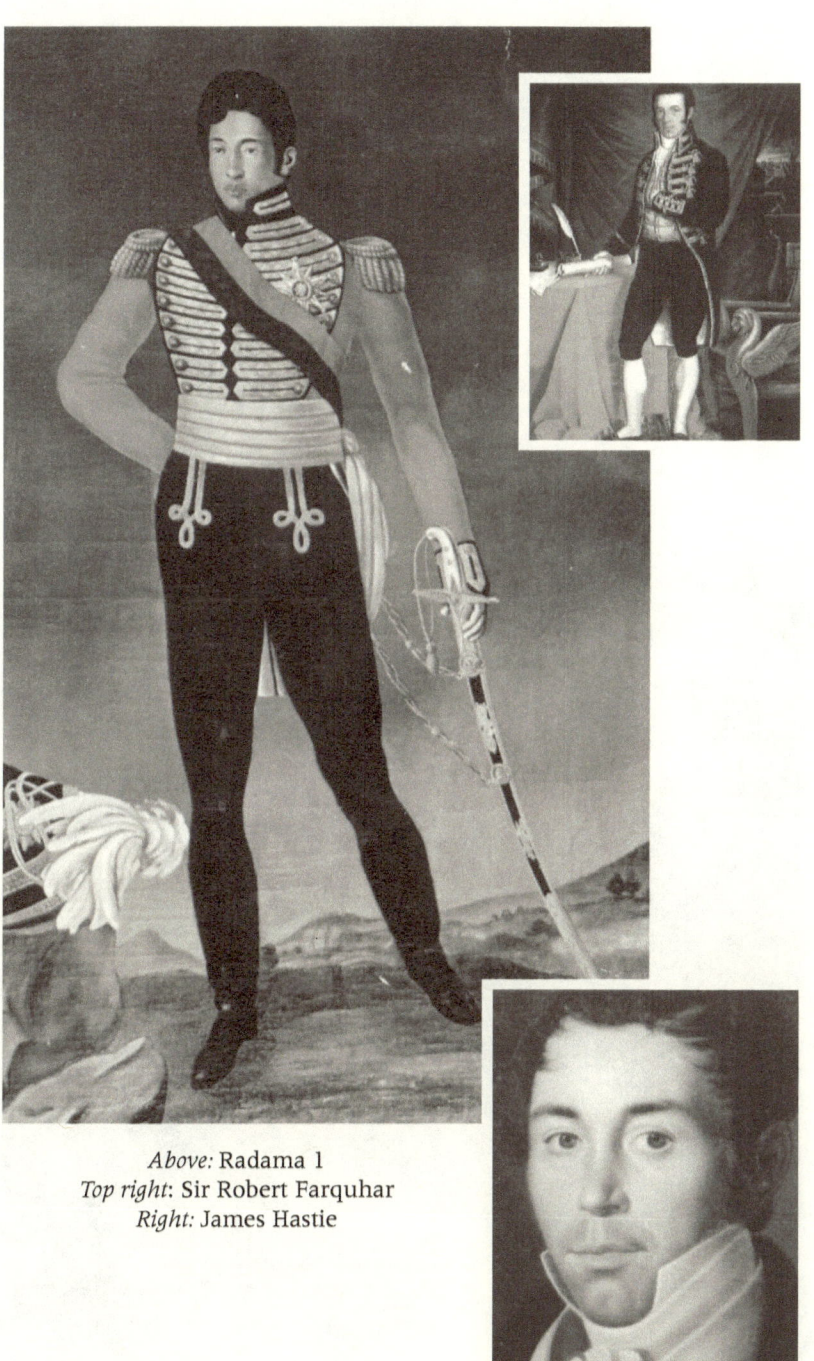

Above: Radama 1
Top right: Sir Robert Farquhar
Right: James Hastie

Audience at the palace, 1856, from a sketch by W. Ellis

Above: Rev. David Jones
Top right: James Cameron
Right: Rev. William Ellis

Above Prince Rakoto (Radama II) and Princess Rabodo (Rasoherina)
Below Queen Ranavalona II

Rainilaiarivony, Prime Minister from 1864 to 1895
Inset: Queen Ranavalona III

Above: Iron smelting, 1860s
Below: Street scene in Toamasina (Tamatave), 1860s

Above: The Queen's Palace and cannons defending Antananarivo. (c. 1865) Note the 'Place of the Hurling' to the right.
Left: The same view with Cameron's stone towers and outer walls added to the Queen's Palace. Note the Martyrs' Memorial Church and other churches.

Above: Convicts in chains (c. 1880)
Below: Garden party in Antananarivo attended by Queen Ranavalona III

Above: Queen Ranavalona III holding a *kabary* in the square
at Andohalo, Antananarivo
Below: James Sibree with Malagasy teaching staff and their wives
at the LMS College c. 1895

Above: General Gallieni
Below: Rainandriamampandry being taken to be executed

Above: Queen Ranavalona III on a *filanzana*,
escorted by French officers, 1896
Below: The execution of Rainandriamampandry

Above: Leon Cayla, Governor-General of Madagascar
1930–1939 and 1940–1941
Below: The remains of Queen Ranavalona III reburied
at the Queen's Palace, Antananarivo, October 1938

Above: The 1947 rebellion. French troops on patrol
Below: The 1947 rebellion. French soldiers interrogate a Malagasy prisoner

Above: President Tsiranana
Below: De Gaulle in Madagascar, 1958

Above: May 18, 1972. Students and workers celebrate the fall of Tsiranana
Below: General Ramanantsoa faces the crowds of demonstrators,
May 1972

President Ratsiraka when he was foreign minister, 1972

PART 5   MADAGASCAR
IN THE MODERN WORLD

Chapter 17

Colonial rule and nationalism

After the traumatic years of conquest, rebellion and pacification under Gallieni, Madagascar settled down to a more peaceful existence as a French colony. For more than half a century the lives of the people were to be governed by policies which, with certain adjustments to local conditions, were decided in their broad outlines in the metropolitan capital, influenced by French domestic politics and at times by the personality of the colony's governor. As with other colonies, much of the story is a humdrum affair of public works, economic development and administrative progress and reform, interrupted from time to time by calls for retrenchment and economy and by the impact of external events. Gallieni's vision and achievements cast a long shadow, and the administrative and economic framework he established lasted remarkably well over the years. His successors were of lesser stature, capable and honest administrators who made their contribution to economic and social progress to the best of their ability and within the limits of the resources available to them. But like most of their contemporaries they lacked the foresight and imagination to respond constructively to the development of nationalist opposition to the colonial régime, if indeed they had been allowed to by the metropolitan authorities. In Madagascar, owing no doubt to the recent experience of relatively sophisticated statehood and the comparatively advanced state of education, such opposition declared itself rather earlier than in the French colonies of black Africa.

As with Britain, the acquisition of a colonial empire faced France with the clear contradiction between her commitment to liberty, equality and fraternity and the maintenance of dominion over subject peoples. In Britain, where there was a long and respectable anti-imperial tradition going back to the loss of the American colonies, the underlying guilt was probably stronger; and the contradiction was at least theoretically resolved in due course by a commitment, however long-term, to prepare the people of the colonial territories for eventual independence. In France the strong centralist tradition and a fervent belief in the civilising power of French culture favoured a policy of assimilation of colonial peoples as extensions of metropolitan France. Assimilation had an undeniable appeal to the intellectuals who were the natural leaders of nationalist sentiment. But it was opposed by French settlers and traders (just as British settlers and business interests opposed eventual independence) who saw it as a threat to their privileged position. Partly for this reason, in Madagascar the policy of assimilation was applied in a confused and half-hearted way, always too little and too late to satisfy Malagasy aspirations.

Gallieni's immediate successor, Victor Augagneur, had no previous colonial experience, being a doctor by profession, a former Deputy and Mayor of Lyons. A typical intellectual of the Third Republic, anti-clerical and anti-military, he came out to Madagascar with generally liberal views and a policy of conciliation and healing the wounds of the conquest. He set about liquidating the remaining military posts which retained administrative functions in certain areas and bringing them under civilian authority. He took steps to limit the abuse of compulsory labour which had continued in various forms after the abolition of *prestations*, partly through levies imposed on the *fokonolona* and partly through the Labour Offices which had been set up to recruit workers for French-owned plantations. The Labour Offices were suppressed and *prestations* were re-introduced but limited to a not unreasonable ten days a year instead of the fifty days required under Gallieni. Maximum sentences under the laws applicable to the Malagasy were reduced, and arbitration courts set up in an attempt to limit exploitation of Malagasy workers by their French employers. All this naturally earned him the hostility of the French settlers, but he declined to court easy popularity with his own countrymen and ignored their vociferous protests.

Augagneur's most innovative measure was a decree of 3 March 1909, permitting a small number of French-speaking Malagasy with certain qualifications to become French citizens. As a firm believer in France's *mission civilisatrice* he gave some encouragement to secondary education, at least in the plateau area. But owing to his anti-clerical views, which were shared by the government which appointed him, the main impact of his policies was to retard educational advancement. He came out determined to enforce in

Madagascar the separation of Church and State which had recently been decreed in France. One of his first acts was to prohibit any teaching in churches. Since in nineteen out of twenty cases the church was also the school-house and few villages could afford to build a separate school-house, this measure put an end to teaching in the great majority of villages and there was a dramatic fall in the number of children attending school. It was not until 1930 that the school population had recovered to approximately the level reached before the colonial occupation.[1] He also closed down the Young Men's Christian Association (YMCA) which had been set up in Gallieni's time by a young Protestant pastor Ravelojaona. For a different reason, budgetary economy, Augagneur closed the *écoles normales* which Gallieni had established in the main provincial centres. This left the *Ecole Le Myre de Vilers* in the capital as the only training school for Malagasy officials, thus giving the plateau a further advantage over the under-privileged coast. It was the low state of education in the coastal areas which led the administration gradually to abandon "*la politique des races*" and to appoint Merina officials to posts in the provinces.

Thus, despite considerable abilities and energy and good intentions, Augagneur's achievements by the time he left in 1910 were decidedly mixed. The colonial lobby in Paris ensured that his wish to return for a further tour was not granted, and he was transferred to French Equatorial Africa.

After these difficult experiences with a politician as governor-general, Paris henceforward played safe and appointed experienced colonial officers, starting with Albert Picquié, an inspector-general of colonies. He avoided controversial policies, restored good relations with the *colons* and devoted himself to sound administration and public works projects. In his time the last army officers occupying administrative posts were replaced by civilians. Relations between Church and State were satisfactorily regulated; and wasteful competition between the various missions was reduced by a decree limiting the number of churches each confession could have in a given area. The railway from the capital to Tamatave was completed and the main road to the south, which had previously reached Antsirabe, was extended to Fianarantsoa. Perhaps Picquié's main claim to fame was his decision to develop Antsirabe as a most agreeable spa town, "the Vichy of the Indian Ocean".

On Picquié's departure in 1914 his secretary-general Hubert Garbit took over as acting governor-general and, because of the outbreak of war in Europe, remained in this position for three years. He knew Madagascar well, having served as an artillery officer in the 1895 campaign and later as Augagneur's *chef de cabinet militaire*.

His first task was to mobilise the island's resources in support of the metropolitan war effort. Over 40,000 Malagasy were enlisted into the French army, most of them as combatants, and nearly one in ten died in the trenches. Malagasy troops distinguished themselves particularly in 1918, both during the German March offensive and the final victorious Allied advance. Their several citations for valour were a proof of their courage under good leadership and helped to efface the dismal record of 1895.

The demands of the war provided a stimulus to the economy as large quantities of rice, beef, leather, graphite and other materials were shipped to France. A considerable boost was given in particular to the production of graphite, which had started in Tamatave province in 1907 and expanded from 1912 when the British Morgan Crucible Company became involved. However the priority given to supplying France and the disruption of supplies from abroad led to shortages of food and imported items and consequent price inflation. Banknotes were issued for the first time instead of the higher-value coins; and the inability of France to provide sufficient smaller coins led to the temporary use of postage stamps stuck on pieces of cardboard for the smaller denominations. But a proposal to set up a separate issuing bank was successfully opposed by the *colons*, who were hostile to any sign of a reduction of Madagascar's total administrative dependence on France.

Garbit's governorship saw the first stirrings of nationalist opposition since the completion of the "pacification". This opposition appeared, as was to be expected, in intellectual circles in Antananarivo. The warrior peoples of the previously unsubdued south and west fought courageously before submitting to French rule; but once the colonial administration was established the sparseness of the population and the low level of education prevented the development of any effective opposition. In other coastal areas formerly under Merina domination, the French occupation was seen as the replacement of one master by another more efficient and generally more just and humane; there was no incentive to throw off the French yoke if it meant a return to Merina rule. The former ruling classes in Imerina had, however every incentive to try to oust the French and regain their former privileges and power; whilst their gradually increasing contacts with French intellectual opinion, much of it left-wing, stimulated directly or indirectly their nationalist aspirations.

Apart from resentment at the loss of political power, nationalist opposition was inspired by French economic and cultural policies. As we have seen, the imposition of the colonial economy, with high tariffs excluding foreign competition, led to increased prices and an excessive dependence on French markets and sources of supply. The economic dominance of French and creole traders and settlers was compounded (as in most of the British colonies) by their attitude to the Malagasy, often tinged with racialism. A constant theme of the colonial period (again as in the British colonies) was the conflict between the *colons* and the colonial administrators who in general sought to protect the Malagasy against the demands of the settlers. In the cultural field Malagasy intellectuals, proud of their own national language and culture, resented the imposition of French as the official language and a necessary medium for advancement in the administration and the professions. The creation of a French-speaking élite, which was an inevitable consequence of the imposition of French rule, was seen as a further factor dividing Malagasy society. The leading intellectuals had been a product of the Anglo-Malagasy culture created by the missionaries and their pupils in an atmosphere of voluntary cooperation. They were obviously unhappy at having to abandon this culture in favour of a new culture which was in effect imposed by force.

An underlying cause of nationalist feeling was resentment at the second-class status, both political and legal, accorded to the Malagasy in their own country. The separate *justice indigène* could be defended on the grounds of respect for traditional laws and customs but in practice it imposed an inferior status. Under the system known as the *indigénat*, which regulated their separate status as French subjects as opposed to French citizens, Malagasy could be sentenced by administrative decree to a fine or up to 15 days in prison for certain offences, such as failure to cultivate sufficient crops, non-payment of taxes or avoidance of *prestations*.

The catalyst for this nationalist feeling which led to the first organised nationalist movement was a series of newspaper articles on Japan, extolling that country's success in becoming a powerful modern nation while preserving its independence and traditions. The author was Pasteur Ravelojaona who is generally considered the father of Malagasy nationalism. After graduating top of his class from the *Ecole Le Myre de Vilers* he became well-known as a teacher and Protestant minister specialising in youth work and also as a journalist and scholar. His articles on Japan inspired the formation in 1913 of a secret society, the VVS (*vy, vato, sakelika* – "iron, stone and 'network' ", the latter word being a reference to the group's secret organisation) which included intellectuals such as Robin, medical students, notably Joseph Ravoahangy-Andrianavalona and Joseph Raseta, Protestant pastors such as Ravelojaona and Rabary and even several Catholic priests, including Venance Manifatra, one of the first ordained Malagasy priests. The aims of the movement were confused and unrealistic: to expel the French and restore the monarchy in the person of Prince Ramahatra, who was in fact a leading Francophile and had nothing to do with the society. It was concentrated in Imerina, with one or two branches among groups of Merina Protestants elsewhere in the plateau area, and its total numbers probably did not exceed five hundred. Secrecy was of the essence: the various groups did not know one another and there seems to have been no active central organisation. A sense of commitment was imposed by special initiation rites, but for the time being there was little prospect of effective action. The intellectuals and students who composed the society had no popular following or military strength, and they posed no immediate threat to the colonial regime. But, partly because of the war atmosphere, the administration and French settlers reacted violently when the existence of the VVS became known at the end of 1915 and members of the society were arrested and brought to trial. Despite the lack of adequate proofs, eight leading figures, including Robin and Ravoahangy, were sentenced to hard labour for life and twenty-six others were given long sentences of hard labour. Over two hundred more, though not charged with any offences, were interned by administrative decision. Another response of the administration was a temporary cutback in higher education for the Malagasy, especially in subjects such as French history which might stimulate nationalist sentiment. However, in the calmer atmosphere after the Armistice in 1918 there was a progressive amnesty, leading to the freeing of all prisoners by 1922.

Meanwhile Garbit, as a reserve officer, was recalled to France for military service in 1917. During his absence his place was filled first by Martial Merlin, who stayed only three months, and then for eighteen months by Abraham Schrameck, a former *préfet*. Schrameck saw his main task as the revival of the economy after the difficult war years. To this end in January 1919 he convened a major economic conference with representatives of the various chambers of commerce and agriculture (still exclusively European). The conference recommended important measures of agrarian reform setting limits on land concessions to the *colons* and reserving other land for the Malagasy. A Madagascar Agency was set up in Paris to market Malagasy produce. And a rudimentary development plan was drawn up, outlining a programme of major public works projects. The settlers also used the opportunity to demand a degree of participation in the colonial government, including representation by elected members on the governor's administrative council.

These demands were not successful but were to lead to the first small beginnings of representative government under Garbit who returned in 1920, this time as titular governor-general. Gallieni had set up consultative chambers in some of the main towns, composed of settlers appointed by him; from 1907 the members were elected by the settlers. In 1920 these chambers were converted into municipal commissions with certain administrative functions and a small Malagasy membership; and the chambers of commerce were given formal legal status and additional functions. In the same year Garbit set up on an experimental basis a national consultative group called Economic and Financial Delegations empowered to examine and express views on the budget, taxation, loans and public works, though decisions remained with the administration. They consisted of two representatives of the governor's administrative council, twelve from the chambers of commerce, twelve from the municipal commissions and, meeting in a separate section, twenty-four Malagasy chosen by a very restricted Malagasy electorate. Strong opposition by the *colons* to the Malagasy representation prevented the Delegations from operating effectively; and it was not until May 1924, after Garbit's departure, that they were formally established by decree. They were significant as the first opportunity for elected Malagasy to be involved in the administrative process. But the limited consultative role in purely economic matters did not begin to satisfy Malagasy aspirations, especially as the Malagasy section met separately and in private. Meanwhile settler aspirations were somewhat appeased in 1921 by the establishment in Paris of the *Conseil Supérieur des Colonies* to which the Madagascar *colons* elected two members.

Like many colonial governors Garbit was criticised from both sides, by the *colons* for being too liberal towards the Malagasy and by the government in Paris for being too paternalistic. But when he finally left in 1923 he had a number of solid achievements to his credit, notably the railway from Antananarivo to Antsirabe (here he completed the development of the spa initiated by Picquié) and the branch line to Lac Alaotra. In the capital his improvements included the road tunnel which for many years bore his name, now the Ralaimongo tunnel. Secondary education was extended, with the two colleges in Antananarivo becoming *lycées*, though at first access was limited to European children. Garbit was also responsible for initiating the commercial production of Maryland tobacco which became a useful addition to the cash crop economy.

The early twenties saw a revival of nationalism, partly inspired by the experiences and contacts of Malagasy soldiers in France and supported by a new movement of left-wing opinion in the metropolis in favour of the colonial peoples. Its leader, a Betsileo Protestant teacher called Jean Ralaimongo, had served with the army in France during the war and stayed on for some time afterwards. He came into contact with various left-wing organisations and at one time shared a room with Ho Chi Minh. In 1920 he founded with some French friends the "French League for the accession of natives of Madagascar to the rights of French citizenship". The League sent him back to Madagascar for six months in 1921 to recruit members for the League and to campaign for improved political rights. He won the admiration of his compatriots for his courage in standing up to the colonial administration and the abuse of the settlers.[2] But the strict censorship of the Malagasy press and the banning of any public meeting he tried to organise limited his effectiveness. He returned to Paris where he campaigned for the freeing of the VVS prisoners, which was achieved in 1922, and in defence of Malagasy peasants deprived of their land or subjected to various disguised forms of compulsory labour. With funds provided by French sympathisers, he founded a newspaper, *Le Libéré*, which was effective in winning support for the Malagasy cause in Paris and was also widely read by the French-educated élite in Madagascar. However, recognising that the battle had to be fought in Madagascar he returned there in 1923, installing himself in Diego Suarez. He quickly became involved in helping peasants complaining of exploitation, by writing letters to the press, intervening with the administration and taking cases to court. His popularity became a matter of concern to the authorities.

The governor-general who had to deal with this new threat to the orderly routine of paternalistic government was Marcel Olivier, who arrived in 1924 from French Sudan with a number of new ideas. These were to lead to a series of important administrative and economic reforms during his five-year stay. In a major structural change the 29 provinces and 90 districts which had provided the framework since Gallieni's time were replaced by 6 regions and 44 provinces. The *chefs de province* became the main work-horses of the administration and, with the abolition of the districts, the Malagasy *chefs de canton* acquired more responsibility. The main aim of the change, and especially the establishment of the regions, was a degree of decentralisation in the hope of improving services in the remoter areas and doing something to reduce the gap between coastal and plateau populations which colonial rule had if anything accentuated. A land registry was set up to protect Malagasy property and the arbitration councils strengthened to reduce exploitation of workers on the plantations. The *lycées* in Antananarivo were opened to Malagasy pupils via a special entrance examination, thus permitting them for the first time to follow a liberal education instead of simply acquiring occupational qualifications. An issuing bank, the Bank of Madagascar, was established in the capital, together with a new private bank, the Bank of the Indian Ocean.

Decentralisation was made easier by improvements in road communications, resulting from Olivier's order that *prestations*, previously used mainly for minor works around the villages, should concentrate on road construction. The main road to the south was extended to Tulear and Fort Dauphin and a network of roads linking the provincial headquarter towns was established throughout the country. A new railway line was initiated from Fianarantsoa to Manakara on the east coast where a new port was constructed. After a major cyclone had destroyed Tamatave in 1927, the town was rebuilt and its port modernised; improvements were also carried out in the other main ports. New loans were raised to finance these major works, which also required a substantial and regular source of labour. Olivier is now remembered mainly for the way he dealt with this problem.

Military service had been established some years previously to provide soldiers for the regiments of *tirailleurs malgaches* in the French army[3]. However only a proportion of the annual call-up was needed for this purpose. Olivier's innovation was to draft the remainder into a labour force called SMOTIG (*Service de la main d'oeuvre des travaux d'intérêt général*) which was established in June 1926. Logically, compulsory labour for public works is no more objectionable, and is less dangerous, than military service. But whereas military service can have romantic, patriotic overtones the labour equivalent is immediately dubbed forced labour, which has much more sinister connotations and is anathema to trade unions and liberal opinion in general. The SMOTIG workers were organised on military lines in camps of 200 or so and required to work 48 hours a week during their three years' service. They were in general well fed and clothed and received a useful training; but there were sufficient cases of abuse of the system to lend force to denunciations in Paris by left-wing politicians and the Communist-dominated *Confédération Générale du Travail* (CGT) and to provoke an enquiry by the International Labour Organisation. Above all, SMOTIG provided a ready-made issue for Ralaimongo and likeminded nationalists

In 1926 Ralaimongo was joined in Diego Suarez by Ravoahangy, who since his release had completed his medical studies, and later by a left-wing Frenchman Paul Dussac who had come from Réunion to work an unsuccessful plantation in the northwest. Ralaimongo was able to get round the problem of censorship of the Malagasy press by establishing in Diego Suarez a French-language newspaper *L'Opinion* with Dussac as Director. Dussac also founded a newspaper in the capital, *L'Aurore malgache*, with Malagasy journalists Jules Ranaivo and Emmanuel Razafindrakoto. With no possibility yet of forming legal political parties, the press was to play an increasingly important role in fomenting nationalist opposition. Through their newspapers, Ralaimongo, Ravoahangy and Dussac continued to denounce abuses by the administration and the settlers and to campaign for the assimilation of Madagascar as a *département* of France with full rights of citizenship for its inhabitants.

In 1929 Dussac came to Antananarivo to organise a massive petition demanding citizenship rights. With the help of two communist workers Edouard Planque and François Vittori, he organised a public meeting in a cinema in the centre of the capital on 19 May. However the police prevented any Malagasy from entering the meeting, whereupon Planque and Vittori led an unauthorized protest march through the town to the governor-general's residence. The acting governor-general (Olivier had departed earlier in the year), yielding to pressure from the *colons*, ordered the dismissal of any Malagasy officials involved in the demonstration and the arrest of the three Frenchmen. They were released a week later after protests against the forcible feeding of Planque and Vittori who had gone on hunger strike. But as they continued their subversive activities they were re-arrested in October along with thirteen Malagasy, including Jules Ranaivo, on a charge of "rebellion". At their trial their defence lawyer, who had been sent out from Paris by a left-wing organisation, secured the acquittal of all except Planque and Vittori (Dussac, though acquitted at this trial, had already been imprisoned on another charge). They were sentenced to eighteen months imprisonment to which two years were added after they had greeted the sentence by singing the Communist anthem "The International".[4]

The French government responded to the increasing unrest by sending out a strong governor-general with instructions to take a firm line. Léon Cayla, who arrived in May 1930, had already served in Madagascar as secretary-general. One of his first acts was an administrative decree confining Ralaimongo and Ravoahangy to house arrest for five years in separate remote and unhealthy spots on the west coast; and Dussac was transferred from Antananarivo to a prison in the less comfortable climate of Majunga. A decree of December 1930 aimed against "acts and manoeuvres calculated to provoke hatred of the French Government" was used to justify numerous arrests and prison sentences for Malagasy linked in any way with the nationalist movement. A clause in the same decree making it an offence to publish anything "which might harm the prestige of France" led to a series of fines and prison sentences for Dussac and his Malagasy collaborators on *L'Aurore malgache*. The implications for the nationalists were clear. Henceforward the idea of assimilation with France was discredited. Abandoning the hope of achieving full citizenship rights for all Malagasy under a French government, the nationalist leaders now publicly called for independence[5] with the slogan, first heard during the May 1929 demonstration, of "Madagascar for the Malagasy".

However, even under Cayla's stern regime, agitation and repression were only a small part of the picture of life on the island. Political agitation was sporadic and largely confined to the capital; whilst exploitation of labour by settlers mainly affected the east coast areas where most of the cash-crop plantations were to be found. Elsewhere in the country the people continued peacefully[6] in their traditional ways under the generally benevolent and just paternalism of the local French administrator. (After criticism that the *chefs de province* were too remote from the people, Cayla restored the *chefs de district* and abolished the provinces, leaving 85 districts grouped in eight, instead of six, regions.) Most importantly, while political and legal assimilation was checked, cultural assimilation made rapid progress. The young élite of the plateau region took full advantage of the greater availability of secondary education, and an increasing number went on to study at universities in France. With their relatively long tradition of literacy and their quick intelligence they adapted readily to French culture and academic studies. In due course some became distinguished in various sciences and made valuable contributions to the Malagasy Academy and to other academic and scientific institutions in the metropolis as well as in the island. Others achieved recognition as writers in the French language, including several poets, notably Jean-Joseph Rabearivolo and later Jacques Rabemenanjara and Flavien Ranaivo. The development of this Malagasy intellectual élite underlined the ambiguities and contradictions of French colonial policy, which were not resolved by granting French citizenship to a few of them. For the intellectuals themselves there was an inevitable conflict between their patriotic feelings and their enthusiasm for French culture which caused tensions and problems of identity for some of them. The suicide of Rabearivolo at the early age of 36 has been attributed to these tensions, although many of his poems revealed a preoccupation with death.

Cultural assimilation operated to some extent also in the other direction. Many Frenchmen, particularly in the administration, were captivated by Madagascar – the charm of the people, the varied beauty of the island, the fascination of its culture and history – and became lifelong *malgachisants*. Educated Malagasy were accepted in French society to a degree which would have been unthinkable for Africans in Britain in the same period. There were many friendships between French and Malagasy, and some intermarriage.[7] These personal links did something to temper nationalistic anti-French feelings, as did the support given to the nationalists by the French left wing in press and Parliament. The advent of the left-wing Popular Front government in 1936 was thus seen as promising a radical change in the relations between the metropolis and its colonies.

In the intervening years, Cayla's main task had been to restore the economy after the world depression of 1929-31. The twenties had seen a modest expansion of the economy and of exports, based on a combination of traditional commodities, such as rice, hides and meat products, and the slowly-expanding new cash crops, mainly coffee, vanilla and butter beans (exported to Britain by the African Mercantile Company). The depression hit these exports hard and stocks of unsold commodities piled up at the ports. In the same period the south of the island was devastated by a severe drought, followed by a plague of cochineal beetle which destroyed the prickly-pear cactus, the main food of the cattle in this dry region. Hundreds of thousands of cattle died and many of the Antandroy people were compelled to migrate elsewhere in search of a living. Cayla could not control these natural disasters. But he tackled the general economic problem with an energy and ability which marked him out as one of the outstanding governors of Madagascar. He encouraged the increased production of the more valuable cash crops, particularly of coffee which expanded dramatically. By improving and standardising quality he made the commodities more marketable and, with the help of protectionist policies in France, by 1934 he had converted the long-standing trade deficit into a surplus. With exports of coffee increasing from 6,000 tons in 1930 to 41,000 tons in 1938 and sustained exports of vanilla, cloves, butter beans, graphite and mica, the trading balance was to remain in substantial surplus until the outbreak of war in 1939.

At the same time Cayla presided over a major programme of public works with the help of a loan from France. The railway from Fianarantsoa to Manakara was completed and modern quays constructed for the ports of Tamatave and Diego Suarez. Extensive building works in Antananarivo included the refurbishment of the famous *zoma* market, the Ambanidia market, the Mahamasina stadium and what is now the *Avenue de l'Indépendance*; the other main towns were also given essentially their modern appearance. The road network was doubled from 12,000 to 25,000 kilometres. Construction work at the district level was encouraged by giving the districts a public works budget instead of relying solely on the *prestations*. All this was achieved within a balanced budget, thanks to pruning of administrative staff and careful control of expenditure. Cayla, who was himself a pilot and flew his own plane on administrative tours, was also instrumental in establishing a commercial air service between Madagascar and Europe and the beginnings of an internal air network.

In the political field the policy of repression failed to extinguish nationalism, which now began to appear also in the main population centres in the regions. The press was still allowed to operate with circumspection, and from prison and detention Dussac, Ralaimongo and Ravoahangy continued to write articles calling for abrogation of the various oppressive laws. All three were released when their sentences expired in 1935. Through a new journal *La Nation malgache* they intensified their campaign, encouraged by the arrival of the Popular Front government in the following year. This brought about an immediate change in atmosphere as Cayla adapted skilfully to the requirements of a more liberal colonial policy. The 1930 decree controlling the press was abolished along with SMOTIG, which was already being gradually replaced by a system of voluntary recruitment controlled by regional Labour Offices; and trade union rights were recognised for the first time. On the advice of French communists, Malagasy nationalists had become involved in trade unions from 1936 when Ravoahangy and Emmanuel Razafindrakoto created worker and peasant unions, which were declared illegal. But after a series of strikes, trade union rights were granted in 1937 to workers literate in French and in the following year to all workers. By 1939 there were fourteen trade unions grouped in a *Union départementale* affiliated to the French CGT and owning two newspapers. In addition there were over twenty non-CGT unions affiliated to the French Catholic trade union organisation.

The Popular Front government headed by the socialist Léon Blum in fact lasted only a year. Colonial reform was only one of many preoccupations and in any case the views of the coalition partners on colonial policy differed widely: the Communists favoured independence, the Socialists assimilation and the Radicals the status quo. So whilst they were able to get rid of some of the more oppressive features of colonial rule they did not tackle the fundamental problem. Thus Malagasy nationalist aspirations were again disappointed. However the brief Popular Front era saw the almost equally brief emergence of the first modern political party in Madagascar. This was the *Parti Communiste de la Région de Madagascar* (PCRM) founded by Dussac in August 1936. Although few of them were Marxists, most of the nationalists joined the PCRM for the good reason that the PCF was the only metropolitan party which supported their aspirations to independence. Members included Ralaimongo, Raseta, Jules and Paul Ranaivo and Emmanuel Razafindrakoto; Ravoahangy did not join but remained as political director of *La Nation Malgache*, which changed its name to *Le Prolétariat Malgache* and became the organ of the party. Adopting Communist methods of organisation, the party rapidly set up a network of cells of supporters and sympathisers in many parts of the country, especially the central plateau and the east coast. It also promoted the establishment of cooperatives for both production and marketing and was particularly active in the formation of trade unions.

However metropolitan politics did not favour the survival of the new party. In order to preserve the unity of the Popular Front in face of the menace of fascism, the PCF abandoned its support for Malagasy independence in favour of assimilation and ordered the Malagasy branch to do likewise. The PCRM reluctantly agreed, but Dussac and other leaders continued to speak and write in favour of independence. This caused the PCF to denounce the PCRM as being "anti-French" and then, in January 1937, to disown it. Dussac went to France in April 1937 to try to resolve the differences but without success, and he died a year later without returning to Madagascar. Meanwhile the withdrawal of PCF's support had been soon followed by the collapse of the Popular Front, which enabled the colonial government to resume some of its oppressive policies. The PCRM, further weakened by internal disagreements, ceased to be an effective party and in December 1938 it formally dissolved itself. However, many of the members remained politically active as trade unionists, organising numerous strikes in the years immediately before the war. Others went "underground" and formed various secret societies to keep alive the nationalist flame, using the network of cells built up by the PCRM. This same network was to help the post-war nationalist party the MDRM to build up support througout the country in a remarkably short space of time.

During Blum's brief second ministry in 1938 a decree further widened the scope for Malagasy to become French citizens, but the small élite who benefited were still numbered only in thousands. The succeeding government headed by Daladier was not particularly sympathetic to nationalist aspirations but it was anxious to ensure the loyalty of the colonies in the war which now seemed inevitable. In a gesture which created a most favourable impression in Imerina the remains of Queen Ranavalona III were returned from Algiers and buried in the royal tomb by the queen's palace in Antananarivo. A Malagasy seat was allocated in the *Conseil supérieur des colonies* alongside the two seats held by French *colons*; and the veteran nationalist Pasteur Ravelojaona was elected by a substantial majority. But these concessions were, as always, too little and too late. The numerous new nationalist journals which appeared in the years immediately before World War II no longer called for citizenship rights but for independence.

Extremist *colons* reacted to the modest political reforms and the calls for independence with violent abuse of the nationalist leaders and occasionally physical assault. In October 1936 Dussac and Ravoahangy were abused and manhandled by a group of *colons* on the outskirts of the capital. At the end of that year Ralaimongo was waylaid by another group of *colons* in Mananjary, beaten unconscious and thrown in a river to drown. He managed to survive but never fully recovered from the assault. He virtually withdrew from the national political scene and retired to a small village near Andapa in the northeast, where he died in 1943.

In the summer of 1939 Cayla exchanged posts with Marcel de Coppet, governor-general of French West Africa. When war broke out in Europe a few months later, de Coppet set about mobilising Malagasy support for the French war effort. In general the Malagasy rallied loyally to the metropolis, recognising the need to oppose Nazi Germany, and the nationalists suspended their press campaigns. By June 1940 there were 34,000 Malagasy soldiers in France, with 72,000 more getting ready to embark from Madagascar, along with 20,000 workers.

The collapse of France in June 1940 was a great shock and ushered in a period of much greater difficulties for Madagascar than those experienced in the first World War. Some of the French community were inclined to support the Vichy regime but the majority, including de Coppet, at first rallied to General de Gaulle's appeal to fight on by the side of Britain. The British bombardment of the French fleet at Mers-el-Kebir produced a decisive switch of opinion, as elsewhere in Africa.[8] De Coppet, though a socialist and antifascist, felt obliged to declare for Vichy, after which he resigned. Fearing a resurgence of nationalist opposition the Vichy regime recalled the "strong man" Cayla for a short time. He interned a number of Communist or pro-Communist nationalists, including ex-VVS member Dr Raseta and Jules Ranaivo, and suspended trade union rights. This had the desired effect and his pro-Vichy successor Armand Annet, arriving in April 1941, found the island politically calm (the Malagasy press had ceased to appear because of shortage of newsprint). But the economic consequences of alignment with Vichy were severe. The British control of the seas imposed an almost total economic isolation. Overseas trade virtually ceased apart from a few authorised convoys and the export of vanilla and graphite to the USA. The island was largely self-sufficient in basic foodstuffs, but lack of petrol, spare parts for vehicles and money for road maintenance caused serious distribution problems resulting in shortages and hardship in many areas. Imported consumer goods became increasingly scarce and it was necessary to revive traditional methods of manufacturing clothes, from local materials such as raffia fibre, as well as tools and utensils of all kinds.

Madagascar was now to be the scene of military action when probably for the last time Britain was to exercise a decisive influence on events in the island. British contacts with the island had inevitably declined steeply after the French occupation. But British missionary activity was still considerable. For example in 1930 there were still 24 LMS missionaries in Madagascar compared with 39 in 1895.[9] The French Protestant mission and the Quakers, working closely with the LMS in the plateau area, numbered 29 and 10 missionaries respectively, although by now the evangelical church on the plateau was largely in the hands of the Malagasy. The small Anglican mission, with branches on the east coast and in the Diego Suarez region, accounted for another 10 missionaries. The Lutherans, operating mainly in the less developed south, were now by far the largest Protestant mission, with 65 Norwegian missionaries and some 50 Americans, divided between the Norwegian Lutheran Church of America based on Fort Dauphin and the Lutheran Board of Missions operating in the Tulear region. The Catholic missions had of course greatly expanded and exceeded in numbers all the Protestant missions combined.

In the commercial sphere however, tariff protection had ensured continued French domination, with France normally accounting for between 75 and 80 per cent of both imports and exports. British and American imports, which had dominated the market in the last days of the Merina monarchy, had virtually disappeared, apart from a few items such as Scotch whisky for which there was no French equivalent. But a useful export trade had developed to Britain and USA in products for which the French demand was limited. The US ice-cream industry took nearly all of the vanilla of which Madagascar was the world's largest producer; whilst the butter beans, developed in the southwest of the island by British pioneers in the early years of the century[10] were exported almost exclusively to Britain. Much of the graphite and mica exported was also taken by the USA and Britain.

As we have seen, the British Government's interest in Madagascar declined after the opening of the Suez Canal. Strategic interest in the great island revived in 1941 with the closure of the Suez Canal route to the East owing to the Axis powers' domination of the Mediterranean. And Madagascar's position astride the Cape route to the Middle East and India became of crucial importance when Japan entered the war in December 1941. General de Gaulle immediately proposed to Churchill a military operation to install the Free French in Madagascar. Churchill favoured the idea, since he feared that the Vichy authorities would not deny use of the great harbour of Diego Suarez to the Japanese navy, which from Singapore was already roaming far across the Indian Ocean. German records show that in March 1942 the Japanese were planning to establish bases in Madagascar in order to attack shipping round the Cape.[11] It appears that at the time Hitler vetoed the plans because of likely political repercussions in Vichy France and French Africa; but it is possible that, if Britain had not taken action, the strong military arguments in favour of the Japanese plans might have prevailed at a later stage. At any rate Churchill could not ignore the potential threat to the sea route round the Cape (which was soon to carry the vital military convoys to Egypt which turned the tide at El Alamein) and he decided to act. But with memories of the disastrous failure of the joint British-Free French attack on Dakar in 1940, he finally determined that the operation would be carried out only by British forces; and that in order to preserve secrecy the Free French would not even be informed.

To ensure surprise for "Operation Ironclad" as it was called, the capture of Diego Suarez harbour was to be effected by British troops who were on their way round the Cape to India and did not know their immediate destination until they had embarked at Durban. They comprised the 29th Independent Brigade and a Commando, both specially trained in amphibious operations, and two brigades of the 5th Division, adding up to some 30,000 men under the command of Major-General Sturges of the Royal Marines. They were transported and protected by a substantial naval force withdrawn from the western Mediterranean, including the battleship *Ramillies* and the aircraft-carrier *Illustrious*, commanded by Admiral Syfret. Early on 5 May, 1942 the British force appeared off the northern tip of Madagascar and the troops were landed, not in the strongly-fortified Diego Suarez bay itself, but on the western coast of the narrow peninsula some 18 miles to the west of the town. The surprise was complete but the greatly outnumbered

French garrison, under orders from Vichy to fight to the death, put up a stubborn resistance in places and it was two days before they surrendered. A few weeks later the *Ramillies* and an oil-tanker were struck by torpedoes. It transpired that they had been fired by a Japanese midget submarine which was then scuttled. It has been suggested that this incident was either invented or contrived by the British to prove the reality of the Japanese threat and so justify their action. In support of this suggestion was the rather curious disappearance of the evidence: it was said that the midget submarine had been scuttled and that the two-man crew were shot and killed after gaining the shore. But the torpedoings were real enough, and it is a little far-fetched to suggest that the British Navy would put one of their precious battle-cruisers out of action for several months in order to prove the existence of a threat which was obvious to anyone with access to a map of the Indian Ocean.

It had been hoped that the occupation of Diego Suarez would persuade Governor Annet to cooperate with the Allies. On the contrary the unprovoked assault and the loss of French lives (one of them was a First War air ace Commandant Assolant) made him more intransigent. Churchill was at first disposed to content himself with denying Diego Suarez to the Japanese. But he was persuaded by Field-Marshal Smuts that the increasing importance of convoys through the Mozambique Channel and the activities of German as well as Japanese submarines in the area made it necessary to control the other main ports of Madagascar. On 10 September, the 29th Brigade under the command of Brigadier Frank Festing (who later rose to be Chief of the Imperial General Staff) was landed at Majunga, which was captured with little opposition[12]. An East African brigade, which had replaced the 5th Division, was then landed and set off on the road to Antananarivo. The 29th Brigade was re-embarked to sail round the north of the island to capture Tamatave and then move on up the escarpment to the capital. The defending troops retreating from Majunga, mainly Malagasy or Senegalese with French officers, in general put up little resistance. The Malagasy had little incentive to fight the British, who they hoped had come to liberate them from the French, and in the later stages of the campaign they deserted in droves. The Senegalese were more disposed to fight but the French officers knew that resistance was hopeless; and those not sympathetic to the Allied cause were concerned mainly to put up a show of resistance to preserve their honour (and also their pension rights just in case the Allies were to lose the war, a not impossible prospect in the dark days of 1942). A brief stand was made on September 22 at Mahitsy some 20 miles to the north of the capital, where one of the the three defending companies was commanded by Captain Gabriel Ramanantsoa, a Malagasy graduate of St Cyr who was to become Head of State of Madagascar in 1972; but the capital surrendered to the East African brigade on the following day. It was something of a shock for the inhabitants to find that their British liberators (as they hoped) were in fact "Zulus";[13] but they nevertheless gave the troops a warm welcome.

Even now Annet, under uncompromising instructions from Vichy, refused to surrender but continued to retreat south with his remaining troops, pursued by the East Africans. The pace was slow because of stretched lines of communication, the onset of rains, the destruction of bridges and the felling of thousands of trees by the French to block the roads. But Annet ran out of space when he reached Ihosy and learned that another British column was advancing on him from Tulear. The surrender negotiations took place at Ambalavao on November 5, but Annet's representative delayed signature until one minute after midnight on November 6. This was done in order to prolong the campaign to precisely six months from the Diego Suarez landing, thus entitling the French participants to a campaign medal and various financial and other benefits for having served six months "in the field".[14] With the Vichy forces disposed of, arrangements were made to hand over the administration of the island to the Free French, as had always been intended. But this did little to assuage General de Gaulle's resentment against the British unilateral action.

The period between the capture of the capital and the arrival of the Free French governor-general in January 1943 was one of considerable difficulty for the British military administration which under Lord Rennell was responsible for running the country. Vichy propaganda had played effectively on the themes of jealousy of the old rival, bitter resentment at the "unprovoked" attacks at Mersel-Kebir and Diego Suarez and the resultant French deaths, and suspicion that the British intended to supplant the French in Madagascar. Not surprisingly many officers in the French army and administration were in varying degrees hostile and disposed to be uncooperative. Even those who sympathised with the Allied cause felt inhibited by their oath of loyalty to Marshal Petain and tended to regard de Gaulle as a deserter.[15] Some of the most intransigently hostile officials had to be arrested, but there was no real alternative to working with the existing French administration. Anglo-French relations slowly improved with closer personal acquaintance and the realisation that the British had no intention of taking over the island permanently. Nevertheless it was a relief when the military administration could hand over its responsibilities to the

Free French authorities and dissolve itself.[16] Most of the British forces could now be withdrawn, but some army, navy and air force elements remained under a British military mission until 1946.

The new governor-general who arrived in January 1943 was General Legentilhomme, one of the most successful Free French commanders. In a short stay of four months he applied himself with military directness to the task of bringing the resources of Madagascar back into the war on the side of the Allies. To this end he and his civilian successor as governor-general, Pierre de Saint Mart, imposed new burdens which the people found hard to bear after two years of isolation and deprivation. Reserve stocks of rice were requisitioned for export to Europe and a Rice Office set up to purchase rice and ration its distribution. This system led inevitably to abuse and, together with the continuing shortage of imports, encouraged a black market organised by unscrupulous Europeans. Rice, for which the grower was paid one franc the kilo, was sold on the black market for ten times that price, with similar increases for cotton goods and petrol. Prices in general quadrupled, far outstripping the wages of salaried workers. Taxes were increased and great pressure was put on those with money to make "voluntary" contributions to various war funds and charities. Greater demands were made on the labour force. To repair the roads and the bridges which had been destroyed by Annet's troops during their retreat, *prestations* were increased from ten to thirty days a year. In addition labour was requisitioned to work on the plantations and to gather rubber in the eastern forests. The difficulties of road transport, compounded by the destruction of bridges, led to the compulsory recruitment of many thousands of couriers and porters. Health inevitably suffered from the hard physical work, malnutrition and shortage of medical suplies. The normal rate of population growth declined during the war, and in 1944 deaths exceeded births for the first time since reliable statistics were established.

The collapse of France in 1940, the British occupation and the squabbles between Vichyists and Gaullists had greatly lowered French prestige and encouraged nationalist hopes of early independence. These were dashed when the British returned the island to French colonial rule. The nationalist leaders were allowed greater freedom by the Gaullists than under the Vichy regime, but in the absence of newspapers there was not much they could do to exploit the discontent caused by food shortages; indeed most of them had no desire to embarrass the government while the war was going on. However they did take advantage of the restoration of trade union rights. Ravoahangy and Raseta, among others, organised trade unions with the help of some French communists, notably Pierre Boiteau.[17] The war years thus consolidated the rather curious alliance between Merina aristocrats and French communists which gave a special character to Malagasy nationalism.

In the last years of the war, there was much discussion of constitutional reform among the Free French authorities. In February 1944 a major conference held at Brazzaville to consider the future evolution of the French colonies in Africa again raised the hopes of the nationalists. But the conference rejected the idea of independence for the separate colonies. Instead it advocated complete assimilation, with the abolition of the *indigénat* and the representation of the colonial peoples in a Constituent Assembly and in the subsequent French parliament. In line with other recommendations designed to prepare the colonies for a degree of internal self-government, de Saint Mart set up at the local level *collectivités malgaches* consisting of village notables. They elected the members of district councils, whose role was only to advise the *chef de district*. At the centre a Franco-Malagasy Mixed Commission of nominated members was established. This was little more than a debating chamber and in March 1945 it was replaced by an elected representative council with powers over the budget and composed of 30 Frenchmen and 30 Malagasy, the latter elected by the corps of 75,000 notables.

The end of the war brought in a period of nationalist ferment with the return of Malagasy soldiers from France (where some had joined the *maquis*) and the holding of a series of elections for local representative bodies and for the Constituent Assembly in Paris. Madagascar was allocated four seats in the Assembly, two for Frenchmen and two for Malagasy. In the elections of November 1945 Ravoahangy (who defeated Pasteur Ravelojaona) and Raseta were elected – both of them Merina, Protestant, medical doctors and veterans of the VVS. In Paris they met a group of young Malagasy intellectuals, notably Dr Albert Rakoto-Ratsimamanga,[18] a distinguished scientist, Raymond Rabemananjara, a well-known journalist, and Jacques Rabemananjara (no relation), the young poet. On February 22, 1946 the old nationalists and the "young Turks" joined in forming a new party MDRM (*Mouvement Démocratique de la Rénovation Malgache*) with the aim of immediate independence within the French Union. This was perhaps the first truly national political party in Madagascar. The struggle against colonialism had already bridged the gap between *andriana* and *hova* among the Merina: Ravoahangy was a member of the highest nobility (Andriamasinavalona) and Raseta came from a leading *hova* family, while most of the other leaders were of modest bourgeois origin. The leadership of the MDRM remained predominantly Merina and Protestant; but the national appeal of the party was greatly strengthened by the inclusion of Jacques Rabemananjara, a Catholic of mixed Merina and Betsimisaraka ancestry who had been born on the east coast. He now became secretary-general of MDRM, while Raseta became president.

The national appeal of the MDRM and the prestige of its two Deputies ensured its preponderance over other more moderate parties which were essentially Merina: the PDM (*Parti Démocratique Malgache*), a Protestant group led by Pasteur Ravelojaona, and the MSM (*Mouvement Social Malgache*), a group of Catholic bourgeois Merina formed at the instigation of the Jesuit mission and led by the historian Edouard Ralaimihoatra. A greater threat to the MDRM was PADESM (*Parti des Désherités de Madagascar*) founded in June 1946 by a group of coastal notables and minor officials led by Pascal Velonjara from Tamatave province, Raveloson-Mahasampo, "native" governor of Tulear, Norbert Zafimahova, head of the leading family of Farafangana on the southeast coast, and a group from Majunga province including Philibert Tsiranana, a Tsimihety cowherd turned schoolteacher. PADESM aimed at uniting underprivileged sectors of the population – mainly the coastal peasants and the former slave classes of the plateau – by awakening fears that early independence as proposed by MDRM would lead to a reimposition of Merina domination. Their preference for a continuation of French rule was made strikingly clear on August 6, 1946, the fiftieth anniversary of the annexation of Madagascar as a French colony, which MDRM had proclaimed as a day of mourning; PADESM regarded it as a day of rejoicing, celebrating " the suppression of Hova hegemony and slavery".

At first PADESM lacked sufficient educated leaders and organisation. And their appeal lacked the heady glamour of MDRM, being essentially negative – anti-Merina and opposed to independence until such time as the *côtiers* could organise themselves and use their greater numbers to outvote the Merina. But memories, often bitter, of Merina rule were still alive among the older coastal population.[19] The colonial administration (de Coppet had returned as High Commissioner, the new title of the governor-general, in 1946) quickly realised that coastal suspicions of the Merina were their best weapon against the independence demands of the Merina-dominated MDRM. In another reversion to *"la politique des races"* they now gave active support and encouragement to PADESM; indeed it seems likely that certain elements of the administration had a hand in its formation.

In the Constituent Assembly the two Malagasy Deputies joined with other colonial representatives and left-wing French parties to secure the abolition of forced labour and the *indigénat*. But their proposal that Madagascar should become an independent state within the French Union was shelved without serious discussion. After the first draft constitution was rejected by a referendum, a second Constituent Assembly finally adopted in October 1946 a constitution which appeared to meet most of the demands of Ralaimongo twenty years earlier. Madagascar became an Overseas Territory of France and all Malagasy became French citizens. But the proposed assimilation was still far from complete. The status of territory was imprecise; the grant of French citizenship was tempered by the continuance of separate electoral colleges for French and Malagasy; whereas all French adults resident in Madagascar were entitled to vote, only Malagasy with certain qualifications could do so (the Malagasy electorate numbered a quarter of a million, about one eighth of the adult population); and whilst the Malagasy electorate, to say nothing of the total population, outnumbered the French many times over, they were allocated only three seats in the National Assembly, while the French had two. In any case assimilation no longer satisfied nationalist demands, and the two Malagasy Deputies abstained in the vote on the Constitution.

The 1946 Constitution also established provincial assemblies in five redefined provinces of Madagascar, with the same separate electoral colleges electing Malagasy and French councillors in the proportion of three to two. The importance of the provincial assemblies lay not only in their considerable delegated powers over budgetary and other matters in local government but also in the fact that their councillors collectively chose from their numbers the members of the national Representative Assembly, in the proportion of seven Malagasy to five French. They also elected senators, three Malagasy and two French, to the French Senate; and, this time in a single college, councillors to the less important Council of the French Union. Thus both in the local assemblies and in representation in the French capital, the Malagasy were in a majority.

In the first elections to the French National Assembly in November 1946, MDRM captured all three Malagasy seats: Jacques Rabemananjara for the east coast, Ravoahangy for the centre and Raseta for the west. But Velonjara won a respectable vote for PADESM in the eastern region and the PADESM candidate came close to defeating Raseta in the west. MDRM was also the overall victor in the elections to the provincial assemblies in January 1947, winning all or a majority of seats in four provinces; but PADESM won a majority in Majunga and a respectable minority in Tulear and Fianarantsoa. In the secondary elections MDRM accordingly took all the Malagasy seats in the Senate and the Council of the French Union. But in the elections to the Representative Assembly on March 30 (much influenced by the outbreak of rebellion the day before) PADESM actually won a majority of the Malagasy seats with twelve to only nine for MDRM.

With its nation-wide organisation and with the help of some brilliant propaganda and not a few rash promises, MDRM had quickly become an effective mass party. But it was far from being united, even within the leadership, and the rapid growth of the party had created problems. The leaders in Paris had difficulty in controlling extremist elements in the party headquarters in Antananarivo. And the movement served as an umbrella for certain secret organisations such as *Jina* (the significance of this name, sometimes written *Jiny*, is obscure) and PANAMA (*Parti Nationaliste Malgache*) which looked back not so much to VVS as to the violent xenophobia of the *menalamba*. The ferment of the frequent elections and the virulence of MDRM propaganda created an atmosphere favourable to extremism and violence. On the day that de Coppet returned as High Commissioner in May 1946 his carriage was bombarded with missiles and fifteen people were wounded in rioting. In June mob attacks on the *Hôtel de Ville* and the *gendarmerie* headquarters followed an incident in which a French *gendarme*, threatened by a MDRM crowd, shot two of them dead. In August Malagasy soldiers invaded the Grand Mosque in Antananarivo and killed several Comorians, who were regarded as pro-French.

The spectacular political advance of PADESM early in 1947, which was attributed to French divisive policies, caused further agitation among the MDRM by threatening to delay independence and to deny to MDRM the fruits of all their efforts. PADESM was bitterly attacked in MDRM speeches and newspapers as agents of the administration and there were more personal attacks on Comorians and Frenchmen. Anti-French feeling was particularly strong among Malagasy soldiers who had been kept on in France after the liberation in 1944 in very difficult conditions and had been repatriated only in 1946. There was increasing talk of armed rebellion, encouraged by the success of the Vietminh revolt in Indo-China.

Rumours of rebellion increased during March 1947 and on March 27 a message from MDRM headquarters signed by the three Deputies called upon all members to remain calm in the face of provocations. On the night of March 29 thousands of armed rebels attacked military posts, administrative headquarters and French settlers at widely-dispersed points. In the areas of Moramanga halfway along the railway from the capital to Tamatave, and Manakara, the terminus of the railway from Fianarantsoa to the east coast, the attacks were successful. Buildings and plantations were destroyed or damaged, rail communications disrupted, weapons seized and numbers of French soldiers, administrators and planters killed along with some pro-French Malagasy. Elsewhere the attacks soon fizzled out. In Diego Suarez, a small mutiny of Malagasy troops was not followed up; some timely arrests at Fianarantsoa forestalled an attack there, and a planned assault on the capital itself was called off at the last moment. With these chances missed on the plateau and with the west and south remaining aloof, indeed hostile to the rebels, the rebellion was in effect confined to the east coast and the forests of the eastern escarpment from approximately the Mananara river in the north to a line west of Vohipeno in the south.The insurgents were organised into two main divisions: a northern zone commanded by Victor Razafindrabe from a village in the forest south of Moramanga and a southern zone where the principal leader was Michel Radaoroson based in the area south of the railway from Fianarantsoa to Manakara.

The core of the insurgent troops consisted of former soldiers and they and others were armed with rifles and a few automatic weapons captured in attacks on military posts; but many were armed only with spears. In the long run they could never have succeeded against the military strength which France, even in its weakened post-war state, could deploy against them. But in the short term their cause did not look hopeless against the small number of French troops actually on the ground in Madagascar in 1947; and they were sustained by rumours (possibly inspired by the anti-colonial stance of the USA in the United Nations) that American troops were on the way to fight on their side. The forested escarpment was favourable to guerrilla warfare and by the end of 1947 insurgent activity had extended to perhaps a third of the countryside; but they were never able to capture and hold any sizeable towns. The fighting continued for two years during which the original political aims of the rebels became mingled with the settling of old scores between rival groups, families and political parties and, in areas like the Tanala, with a traditional hostility to central authority.

The massacre of Europeans in the early days of the uprising produced a violent reaction among the settlers. They called for stern measures of repression, and de Coppet, a socialist regarded as too sympathetic to nationalist aspirations, was fiercely attacked in the press for being insufficiently firm. In March 1948 he was replaced by Pierre de Chevigné, an ex-army officer and right wing (MRP) Deputy who made it clear that his mission was to crush the rebellion and repress all political activity aimed at independence. Large military reinforcements had already arrived, both French and West African, and by a combination of Gallieni's *"tache d'huile"* tactics and occasional brutal reprisals, amounting in a few cases to atrocities, the whole country was gradually brought back under government control. By March 1949 the last of the rebels had surrendered.

The death roll of the repression was substantial. Apart from those killed by the French troops, many thousands fled to the forest to escape indiscriminate reprisals or were carried off by rebels; and large numbers died of disease and starvation. When the insurrection was over, de Chevigné mentioned in a press statement (subsequently withdrawn) a figure of over 100,000 Malagasy deaths. The French military headquarters privately estimated that 89,000 Malagasy had died, mostly from disease and starvation rather than direct military action. Later two detailed enquiries by the administration in 1950 and 1952 produced the much lower figure of 11,200. Whether or not the administration deliberately underestimated the death toll with the aim of minimising the scope of the insurrection and the brutality of the repression, this lower figure was convincingly demolished by a later academic study.[20] This concluded that the military estimate of 89,000, based on the admittedly crude method of comparing the population of the insurgent areas before and after the rebellion was probably close to the truth, and a figure of this order is now generally accepted.

While the insurrection was being defeated in the field, steps were taken to crush it politically and legally. MDRM was dissolved and membership of *Jina* and PANAMA made illegal. Hundreds of MDRM leaders were arrested. Although Ravoahangy and Rabemananjara had, on the outbreak of the fighting, offered to appeal for calm and disown the insurrection, they too were arrested. Their parliamentary immunity was removed along with that of Raseta, although he had been in Paris at the time of the outbreak. The administration had a strong interest in discrediting MDRM as the party of independence – indeed it was suggested at the time that elements in the administration had actively provoked the insurrection for this purpose. At their trial the prosecution accused the Deputies of responsibility for the insurrection and claimed that the appeal for calm of March 27 was a secret signal to start the fighting. But evidence against them was confused and in some cases extracted by torture (Ravoahangy and Rabemananjara also stated that they had been tortured) and the court was blatantly biased against them. It may be true that their sometimes fiery speeches in favour of independence helped to create an atmosphere favourable to violence and that they might have done more specifically to discourage the idea of an armed rebellion. But the MDRM's policy was clearly to win independence by parliamentary means through argument and negotiation. The three Deputies knew France well enough to realise that armed rebellion was not only certain to fail but would be a major setback to their aspirations for independence. The defence[21] claimed that the insurrection was the work of extremist groups such as *Jina* and PANAMA operating under cover of the MDRM. This seems the most likely explanation, and most of the military leaders of the insurrection, such as the "generalissimo" Samuel Rakotondrabe who was regarded as its principal organiser but who was arrested less than two months after it broke out, were members of *Jina*.

The military chiefs were tried by a military tribunal and some twenty of them were executed by firing squad. The civilian courts also passed severe sentences, despite the lack of clear proof. In the main trial involving the MDRM leaders, six were condemned to death (including Raseta and Ravoahangy), eight to forced labour for life (including Rabemananjara) and two to life imprisonment (including Jules Ranaivo). Thanks partly to agitation by Communists and Socialists in France, helped by considerable unease about the way in which the trial was conducted, the death sentences were commuted to life imprisonment. The prisoners were in due course moved from the convict island of Nosy Lava to prisons in France and over the years their sentences were gradually reduced or converted to house arrest; but the principal MDRM leaders were not permitted to return to Madagascar and remained in exile in France until after independence in 1960.

The 1947 insurrection was a traumatic event in the history of Madagascar. It shattered the MDRM and created deep divisions, not only between French and Malagasy but between French *colons* and the administration and not least among the Malagasy themselves. The people of the east coast who bore the brunt of the casualties accused the Merina-dominated MDRM of stirring up the rebellion and then taking no effective part in it. MDRM nationalists regarded the PADESM as traitors for failing to support the rebellion, indeed for actively opposing it. PADESM leaders and other Malagasy regarded as pro-French had been a principal target of rebel attacks; and PADESM delegates to the Representative Assembly had called formally for the dissolution of the MDRM, the death penalty for its leaders and the deportation of other militant members. In France the insurrection itself and the subsequent trials became a subject of major political controversy in which the Left wing and some Centre elements denounced the treatment accorded to the MDRM leaders and agitated for an early amnesty. The widespread support in France for the cause of the nationalist leaders undoubtedly did much to assuage the bitterness and to prevent the breach between French and Malagasy from becoming irreparable. In Madagascar the shock and pain had been so great that a tacit agreement seemed to develop to draw a veil over the episode. The traditional "Malagasy wisdom" helped to ensure that the wounds did not fester and that too much effort was not squandered on bitterness and recriminations. But differing attitudes to the rebellion and to the treatment of the MDRM leaders were a major political issue in the years leading to independence and an important factor underlying political divisions for a long time afterwards.

Chapter 18

The road to independence

The failure of the rebellion and the harsh measures employed in its suppression put an end to hopes of early independence. The dissolution of MDRM and the imprisonment of its leaders left the nationalists in subdued disarray and their opponents in PADESM apparently triumphant. But with their *raison d'être* – fear of independence under Merina domination – removed, the fragile unity of the various regional elements of PADESM began to disintegrate.[1] Having no positive programme, the *côtier* movement lacked the dynamism to develop into an effective political party; and underlying divisions remained between those who were content with an indefinite continuation of French rule and those who were prepared to envisage a cautious approach to autonomy within a French Union.

In the aftermath of the insurrection moderate nationalist elements regrouped in the first incarnation of a Third Force which in various forms was to be an enduring feature of the political scene for the next twenty years. The components were the Protestant PDM, led by the ageing Pasteur Ravelojaona and a leading journalist Gabriel Razafintsalama; the Catholic MSM; a moderate socialist party PSM; the Association of Parents and Friends of Malagasy Students (APAEM); and the Association of French Citizens of Malagasy Origin (ACFOM) which was led by a *métis* journalist and prominent member of MSM Louis Rakotomalala. They were joined by a small group of "liberal" Europeans led by Roger Duveau, who foresaw the inevitability of independence and preferred to channel nationalism in the direction of gradual autonomy rather than oppose it.

The MDRM never re-emerged as a nation-wide party, even under another name, although several groups claimed to be its true successors. Some of its hard-line nationalist members turned to Communism for support and inspiration, under the influence of French Communists sent out to Madagascar to proselytise for the party. One of these, Pierre Boiteau, had been active for years in organising trade unions and had been joint Secretary-General with

Ravoahangy of the Malagasy CGT, affiliated to the French CGT, set up in 1943. He also set up in 1946 a *Groupe d'Etudes Communistes* (GEC) which was effective for some time as a nucleus of hard nationalist opinion. Many Malagasy were influenced by Communism while studying in France, and the Association of Students of Malagasy Origin (AEOM) in France developed close links with the French Communist Party (PCF) and with international communist organisations such as the World Federation of Democratic Youth. Whilst card-carrying Communists in Madagascar remained few in number they exercised disproportionate influence through the trade unions, their newspapers and their identification with anti-colonialism. They effectively controlled COSOMA (*Comité de Solidarité de Madagascar*), a small but influential group set up in 1950 to promote nationalist causes, especially the campaign for amnesty for the condemned MDRM leaders.

The suppression of political activity after the rebellion enabled the colonial administration to concentrate on economic development and administrative reform. The economy had made a good recovery from the low point in 1942 when overseas trade had almost ceased. By 1947 imports had overtaken the pre-war level while exports were understandably taking rather longer to recover. The main export crop, coffee, had especially suffered from years of neglect and its revival was delayed by the insurrection which had been most active in the main coffee-growing areas. The poor state of the infrastructure also contributed to the stagnation of exports over the next few years. A development plan introduced by de Chevigné in 1948 and supported by French government loans provided for an energetic programme of replanting, development of new crops and minerals and investment in improved communications. A series of parastatal commercial and industrial enterprises were set up and some major agricultural projects initiated, notably the draining of part of Lac Alaotra for intensive rice cultivation. In the short term the requirements of the plan led to a large increase in imports and a bigger trade deficit; in 1951 export earnings covered only 58 per cent of imports. Visible trade was to remain in deficit but increased production of export commodities during the fifties improved the commercial balance so that by the time of independence exports covered 75 per cent of imports.

Mineral production, mainly of graphite and mica, remained disappointingly low, though there was some increase in the production and export of semi-precious stones, notably garnets. Oil exploration in the 1920s had proved negative; and hopes of exploiting the Sakoa coal deposits in the southwest to meet the post-war world shortage were as short-lived as the shortage proved to be. The economy therefore remained overwhelmingly agricultural and pastoral. Coffee strengthened its position as the leading cash crop, with production rising to 60,000 tons by 1960, of which 50,000 tons were exported. Vanilla and cloves remained valuable export crops, but never recovered the volumes they achieved in the 1930s. Butter bean production continued in the arid southwest, supplemented by the development of groundnuts as a substantial export crop. The post-war period saw the emergence of two new important export commodities – sugar and sisal. Sugar cane had been grown on the east coast and in the north west for centuries, but had mostly been converted into rum or a little coarse sugar consumed locally. In the 1950s the distilling of rum was limited by government decree and new refineries producing high-quality sugar led to sugar becoming the second largest export crop by the time of independence. Sisal had been introduced in 1922 but production, mainly in the Androy region west of Fort Dauphin, only took off after 1947, especially when the Korean War stimulated world demand. By 1960 over 20,000 tons a year were being exported, but production was already on the decline owing to competition from synthetic fibres. Tobacco and cotton featured little in the export statistics, most production being absorbed by local cigarette factories and textile industries. As always, rice remained by far the largest single crop, but the legendary Malagasy consumption of rice, the highest per head in the world, left only a small amount of high-quality grain for export. The huge herds of cattle remained unexploited commercially, except for local meat production and modest exports of live cattle to Mauritius and Réunion.

The hope of increasing agricultural production at the peasant level was one reason behind the administration's attempt to revive and modernise the *fokonolona*, the traditional village assembly established by Andrianampoinimerina. Another aim was to increase the political awareness of the peasant masses as a counterweight to the dominance of the Merina in both politics and the administration. A decree of June 1950 revived the *fokonolona* in the form of *collectivités autochtones rurales* (CAR) each with a president and a council and duties including hygiene and the development of agriculture, stock breeding and local crafts. A select number of CARs, 125 in the first instance, were given special status as *collectivités rurales autochtones modernisées* (CRAM) with additional support in the way of training, more sophisticated equipment such as tractors, and the right to raise loans.[2] The CARs and CRAMs undoubtedly contributed to the increase in agricultural productivity but were less successful than had been hoped in improving agricultural techniques. As elsewhere in colonial territories the administration found it easier to supply equipment (the number of tractors increased from 50 in 1939 to 750 in 1952), than to train the peasants in new skills and persuade them to abandon the traditional methods practised by the ancestors.

The economy probably benefited more from improvements in the infrastructure, especially in the road system. Before 1950 asphalted roads were limited to a few kilometres within and immediately outside the main towns. All other roads were made of laterite, classified as all-weather (reinforced by stone), dry-season or *"jeepable"*, the last category including some truly horrendous surfaces. Even the all-weather roads were dusty in the dry season and dangerously slippery in the wet, and needed to be re-graded every year. From 1950 a programme of asphalting some of the main roads was instituted, starting with the roads from the capital to other main towns on the plateau, to Tamatave and in due course to Majunga. At the same time bridges were strengthened and widened, and maintenance of the laterite roads was improved by the use of mechanical graders. With increasing reliance on roads and motor transport there was no question of further extending the rail network. But the size of the country and the continuing poor state of most of the roads favoured the extension of air transport. In the fifties many new air-strips were built to cater for virtually all towns of a reasonable size so that in due course Madagascar could claim to have, in relation to the small population, the densest air network of any country in the world.

Meanwhile political activity slowly revived, under the impulsion of existing legislation and developments in the metropolis and elsewhere. In advance of the French legislative elections in June 1951, High Commissioner Robert Bargues, who had succeeded de Chevigné at the beginning of 1950, approved a law widening the qualifications for voting so that the Malagasy electoral roll was greatly increased from some 235,000 to over 850,000. The main beneficiaries were the less well educated coastal people, and one object of the change was to "drown" the troublesome Merina in the mass of docile *côtiers*. In this it was successful. In the elections to the Chamber of Deputies, Pascal Velonjara of PADESM was returned unopposed for the eastern region while Raveloson-Mahasampo won the western seat by a huge majority. For the central region an ambitious Catholic Merina, Stanislas Rakotonirina, an ex-member of MDRM who had been arrested, tortured and acquitted after the rebellion, attempted to revive the nationalist cause. But he could not prevail against the conservative pro-French candidate Jonah Ranaivo who, with the full backing of the administration, won by a comfortable majority. In what was to be his last electoral campaign the elderly Pasteur Ravelojaona came a very poor third. The two French seats were won by the liberal Roger Duveau and a conservative Louis Labrousse. The same pattern was repeated in the elections to the Senate. The three Malagasy seats went to two PADESM members, one of them Norbert Zafimahova, and a Betsileo supporter of the *"Présence Française"*; whilst the French seats went to the leader of the conservatives, former Deputy Jules Castellani, and a relative liberal Paul Longuet.

The election results ensured that there would be very little pressure from the Malagasy representation in the National Assembly to push the French government towards granting autonomy to Madagascar. Pressure of another kind came from Indo-China, where the liberation war culminating in the French disaster at Dien Ben Phu led to independence for Vietnam, Cambodia and Laos in 1954. The Indo-China peace settlement was achieved during the short-lived administration of Pierre Mendès-France, who was sympathetic to the aspirations of the colonial peoples. He had been a member of a Committee for Aid to Political Prisoners in Overseas Territories which campaigned for amnesty for the imprisoned MDRM leaders. As prime minister he appointed Roger Duveau as state secretary (ie junior minister) for overseas affairs, where he was able to achieve an amnesty for some of the lesser MDRM leaders and a reduction of sentences for the others. The Mendès-France government also instructed colonial governors to accelerate progress towards independence. In Madagascar a new High Commissioner, appointed in 1953, proved well fitted to carry out these instructions. He was André Soucadaux, a Socialist with considerable colonial experience, and he was to play a key role in steering Madagascar to independence in conditions of peace and harmony with the metropolitan power.

The change in the political climate in France caused the various interests and factions within Madagascar to regroup and define their attitudes and policies, especially in relation to the main political issues of the day, namely the speed of progress to independence and amnesty for the imprisoned MDRM leaders. Attitudes to independence varied from the conservatives of PADESM who wanted Madagascar to remain an overseas department of France, to the communists and other "hard" nationalists who called for an immediate and complete separation from the metropolis. In between were a majority who favoured a more or less speedy progress to some degree of autonomy or independence in continuing close association with France. Similarly PADESM conservatives opposed any form of amnesty; the hard nationalists called not only for amnesty but for a full pardon and annulment of the trial;

whilst the moderates, a number of whom viewed with apprehension the return of the charismatic ex-Deputies, supported a simple amnesty without going so far as a pardon and annulment.

The colonial administration, which still exercised a predominant influence, adapted skilfully to the changed political scene. While continuing to oppose the communists and other nationalists calling for immediate independence, they distanced themselves from the right-wing French *colons* and pro-French Malagasy conservatives and gave their support to French liberals and moderate progressives among the Malagasy. Senator Castellani and his supporters of the *Presence Française*, whose main strength lay in the big commercial companies and the larger plantations, denounced the administration for its "betrayal" of French interests. But the majority of the French population became reconciled to the inevitability of some form of autonomy and increasingly transferred their electoral support to the liberals. The latter sought to strengthen their links with moderate Malagasy politicians of the amorphous Third Force by setting up various groups such as *Action Madécasse*. Personal rivalries and the march of events led in due course to the disintegration of these groups, but they served as a vehicle for liberals like Roger Duveau to make themselves more acceptable to the Malagasy as well as the French electorate.

In this period the Catholic Church in Madagascar, and in particular the Jesuit mission, became an important political factor. In the post-war years the Vatican's main political concern was to arrest the tide of communism. It accurately foresaw the inevitable success of the anti-colonial struggle and was worried about the long-term effects if the Church remained aligned with the colonial administrations in resisting nationalism while the nationalists received their main support from the Communist world. A policy accordingly emerged of lending support to moderate (preferably Catholic) nationalists in their demands for independence, and Madagascar was one of the first countries where it was applied. On December 20, 1953 the Catholic bishops of Madagascar issued a statement supporting the nationalists' aspirations for independence. Despite the disapproval of the administration and the outrage of the *colons*, this was followed in 1955 by a statement in support of amnesty for the condemned MDRM leaders. In July of the same year a *communiqué* instructed Catholics how to exercise their vote in the forthcoming French legislative elections and threatened excommunication for those who supported Communist candidates. The moving spirit in all this was a strongly anti-Communist Jesuit priest, Father Boué.

In contrast the Protestant churches as such never sought a political role. The Protestants were of course divided among several denominations and there was no single powerful and politically-motivated foreign mission comparable to the Jesuits: in the plateau area the Protestant churches were by now largely in the hands of the Malagasy. On the other hand the historical links between the ex-LMS Protestant church and the Merina aristocracy and bourgeoisie meant that most of the early nationalist leaders had been Protestants, including a number of ministers such as Pasteur Ravelojaona. Individual Protestants, including a few pastors, continued to figure prominently among the "hard" nationalists. But although a small number flirted with communism, most of them drew the line at overt collaboration with the Communists.

Because of the strength of the Christian churches, the importance of family and tradition and the absence of any sizeable industrial proletariat, Madagascar was stony ground for the Communists. Nevertheless, and despite their small numbers, they were an important factor in the pre-independence years thanks to their dedication and organisational skill backed by advice from the French Communist Party (PCF). The main advice was to make no serious attempt to proselytise on behalf of Marxism, indeed to play down their own Communist beliefs, but to identify themselves with the nationalist anti-colonial cause and seek to infiltrate and control the "respectable" nationalist organisations such as COSOMA and the *Comité Nationale pour l'Amnistie des Condamnés* (CNAC). A central rôle was played by a young woman, Gisèle Rabesahala, who had worked as a secretary to Communist leaders in France and had acquired prestige by meeting both Mao Tse Tung, at a Congress of Asian Women in Peking in 1949, and Stalin, in Moscow on the way to the Congress. Over the next decade she edited Communist newspapers, organised trade unions and served on the committees, often as Secretary-General, of many of the hard nationalist groups. She was joined by others who had been trained in Eastern Europe, such as Rémi Rakotobe and his brother Henri; and by some of the ex-MDRM leaders, such as Jules Ranaivo, who had been released by amnesty in the mid-fifties.

Trade unions were an obvious field for Communist infiltration. Although memberships were never large, trade unions were important in providing a means of political expression and an apprenticeship in political organisation in the period when political parties as such were banned. As we have seen Communists were involved in the establishment of the *Confedération Générale du Travail Malgache* (CGTM), which was affiliated to the French Communist-controlled CGT, and they remained active in its leadership. In the early fifties objections to the strong Communist links caused a number of members to leave to join Christian unions. The leadership responded by dissimulating their Marxist beliefs and emphasising their support for anti-colonial nationalism. Criticisms of subordination to a metropolitan body led in 1956 to disaffiliation from the French CGT and the adoption of a new Malagasy title with the acronym FISEMA. However the organisation remained effectively under PCF control through local Communists such as Gisèle Rabesahala and Rémi Rakotobe.

The main Christian (Catholic) trade union was the Malagasy branch of the *Confédération Française des Travailleurs Chrétiens* (CFTCM) set up in 1945. It had many more members than the CGTM (34,000 in 1954 compared with 7,000 for CGTM) but before the "bishops' communiqué" of December 1953 it confined itself largely to the social aspects of trade union work. Thereafter, inspired by the Jesuits (notably Father de Puybaudet), it became actively involved, in competition with the CGTM, in support of the nationalist causes of amnesty and independence. Also like the CGTM it broke away from its metropolitan parent in 1956, changing its name to the *Confédération Chrétienne de Syndicats Malgaches* (CCSM). In the following year a new body, the *Confédération des Travailleurs de Madagascar et des Comores* (CTMC) was set up as the trade union branch of the progressive *côtier* movement. Thus trade unionism as an independent political force hardly existed in Madagascar, each union acting mainly as the syndicalist arm of a political party or movement.

With no university in Madagascar, student activism played little role there. But in France the main Malagasy students' association AEOM became inevitably a centre of nationalist agitation and, as already noted, was in close contact with the PCF and international communist organisations. Freed from the restrictions of colonial government they were able to express themselves uninhibitedly; and their conferences, declarations and communiqués had a considerable impact when reported in Madagascar. Many of their leaders, such as Alfred Ramangasoavina and Richard Andriamanjato, later returned to play significant parts in pre- and post-independence politics, usually though not always on the left. Another, more moderate, nationalist voice in France was the *Conseil National Malgache* (CNM) set up in 1949 by Dr Rakoto-Ratsimamanga and Raymond Rabemananjara, two of the founder members of MDRM who had remained free of any suspicion of involvement in the rebellion. During the imprisonment of the three ex-Deputies they came to be regarded as the guardians of MDRM nationalism, whose aims they continued to propagate through the press and their contacts with French politicians and the emerging political parties in Madagascar. However the three ex-Deputies continued to be regarded as the true leaders of Malagasy nationalism and their long-range influence was an important factor in Madagascar, especially after they were released from prison. In August 1955 Raseta was transferred from prison to house arrest in Grasse; and in March 1956 Ravoahangy and Jacques Rabemananjara were conditionally released but required to remain in metropolitan France. However the divisions appearing among the various nationalist groups in Madagascar were soon reflected in the Deputies themselves. Raseta moved closer to the Communists while the Catholic Rabemananjara became the great hope of the Jesuits, with Ravoahangy occupying a middle position and developing close links with the French Socialist Party (SFIO).

News of the Deputies' release was an encouragement to the nationalists who now called for the return of the Deputies to Madagascar. But it was received with consternation by the conservative *côtiers* as an indication that the French will to rule had weakened. They now saw the need to come to terms with the nationalists but never adjusted satisfactorily to the new situation. Among the progressive *côtiers*, however, a new leader emerged as a natural ally of the French liberals and protagonist of the administration's new policy of steady progress towards independence.

Philibert Tsiranana was a Tsimihety born of humble parentage near Mandritsara probably in 1910. As a boy he tended his family's few zebu cattle, but later he received sufficient education to be admitted in 1930 to the teacher training section of the *Ecole Le Myre de Vilers* in Antananarivo. After qualifying, he taught as an assistant teacher in the capital for a decade and became an official in the teachers' union. He was one of the founders of PADESM in 1946, but at the end of that year he went to France to spend the next four years obtaining a higher teaching qualification in Montpellier. This experience both developed his political ideas in the direction of moderate socialism (he subsequently joined the SFIO) and left him with a respect and affection for the French. His contacts with other students, mainly Merina, in the AEOM would also be useful to him later on. After his return he was elected to the Representative Assembly via the Majunga Provincial Assembly, and soon established himself as the leader of a progressive group among the *côtiers* aiming at gradual movement towards autonomy within some form of French Union. While avoiding the reverse racism of the conservative *côtier* leaders and seeking allies among the Merina as well as other ethnic groups, Tsiranana insisted that a prerequisite of autonomy was educational and political advance among the *côtiers* to enable them to compete on more equal terms with the plateau people. But his firm views in support of autonomy and a single non-racial electoral college made him acceptable to moderate Merina nationalists, both Protestant and Catholic (he was himself a Catholic, though originally brought up as a Protestant). Beneath a bluff peasant demeanour he concealed a shrewd political brain which was to serve him well in the manoeuvrings for power over the next few years.

The next electoral test came with the French legislative elections of January 2, 1956, which produced some surprising results. Roger Duveau's success in working for racial harmony and defending Madagascar's interests in the National Assembly was rewarded by his being elected unopposed for the *Malagasy* seat representing the east coast, the sitting PADESM Deputy Velonjara withdrawing in his favour. For the west coast, Tsiranana enjoyed the solid support of his own Tsimihety people and of progressive *côtiers* generally. As he was also favoured by the administration and supported by a significant number of moderate Merina nationalists, he comfortably defeated the sitting PADESM Deputy, the arch-conservative Raveloson-Mahasampo.

For the plateau seat Stanislas Rakotonirina again raised the standard of traditional Merina nationalism, with the enthusiastic support of the Jesuit mission. But, as he did not wish to appear as the "Jesuit candidate", he repudiated their support and successfully sought the endorsement of the Communists and hard-line nationalists who had set up the *Union du Peuple Malgache* (UPM). However this endorsement alienated many anti-Communist Merina who preferred to support other Merina candidates such as Louis Rakotomalala. Moreover the socialist High Commissioner, disapproving of the Jesuit interference in politics, gave his support to a conservative Betsileo candidate Rakotovelo, who emerged the comfortable winner. Rakotonirina appealed without success to Paris, alleging fraud and administration interference. But whilst administration influence might have helped, especially in the rural districts, Rakotovelo's victory was due to other factors: his solid Betsileo support, the anti-Merina vote of other peoples living in the plateau region and the split of the Merina vote among several candidates. Thus the Merina nationalists were again denied the victory which they considered their due. And their bitter complaints against the Betsileo victory further widened the division between them and the other peoples of the island.

This was a period of intense political activity, especially in Antananarivo, as electoral committees set up for the legislative elections registered as political parties, formed alliances, split, formed new parties and regrouped in a bewildering manner. The aim was in the short term to win elections and in the longer term to form a national party which would inherit the mantle of MDRM and lead the country to early independence. But Merina hopes of resuming their dominant role were doomed not only by their numerical inferiority[3] but by their internal divisions – Catholic and Protestant, Communist and anti-Communist, extremist and moderate, anti-French and pro-French – compounded by the conflict of personal ambitions.[4] Almost the only stable element was the UPM, at the extreme left of the political spectrum. One of the leading non-Communist nationalist groups was the *Front National Malgache* (FNM), essentially Merina protestant bourgeois, though at one stage it had some support among progressive *côtiers* including Tsiranana. But it soon split between "hard" and moderate nationalists. The *"durs"*, including young intellectuals such as Henri Razanatseheno and Emile Ramarosaona, remained in control of FNM, while the moderates left to form the *Rassemblement du Peuple Malgache* (RPM).[5] Both FNM and RPM tried to widen their support among Catholics, trade unionists and *côtiers*, but had little success in disarming coastal suspicions of the Merina, which were compounded by the arrogant paternalism of some of the Merina élite with regard to the coastal people.

Meanwhile in Paris the 1956 elections had produced a left-of-centre Republican Front coalition government led by the Socialist Guy Mollet and dedicated to a more liberal colonial policy. In June 1956 the National Assembly adopted the *loi cadre* proposed by the Minister for Overseas Territories Gaston Defferre as a framework for constitutional advance in the territories. It provided for all the territories universal suffrage and a single electoral college. For Madagascar it extended the powers of the elected assemblies and provided for a partly elected executive, with a central council of government and provincial councils for the five provinces, which became six after the addition of Diego Suarez. Despite suspicions by the nationalists that it was a tactic to delay independence,[6] and resentment by the Merina at the perpetuation and extension of provincial decentralisation, the *loi cadre* was generally welcomed as a decisive step forward.

The first elections under the *loi cadre*, for the municipal councils, took place on November 18, 1956. Though not of great political significance in themselves, the municipal elections were symbolically and psychologically important in enabling Malagasy to assume positions of authority, notably as mayors of the main towns, for the first time. Moreover, success in the municipals could have a bandwaggon effect on later national elections. All parties therefore made a major effort. The hard left set up a coalition CEAP

(*Comité d'Entente et d'Action Politique*) but after suspicion of the Communist elements, heightened by the Soviet suppression of risings in Hungary and Poland, had caused the withdrawal of some parties, it was limited to the UPM and the *"durs"* of FNM. Stanislas Rakotonirina, still seeing himself as the future national leader, this time welcomed the support of the Jesuits. With their help he set up a coalition, the *Union des Indépendants de Tananarive* (UIT), embracing not only Catholics but also Protestant anti-Communists, including the RPM, as well as European liberals. By emphasising social and economic issues and the support of the Catholic trade unions he widened his appeal from the Merina bourgeoisie to embrace a much more popular constituency; and through the missions he gained powerful allies in other towns

The outcome was a victory for Stanislas Rakotonirina and the Catholic missions. In Antananarivo, UIT won twice as many seats as CEAP, and Rakotonirina became mayor. UIT allies also prevailed in Antsirabe and Majunga, whilst in Fianarantsoa mainly Catholic candidates swept the board, electing an ex-MDRM member Dr Michel Randria as mayor. In Diego Suarez the strength of the FISEMA trade union among the naval base workers ensured a victory for the CEAP list, led by ex-MDRM senator Justin Bezara. Tamatave saw a landslide for a local list led by another, but more moderate, ex-MDRM member Alexis Bezaka, a close friend of Jacques Rabemananjara. In Tulear the ultra-conservatives under Raveloson-Mahasampo won most seats, although the CEAP list led by another ex-MDRM member, Monja Jaona[7], made a respectable showing.

With UIT and its allies successful in four out of seven towns and ex-MDRM leaders in control in two others, the prospects for Rakotonirina's ambitions looked good. But these elections had been limited to the small urban population; the mass of the peasants, mainly non-Merina, had not yet spoken. The provincial elections, due on March 31, 1957, were far more significant, since the provincial assemblies would designate the members of the national Representative Assembly who would then elect members of the council of government. They would thus in effect determine the country's future political orientation and leadership; especially as it transpired that there would not be another general election before independence.

For the provincial elections two new parties were set up to compete for the coastal vote, thus formalising the growing split between the conservatives and progressives of the old PADESM. In December 1956 the conservatives set up the *Union des Démocrates Sociaux de Madagascar* (UDSM). Its President was Raveloson-

Mahasampo but the real leader was the Vice-President, Senator Norbert Zafimahova. UDSM had a potentially large following in the south and east but was handicapped by an essentially negative or passive programme: opposition to Merina domination, defence of provincial autonomy and close relations with France, though by now even the conservatives felt obliged to accept, without much enthusiasm, the aim of autonomy within a federation and, even more reluctantly, the concept of amnesty.

In the same month Tsiranana and a group of progressive *côtiers* meeting in Majunga founded the *Parti Social Democrate* (PSD).[8] The founding members were mainly from Majunga province, which was to remain the heartland of PSD, but they included representatives of other coastal provinces, notably André Resampa from Morondava. Early recruits included Calvin Tsiebo from Tulear and Eugène Lechat, a French schoolteacher from Mananjary on the east coast. PSD's political philosophy was a very moderate socialism, with little ideology and the emphasis on hard work, realism and practical solutions. Its immediate programme was autonomy and the working out of a new relationship with France within a Community (Tsiranana appears to have originated this concept) something on the lines of the British Commonwealth. In due course it also came out in favour of total amnesty for the MDRM leaders. This platform enabled it to attract some support from moderate Merina nationalists; and the energy and organising ability of its leaders soon built up a network of party branches which gave it a broader base than any other party.

In Antananarivo the contest appeared to lie between the extreme left-wing CEAP and the mainly Catholic nationalists of UIT. For the latter the new mayor Stanislas Rakotonirina, hoping to repeat his success in the municipals, adopted a tough nationalist programme calling for full independence and total amnesty. Again Father Boué and the Jesuits were active in his support. They concentrated on exposing the Communist elements of CEAP, to such effect that several FNM members withdrew from the CEAP coalition. They included the former AEOM student leader Alfred Ramangasoavina, who joined Louis Rakotomalala and other moderate nationalists such as Gabriel Razafintsalama in a *Liste de Défense des Droits du Peuple* (LDDP).

In the country as a whole the provincial elections offered a choice between the "nationalists", based mainly in the capital and calling for immediate and total independence, and the "moderates" favouring negotiated independence in continuing close association with France. The latter group included the main coastal parties PSD and UDSM and several more locally-based Christian parties in

Fianarantsoa and Tamatave provinces. The result was a clear victory for the moderates. In the capital the nationalist but non-Communist UIT took two-thirds of the seats, with LDDP taking the remainder; the left wing CEAP did not win a single seat. CEAP had the consolation of a majority in Diego Suarez, though its list included a prominent moderate *côtier* Victor Miadana, who was elected leader of the provincial council but then defected to PSD; and Monja Jaona picked up a few seats for them in Tulear. Elsewhere the moderates won comfortably, with UDSM ahead in Tulear and Fianarantsoa and PSD leading in Majunga but also doing well in the other coastal areas.

Each provincial assembly now elected nine of their number to sit in the national Representative Assembly. Next came, on May 25 1957, the crucial election, from the Representative Assembly, of seven members of the Council of Government, who would have ministerial portfolios in the colonial administration. UDSM's numerical strength would have justified two ministerial posts. But Norbert Zafimahova, fearing that ministers might be required to take unpopular decisions, made a tactical blunder in not putting himself forward as a candidate and in agreeing to only one ministerial post[9] for UDSM (Philibert Raondry). Instead he accepted the prestigious position of President of the Assembly, with his UDSM colleague Raveloson-Mahasampo as Vice-President. The PSD took a more robust attitude and Tsiranana was elected Vice-President of the Council of Government (presided over by the High Commissioner) while Resampa became Minister of Education and Youth. Widespread resentment of Jesuit interference and Rakotonirina's arrogance ensured that UIT was denied a ministerial post; the only Merina appointed was Alfred Ramangasoavina as Minister of Finance.[10] The CEAP were content with the appointment of Justin Bezara of Diego Suarez as Minister of Supply; and drew comfort from the nationalist backgrounds of Ramangasoavina and Alexis Bezaka from Tamatave who became Minister of Health.

By now independence was no longer an issue. The questions discussed by politicians and press over the next year were when and in what form. In the Representative Assembly three separate motions were debated without a decision being reached: for immediate independence as an associated state; for independence followed by a referendum on the new status; and (the PSD proposal) for two-stage independence, with internal autonomy followed by full independence within a French Community. In this national debate the Merina intellectual élite attempted to reassert itself. In 1956 a group of them including Ramangasoavina and Emile Ramarosaona had set up a *Union des Intellectuels et Universitaires Malgaches*

(UNIUM). In June 1957 UNIUM issued a manifesto recalling the unification of Madagascar under the Merina monarchy and the rôle of the MDRM as a national party. It demanded recognition of the country's right to independence as an associated state within a French Union, the dissolution of the Assemblies and new elections. This was badly received by the *côtiers* as a revival of Merina ambitions, especially when UNIUM subsequently called for a unitary state and the abolition of the provincial governments. But it was welcomed by the non-Communist nationalists and for a time UNIUM was recognised as the spokesman of Malagasy nationalism. The intellectual voice was reinforced by the student movement in France. By now AEOM was even more left-wing under the leadership of Richard Andriamanjato, a theology student at Strasbourg who, though not himself a Communist, favoured alliance with Communists, both in Madagascar and abroad, to achieve early and complete independence.

Having fallen out with Stanislas Rakotonirina, the Jesuits now regarded UIT as a lost cause and instead advocated the establishment of separate Christian Workers' parties in each province. Curiously, despite PSD's moderate programme and the fact that Tsiranana and most of the leading members of the party were Catholics, the fanatically anti-Communist Jesuits continued to denounce PSD as Marxist and to work against it, thus missing their best chance of influencing the post-independence government. The decline of UIT also left a vacuum among nationalists in the capital which CEAP sought to fill. Its senior partner UPM moved further to the left, with Communists taking over most positions in the leadership. They adopted an even tougher line, advocating immediate independence of a "Malagasy Democratic Republic", the direct election of a national parliament and various measures of nationalisation. With help from COSOMA and FISEMA they began late in 1957 a campaign of political and social agitation, including a call for a general strike which had some success in Diego Suarez and Antsirabe. Their FNM partners, while not agreeing with all UPM's programme, felt obliged to go along with this intransigent line, which attracted increasing support in the Representative Assembly. In Tamatave, Bezaka set up a *Comite d'action sociale et politique pour l'indépendance de Madagascar* (CAPSIM) and moved closer to UPM's position on repeal of the *loi cadre* and immediate independence. Thus the moderates' victory in the 1957 elections appeared threatened by a re-grouping of the nationalists on a broader base than hitherto.

A more formal alliance of the nationalists was brought about by the question of amnesty. This was no longer a domestic issue: in

November 1957 the Representative Assembly had voted unanimously for a total amnesty and the return of the MDRM exiles. In March 1958 the French National Assembly also adopted an amnesty resolution, but it incorporated a Socialist amendment (no doubt inspired by Tsiranana) excluding the ex-Deputies from political activity and preventing their return to Madagascar for five years. This provoked Bezaka and UNIUM to call an "Independence Congress" in Tamatave early in May to coordinate nationalist campaigns to end French rule. The Congress was attended by the three nationalist ministers – Bezara, Bezaka and Ramangasoavina – and representatives of all the nationalist groups except UIT, together with regional Christian parties from Fianarantsoa and Tamatave. Members of UNIUM and AEOM played a leading role, with Andriamanjato, recently returned from France as an ordained Protestant minister, particularly prominent despite his youth. The Congress called for negotiations with France for the establishment of a democratic and unitary Malagasy Republic under a constitution prepared by a constituent assembly chosen by direct elections under UN supervision. A permanent delegation of the Congress was appointed to coordinate nationalist activity to achieve these goals.

Once again, however, events in Madagascar were pre-empted by developments in the metropolis, where the Algerian crisis brought de Gaulle back to power. He proposed a new Constitution for the Fifth Republic with a new autonomous status for the overseas territories within a French Community. The overseas territories were to take part in the referendum on the new Constitution, it being made clear that a negative vote would mean immediate independence and a severance of all links with France.[11] The referendum campaign divided the Malagasy on predictable lines. The nationalists represented at the Tamatave Congress, plus a new party MONIMA (*Mouvement National pour l'Indépendance de Madagascar*) founded by Monja Jaona, advocated "no" as did UIT, most of the Protestant churches and the Jesuits in Antananarivo. But the Catholic bishops and missions elsewhere favoured "yes" as did the coastal parties and the moderate nationalists who together outnumbered the "hard" nationalists. The "yes" vote was reinforced by de Gaulle's visit in August, when he addressed a great crowd in the stadium at Mahamasina, at the foot of the "place of the hurling" surmounted by the queen's palace, by now a national museum. With typical grandiloquence he pointed to the palace, saying: "Tomorrow you will once more be a State, as you were when that palace was inhabited".

In the referendum held on September 28 1958 an overwhelm-

The road to independence

ing majority voted "yes" – 77 per cent to 22 per cent "no". Those who voted "no" had a clear majority in the capital and a very narrow majority in Antananarivo province. Elsewhere the "yes" vote was very large, rising to over 90 per cent in Majunga, Tulear and Fianarantsoa provinces. The victors moved swiftly against the partisans of the "no" vote. Tsiranana dismissed Bezaka and Ramangasoavina from the government, though Bezara, who also voted "no" but had kept a low profile, was allowed to remain. In Antananarivo defectors from UIT joined with the LDDP to force Rakotonirina from his posts of Mayor and Vice-President (ie leader under the *Chef de Province*) of the provincial council, replacing him with Rakotomalala and Razafintsalama respectively.

The government decreed that the decision on the precise future status of the country should be made not by the indirectly elected Representative Assembly but by a Congress of all the Provincial Assemblies. On October 14 1958, the Congress voted unanimously (apart from a small number of abstentions) for autonomy within the Community. On the following day the High Commissioner formally proclaimed French recognition of a Malagasy state and abrogation of the annexation of 1896. Under provisional arrangements pending adoption of a new constitution the Council of Government became a provisional government headed by Tsiranana with the powers of a prime minister; and the Vice-Presidents of the Provincial Councils became Presidents. The Representative Assembly was dissolved and replaced by a Constituent Assembly of 90 members, to be elected by the Congress of Provincial Assemblies meeting together, rather than each Assembly choosing its own quota of members. This clever move meant that the strength of "no" voters in Antananarivo province would count for nothing against the massed votes of the other provinces. Accordingly only members of parties which had voted "yes" in the referendum were elected to the Constituent Assembly.

The "no" voters were thus eliminated from power, but not yet crushed. The Permanent Delegation of the Tamatave Congress invited all parties who had attended the Congress to regroup in opposition to the provisional government. Once again fear of the UPM Communists who dominated the Permanent Delegation led most parties to decline, leaving only UPM, FNM and two other small left-wing parties to form on October 19 the *Parti du Congrès de l'Indépendance de Madagascar*, known by its Malagasy acronym AKFM, of which Andriamanjato, aged only 29, became President. AKFM immediately adopted a hard line against the Government, insisting on complete independence rather than an intermediate solution within the Community. They still hoped that the appeal of their independence slogan and the return of the MDRM ex-Deputies would generate sufficient nationalist emotion to sweep the moderates from power. The other Congress parties, notably Bezaka's CAPSIM and some moderate nationalist groups from Antananarivo and Fianarantsoa, formed another new party the *Rassemblement National Malgache* (RNM). It incorporated most of the remaining members of UIT apart from its leader Rakotonirina who refused to join and was left without a party. Like AKFM, RNM called for complete independence outside the Community and opposed the government but from a more moderate standpoint, partly because Bezaka hoped to rejoin the government. As for the Catholic groups, the various provincial Christian Workers' parties, meeting in Tamatave in December, formed the *Rassemblement Chrétien Malgache* (RCM) with Dr Michel Randria from Fianarantsoa as President. The RCM represented a sizeable number of voters, but disagreements on policy among Church leaders prevented them from exercising much influence. The Jesuits in the capital continued to oppose any dealings with the "Marxist" PSD,[12] while a majority of RCM including Dr Randria followed other Church leaders who favoured cooperation with the government. However, suspicions of the Jesuits led Tsiranana to rebuff offers of RCM support in return for a ministerial post.

At the beginning of 1959 Tsiranana appeared to be in a strong position as head of the provisional government and leader of the largest party in the Provisional National Assembly. He also continued to enjoy the sympathetic support and advice of the High Commissioner Soucadaux. But his position was still far fom secure. With 37 seats out of 90 in the Assembly, PSD was some way from being the majority party. Its somewhat reluctant coalition partner UDSM, which disagreed with PSD on some fundamental issues such as the shape of the new constitution, had no less than 36 seats in the Assembly with Zafimahova as President; it also had three ministerial posts (a third UDSM minister Albert Sylla from Ile Sainte-Marie had been appointed in place of Bezaka). Moreover Tsiranana was vulnerable to attack from AKFM and RNM on the limitations of Malagasy sovereignty within the Community. France remained responsible for foreign affairs and for defence: Madagascar had neither army nor *gendarmerie* of its own, was not a member of the United Nations and its relations with other countries were conducted through the High Commissioner by the French Government. After the euphoria over the achievement of autonomy had faded, more and more Malagasy began to call for the completion of the independence process.

Tsiranana therefore had to steer a difficult middle course: expanding PSD's electoral base, largely at the expense of UDSM, without losing UDSM's support in the Government; and fending off nationalist attacks while retaining his moderate nationalist support. In the competition with UDSM, PSD had the advantages of a more positive programme, dynamic leadership and efficient organisation. At a party congress in January 1959 it was decided to set up a PSD section in every administrative unit in the country; and by August they could claim to have increased their membership from 70,000 to 250,000. But their key advantages were PSD's control of the administration and Tsiranana's powers of patronage. In February 1959 he created three new posts of state secretary (junior minister) and appointed to them two members of PSD and Louis Rakotomalala, who now joined PSD. In contrast UDSM was less well organised and disciplined, and tended to be split between those who were generally willing to support PSD, perhaps in the hope of sharing in government patronage, and others led by Zafimahova who preferred to maintain a separate identity in the hope of replacing PSD as the dominant party. By now Zafimahova was becoming almost obsessively jealous of Tsiranana. His proposals for the new constitution – a parliamentary rather than a presidential system, a National Assembly elected by proportional representation, a referendum and new elections – were at least partly designed to limit Tsiranana's powers and prevent PSD from swamping the Assembly on a first-past-the-post, single-constituency election. However opinion generally favoured the PSD preference for a presidential system roughly on the American style. After much discussion and amendment in a special Constitutional Consultative Committee and then in the Provisional National Assembly as a whole, a presidential-style constitution was adopted on April 28 1959 by a unanimous vote of the Assembly, with only Zafimahova abstaining.

Under the Constitution the President of the Republic was also Head of the Government; he was elected for seven years, not by popular vote but by an electoral college consisting of the members of the National Assembly and Senate and all elected members of provincial and local governments. The National Assembly was to be elected for five years by universal suffrage, with one member for each constituency of approximately 50,000 inhabitants. The Senate would contain 54 Senators, six from each province elected indirectly by delegates of the provincial and local assemblies and 18 nominated by the government to represent economic, social and cultural forces.

A *Conseil Supérieur de la République* of five members would act as a constitutional high court to interpret the Constitution and arbitrate on any disputes between executive and legislature. In each province there would be an elected *Conseil Général de Province* and an executive *Secrétaire d'Etat Délégué* appointed by the President and assisted by two appointed *Contrôleurs-Généraux de Province*. Tsiranana and the PSD, having taken charge of the central government, had become less keen on decentralisation and provincial autonomy, and wished to extend their control over provincial as well as national institutions. Under transitional arrangements the Constituent Assembly would remain as the Provisional National Assembly until the new Assembly was convened; the members of the Constitutional Consultative Committee would become the first Senate; and the Provincial Assemblies would act as *Conseils Généraux de Province* until new councils were elected. Thus PSD dominance of the government machine would not be disturbed by immediate new elections.

The first act of the new transitional parliament was to elect the President. On May 1, 1959 Tsiranana was elected by the unanimous vote of all members present. One of those absent was Zafimahova who, although still President of the Assembly, had gone off to France rather than witness the triumph of his rival. Following this act of pique a majority of the Assembly signed a motion of no confidence in him, after which he resigned, being replaced in due course by Jules Ravony,[13] a UDSM member who had joined PSD. Other UDSM members also defected to PSD which now had a majority with 46 members, while UDSM declined to only 18. The new government appointed by Tsiranana reflected the new balance of power. There were six PSD ministers – Resampa as Minister of the Interior, Botokeky and Lechat of the original PSD, plus Rakotomalala, Paul Longuet and Ramangasoavina, who returned to office by joining PSD. Of three UDSM ministers, Albert Sylla (who was made Vice-President of the government) and Raondry were preparing to join PSD, and Randrianasolo would later leave UDSM and found a Betsileo party (Malagasy initials AVM) supporting the Government. In his frustration and bitterness at his rival's success Zafimahova forgot his principles and joined in the left-wing call for immediate full independence, amnesty and the return of the ex-Deputies. This led to some sharp exchanges with the President. But with municipal elections covering 26 communes due in October 1959, Tsiranana needed UDSM support against AKFM. The latter was now firmly in the hands of the ex-UPM extreme nationalists (the leading ex-FNM members had resigned after a disagreement over participation in an anti-government demonstration). The rousing oratory of Andriamanjato and the propaganda skills and organising ability of Gisèle Rabesahala as Secretary-General were winning more support for their intransigent demands for full independence and amnesty, especially among the educated classes. Tsiranana, whilst reasonably confident of victory in the country as a whole, feared the possibility of a humiliating defeat by AKFM in the main towns. He accordingly held out an olive branch to Zafimahova, baited with offers of government posts for two of his brothers. Zafimahova agreed to moderate his opposition and to cooperate with PSD in the elections in those areas where AKFM posed a serious threat.

Tsiranana's fears were well founded. PSD won a majority in only one of the main towns, Majunga, and even here AKFM won ten seats to PSD's 18. AKFM triumphed in the two communes of the capital as well as in Diego Suarez and two other smaller communes. Tamatave went to Bezaka's RNM and Fianarantsoa to a joint UDSM/RCM list. Even in Tulear a joint UDSM/PSD list lost to MONIMA. Taking the six main towns together, PSD won only 40 out of 192 seats. However PSD's strength in the countryside, greatly helped by the prestige of being the party of the *fanjakana* (government), prevailed in 16 of the remaining 19 communes. This rural strength also ensured that PSD dominated in the elections to the Provincial Councils. PSD candidates were elected Presidents of the councils in Majunga, Tulear, Tamatave and even Diego Suarez, while the Presidents elected in Antananarivo and Fianarantsoa provinces were from parties allied to PSD.

Tsiranana's success has been attributed by many writers to the support of the colonial administration, which saw in him a suitably malleable moderate who would lead the country to independence at a measured pace in close collaboration with France. Administration support and Tsiranana's close and friendly relations with Soucadaux were certainly helpful, but there were many other reasons. Anti-Merina feeling in the majority of the population and divisions among the Merina ensured that the wishes of the coastal peoples would prevail. Among the coastal parties PSD was the best organised, with Resampa as an outstandingly able and energetic admininistrator; and Tsiranana proved to be the shrewdest of the coastal politicians, especially in judging the pace of events and in appealing to a wide spread of voters from the less conservative *côtiers* to the moderate nationalists of the plateau and the French liberals. He also reassured the French population as a whole by telling them that they would be welcome to stay on and referring to them as the nineteenth tribe of Madagascar. He was tactically skilful in isolating his most dangerous opponents such as UIT and combining with others to defeat them; and then repeating the same manoeuvre on erstwhile allies such as Zafimahova and UDSM. He used his considerable powers of patronage as head of the government to win over many former opponents and to infiltrate the administration with PSD members, especially after Resampa became Minister of the Interior while remaining Secretary-General of the party. Thus the administration became more and more identified with PSD, which accordingly benefited from the traditional Malagasy respect for authority and tendency to vote for the party of the *fanjakana*. Moreover, having secured the key appointment of Vice-President of the Council of Government via the doubly indirect election of 1957, he resisted all proposals which might have put his position at risk either by new parliamentary elections, a referendum on the Constitution or a direct election of the President. Whilst paying lip service to amnesty he also made sure, with the collaboration of the French authorities, that the three ex-Deputies, potentially his most serious rivals, did not return until his position as President of the Republic was unassailable.

For the moment, however, the AKFM relative success in the municipal elections showed that his position was vulnerable to the growing clamour for full independence, which was finding support even within PSD. He therefore decided to take away AKFM's strongest weapon by coming out in favour of full independence himself. After a visit to Paris to obtain de Gaulle's approval he summoned a joint meeting of the Senate and the National Assembly on December 22 1959 at which he announced his intention of starting negotiations immediately for "the transfer to Madagascar of the residual powers held by the Community". A week later in his New Year speech he emphasised the need to achieve the transfer amicably and to maintain links with France as a guarantee of protection against Communism.

Tsiranana appealed for the support of all parties in the negotiations. Apart from PSD and UDSM, and other smaller pro-government parties, support was forthcoming from Bezaka's RNM and significantly from the Merina intellectuals of UNIUM and the remnants of FNM. The AKFM leaders were caught off balance as they could not appear to be against independence. So they demanded that a proclamation of independence, new elections and the return of the ex-Deputies should precede negotiations, in which the ex-Deputies should participate. A similar attitude was taken by MONIMA, the rump of UIT and even by the Christian RCM. Tsiranana had no intention of acceding to these demands, although by now he had little to fear from the ex-Deputies. Raseta, closely linked to the AKFM extremists, remained hostile. But Ravoahangy and Rabemananjara were well informed on the popularity of Tsiranana and the strength of PSD. Recognising that there was no hope of reviving the MDRM dream, they had for some time been advising their friends among moderate nationalists in Antananarivo and Tamatave to cooperate with Tsiranana, whom Rabemananjara was later to describe as "the only man capable of uniting all the Malagasy".[14] Their views were in fact quite close to Tsiranana's on the need for a friendly association with France after independence and for Madagascar to remain in the Western camp.

The independence negotiations in Paris led rapidly to agreement that Madagascar would become completely independent while staying within the Community (this had not been foreseen and required amendment of the French laws governing the Community). The agreement on the "transfer of powers" was signed on April 2 1960 and on the same day a series of Cooperation Agreements governing future relations with France was initialled. These covered a wide range of subjects such as nationality and the status of French residents in Madagascar and of Malagasy residents in France; but the most significant agreements related to defence, foreign policy, education, finance and economic policy.

Under the defence arrangements a Malagasy army was to be set up, consisting initially of Malagasy soldiers serving in the French army, to be commanded by the senior Malagasy officer Colonel Gabriel Ramanantsoa,[15] and with France providing financial support, equipment and training. France would retain control of the naval base at Diego Suarez and an air base at Ivato (now the international airport for Antananarivo), the right to station troops in Madagascar and the right to use Malagasy air space, territory and territorial waters as necessary for defence purposes. The foreign policy arrangements provided for close consultation and exchanges of information. In the field of education, a new University of Antananarivo, to be named after General de Gaulle, was to be financed by France, which would appoint the Rector. The teaching staff, who would be appointed by France in agreement with the Malagasy authorities, would be equated to French university personnel; and Malagasy degrees and diplomas from the *baccalauréat* upwards would be equivalent to French qualifications and would be regulated by standards and examinations controlled by the French Ministry of Education. Cooperation would be equally close in financial and economic affairs based on Madagascar's continued membership of the Franc Zone and a mutually preferential trade system. A new currency, the Malagasy franc (FMG), would replace the CFA (*Communauté Française Africaine*) franc at the same exchange rate of 50 = 1 French franc, and with its convertibility guaranteed by France. A Mixed Economic and Financial Commission would control the Malagasy import programme and development projects financed by France.

These arrangements left the French in a dominant position in key sectors of the country's life; the financial arrangements in particular meant that Madagascar was not in a position to pursue an independent monetary or economic policy. But the agreements were not imposed by the French; they were freely negotiated and willingly accepted by Tsiranana, who made no secret of his belief that French underpinning by way of key personnel, finance and military protection would be needed for some considerable time before Madagascar could stand on its own feet. The continuing close links with France were welcomed by the conservatives and accepted by most moderate nationalists as necessary for at least a transitional period. Even Andriamanjato, in a communiqué of April 29, welcomed the agreements and expressed AKFM's readiness to respond to Tsiranana's appeal for national unity. He did not however speak for the communists and other hard-line elements in AKFM who opposed the agreements and agitated for a neutralist Afro-Asian foreign policy, the removal of all French forces, withdrawal from the Franc Zone and nationalisation of the banks, utilities and railways. But they were a tiny, though noisy, dissentient voice in the chorus of approval and support for Tsiranana, "the father of independence".

In France Ravoahangy and Rabemananjara, though not Raseta, joined in the chorus. In return Tsiranana arranged for the return of four other remaining MDRM exiles on June 4 and announced that the three ex-Deputies could return after the independence date. Apart from other considerations he presumably did not wish to share the glory of the independence ceremony. This took place on June 26 1960 in the famous arena of Mahamasina where independence was proclaimed on the *vatomasina* or sacred stone of the old monarchy. A message from de Gaulle, read by the French Deputy Minister for Relations with the Community, stated that "France's fraternal collaboration will not be withheld from the 'Great Island', an old and a new independent state".

Thus ended the colonial period, which lasted less than the biblical span of a human life, and which will appear to future centuries as a brief interlude in the development of the Malagasy nation. Indeed many parts of the country were little changed even after 65 years of colonial rule. The sheer size of the island, the sparse population (little more than five million at independence) and lack of governmental resources limited the effectiveness of French efforts to modernise the country. Away from the main towns life in the villages and isolated hamlets and the nomadic existence of the herders of cattle continued as they had been before

The road to independence

the French occupation, virtually untouched by the twentieth century. Most of the population lived in a subsistence economy, growing their own food and building their own homes, and only occasionally entering the fringes of the monetary economy when they would barter or sell surplus produce at a local village market in return for basic items of household furniture or farm equipment. With no electricity or gas, their lives were governed by the sun. Villages would stir into life at dawn and would close down at sunset with doors and shutters firmly closed to keep out hostile spirits and unwelcome intruders such as the *mpakafo* (heart-stealers) who were believed to roam around after dark. The pattern of life would vary through the year according to the seasons, the requirements of the crop cycle and the incidence of family ceremonies such as weddings and circumcisions. Because of the special role of ancestors in Malagasy thinking, funerals were especially important, though the actual funeral rites and types of tombs varied considerably in the different regions. The high cost of these ceremonies, including in the plateau area the periodic *famadihana* or "turning of the bodies", were and would remain an obstacle to improving living standards since they absorbed potential savings and often drove families into debt. The consequent lack of resources, together with reluctance to alter ancient agricultural methods as practiced by the ancestors, contributed to the unchanging face of the countryside.

However, in other areas colonial rule had a profound effect on the intellectual and cultural life and on the economic and administrative structure of the country. Building on the educational work of the British missionaries, the French had created a French-speaking élite who were at home in the universities and salons of metropolitan France and appeared to be fully equal to the task of governing their own country. They had established a reasonably efficient and economical administrative framework which, while taking account of regional differences, had helped to create a sense of nationhood in a country which they had united for the first time under one government. Alongside the old subsistence economy they had developed a modern trading economy based mainly on the export of plantation crops such as coffee, sugar, vanilla and cloves, many of which they had introduced into the island. To service the economy they had built up a basic infrastructure of ports, a few railways and a road system, the inadequacies of which were partly compensated for by an intensive air network. They had developed or created modern-looking towns, mainly the national and provincial capitals, supplied with electricity, piped water and in some cases main drainage. For the traveller, hotels with basic amenities were to be found in any sizeable town, together with restaurants, often run by Frenchmen or creoles from Mauritius or Reunion and serving French meals, based on the ample supplies of excellent meat and fish and both tropical and temperate fruits and vegetables, as well as the traditional Malagasy food.

The independent Malagasy Republic of 1960 was thus very different from the independent kingdom of Madagascar of 1895. Yet the difference was less than in comparable situations in black Africa, where in many cases colonial rule created a country and imposed a common language where none existed before. In Madagascar one can talk of the recovery of independence, the restoration of a separate national identity based on a common culture and language. And it is arguable[16] that the political impact of colonial domination was less far-reaching than that of the internal changes brought about in the nineteenth century by the expansion of the Merina monarchy. The mistrust between various regions resulting from this upheaval, and to some extent exacerbated by French colonial policies, was still unresolved in 1960. But Tsiranana's skill in bringing together various parties and interests, and in particular his *rapprochement* with two of the ex-MDRM leaders, meant that the Malagasy Republic started its new independent life in a spirit of reconciliation which augured well for the future.

Chapter 19

Independence and neo-colonialism

The general euphoria and optimism at the time of independence proved to be justified, at least for a time. For over a decade Madagascar was to enjoy a political stability and internal peace virtually unmatched in any of the African countries which came to independence around 1960.[1] Political differences and ethnic problems remained but were largely concealed under the widespread support for the coalition of moderates grouped in the PSD government of President Tsiranana. Merina intellectuals' resentment at being ruled by an essentially *côtier* government was to some degree appeased by their share of the spoils of independence in the shape of most of the senior posts in the administration, the parastatals, the diplomatic service and the army. The overwhelming dominance of the PSD in the national and provincial assemblies provided a political stability unlikely to be threatened by the normal democratic process; and there was little risk of intervention by the armed forces under the command of the thoroughly professional, French-trained and loyal General Ramanantsoa.

Much of the credit for the decade of stability belongs to Tsiranana's cautious and pragmatic policies and to his own personality. With his paternal air and good-natured *bonhomie*, perhaps deliberately exaggerated to conceal his shrewd political brain, he fitted easily into the role of Father of Independence. And it is perhaps significant that the decline in his health towards the end of the decade was followed quickly by the collapse of the PSD régime. Meanwhile, peace and stability were maintained, not by harsh dictatorial rule as in some "stable" countries, but in an atmosphere of easy tolerance with most of the trappings of multi-party democracy, including the rule of law and a considerable degree of freedom of speech and of the press.

At the time of independence, PSD dominance was still some way from being absolute. AKFM controlled the capital, whilst PSD came second to other parties on the east coast and the southern plateau.

There was a danger that the return of the charismatic ex-Deputies might swing the balance of power against PSD, especially if they could remain united. The ruling party accordingly decided to bring forward the parliamentary elections, which under the Constitution could not take place before March 31 1961, in order to exploit the President's popularity and the euphoria of independence. The Constitution was amended to permit the President to dissolve the elected Assemblies, and elections for the National Assembly, to be followed by those for the Provincial Councils and the Senate, were fixed for September 4 1960.

Meanwhile Tsiranana had skilfully defused the threat posed by the ex-Deputies. By bringing them back to Madagascar on July 19 1960 in his own aircraft he ensured that he personally was given most of the credit for their return. At the same time he appealed for national unity, stating that "our friends" could stand for election and that, while he hoped that they would work with the Government, they were equally free to join the opposition. He then organised a series of meetings with leaders of the various parties and the ex-Deputies in an attempt to define a common programme. Ravoahangy and Rabemananjara were prepared to accept most of PSD's ideas, but Raseta joined AKFM extremists in pressing hard left-wing demands – for a programme of nationalisation, leaving the Community and cancelling the cooperation and military agreements with France. The meetings therefore broke down with the blame for failure placed clearly on the AKFM, and Ravoahangy publicly dissociating himself from Raseta. In contravention of a joint statement by the ex-Deputies that they would join no party, Raseta now joined AKFM. Whilst he had been expected to contest his old seat in Tulear, he joined the AKFM list in Antananarivo for the September elections, where he would compete with Ravoahangy who was standing as an independent. In outraged response Ravoahangy joined the government list in Antananarivo, without joining PSD, and Rabemananjara did the same in Tamatave. The breach between Raseta and the other two was thus finalised, to the great advantage of the PSD.

For the National Assembly elections a system of proportional representation by party list was adopted, with only seven constituencies, the six provinces and the capital. But in an outrageous manoeuvre to favour the government party, it was decreed that any party gaining over 55 per cent of the vote would take all the seats, thus defeating the object of proportional representation. Even more blatantly, this rule did not apply to Antananarivo town, the one constituency where AKFM might achieve a 55 per cent majority. These manoeuvres were successful. PSD won large majorities and all the seats in Majunga, Tulear and (in alliance with RCM) Diego Suarez provinces. In Fianarantsoa even a UDSM/RCM "Third Force" alliance could not prevent PSD from taking 62 per cent of the vote and all the seats. In Antananarivo province a bare 55.18 per cent of the vote again gave PSD all the seats. In Tamatave Rabemananjara led a new pro-government grouping Miara Mirindra (MM) comprising Bezaka's RNM, the local RCM and UDSM (Sylla) and some PSD (with Tsiranana's blessing) to a 63 per cent victory, with all the seats, against an official PSD list put forward against Tsiranana's wishes. In Antananarivo town AKFM won 54 per cent of the votes and 3 seats against 42 per cent and 2 seats for the independent pro-government list led by Ravoahangy. In the whole country PSD, with under 63 per cent of the vote, took 82 out of a total of 107 seats, MM and other smaller pro-government parties took 22 seats and AKFM with over 13 per cent of the vote had only its three seats in the capital.

The same unfair rules were applied to the elections of provincial councillors, with the same results, PSD sweeping the board in all provinces except Tamatave where its ally MM took all the seats, and AKFM taking two of the four seats in the capital. The elections to the Senate, for six Senators from each province, were then a formality, since PSD controlled more than half the electoral college (all elected officers at national, provincial and local level). With AKFM and MONIMA accordingly refusing to take part, PSD and its allies took all the 36 elected seats.

The 1960 elections saw the final demise of UDSM as an effective party. Their only successful candidate as Deputy, Sylla, had been elected on the MM list in Tamatave, and most of the remaining leaders defected to PSD, leaving Zafimahova isolated[2]. PSD's political control at national and provincial level was now greatly strengthened. However the huge vote for PSD did not necessarily mean that the bulk of the population were convinced supporters of PSD and its policies. In a perceptive editorial the Catholic weekly *Lumière* stated that the mass of the Malagasy were not yet ready for Western-type democracy and that much of the PSD vote was a vote for the party in power. "The country seems ready for a 'popular democracy'. Paradoxically the PSD victory risks preparing the way for an AKFM victory."[3] Thus districts with a 90 per cent pro-government vote today could have the same majority for another régime tomorrow – as indeed was to happen in the 1970s.

Such thoughts were far from the minds of the PSD leaders most of whom, led by Resampa, looked forward to exclusive enjoyment of the spoils of power. However Tsiranana as usual preferred the path of conciliation and formed in October 1960 a governmentof national union to include other pro-government parties. MM was given three posts, two of them very important: Rabemananjara as Minister of National Economy and Sylla as Foreign Minister;[4] and Ravoahangy was made Minister of Health. The remaining posts were filled by PSD stalwarts led by Tsiebo as Vice-President of the government and Resampa again as Minister of the Interior; and the two Frenchmen were retained, Longuet as Minister of Finance and Lechat as Minister of Public Works, Supply and Transport[5]. The PSD also took most other senior political posts such as the Presidencies of the Senate, the National Assembly and all the Provincial Councils except for Tamatave which went to MM. The only part of the country not under the control of the PSD and its MM ally was Antananarivo municipality and even here the government was not prepared to leave AKFM wielding effective local power. Using a precedent established in Paris the municipal statutes of the capital were altered to provide for the appointment of a *Délégué-Général du Gouvernement* as head of the Commune of Antananarivo with most of the powers of local government. Andriamanjato, the Mayor and President of the Municipal Council, was left with little more than ceremonial functions.

With PSD dominance now firmly established there was inevitably talk of setting up a one-party state, using the familiar argument of the need for national unity to tackle the problems of under-development. But Tsiranana preferred the reality of one-party control combined with the outward semblance of multi-party democracy rather than the legal establishment of a totalitarian one-party state. He was however prepared to consider coalitions and consensus in support of a national programme for development, and to this end organised several all-party seminars around the end of 1961 and 1962. At these seminars the left wing of PSD and AKFM moderates led by Andriamanjato were willing to make concessions of principle to permit AKFM to amalgamate with PSD or at least participate in the government. But the wide gap between the PSD right wing and the communists with Raseta on the left of the AFKM, together with Resampa's fears of Andriamanjato as a rival for the presidential succession, made this impossible. The main result was the rallying to PSD of Jacques Rabemananjara bringing with him most elements of MM, including Sylla, most of FNM and some coastal sections of RCM; and also of Ravoahangy and the ex-AKFM Bezara from Diego Suarez. The PSD now mustered 91 votes in the National Assembly and became the dominant party in Tamatave and Diego Suarez as well as the other four provinces. The remainder of RCM joined with the rump of UDSM and the Betsileo party AVM to form a new "Third Force" Catholic group which remained outside PSD but affirmed its support for Tsiranana's policies. The only parties left opposing PSD were AKFM and MONIMA.

To reinforce the government's control of the provinces, each province was divided into three *préfectures* and the old districts became *sous-préfectures*, with the *préfets* and *sous-préfets* appointed by the government and in effect also representing PSD. A decree of June 1962 revived the *fokonolona* as a means of carrying out development projects at the grass-roots level under the direction of the *préfets*, thus providing another means of political control. The government administrative structure was underpinned at every level by the party organisation, with sections in every commune, grouped into federations at the *sous-préfecture* level. For most people, especially in the rural areas, the party became synonymous with the *fanjakana* or government; and membership of the party was generally regarded as essential for advancement in the government service or in areas of government patronage. Government and party control were reinforced by two government newspapers, the Malagasy-language *Vaovao* and the French-language *Courrier de Madagascar*; and by exclusive access to the most influential media, radio and later television.

The PSD also sought to extend its influence in social areas through trade union, youth and women's organisations. The official *Confédération des Travailleurs Malgaches* worked closely with the government and was underpinned by several "social-democratic groups of workers" for various professions. In 1960 the PSD set up the *Jeunesse Sociale-Démocrate* (JSD) to compete with various Christian or Communist-inspired youth movements; and two years later the *Union des Etudiants Socialistes Malgaches* (UESM) in opposition to other student movements which were generally critical of the government. There were feminine sections of PSD, led by Madame Elise Rasoamampionona; and the President of the National Council of Women's Associations of Madagascar was the wife of a minister, Madame Zaïveline Ramarosaona. Curiously, despite the advanced state of women's education – there were many women doctors and lawyers as well as teachers, and Madame Andriamanjato was a qualified engineer – there were no women in the PSD government.[6] It was not until 1964 that there was a woman Deputy in the National Assembly (Madame Rasoamampionona) and it was another two years before a woman Senator was appointed.

Certain areas of national life escaped total PSD dominance. Despite government interference in its municipal affairs, the capital city remained an AKFM fief; and the bulk of the many small newspapers printed in Antananarivo supported the opposition against the government. The large measure of press freedom permitted them to denounce the government, often in violent terms; and only when they were particularly abusive or scurrilous did Resampa intervene to suspend the paper and have the editor fined or briefly imprisoned. Although small in circulation these journals were widely read and a constant irritant to the government. The churches were also a powerful influence outside government control; and although Christianity and freedom of conscience were enshrined in the Constitution and nearly all government ministers were practising Christians, this influence was often hostile. Jesuit suspicions of the socialist element of PSD were responsible for continuing coolness towards the government and the constant search for an effective Catholic "third force" in politics. However relations improved after a Malagasy Archbishop (later Cardinal) Jérome Rakotomalala became head of the Malagasy Catholic Church and established good relations with Tsiranana, himself a Catholic. The Anglicans and Lutherans kept out of politics and stayed on good terms with the government. But the "non-conformist" churches deriving from the LMS, the Quakers and the French Protestant mission, which in 1968 joined together to form the FJKM (Malagasy Church of Jesus Christ), remained antipathetic to the government. Because of these churches' close links with the nationalist opposition to the French, they tended to align themselves with the AKFM against the pro-French PSD. The Protestant daily paper *Fanasina* usually followed the same line as the AKFM papers to the extent that the government sometimes intervened to prevent its distribution. PSD also had little success in winning over youth and student opinion, especially in the capital where the student population was predominantly Merina: normal student radicalism and anti-establishment feeling were therefore reinforced by lack of sympathy for the conservative *côtier* government. The leaders of the PSD movements JSD and UESM felt obliged to keep a low profile or even to oppose PSD policies in order to win support. The opposition student movement, the *Fédération des Associations d'Etudiants de Madagascar* (FAEM), dominated at the University and often adopted attitudes more radical than those of AKFM.

However these areas of opposition were for the time being little more than irritants and had little effect on the government's total control of the country or its ability to carry out party policies. What was perhaps lacking in PSD was a clearly defined political and social philosophy underlying and motivating policies. This was partly because the party was a coalition of many diverse interests; but perhaps mainly because of Tsiranana's pragmatic nature and his mistrust of theory and dogma. He was particularly opposed to Communism, both its theory and its totalitarian practice, and Marxist–Leninism had little place in his concept of democratic socialism. Heavy industry and grandiose agricultural schemes were rejected in favour of light industry and grass-roots agricultural projects. Although some PSD leaders including Resampa favoured some degree of nationalisation, this was opposed by Tsiranana, partly on moral grounds ("to nationalise is to steal") and partly because the main candidates for nationalisation were foreign enterprises and the country needed foreign capital to develop its economy. The essence of PSD's socialism was perhaps the primacy of economic development to improve the living standards of the people and the importance of planning in the framework of a mixed economy. The private sector was left free to develop, mainly on the basis of foreign capital since domestic capital formation was at a low rate, partly because in the plateau which was the richest part of the country the ruinous practice of *famadihana* used up the savings of all but well-off families. State intervention was reserved to sectors where private capital was reluctant to invest, mainly agriculture.

With hardly any industrial base and with exploitable mineral deposits on a modest scale, agriculture remained by far the prime sector of the economy. In an under-populated country there was no serious land problem and most peasants owned the land they worked. There was some agitation to nationalise or expropriate some of the land granted to French *colons*, especially the large plantations; but the government preferred to tax unused land to persuade the owners to surrender it for distribution to landless peasants. The main problem was to persuade a passive, conservative peasantry to produce more by working harder and adopting more modern methods. From the beginning PSD had adopted the slogan *"asa fa tsy kabary"* ("work, not speeches"), but appeals for harder work had limited effect on a people who in general were "more inclined to revery than to Stakhanovism".[7] In trying to overcome this problem PSD took as its main inspiration the Israeli Labour Party (MAPAI) which was a more relevant model than the SFIO or the German SDP with which close links were also established. A *Commissariat à l'Animation Rurale* was set up under the energetic Emile Ramarosaona to motivate and educate the peasants in more modern techniques. A *Service Civique*, denounced by students and the opposition as a revival of SMOTIG, was established, again under Ramarosaona, to direct young people not called up for military service to work in various capacities mainly in the least developed areas. Extension services, tractors and agricultural machinery were supplied through *syndicats de commune* under the control of the Interior Minister. Ramarosaona was also later appointed *Commissaire à la Coopération* to promote cooperatives for agricultural production and marketing. These in general proved to be less efficient than the Indian and Chinese middlemen who traditionally advanced loans and marketed the crops, and they suffered, along with some state farms set up from 1966 onward, from petty corruption and local political interference. More successful were some major aid-financed agricultural schemes such as SOMALAC, an intensive rice-growing project in the drained marshes south of Lake Alaotra, and SOMASAK,[8] a mixed farming enterprise around Sakay on the plateau to the west of Antananarivo.

The government's foreign policy was also strongly marked by Tsiranana's realism and anti-Communism and the priority he accorded to economic development. It was based on close friendship with France, reliance on the West for economic aid and defence, and fear of Communist subversion. The latter was compounded by a more fundamental fear of the countless millions of Asia as contrasted with the empty spaces of Madagascar; the example of Mauritius, where imported Indian labour had multiplied to outnumber the original Creole population, was ever present. Anti-Communist feeling was therefore directed particularly against China which in the early sixties was in the throes of the Cultural Revolution and pursuing an aggressive and for a time apparently successful policy of Communist subversion in such African countries as Ghana, Mali, Burundi and Zanzibar. Madagascar accordingly maintained diplomatic relations with Taiwan throughout the years of Tsiranana's presidency, long after France and other Western countries had recognised the Chinese People's Republic in Peking. Even more unusually Madagascar during this period never established diplomatic relations with the USSR or any of the Soviet bloc countries; and it was only in the late sixties that commercial agreements were signed with USSR and several East European countries, to little practical effect.

Fear of Communist invasion or subversion was the main justification for the stationing of French forces on the island. France also continued to be by far the largest supplier of economic aid and technical assistance. But close cooperation with France did not mean subservience to De Gaulle in all matters of foreign policy. Apart from his more uncompromising hostility to Communism, Tsiranana differed more or less publicly with De Gaulle in his condemnation of the Biafra secession, in his more friendly relations with USA and his closeness to Israel. And when in 1966, following the Rhodesian declaration of independence, Britain wished to station a small detachment of patrol aircraft at Majunga to help enforce the oil blockade of Beira, Tsiranana agreed despite strong pressure from De Gaulle, who still remembered and resented the British invasion of 1942.[9]

Tsiranana was fond of saying that Madagascar was the only true Afro-Asian country. The Malagasy in general do not regard themselves as African, and Madagascar joined the Organisation of African Unity (OAU) only after failing to get the name changed to the Organisation of African and Malagasy Unity. With his pragmatic outlook Tsiranana had little time for the pan-African rhetoric of Nkrumah, Nasser and the other radicals who dominated the OAU meetings, and in several major speeches, notably one in Cairo in July 1964,[10] he effectively ridiculed their pretensions and impracticality. In return they denounced his "reactionary" views, eg his support for Tshombe and the Belgian/mercenary intervention at Stanleyville, his friendship treaty with Israel and his lukewarm attitude to sanctions against South Africa. Not surprisingly Tsiranana attended few OAU summit meetings. He was much happier attending meetings of the moderate francophone group OCAM (*Organisation Commune Africaine et Malgache*) and had excellent relations with the individual leaders, notably Senghor of Senegal and Houphouet-Boigny of the Ivory Coast, as well as with his fellow conservative Dr Banda of Malawi.

Tsiranana's conservative foreign policy fuelled attacks on the government by the left-wing opposition, which favoured Bandung-type non-alignment (ie generally pro-Soviet and anti-Western) and denounced the cooperation agreements with France along with "American imperialism" in Vietnam and elsewhere. (AKFM's support for the Soviet Union was to extend as far as justifying the invasion of Czechoslovakia in 1968). However for the time being foreign policy was not an important domestic political issue and opposition attacks could make little impression on PSD's dominance. In the legislative elections of June 1965, AKFM retained its three National Assembly seats in the capital, but disagreements among the various Third Force parties led to the loss of all their seats, leaving all the remaining 104 to PSD which also won all the elected seats in the Senate. In the presidential elections[11], brought forward a year to May 1965, AKFM did not think it worthwhile to field a candidate. The only serious candidate to oppose Tsiranana was Raseta who, frustrated in his hopes of leading AKFM, left in 1963 to set up his own party FIPIMA. When the bulk of AKFM refused to follow him he repudiated his Communism, formed an alliance MORENA with Bezaka's neo-RNM and established good relations with MONIMA. However his decision to contest the presidency lost him the support of Monja Jaona, who had intended to stand himself; and AKFM, resenting his defection, secretly advised its supporters to vote for Tsiranana. Accordingly even in Antananarivo Raseta won only 35 per cent of the vote, and in the country as a whole only 2.3 per cent, while Tsiranana recorded 97.4 per cent of the votes cast.[12] This humiliating defeat ended Raseta's political career which had started with the VVS movement fifty years earlier.[13]

In the second half of the sixties Madagascar appeared to the outside observer as a fortunate country, often referred to as *"l'ile heureuse"*. There was no apparent external enemy. Internally, despite the ethnic division between plateau and coast there was a genuine feeling of unity arising from the common culture and language. Strict controls had limited immigrants from China and the Indian sub-continent to a few thousand each; and although there was some resentment at their success in the small retail trade their numbers were not sufficient to create any serious racial problem. Tsiranana and the PSD ruled as virtual dictators but it was a benign dictatorship. There was freedom of political association, with a number of small parties active as well as AKFM, freedom of expression and freedom of the press exploited by many publications often hostile to the Government. There were no political prisoners and the occasional clampdowns on particularly vituperative newspapers were short-lived. The underlying coast-plateau hostility symbolised by the PSD/AKFM political division was tempered by Andriamanjato's moderate leadership and his good personal relations with Tsiranana. Merina resentment at *côtier* domination was somewhat assuaged by the presence in the government of respected Merina nationalists such as Ravoahangy and Ramangasoavina and, at a more junior level, Ramarosaona and Césaire Rabenoro,[14] the first *Commissaire au Plan*; and by the continuing prominence of Merina in senior official and diplomatic posts. Ordinary people everywhere enjoyed the inestimable, though frequently underestimated, benefit of law and order: in the nineteen-sixties it was possible for anyone, Malagasy or foreigner, to travel the length and breadth of the country by vehicle or even on foot without fear of molestation. In international statistics, Madagascar ranked as one of the twenty poorest countries in the world, with a *per caput* income of only US$80 in 1960, but it did not appear so. Many of the peasants outside the monetary economy lived relatively comfortably in well-constructed houses with their own rice-patch, poultry and cattle. In a generally benign climate nearly everyone had access to the basic requirements of food, shelter and clothing and there was little sign of real hardship or deprivation. The welcome given to Tsiranana on his frequent tours did not merely reflect traditional Malagasy respect for authority: his benevolent paternalism was genuinely popular.

Tsiranana's popularity and PSD dominance reached their peak around 1967 when they seemed likely to endure for a long time. Why then did the régime collapse so completely only a few years later? Economic stagnation has been suggested as one reason, but statistical evidence[15] does not support this. During the first decade of independence percentage growth in GNP comfortably exceeded the growth in population from 5.39 million in 1960 to 6.93 million in 1970; and most other economic indicators showed a steady improvement. Much has been made of the fact that rice had to be imported for the first time[16] during the decade, but only in one year (1965) did imports of (low quality) rice exceed the volume of (high quality) rice exported, and overall rice production more than kept pace with population increase. Production and exports of the main cash crops – coffee, vanilla and cloves – also increased. Industrial production grew steadily, from a very low base, at a rate of 13.5 per cent per year and employment in industry rose from 200,000 in 1960 to 500,000 in 1971. Apart from light industries mainly processing agricultural products – cigarettes, vegetable oil, beer, fruit juice – industrial investment included a cement factory, a paper mill, a large textile complex at Antsirabe and an oil refinery at Tamatave. The small mineral sector, mainly graphite and mica, remained fairly static but towards the end of the decade mining of chromite began at Andriamena on the eastern escarpment. Prudent financial management kept inflation at a low average 4 per cent and ensured that there was a budget surplus on current expenditure; capital expenditure produced an overall budget deficit but extravagant prestige projects were avoided. During the decade exports tripled in volume although, owing to declining agricultural prices, they only doubled in value; and as imports also increased in value by a similar amount the balance of trade remained in deficit, with coverage of imports by exports varying from 65 to 85 per cent. But the balance of payments was never a problem thanks to membership of the Franc Zone and the substantial inflow of aid funds both multilateral and bilateral, with France providing on average 85 per cent of the latter. As the bulk of the aid was in the form of grants, the external debt remained low, with debt servicing in 1970 amounting to only 3.5 per cent of export earnings.

The steady economic progress was recognized when in 1970 UNCTAD removed Madagascar from the list of the world's poorest countries. There was even talk of Madagascar approaching the economic take-off point. Whilst this was wildly optimistic, the economy as a whole certainly seemed in better shape in 1970 than at independence. Unfortunately the benefits of the economic improvement were unevenly spread and there were two areas of major concern for the future. Investment in agriculture had been very disappointing and limited mainly to the cash-crop plantations and a few major projects such as SOMALAC at Lac Alaotra. Elsewhere the various government programmes to "animate" and modernise the rural areas had made little impact, and the bulk of the peasantry still practised subsistence agriculture using the traditional tools, the *angady* for digging and hoeing and the *antsy* for clearing forest land. As prices of basic necessities increased with inflation while prices paid to farmers stagnated, the standard of living of the peasant, unlike the town-dweller, actually declined. With little hope of a better life on the land, youngsters from the growing peasant families deserted in increasing numbers to the main towns, and especially the capital, where they formed a hard core of uneducated unemployed and a future source of crime and unrest. At the same time the rapid expansion of higher education, desirable and worthy in itself, greatly outpaced the capacity of the economy to produce extra jobs for the educated élite. An alliance of dissatisfied students and urban unemployed was to play a leading part in the downfall of Tsiranana in 1972.

In the political field PSD's continuing dominance inevitably induced complacency among its leaders. Originating mostly from petty officialdom in the coastal towns with little direct contact with the peasantry, they became increasingly isolated from and paternalistic towards their grass-roots support as their lifestyle adapted to their new bourgeois status. The lower ranks of the party became discontented with the lack of promotion prospects as the ministers, most of them quite young on appointment, stayed on and on in the same jobs with only rare government reshuffles. With no serious opposition threat to impose the need for party unity and discipline, internal divisions based on doctrinal differences, personalities and ethnic or regional origin began to appear in what was a very broad-based coalition. So long as he was in full vigour Tsiranana could contain these divisions. But as his health declined in the late sixties the divisions became increasingly open and were sharpened by competition for his succession.

Long periods of unchallenged power tend to breed corruption and it has been suggested[17] that this was an important factor in the growing unpopularity of the government. There was no lack of accusations from the opposition press, but at the ministerial level allegations of corruption were never satisfactorily proved and were not supported by the ministers' life-style.[18] The detailed involvement of French advisers in the country's financial management would in any case have impeded corruption on any substantial scale. Petty corruption certainly existed in the countryside where small-scale bribery was common and local PSD and government officials were able to exploit the management of cooperatives and *syndicats de commune* to their own advantage; and this undoubtedly contributed to unrest in the southwest in 1971. But corruption at the centre was not a significant factor in the collapse of the regime.

A major factor, some would say *the* major factor, in the decline in the popularity and authority of Tsiranana was the growing perception that little had been changed by independence and that behind the facade of a Malagasy government the French were still running the country. Under the Franc Zone arrangements the French had a major say in economic decisions in return for backing the Malagasy franc. Import-export trade was largely controlled by three French companies known as *"les gros caimans"* – the Lyonnaise, the Marseillaise and the Rochefortaise (through the *Société de l'Emyrne*); whilst another company the Havraise enjoyed a shipping monopoly and controlled two banks. French advisers (*conseillers techniques*) in the economic ministries helped to ensure that the bulk of imports came from France, even after the tariff protection enjoyed by the French was extended under the Lomé Convention to other members of the European Community. The French occupation of the naval base at Diego Suarez and the presence of French military aircraft and paratroops at the capital's airport were a constant affront to nationalist feeling. But it was in education that French influence was most pervasive and prominent. At the end of the decade the Rector of the University was still a Frenchman, appointed by the French Minister of Education. Despite the availability of many qualified Malagasy academics, eighty per cent of the teaching posts in the University, and nearly all of the highest posts, were filled by Frenchmen, who also accounted for 80 per cent of the teaching staff of the state secondary *collèges* and *lycées*. Instruction was of course in French and the curriculum was virtually the same as in France, with prominence given to French rather than Malagasy history and geography; and the external examinations were set and administered by the French Ministry of Education. Whilst the resultant "equivalence" of Malagasy and French qualifications had obvious advantages, it facilitated a "brain drain" to France. And there was growing concern that a French academically-oriented education was not a very suitable preparation for life in Madagascar and tended to widen the gap between the educated élite and the mass of the population.

In addition to roughly 1,000 university and secondary teachers, a similar number of French technical assistants filled half the senior posts in the central administration, while a substantial number of French officers and NCOs served as instructors and advisers with the Malagasy armed forces. The influence on policy of the *conseillers techniques* attached to all ministers was probably not very great, but their presence seemed to be a restraint on Malagasy sovereignty; whilst the proliferation of technical assistants reduced the scope for promotion of Malagasy civil servants and jobs for graduates. The most glaring example of neo-colonialism was in the President's office and the services it controlled, where there were over a hundred technical assistants. The head of the President's office, the secretary-general, was French, as were the head of security and the President's personal chief of staff, a colonel who also (until 1969) commanded the *gendarmerie*. Such arrangements were quite common for a brief transitional period in other newly-independent African countries; but in Madagascar they were still in place a decade and more after independence and showed no signs of being changed. What was particularly galling was that there were enough Malagasy well enough qualified to fill virtually all the posts occupied by Frenchmen, apart from a few technical positions. But nearly all the Malagasy in question would be Merina. Hence it was not the French but Tsiranana and his coastal ministers who insisted on retaining the French advisers in the face of growing demands for "Malgachisation" from within PSD as well as from the opposition. The reason was that they needed the French as a defence against the Merina on whom they would otherwise have had to depend for the running of the government. The plateau-coastal division was thus at the heart of this major weakness of the régime.

A considerable degree of French influence after independence was to be expected, especially in view of the substantial volume of French aid and investment. What was unusual was not only the extent of the influence but also the lack of discretion in exercising it. The French not only continued to run the country but were seen to be doing so. Under a clause of the Cooperation Agreements their ambassador was automatically *doyen* of the Diplomatic Corps, an apparently trivial matter which nevertheless had a symbolic importance placing him in a different category from other ambassadors and tending to encourage pro-consular behaviour; while the French Embassy-financed *Courrier de Madagascar* often seemed to give as much coverage to the ambassador's activities as to the President's. With astonishing lack of tact the French had retained the residence of the former governor-general in the centre of Antananarivo as their ambassador's residence, a situation without parallel in any other ex-French or indeed ex-British territory where the

Independence and neo-colonialism

governor's residence invariably became the residence of the new Head of State after independence.[19] It is hardly surprising that many ordinary Malagasy were far from certain that colonial rule had ended; and that senior Malagasy would in private refer to the French Ambassador as "Monsieur le Gouverneur". France's loss of her special position in 1972 was to some extent a self-inflicted wound.

Chapter 20

The fall of the First Republic

Things started to go wrong for the government at the end of 1967 with the affair of the *Grands Moulins de Dakar*, a French company which had obtained a monopoly for the importation of flour into Madagascar. In an agreement of December 1967 the government authorised the company to construct a cement factory, a wine warehouse and a flour mill at Tamatave in return for an undertaking to invest 7 billion Malagasy francs (about $25 million) in developing a large forestry concession. The left wing of PSD joined with AKFM in denouncing what they saw as a reversion to colonialist exploitation. Rabemananjara, who had become foreign minister after the death of Sylla in an air crash in July 1967, and who considered his main task to be the attraction of foreign investment, was the main target of attack as the signatory of the agreement. The agitation was kept up for many months and led to a rare revolt against the government by PSD Deputies in the National Assembly. Tsiranana finally gave way and the agreement was revoked in December 1969.

Earlier in 1967 the Six-Day War between Israel and its Arab neighbours led to the closing of the Suez Canal for the next eight years. This caused short-term disruption of Madagascar's trade with Europe and long-term higher shipping costs for the longer route round the Cape. It also strengthened the arguments in favour of developing economic links with neighbouring South Africa which but for the apartheid problem would normally have been a principal trading partner for Madagascar and a major source of investment and tourism. Tsiranana decided that the economic needs of the people were paramount and was prepared to face the predictable hostility, both internal and external. As additional justification he used the rather naive argument that the situation in South Africa could be favourably influenced by exposing South Africans to a peaceful, well-run and racially harmonious "black" state.[1] Informal contacts were developed with South Africa through Malawi in the course of 1968. In the following year the

[310]

new policy became public with visits by groups of South African businessmen, the inauguration of an air service between Antananarivo and Johannesburg and a visit by an official South African delegation to consider the construction of a hotel at Nosy Be, the main Malagasy tourist resort. Further exchanges of official delegations followed, leading to the signature of agreements for the construction of the hotel and other investment totalling some $7 million, together with vast mineral prospecting rights for De Beers. The potential benefits to Madagascar were considerable, but so was the political cost. Tsiranana could afford to shrug off the predictable outrage of the OAU, but the unpopularity of the South African policy at home among intellectuals, students and the opposition and even within PSD was an important factor in the decline of his authority.

Meanwhile Tsiranana's health had become a matter of public concern. He was still only in his fifties, but the pressure of his high-profile life and frequent travels was taking its toll. A mild stroke during the inaugural meeting of OCAM in Antananarivo in 1965 and a slight heart attack in September 1966 were kept quiet and he soon resumed his energetic routine. However, following a more serious attack in August 1969, specialists flown from Paris prescribed several months' rest. Speculation about the succession now widened rifts which had appeared in the government and party between left and right wings and among various personal factions based on region of origin. The benign and popular Vice-President of the government, Calvin Tsiebo, was not a serious contender because of his age and poor health, though he was a potential stopgap or compromise candidate. The obvious *"dauphin"* was André Resampa who stood somewhat to the left of the centre of the party. Despite more than a decade in office he was still a young man, and if Tsiranana had died suddenly in 1969 he might well have become President. However his authoritarian exercise of his power as both Secretary-General of the ruling party and Minister of the Interior aroused resentment and fear, especially after he had set up in 1966 the *Forces Républicaines de Securité* (FRS),[2] a mainly *côtier* paramilitary force under his personal control as Interior Minister. Within the PSD leadership a split developed between the supporters of Resampa, mainly from the southwest of the country, and a group from PSD's heartland in the northwest. However this latter group had no obvious candidate of its own and was lukewarm about the other main candidate, Jacques Rabemananjara. The foreign minister had an international reputation as a poet in the French language. His arrest, torture and threats of execution in 1947 followed by 13 years of imprisonment and exile had left his admiration for

France and its culture undiminished and, next to the President, he was the most prominent advocate of close relations with the former colonial power. As the leading member of the liberal Christian wing of the party he was the favoured candidate of the Jesuits and, it was believed, the French Embassy. But the liberal wing, based mainly on Tamatave, was a minority in the party. To the majority, and especially the left wing, he was suspect as an intellectual, a former MDRM leader and a lukewarm socialist. His close links with the French Embassy and his rôle as executant of the South African policy further limited his appeal.

Emerging from his enforced rest, Tsiranana surprised everyone by dissolving the government at the beginning of December 1969. But this was intended merely as a warning to ministers to toe the line, and all ministers were re-appointed with only minor re-allocations of portfolios. Another disagreeable surprise came with the municipal elections later in the month. While easily defeating AKFM in the rest of the country, PSD narrowly lost its overall majority in Tamatave; and despite fielding a strong team of candidates it lost badly in the capital to AKFM which doubled its vote and seemed to have captured most of the young voters who had swelled the electoral roll.

Then at the end of January 1970, while attending an OCAM meeting in Yaoundé, Tsiranana suffered a more serious stroke which this time almost killed him. He was saved only by expert French medical care and evacuation to a hospital in Paris where he remained out of action for nearly four months. During this time the government was directed by a *troika* of Tsiebo, Resampa and Rabemananjara, with the latter two obliged to put out a public statement denying newspaper reports that there was a serious rift between them. Tsiranana returned in time for the celebration of the tenth anniversary of independence on June 26 but he was both physically and mentally impaired. Apparently convinced by his near-miraculous escape that he was the divinely chosen leader of Madagascar he became increasingly autocratic in his behaviour and suspicious of any sign of disloyalty among his colleagues.

National Assembly elections in September 1970 produced no change. They were followed by another reshuffle involving mostly the same people but with the creation of four Vice-Presidents, apparently to lighten the load on Tsiranana. Resampa was made First Vice-President ahead of Tsiebo and therefore front runner for the succession, though control of the FRS was taken away from him. Ominous signs of discontent now began to appear both in the towns, where some sharp price increases caused hardship, and in the countryside. The environmentally damaging practices of burning the forest and the pasture seemed to be on the increase partly, it was suggested, as a political protest against the government which prohibited them. A wide-ranging tour of the country by the President around the end of the year did little to revive party and government morale. Like other ageing rulers Tsiranana now became suspicious and jealous of his likely successor. In yet another reshuffle in February 1971 Resampa was demoted to Second Vice-President behind Tsiebo (the other Vice-Presidents being Rabemananjara and the Finance Minister Victor Miadana) and was switched from the Interior to Agriculture. Tsiranana himself took over the Interior ministry, assisted by a junior minister Johasy.

The 1968 university troubles in France had had little echo in Antananarivo, where the Malagasy students had the reputation of being serious and docile. But there was a delayed reaction, mainly through the influence of AEOM, the union of Malagasy students in France. In March 1971 came the first strike at the university, organised by medical students protesting against tougher examination requirements imposed by the French Ministry of Education. This soon expanded into a general sympathy strike led by the AKFM-linked students' union FAEM. The cause was partly difficult living conditions for students and the lack of job prospects for graduates; but the strikers also called for greater use of the Malagasy language in the educational system, the replacement of French teaching staff and study courses more adapted to the realities of Malagasy life. The government immediately closed the university and refused to recognise the FAEM strike committee. But the strike resumed when the university reopened and it survived attempts by the PSD union UESM to break it. The students returned to work only after a Mixed Commission had been set up to examine their grievances.

Meanwhile far more serious troubles had emerged in the arid regions of the south and southwest. An outbreak of anthrax followed by a prolonged drought had decimated the herds of zebu in the Antandroy and Mahafaly regions causing great hardship and even famine. The poll tax and the tax on cattle, always a problem in a non-monetary society, became increasingly burdensome; but the tax-collectors, paid on a commission basis, were unrelenting and often continued to demand cattle tax based on the numbers as they were before the epidemic and the drought. The exactions of a corrupt petty bureaucracy added to the misery and discontent. Monja Jaona and MONIMA organised protests but these were ignored by the government as were warnings of impending revolt. On the night of April 1 1971 bands of up to a hundred, armed mainly with spears and axes, attacked *gendarmerie* posts and other government buildings in several places. The biggest attack was at Ampanihy where government buildings and residences were sacked before the rebels, led by a Malagasy Lutheran pastor, dispersed into the countryside. The revolt was suppressed by the gendarmerie with considerable brutality. An official communiqué of 15 April mentioned 45 rebels killed (but only one *gendarme*) and 847 arrested; but later unofficial reports of 1,000 dead and 1,500 (or even 5,000) arrested seem to have been closer to the truth. Monja Jaona, who was arrested after several weeks hiding in the forest, accepted full responsibility for organising the attacks because the authorities had refused to listen to MONIMA's complaints.

The government at first tried to distinguish between Communist-inspired MONIMA leaders and the duped populace. But press accounts of the repression and growing awareness of the appalling conditions in the south swung opinion in the capital, led by the Churches, in favour of the peasants. Tsiranana admitted publicly that the people in the south had genuine grievances, and instructions were given to the local authorities to remedy them as far as they could. On May 11, accompanied by Tsiebo, Resampa and other ministers, he toured the areas of the disturbances dispensing a mixture of conciliation, with offers of pardon to those who had been "led astray", and threats of the consequences of further rebellion.

Tsiranana's obsession with Communism led him to link the revolt in the south and the student strike in Antananarivo as parts of a single "Maoist" plot. In fact they were not connected, but common opposition to the government was to lead in due course to a potentially revolutionary alliance between MONIMA and the radical student leaders of FAEM. At the same time the students became disillusioned with AKFM which in its initial reaction to the disturbances appeared to support the government by calling for respect for law and order.

The disturbances in the south further widened the breach between Tsiranana and Resampa, whom he suspected of sympathising and even colluding with Monja Jaona. On May 25 Resampa submitted the resignation of the whole directing committee of PSD to Tsiranana and asked him to take the destiny of the party into his own hands. On May 30 the President accused an unnamed foreign embassy of interfering in internal Malagasy affairs. Two days later Resampa was arrested and convicted of plotting with an embassy, still unnamed but obviously the American since the American Ambassador was expelled at the same time.

The arrest and imprisonment of Resampa was a crucial step in the collapse of the PSD régime, though it was to last another year The real story behind the arrest is still in dispute. There is agreement only that the stated reason, the plotting with the American Ambassador, was patently absurd or at the very most amounted only to the ambassador carrying out the normal diplomatic function of cultivating good personal relations with an important minister and likely future President. According to one popular theory the French Embassy, apprehensive of Resampa's relatively left-wing and nationalist views and his close links with Germany through the SDP, fabricated the 'evidence" in order to remove Resampa and clear the way for their own candidate for the Presidency, Rabemananjara. It is indeed likely that the Embassy was involved in "the game of the succession". But there are indications that by then they had realised that Rabemananjara lacked the party and popular support to succeed to the Presidency and were themselves cultivating closer relations with Resampa[3] as the most likely successor. On the whole the most likely explanation is that the arrest was decided upon by Tsiranana himself and was the result of the President's paranoiac jealousy of his "dauphin", perhaps fuelled by the attentions paid to him by the leading embassies, and egged on by Resampa's enemies within the party.

The general malaise was heightened by the discovery of more "plots", first a "Maoist" plot involving a Frenchman and a Malagasy at ORSTOM, the main French scientific research organisation in Madagascar. Some members of the Catholic Church, which had taken the lead in criticising the repression in the south and organising relief in that region, were also said to be involved. Leaders of Catholic associations were among ten Antananarivo intellectuals who, together with about a hundred peasants from the surrounding area, were arrested in September for alleged involvement in another ill-defined plot against the régime. The increasingly open pursuit and defence of the South African policy aroused fears of a new foreign domination, bringing with it racial discrimination. The demoralised PSD could do no better than rally round Tsiranana who now more than ever believed that he was the elect of God and the ancestors. In the presidential elections of 30 January 1972 there was no other candidate, and Tsiranana was re-elected with an absurd 99.97 per cent of the votes cast.

Almost unnoticed during the presidential campaign, the students at the Befalatanana medical school in Antananarivo went on strike. This was not part of the university but the old colonial medical school set up by Gallieni to train auxiliary doctors to work under French doctors in the main population centres and to run basic health-care clinics in the countryside. The strike was motivated partly by economic grievances but later it developed into a protest against the low status of auxiliary doctors, their permanent inferiority to fully qualified doctors, French or Malagasy, trained in France[4] and the impossibility of ever improving their status (as they did not possess the *baccalauréat*). As with the previous year's strike the government rejected the students' demands and closed the school, and again the students remained on strike when the school was reopened. The Befalatanana students' union AEMEP attracted the support of FAEM and also the union of university teachers who, since 1968, had become more left-wing and were to play an important part in subsequent events by helping the students to organise and encouraging radical ideas.

After waiting several months in the hope that the strike would peter out, the government acted on April 22 to dissolve AEMEP. Two days later all the pupils of the secondary schools in the capital came out in support of AEMEP, followed the next day by the university students. On April 26 30,000 striking students paraded through the town carrying placards which not only protested against the dissolution of AEMEP but also called for a fundamental reform of the education system, denounced French cultural imperialism and demanded the suppression of the cooperation agreements with France. They were received in the Mahamasina stadium by the Education Minister Botokeky[5] who rejected their demands, ordered them to return to their schools and accused them of abusing their privileges. He was interrupted by shouts and chants and the students decided to continue the strike. They constituted themselves as a general assembly of all the students with a permanent council of 400 representing all the striking establishments, who elected a strike committee of ten. Over the next three weeks the students were in almost constant session and the membership of the various representative groups was frequently changed. In the process moderates (who by now included those linked to AKFM!) were eliminated and a 50-member Committee of Animation and Propaganda consisting mainly of militant radicals gradually assumed political direction of the strike. During this period the strike spread to secondary schools throughout the country, provoked partly by an ill-timed announcement by the government on April 9 that plans for a national competition for entry into the upper forms of the *lycées* had been abandoned. This decision effectively excluded the bulk of secondary students from the hope of advancing to the *baccalauréat* and a university education.

After the rebuff of April 26 the government was uncertain how to act. In accordance with their general spirit of popular democracy the students had avoided choosing specific leaders or delegates whom the government might have arrested; and to arrest all 400 of their permanent council would risk provoking more serious trouble. The best hope seemed to be to wait for the enthusiasm to wane and support for the strike to decline. This hope was destroyed when on May 3 striking students at Ambalavao on the southern plateau were fired on by the FRS, killing two, one of them a Merina. On May 6 in the capital the students organised an impressive, silent procession of mourning with placards denouncing the government's "despotism". Feelings ran even higher when it was learned that the government had refused to allow the family of the dead Merina student to bring him home for burial in the family tomb, thus flouting one of the most basic ancestral customs. The militants now took decisive control of the strike and circulated tracts calling on the workers of the capital to join them in a common assembly on the *Avenue de l'Indépendance* in the heart of the city on May 13. In an effort to prevent this, on the night of May 12-13 *gendarmes* surrounded the university and FRS troops went in to arrest the 400 members of the permanent council, who were taken immediately to the airport and flown to the convict island of Nosy Lava. At dawn on May 13 Johasy, now titular Minister of the Interior, announced on the radio that with the ringleaders arrested the strike was over and the schools would reopen; he also declared a state of emergency and forbade any assembly.

Undeterred, thousands of students gathered in the Avenue in front of the City Hall which was occupied by the FRS. After tear gas had failed to disperse them, the FRS opened fire with automatic weapons, killing a number of students. But the students and groups of unemployed youths calling themselves ZOAM[6] quickly formed commandos and counter-attacked the FRS, seizing weapons from them. Now many workers swelled the crowd of demonstrators. Detachments of *gendarmerie* and the army took up position on the Avenue but did not intervene in support of the FRS. After several hours they withdrew, followed by the FRS, leaving some 40 dead[7] and the students and workers in charge of the streets. A government curfew was ignored and throughout the night and the next day bands of insurgents roamed the streets seeking out the FRS. Meanwhile Tsiranana had further weakened his authority by an intemperate radio broadcast in which, imitating the sound of an automatic rifle, he threatened that law and order would be maintained even if it cost 2,000 or 5,000 or 100,000 deaths. Apart from being unwise, this was an empty threat. The army and *gendarmerie* had already made it clear that they would not fire on the crowds; and the French had sensibly refused a request from Tsiranana for military support. However the presence of the paratroops at Ivato no doubt helped to ensure that, although the main motivation of the insurgency was anti-French, no French targets were attacked by the commandos.

On May 15 trade unions and church organisations called for a general strike. A crowd of 100,000 representing most sectors of the capital's population marched on the Presidential palace (the old prime minister's palace at Andafiavaratra) with placards denouncing the French presence and the cooperation agreements and calling for the return of the deportees and the dissolution of the FRS. After intercession by church leaders, Tsiranana agreed to the return of the deportees and the crowd withdrew but did not disperse. Instead they attacked and burned down the City Hall, in protest at AKFM's ambiguous attitude[8] to the events of the last few days, and the offices of the *Courrier de Madagascar*. Sporadic clashes between the FRS and insurgent commandos continued and another violent radio statement by Tsiranana made things worse. Following the return of the deportees on the same day the students' organisation was reconstituted and was joined by committees of teachers and striking workers. The militants, led by Manandafy Rakotonirina, a Betsileo sociology lecturer and formerly a leading member of M0NIMA, formulated demands for the resignation of the government and the temporary assumption of power by the army pending the convening of a People's National Congress which would install a radical new political régime. This programme was approved on 18 May by the crowds gathered in the Avenue. They were about to march on the Palace when General Ramanantsoa arrived to announce that Tsiranana had named him prime minister and given him full powers. Rakotonirina attempted to get the general to accept the insurgents' programme but he skilfully evaded any precise commitment. Nevertheless amidst great enthusiasm the general was carried to the radio station where he announced the news to the nation.

Next day the euphoria faded somewhat when it was realised that Tsiranana was still President. A large crowd marched on the palace to insist on Tsiranana's departure, the denunciation of the cooperation agreements and the other conditions drawn up by the militants. Ramanantsoa, surrounded by a powerful military escort, rejected their main demand, arguing that Tsiranana's dismissal would risk a *côtier* uprising and civil war. This was a genuine fear and another argument was that as virtually the whole administration of the country was in the hands of PSD appointees, Tsiranana's departure could lead to administrative chaos. But the main reason was that Ramanantsoa wished to base his own legitimacy on the transfer of powers from the legitimate President rather than appear to be the creature of the popular movement. In this way he could control any reshaping of the state structure himself rather than have to accept conditions imposed by the mob. However at a meeting with insurgents' representatives the same evening he made some concessions, accepting the convening of a National Congress, the release of political prisoners and the payment of wages to workers during the strike period. On the next day, May 20, the committees reluctantly and the crowd with general relief accepted these concessions, the general strike was called off and the main crisis was over. Church leaders and responsible opinion generally rallied behind Ramanantsoa, and the militants' hopes of achieving a political and social revolution faded rapidly. This was in part because the militants were few in number and far from representative of the mass of the demonstrators. These were not interested in altering the structure of society. Their target was first of all French neo-colonialism, especially in education, and secondly the Malagasy government which sustained it. Once that government had collapsed and there was a reasonable prospect of "completing independence" by re-negotiating the agreements with France, their enthusiasm for demonstrating in the streets rapidly declined.

The militants were not yet ready to give in. The three committees of students, teachers and workers now joined with the ZOAM to form KIM (Joint Committee for the Struggle) which claimed to be the true voice of the masses and the only source of legitimate power. At well-attended weekly assemblies, while preparing their proposals for the forthcoming National Congress, they continued to call for the departure of Tsiranana. But on May 27 when Ramanantsoa formed his new government, consisting of 5 military officers and 6 civilian "technicians" and drawn from different ethnic groups, he had the ministers sworn in by Tsiranana thus emphasising his position as the source of legitimacy. KIM had one minor success, significantly in an anti-French context. The disturbances had caused the abandonment of the *baccalauréat* examination in the *lycées* which normally took place in June. The French Ambassador obtained permission from Ramanantsoa to hold a special examination for French students inside the French air base at Ivato airport. On 17 June a large assembly at the university campus denounced the special treatment of the French students and called for the withdrawal of all French forces. Ramanantsoa, not wishing to appear as an ally of the French, withdrew permission for the examination. Encouraged by this success KIM demanded that May 18 should replace June 26 as the national day; and when this was ignored they announced that they would hold their own June 26 celebrations separately from those of the government. Ramanantsoa responded by declaring a state of emergency and effectively confining the KIM assembly to its usual meeting-place in a scholastic complex, while the government celebrations proceeded under the joint presidency of Tsiranana and Ramanantsoa. This put an end to KIM's pretensions to being the source of government power, though for some time ZOAM remained active and a constant threat to the government's control of the capital. Meanwhile Ramanantsoa strengthened his position in the country by securing the withdrawal of the most senior French *conseillers techniques*, increasing the minimum wage, abolishing the poll and cattle taxes, appointing a Malagasy rector at the university and releasing political prisoners, including Monja Jaona and Resampa.

The KIM militants now concentrated their hopes on the National Congress due to meet on September 4. But Ramanantsoa effectively pre-empted the Congress by announcing that a new Constitution would be put to a national referendum on October 8. The Congress was thus reduced to a discussion group or at best an advisory body in which in any case the Antananarivo militants were outnumbered by the provincial delegates. Since May, KIM and especially ZOAM had sent militants to the provinces to set up local KIMs and preach direct democracy, but they failed to stir up revolutionary zeal. The provincial delegates generally supported the new government as the best hope of getting rid of the oppressive PSD structures in the provinces. Proceedings in the Congress were overshadowed by the referendum campaign in which Tsiranana opposed Ramanantsoa by calling for a "no" vote. But Tsiranana was now so discredited (and no longer the beneficiary of the massive pro-government vote) that only 3 per cent voted "no", with 81 per cent voting "yes" and the rest abstaining. Ramanantsoa now had his own legitimacy as Head of State, and Tsiranana retired as President, after a dignified farewell speech on the radio.

The referendum granted Ramanantsoa full powers to govern for five years in order to implement a "structural transformation" and "to bring about a climate of public life consonant with the wishes of the people". His government would be assisted by a People's National Council for Development (CNPD) elected by the *fokonolona* but with purely advisory functions. Ramanantsoa's policies in broad terms were Malgachisation of the administration, the economy and education to complete the independence only partially achieved in 1960; and economic development and a degree of democratisation based largely on the *fokonolona*. But he was essentially a professional soldier with no political ambitions and, after the upheavals of the previous two years he saw his main role as providing a period of peace and tranquillity during which politics would be set on one side. There was no chance of that, especially as political parties had not been banned. AKFM and MONIMA were still active in their own constituencies and KIM militants reformed as a Marxist or "revolutionary" party MFM (*Mpitolona ho amin'ny fanjakan'y madinika* – literally "fighters for government by the little people") under Manandafy Rakotonirina.

Though in some disarray and no longer monolithic, PSD with Tsiranana still its leader was by far the largest organised political group. In September 1972 Resampa, understandably resentful of Tsiranana, joined with Botokeky in forming the *Union Socialiste Malagasy* (USM) which campaigned for a "yes" vote in the referendum, the overriding aim being to support Ramanantsoa in containing the left wing. But Resampa and USM soon began to vie with PSD in defending *côtier* interests against a government which was increasingly seen as dominated by Merina. The threat of reversion to ethnic politics caused another group of ex-PSD, mainly from the plateau and led by Dr Razanabahiny, to form another new party *Vonjy* (Support for National Unity) which supported Ramanantsoa.

Politics could not be set aside when there were so many problems, notably the economy and urban unemployment, requiring urgent political answers; and the coastal/plateau division had if anything been sharpened by the events of May 1972. The *côtiers*, while accepting Ramanantsoa because of his professional reputation and lack of political ambition, were acutely aware of the loss of *côtier* power at the centre and concerned at the replacement of French advisers by Merina officials. Merina students and others welcomed the Malgachisation of the educational system and the prospect of the departure of French military forces. For coastal students Malgachisation meant that French teachers would be replaced mainly by Merina, and use of the Malagasy language instead of French meant using the official (Merina) dialect which again would place the *côtiers* at a disadvantage. In November 1972 *lycée* students in Tamatave went on strike against Malgachisation and this soon led to anti-Merina violence which paralysed the port and caused thousands of Merina to flee to Antananarivo. There were smaller protests in other coastal towns and in February 1973 a more substantial demonstration in Diego Suarez, provoked by fears of unemployment if the French were compelled to leave the naval base. A number of PSD leaders, including some ex-ministers, were arrested on suspicion of inspiring these protests.

In general however the dismantling of the French special position and the accompanying Malgachisation were the most popular cards in the government's hand. The renegotiation of the cooperation agreements was in the hands of the new foreign minister, Lieutenant-Commander Didier Ratsiraka, a young naval officer. He was a Betsimisaraka whose father had been a governor in Tamatave province and an early supporter of PADESM (as was Ratsiraka's father-in-law Pascal Velonjara). He had done well in his *baccalauréat* (mathematics) in Paris and in his naval and staff college training, also carried out in France, and in 1972 he was Military Attaché in Paris.[9] He soon made a name for himself by reversing Tsiranana's pro-Western policy and pursuing "non-alignment" with a new slogan *"tous azimuts"*. The commercial agreements with South Africa were cancelled, diplomatic relations broken off with Israel, South Vietnam and Taiwan and relations established with the USSR, Eastern European countries and the People's Republic of China.[10] Madagascar withdrew from OCAM and became an active member of the radical wing of the OAU and of the African group in the UN, with Ratsiraka in the forefront of any attack on imperialism. But his main achievement was the renegotiation of the agreements with France in the first half of 1973. The main features were that Madagascar left the Franc Zone and France handed over all its military bases in Madagascar[11] together with certain buildings including the French Embassy, the former residence of the governor-general. But France also agreed to continue to supply, and pay for, teachers and technical assistants (*coopérants*) at the request of the Malagasy government and scholarships for students whom the Malagasy wished to send to France. Despite the cooling of relations, the French sensibly took a long-term view and their aid programme in fact continued at a high level.

These foreign policy successes helped to sustain Ramanantsoa, who also won respect for his even-handed firmness. Having dealt with PSD trouble-makers at the beginning of 1973, he cracked down on MFM militants when they tried to organise a demonstration to celebrate the first anniversary of the May 13 uprising, arresting Rakotonirina and some 60 MFM members.[12] The successful negotiation with the French also won considerable popularity for Ratsiraka, especially among the left-wing parties AKFM, MONIMA and MFM. But within the government, as a junior officer from the smallest service, he lacked a power base and for a time carried little weight. The two main figures to emerge in the government, leading opposing tendencies, were Colonel Ratsimandrava, the Minister of the Interior, and Colonel Roland Rabetafika, Director-General of the government.

Richard Ratsimandrava came from a modest bourgeois family in Antananarivo, but of *andevo* (slave) origin. He had served in the French army in Morocco and Algeria and graduated from St. Cyr before returning to Madagascar after independence. Attracting the favourable attention of Tsiranana, he rose rapidly to become in 1969 the first Malagasy head of the *gendarmerie*. He was therefore in charge of the repression in the south in 1971. This experience contributed to his refusal to use force against the demonstrators in May 1972, which was a major factor in Tsiranana's downfall. He remained in command of the *gendarmerie* when he became Minister of the Interior with the main task of carrying out the reform of local government based on the *fokonolona* which the new government hoped would win the support of the people in the countryside. Working hard to overcome the unpopularity deriving from the 1971 repression, he travelled extensively over the island talking and listening to the peasants while elaborating a radical, almost revolutionary, reform programme. In March 1973 the old rural communes were abolished, and in August the *fokonolona* were restored with a new autonomy in management of local production and use of financial resources, with the government intervening only to provide technical services on request. The old hierarchy of government-appointed local officers was to be replaced by officials directly elected by the people, first at the lowest level (the *fokontany*, the area of the *fokonolona*) and then at the successive higher levels. This programme won the enthusiastic support of left-wing intellectuals in the capital as well as rural peasants and the urban poor. It was less well viewed by the "establishment" of notables and local officials, mostly with links to PSD, whose power base and jobs would be eroded by this form of popular democracy.

Ratsimandrava's reforms also threatened the bourgeois Merina establishment in the capital. Their main representative in the government was Colonel Rabetafika who, though not a minister, probably wielded more influence than anyone as Director-General with constant access to the Head of State and responsibility for coordinating government programmes, particularly in the economic field. He came from one of the leading families of the *haute bourgeoisie* of Antananarivo and was said to be a member of the "Club of 48", a shadowy and possibly mythical group of leading Merina in positions of responsibility in government service, the armed forces and business. He and his colleagues favoured a mixed economy, with state capitalism rather than socialist structures to drive economic development. In addition to the parastatals inherited from the Tsiranana regime they set up a number of "Societies of National Interest" such as SONACO (for external trade) and SINPA (for the marketing of agricultural products). These were intended to replace the Chinese and Indian middlemen who bought and marketed crops from the peasant farmers and take over many of the activities of the big French companies. For the time being the only French company nationalised was the utility company *Electricité et Eaux de Madagascar*. But the government took substantial share holdings in the leading French banks and became the majority shareholder in Air Madagascar.

Whereas Ratsimandrava's populist activities were highly visible, Rabetafika operated behind the scenes in government. The conflict between the two took place for the most part out of the public eye, in the absence of any effective public forum in which government policies had to be defended before elected representatives of the people. Elections for the CNPD in October 1973 produced a pro-government majority: *Vonjy* did well winning 30 per cent of the seats, while PSD and USM suffered from the split of the coastal vote, with Resampa failing to be elected. But the Council met only briefly twice a year and its role was effectively limited to discussing the Development Plan.

Ramanantsoa might have been able to impose unity on his government if he had developed a wider personal power base in the shape of his own party with a dynamic political programme. Instead, lacking political ambition and the necessary taste for intrigue, and not having any clear political ideas of his own, he presided uneasily over the growing split in the government. Problems multiplied in 1974. The economy, which had been disrupted by the disturbances in 1972, suffered a further setback with the steep increase in world oil prices in 1973 and the consequent increased cost of imports of manufactured goods. Inflation and recession caused growing hardship in the towns. The new parastatal societies proved to be less efficient than the Asian middlemen and French commercial companies they sought to replace. The Asians paid low prices and charged usurious interest rates on money advanced for the next crop, but at least they made things work. The societies did not advance funds and did not always pay on time, and so peasants held back production, causing shortages of rice, oil and other foodstuffs in the towns. Both SINPA and SONACO became riddled with corruption and a flourishing black market developed. There were suspicions that the French trading companies, and especially the *Compagnie Marseillaise*, were bribing senior people in the government in the hope of staving off nationalisation. The opposition to the government strengthened in March 1974 when Resampa became reconciled with Tsiranana and USM and PSD merged to form the *Parti Socialiste Malgache* (PSM). They were able to play on the plateau/coast division and exploit the economic difficulties: at one time they embarrassed the government by distributing cheap rice, subsidised from PSM funds, along the west coast.

The divided government seemed incapable of dealing with the many problems. Ratsimandrava's reforms were being sabotaged or delayed by his opponents in the government and by territorial officials who would lose their jobs if the reforms were implemented. He responded with more country-wide travels and speeches and interviews with peasants on the radio, which increased his popularity with the peasants, the urban poor and the left-wing politicians. Enjoying the support of the *gendarmerie* and even some left-wing army officers, he had become the most powerful figure in the government with obvious ambitions to become its leader. His right-wing opponents were directly threatened when he used his powers as Minister of the Interior to begin an investigation into corruption that he promised to pursue to the highest levels. Within the government, Ratsimandrava's only regular supporter was Ratsiraka, but this was merely a tactical alliance between two rivals who both had their eyes on the succession to Ramanantsoa. Although both could be classed as left-wing, Ratsimandrava's grass-roots socialism and participatory democracy were far removed from Ratsiraka's intellectual leanings towards Marxist centralism, and personally they were never close. As foreign minister, Ratsiraka was able to stand aside from internal problems; and as things got worse towards the end of 1974 he skilfully avoided public statements on domestic issues so as to leave his options open.

Several issues came to a head at the turn of the year. On January 3 Ratsimandrava ordered the arrest of three managers of the *Compagnie Marseillaise* and made threatening noises about those who were sabotaging economic reconstruction and his *fokonolona* policy. In mid-January the *Madagascar Matin* (successor to the *Courrier de Madagascar*) published news of an attempted coup against the government. On December 31 several *côtier* army officers had been arrested for plotting to replace Ramanantsoa with Colonel Bréchard Rajaonarison, the senior *côtier* officer in the army. Rajaonarison had been promoted by Tsiranana as a counter-balance to the Merina domination of the senior ranks. Unlike the other two colonels (Rabetafika and Ratsimandrava) he had been given only a very minor post (Military Adviser to the Head of State) under the Ramanantsoa government. He attributed this to anti-*côtier* bias and he felt that further promotion was unlikely when all three generals in the army were Merina. After the arrests he went into hiding for some weeks until on January 22 he took refuge in the encampment of the *Groupe Mobile de Police* (GMP) on the outskirts of Antananarivo. The GMP was formed from members of the FRS which had been disbanded after the events of May 1972 and, like the FRS, was predominantly *côtier*. When ordered to hand over Rajaonarison the GMP refused, thus placing themselves in a state of rebellion. Statements by Rajaonarison made it clear that the motivation of the rebellion was resentment at Merina domination in the armed forces and the government. Tsiranana and Resampa, along with MONIMA and even some *côtier* members of the government, gave moral support to the rebels, and it became apparent that an assault on the GMP camp would risk a Merina/*côtier* split in the armed forces and even civil war.

On January 25 Ramanantsoa dissolved his government and tried to form a new one. But by now even his former supporters in the CNPD, including *Vonjy*, were calling for his resignation. During ten days of complex manoeuvrings (in which for perhaps the only time the CNPD played a significant role) Ramanantsoa at first tried to form a government without Ratsimandrava, but this failed when Ratsiraka stood by his left-wing rival; and the two of them were able to insist that Rabetafika be excluded from the new government. But their alliance fell apart when the CNPD persuaded Ramanantsoa to propose that Ratsiraka should head a new government with Ratsimandrava as his deputy. Ratsiraka overplayed his hand by demanding that Ratsimandrava give up the Interior, command of the *gendarmerie* and control of the *fokonolona* programme. Ratsimandrava, whose political base was far stronger than Ratsiraka's, naturally refused. Under further pressure from the CNPD, who called for the dossiers dealing with corruption in the government, Ramanantsoa finally resigned on 5 February and handed over power to Ratsimandrava.

Ratsimandrava's new government consisted of seven military and nine civilians, with a preponderance of *côtiers*. Apart from himself, only two ministers survived from the previous government and, not surprisingly, neither Rabetafika nor Ratsiraka was included. But the new government had no chance to show how it would deal with the tense situation. Six days after his appointment as Head of State, Ratsimandrava was ambushed by a party of GMP at a crossroads in the heart of old Antananarivo. In a brief exchange of fire Ratsimandrava was killed along with two of his bodyguard and two of his attackers.

The assassination was a profound shock to the country and swift action was needed to restore order. A Military Directorate consisting of eighteen officers from the armed forces, and including Ratsiraka but not Rabetafika, was immediately set up under General Gilles Andriamahazo, the senior officer after Ramanantsoa, but the ministers appointed by Ratsimandrava remained in place. International air services were suspended and external telecommunications censored so that for some weeks Madagascar was cut off from the outside world. Martial law was proclaimed and all political parties dissolved. On February 13 the GMP camp was attacked and

15 defenders and 20 attackers were killed before the camp surrendered. On the next day the PSM headquarters in the centre of the town, where some GMP had taken refuge along with Resampa, was also attacked and taken.

Normal life could now be resumed, but for the next three or four months the attention of the nation was riveted on the trial, by military tribunal, of those accused of responsibility for the assassination. They numbered no less than 297, mainly members of the GMP but including Tsiranana, Resampa and other PSM leaders. At first it seemed a fairly straightforward matter, with the GMP or some of them obviously guilty of carrying out the assassination, and the PSM leaders possibly guilty of incitement or complicity. But it turned out to be much more complicated. The GMP ambush party consisted of a sergeant-major and four men. The three survivors testified that they had orders (denied by their superiors) only to kidnap Ratsimandrava, and not to open fire unless the bodyguard did so first. But the party seemed ridiculously inadequate and low-level for the task, given the size of Ratsimandrava's bodyguard; and curiously the two who had opened fire were both killed. There was evidence indicating that some bullets hitting the car came from the opposite side of the street from the ambush party; and there were persistent rumours that Ratsimandrava had been killed in his office before being taken to the scene of the alleged assassination. Perhaps there was another assassination plot for which the GMP ambush provided a convenient cover.

If other people were involved, there was no shortage of suspects who stood to gain by Ratsimandrava's removal from the scene. The ex-PSD leaders, hoping to return to power, were the most obvious and they had close connections with the GMP. But Colonel Rabetafika and the "Club of 48" were faced not only with the loss of Merina bourgeois power but possible exposure of corruption from the dossiers held by Ratsimandrava; and Rabetafika was the first senior officer to arrive at the scene of the crime. Rabetafika was in fact arrested during the trial and brought before the Tribunal; but there was no clear evidence against him, and the idea of collaboration between him and the GMP was highly implausible. The one who ultimately benefited most from the assassination was Ratsiraka and there were suggestions at the time and subsequently that he was the mastermind behind the plot. But there was no serious evidence and he was not brought to trial. The Tribunal failed to unravel the truth from the mass of confusing and conflicting evidence.[13] Amid suspicions of a cover-up, the "trial of the century" came to an end on June 12 with the release of all the accused except the three survivors of the ambush party, who were sentenced to five years hard labour. In the short term the failure to convict any of the leading personalities at least avoided exacerbating political divisions. But the continuing mystery cast a long shadow over a number of reputations.

While the trial monopolised attention, a struggle for power was going on inside the Military Directorate, to decide who would lead a new government once the emergency was over. General Andriamahazo, like Ramanantsoa a non-political professional soldier, was the obvious candidate of the Merina bourgeoisie, while a Major Soja of the *gendarmerie* was the leader of the Ratsimandrava faction. But neither was a match for Ratsiraka who, with Ratsimandrava dead and Rabetafika excluded from the Directorate, was now well placed for the succession. At first he was in a minority in the Directorate and viewed with some mistrust because of his equivocal behaviour in the last weeks of the Ramanantsoa regime. But during months of skilful manoeuvrings he was able to acquire a dominating position. The more conservative *côtiers* did not care for his political views, but his *côtier* origins and promises of decentralisation won them over. His intellectual credentials and his non-aligned foreign policy made him acceptable to the left-wing bourgeois intellectuals in Antananarivo, including AKFM; and his brother Etienne, a businessman, had links with the "Club of 48". Ratsimandrava's followers were disarmed by a commitment to pursue the *fokonolona* reforms; and he was able to convince the committed socialists that he was one of them. When the trial ended Ratsiraka was chosen as the new Head of State by a two-thirds majority of the Directorate. On 15 June the Directorate was dissolved. Ratsiraka, at the age of 38, assumed the leadership of a country which, after four years of turmoil, could no longer be described as "the happy island".

Chapter 21

Revolutionary Socialism

Ratsiraka's intentions were clear from the outset. The country was renamed the Democratic Republic of Madagascar and he assumed power as President of the *Conseil Suprême de la Révolution* (CSR), a group of officers appointed by him from the Military Directorate.[1] The CSR, which soon acquired civilian members and later became predominantly civilian, was to play the role of the Politburo or Central Committee in Communist states, namely to decide broad policy, leaving it to the ministries of the government to implement it. The government was to be predominantly civilian but, no doubt in order to ensure the loyalty of the armed forces, the posts of prime minister and Minister of Defence were usually held by a military officer, the first prime minister being Lieutenant-Colonel Joël Rakotomalala.[2] In his first speech as President, Ratsiraka stated that "the only road to development is that of socialism". To underline the point and reassure his left-wing supporters he immediately nationalised the banks, insurance companies, the port and oil refinery of Tamatave and the main shipping company. "Non-alignment" was emphasised by the closure of the American satellite tracking station west of Antananarivo.

In a series of radio broadcasts in August 1975 Ratsiraka expounded his Charter of the Socialist Revolution which was then published and became known as the "Little Red Book". Its inspiration came partly from Chinese Communism, partly from Nyerere's Arusha Declaration of 1967 and partly from the general pool of Soviet-inspired left-wing thought which predominated in intellectual circles in France and elsewhere in the 1950s and 1960s. Strong on sonorous rhetoric but rather weaker on detailed practical proposals, it was as much an electoral platform as a statement of political philosophy. Alongside socialism, a principal feature of the Charter was nationalism, expressed internally by a denunciation of French neo-colonialism and externally by condemnation of Western imperialism, together with a firm rejection of the *francophonie* movement and support for nationalist liberation movements. It advocated the dismantling of the remaining features of economic neo-colonialism and the gradual abandonment of the use of French as a joint official language and as the main vehicle for secondary and university education.

The principles of the Charter were enshrined in a new Constitution which was presented to the Malagasy people at the same time. This was remarkable for the prominence given to socialism as an unalterable part of the political and economic structure of the country; and for the powers given to the President. Whereas the normal pattern in Communist countries was for the leader to be elected by a Central Committee and therefore in theory removable by it, in the new Malagasy Constitution the President was directly elected by the people for a period of seven years and it was he who appointed and dismissed the members of the CSR as well as the prime minister, the ministers of the government, the members of the Supreme Court, the heads of the armed forces and many other holders of senior government posts. With considerable powers of government by CSR decree as well as the power to withhold approval of legislation originated by the National Assembly, the President was in a position of virtually unchallengeable dictatorial power.

The new Constitution, like the Charter, emphasised the role of the *fokonolona*, thereby appearing to continue the work of Ratsimandrava. But there was an important difference from the Ratsimandrava concept. This had envisaged a genuine popular democracy with decisions taken at the village level by the elected representatives of the *fokonolona* and then at the higher levels of district, province and finally nation by representatives chosen by those elected at the lower level. Thus the national parliament and in theory national policies would originate in the *fokonolona*. The Constitution enshrined this system, but only up to the level of province: direct popular elections intervened for the National Popular Assembly. And the *fokonolona* were not encouraged to initiate policy: on the contrary, in the name of "democratic centralism" they were required to carry out the socialist policies decided by the central government.

The Constitution guaranteed individual human rights and liberties, but only "within the framework of the Charter of the Socialist Revolution"; and these rights would be withdrawn from anyone abusing them to oppose the Revolution. Political rights were similarly restricted. Elections were by universal suffrage, but the only candidates permitted were those supporting the socialist ideal and members of progressive parties grouped within a National Front for the Defence of the Revolution (FNDR).

On December 21 1975 a national referendum put the question: "To build a new society, based on justice and equality, do you approve the Charter of the Socialist Revolution, and the Constitution that will apply it, and in consequence Commander Ratsiraka as President of the Republic?" The heavily loaded question, an intensive propaganda campaign and a general desire for stability and firm leadership after years of uncertainty ensured a massive "Yes" vote of 94.7 per cent of a high turnout. On January 4 1976 Ratsiraka formally assumed the Presidency, moved into the former residence of the French Ambassador[3] and began putting in place the institutions of the socialist revolution.

In his early years of government Ratsiraka sought to reassure Western ambassadors by explaining that it had been necessary for him to assume leadership of the revolutionary movement in order to control it, with the implication that he was not himself a committed socialist. But there can be little doubt that the "Little Red Book" reflected his own political beliefs, developed during the 1960s when it was generally accepted gospel that socialism was the only solution for the newly independent countries of Africa and elsewhere. By 1975 the image of socialism was somewhat tarnished in some third-world countries where it was increasingly seen as providing the framework and justification for personal dictatorship. But Nyerere's grassroots, egalitarian African socialism was still widely respected, especially in European democratic socialist countries. And in 1975 a socialist revolution had recently taken place in Ethiopia, whilst the collapse of the Portuguese colonial empire was about to bring Marxist governments to power in Angola and Mozambique. So Ratsiraka could claim that he was taking Madagascar back into the mainstream of third-world politics. What he could not plausibly claim was that revolutionary socialism expressed the wishes of the Malagasy people, apart from the "mob" in Antananarivo and its intellectual leaders. The mass of the Malagasy people remained profoundly conservative. Indeed the concept of revolution, implying rejection of ancestral beliefs and behaviour, was so alien to the Malagasy spirit that no suitable word for it was current in the language; hence the speeches in Malagasy made by the new leaders tended to be liberally sprinkled with the French word *"révolutionnaire"*.

The rhetoric of the new regime was certainly revolutionary but its practice fell in some respects short of the Marxist ideal. The most obviously revolutionary feature was Ratsiraka's foreign policy which, officially non-aligned and omni-directional (*"tous azimuts"*), was in practice anti-Western and pro-Soviet. The USSR replaced France as the main supplier of defence equipment and military training; and in contrast to the closure of the NASA station, the Russians were allowed to set up radar stations along the West coast of Madagascar. (However Ratsiraka resisted Soviet pressure to permit their warships to use the Diego Suarez naval base, which would have been in too obvious contradiction to his support for demilitarisation of the Indian Ocean.) In the OAU Madagascar was always in the vanguard of the radicals: it was, for example, one of the first countries to recognise the Polisario movement as the government of the Western Sahara. In the UN Madagascar spoke and voted consistently in support of Soviet positions and was one of the small group of third-world countries which abstained on resolutions condemning the Soviet invasion of Afghanistan. Special relations were cultivated with North Korea, one of the most hard-line Communist states which at first sight did not have much in common with Madagascar or many good features to emulate. President Kim Il Sung's personal philosophy of *Chuche* (*Djoutché* in French) was held up to admiration and made the subject of seminars and conferences, while exchanges of visits proliferated. North Korea was given an important role in providing equipment and training to the army and President Ratsiraka's bodyguard, which included a substantial number of North Koreans. Various economic aid projects were financed by USSR and other Communist countries (notably China's rebuilding of the Antananarivo-Tamatave road). But the new Communist friends lacked the resources to supplant Western aid donors who, led by France, continued to provide the bulk of external economic and technical aid.

Economic policy was also clearly Marxist, at least in the early years. The initial nationalisations were followed in 1976 by the nationalisation of petroleum distribution and of the three main French commercial companies who controlled so much of the import-export trade and the marketing of cash crops. Later came the takeovers of all sugar refineries, chrome mining and the two largest textile factories. There was thus central control and planning of banking and insurance and much of the import and export trade and industrial production. The agricultural sector also saw an increase in state intervention with the establishment of a rural credit bank and the formation of new co-operatives, while SINPA and SONACO remained responsible respectively for rice collection and distribution and the main aspects of foreign trade. With most peasants already owning their land there was little scope for land reform, except in some areas around the capital where the political power of the absentee landlords inhibited any action. Abandoned colonial plantations were taken over and a few active foreign-owned plantations in the southeast expropriated and run as state farms or cooperatives. But there was no serious attempt to introduce the alien concept of communal farming, and individual peasant smallholdings remained the dominant feature of the agricultural landscape.

The most striking variation from the standard Communist pattern was that the Democratic Republic was not a one-party state. Ratsiraka clearly would have liked to establish a single party dedicated to the revolution and led by himself. But the existing left-wing parties which would naturally have formed the nucleus of such a party were reluctant to abandon their independence or accept Ratsiraka as their party leader. He accordingly had to settle for the concept of a coalition of "progressive" parties, the FNDR, which was enshrined in the Constitution. But first he needed to establish his own party base. In March 1976 he founded AREMA (*Avant-garde de la Révolution Malgache*) as a government party with himself as Secretary-General and the Little Red Book as its political programme. With the help of the administrative network, party cells were established throughout the country and AREMA rapidly acquired more branches and members than any other party. Only then, at the end of 1976, was FNDR set up, comprising AREMA, AKFM, MONIMA, the PSD-derived *Vonjy* and a Christian party, UDECMA; MFM had been banned, and Manandafy Rakotonirina imprisoned, following a university strike in August 1976, but joined FNDR when the ban was lifted early in 1977. FNDR's controlling body was the Political Committee consisting of the President, the prime minister, the President of the National Assembly and three representatives from each of the component parties. The leaders of these parties were also usually invited to sit on the CSR.

The FNDR was intended to be an interim stage on the way to a one-party state, but owing to policy and personality differences it never progressed beyond a loose and at times fragile coalition. AKFM was generally loyal to Ratsiraka: Andriamanjato was a member of the CSR while Gisèle Rabesahala became a long-serving Minister of Revolutionary Arts and Culture in the government. *Vonjy* and UDECMA, neither of them "revolutionary" in outlook, were content to maintain a low profile while benefiting from their participation in the government. But Ratsiraka's relations with the leaders of the two populist parties, MFM and MONIMA, were often difficult. Both Rakotonirina, as a leading figure in the overthrow of the old regime in 1972, and Monja Jaona, as head of the oldest party and the only leader with a genuine peasant base, were seen as serious rivals for the left-wing leadership. Relations with the somewhat irascible Monja Jaona were to prove particularly stormy.

The relative strength of the parties within FNDR was first tested in local elections in the spring of 1977. AREMA, profiting from the support of the administration and the traditional pro-government vote, recorded 88 per cent of the vote, which inevitably provoked accusations of electoral fraud. Monja Jaona withdrew MONIMA from FNDR (a breakaway faction, VSM-MONIMA, later rejoined FNDR) and boycotted the legislative elections on June 30, when AREMA won 112 out of 137 seats. Paradoxically AREMA had inherited much of the vote and clientèle of its ideological opposite, Tsiranana's PSD.

In retrospect, 1977 can be seen as the high point of Ratsiraka's power and authority. He had successfully installed the political and economic framework for his socialist revolution; and though he had failed to establish a one-party state, the overwhelming dominance of AREMA produced very much the same result. He stood apart from the other leaders in that he alone had been able to assemble a broad national coalition running from the mass of the coastal and rural people to the intellectuals and business circles of the capital. He now set about the task of economic recovery and transformation by the application of the socialist principles set out in the Charter. The main instrument was to be an Investment Plan, approved in December 1977, which envisaged, over a twenty-year period, the doubling of GNP via the establishment of heavy industry, the achievement of self-sufficiency in food and ultimately the export of manufactured goods. This ambitious programme was to be financed mainly by investment and borrowing from abroad under the slogan *"investissement à outrance"* – "all-out investment", which soon however became transmuted in general parlance to "outrageous investment". Given the rundown state of the economy it was indeed an outrageously optimistic programme, partly because a steep increase in the price of coffee, from 209 FMG a kilo in 1975 to 806 FMG in 1977, encouraged optimism. But the 1977 price was a freak caused by frost in Brazil and was never attained again.

Within three years of the launching of the Investment Plan the economy was in ruins. By 1981 the budget deficit was running at over 40% and exports were covering less than 50% of imports, partly because of the need to import large quantities of rice; industry was running at less than one-third capacity because of lack of raw materials and spare parts; inflation had risen to 27%; and foreign debt had mounted to over US $1 billion. The country could no longer meet its debt payments and Ratsiraka had to appeal to the international financial community for help. In June 1980 the first IMF standby agreement was signed under which the main donors agreed to a rescheduling or refinancing of the debt and in return Ratsiraka had to accept an IMF stabilisation programme, involving devaluation, a pruning of the investment plan in favour of a rehabilitation programme, budget austerity and some degree of liberalisation of the economy. The "conditionality" of IMF support did not for the time being call seriously into question Ratsiraka's socialist policies. He continued to proclaim the virtues of the revolution and the Little Red Book as the basis of economic recovery. But the dream of a socialist Utopia had receded far into the distance.

The collapse of the economy was blamed by the government on the second oil price shock, when the oil price trebled around the end of the seventies, and the severe worsening of the terms of trade for developing countries resulting from the fall in commodity prices. It is fair to say that for these reasons any government in Madagascar, as in most Third World countries, would have been in serious difficulties by the mid-eighties. But the effect of the oil price increase did not begin to be felt until 1981, after the IMF had been called in; and the terms of trade did not seriously worsen until later: for example in the years 1978 to 1982 the coffee price, although on average 25% below the exceptional year of 1977, was still three times what it had been in 1975. Other reasons, mostly internal, must be sought to explain why the economic crisis hit Madagascar earlier and more severely than most other developing countries.[4]

One reason was certainly the "outrageous investment" programme, not only for its disproportionate scale and the unsuitability of some of the projects but also for its dependence on heavy foreign borrowings, contrary to the self-reliance advocated in the Little Red Book. In this area some of the blame belongs to the international financial experts who encouraged the government to seek additional foreign loans on the ground that Madagascar was "under-borrowed". It is true that, because of prudent financial management in the sixties and early seventies, Madagascar had a lower debt ratio than many developing countries. But the experts overestimated the country's capacity to service a larger debt. And their estimates of future productivity and earning capacity did not take account of the disastrous effect of imposing socialist central planning on an economy for which it was singularly unsuited.

The adverse effects of centralised control of the purchase, collecting and marketing of agricultural products, already apparent under Tsiranana's moderate socialist régime, became more pronounced as socialist control was extended further. With the price of rice kept artificially low for the benefit of town dwellers, rice producers lost interest in producing a surplus, and the amount coming to market declined by 50% between 1977 and 1981; hence the need to import large quantities to the detriment of the balance of payments. Producers of cash crops such as coffee, vanilla and cloves were paid (usually late) only between 20 and 30% of the FOB export price. Not surprisingly production stagnated and in the northwest much produce was smuggled to the Comoros where prices were far higher. Productivity also declined owing to inefficiency, corruption and poor maintenance in the state farms and cooperatives which had taken over the former French-owned plantations. Agriculture generally suffered from the lack of foreign exchange to import fertiliser and insecticide. Meanwhile the cost of the expanding bureaucracy and of supporting the mostly disastrous new industrial investments left insufficient funds for maintaining the infrastructure. The problems of collection and distribution were compounded by the worsening state of the roads and the shortage of vehicles due to lack of spare parts. Many villages away from the main roads were virtually cut off from the rest of the country and had to revert to a self-sufficient subsistence economy.

The IMF support averted the immediate financial crisis but failed to halt the economic decline. As the eighties progressed the collapse of the world oil price afforded some relief, but much less than it should have done since Madagascar was locked into a long-term Soviet oil contract at a price which was often double the world price. Meanwhile terms of trade continued to worsen as the price of imported manufactured goods rose dramatically while commodity prices languished or declined. Further recourse to the IMF became necessary in 1982 and at regular intervals thereafter, with each time more stringent conditions such as devaluation, some degree of privatisation, a reduction in price controls and subsidies and other measures of liberalisation. In the negotiations Ratsiraka fought stubbornly to retain as much of his socialist policies and government control as possible, but in the last resort the desperate economic situation compelled him to give way. His acceptance, however reluctant, of IMF conditions made Madagascar a favourite recipient of Western aid, which rose from US $220 million in 1983 to $330 million in 1985.

The continuous economic decline, the failures in distribution and the price rises resulting from devaluation and the IMF liberalisation measures had serious social and political consequences. In the late seventies prolonged drought added to rural misery, especially in the south and west. Sporadic violence became more widespread in the eighties with more serious rioting in Diego Suarez, Tulear and other west coast towns. Groups of *dahalo* (bandits) appeared for the first time since the early years of the century. At first they engaged mainly in cattle-stealing but later they would also attack and rob travellers so that travel was no longer safe away from the main highways. Growing unemployment and the steady drift to the towns caused a steep rise in urban crime, especially in Antananarivo.

The university was in an almost constant state of unrest throughout this period. Ratsiraka's government had embarked on a rapid expansion of secondary and higher education, including the creation of regional university centres in all the provincial capitals. Numbers of university students rose from 6,000 in 1972 to 20,000 in 1979 and 40,000 in 1984 (partly because students who failed their exams were allowed to try again or switch to a new subject) and inevitably standards declined. Contributory factors were the decline in competence in French, still the language of higher education, because of the Malgachisation of secondary education; the departure of most of the French teachers, many of them replaced by Russians; the politicisation of the grant of university scholarships; and the shortage of money and therefore of equipment and books. The students and teachers suffered like the rest of the population from rising prices while the growing numbers created an accommodation crisis, especially as graduates who could not find employment often stayed on in their quarters and were difficult to dislodge. The lack of employment opportunities for graduates was a major grievance, along with the compulsory pre-university national service, especially when this was increased to two years (mainly as a short-term measure to reduce the number of unemployed). The Malagasy teachers were also discontented with their status, salaries and living conditions and in 1979 they went on strike. A year later all the students went on strike, calling for the resignation of the Minister for Higher Education and the President himself.

As in 1971-2, the fortunes of the university became linked with those of Monja Jaona, whose peasant-based party MONIMA had attracted much support in intellectual circles in Antananarivo.[5] Despite his withdrawal from FNDR in 1977, which under the Constitution excluded him from participation in politics, Monja Jaona and MONIMA continued to criticise the government and in November 1980 he called for a general strike. His subsequent arrest provoked student demonstrations in the streets of the capital. On February 3 and 4 1981 a demonstration of 4,000 students was suppressed by security forces at a cost of 6 dead and 45 wounded; and a number of senior university teachers were arrested. Monja Jaona was released in March but it was not until the end of June that the university teachers were released and university life returned to normal. In August MONIMA rejoined FNDR and Monja Jaona was appointed to the CSR where by virtue of his age he was the senior member. But this did little to abate his criticisms of the régime.

From time to time rumours of attempted *coups* added to the political tension. In January 1977 a minor incident, in which two South Africans and an American flying from South Africa to Mauritius in a light aircraft made a forced landing on the east coast, was inflated into a mercenary threat to the régime. In October of the same year Commandant Andriamaholison, who had been a minister in Ratsimandrava's government, was arrested with two other officers on a charge of plotting against State security; they remained in prison for six years before being brought to trial before a Military Tribunal and sentenced to exile for life (although in fact they remained in prison in Madagascar). In 1982 a plot to assassinate the President was discovered allegedly involving South African mercenaries and Malagasy *ombiasy*; among thirteen arrested were several senior officers and politicians and a Catholic priest. At the trial in September 1983, five were acquitted and the rest given suspended sentences. In contrast to this leniency, another trial in November 1983 condemned 29 alleged conspirators led by a businessman Gaston Ramaroson to sentences ranging from six months' imprisonment to ten years' hard labour.

Meanwhile, Ratsiraka's position seemed to be weakened by the development of a split within AREMA itself between hard-line socialists in what came to be called Red Arema and more liberal, market-oriented elements in White Arema. The latter were strong in Antananarivo and were led by Rakotovao-Razakaboana who as Minister of Finance had won the approval of the World Bank and IMF for his prudent management and acceptance of structural reforms. However Ratsiraka was able to hold the party together and maintain his authority by skilfully playing off one side against the other; and Razakaboana's influence was eroded by moving him from the Ministry of Finance and "promoting" him to the CSR.

In January 1982 Ratsiraka announced his candidature for the presidential election which for tactical reasons he postponed until November. This time, in another departure from standard Marxist practice, he had an opponent, Monja Jaona. But despite the serious economic problems Monja Jaona won less than 20% of the national vote (though very nearly 50% in the capital) and again he denounced electoral fraud. He also demanded fresh elections and a new constitution and called for a general strike. This led to rioting and his arrest and removal from the CSR. After eight months of detention he was released in August 1983 in time to take part in the elections for the National Assembly, when he stood as a candidate in Antananarivo and won a resounding and, for a *côtier*, astonishing victory. In the country as a whole widespread apathy caused an abstention rate of 25%. AREMA won a reduced majority of 65% of the votes cast, but the "first past the post" system gave them 85% of the seats (117 out of 137).

One reason for the decline in Ratsiraka's popularity was the activity of the secret police DGID (*Direction Générale d'Investigation et de Documentation*), commanded by the President's brother-in-law Colonel Christophe Raveloson-Mahasampo,[6] in searching out anti-government "plots" and suppressing opposition. They were supported by gangs of unemployed youth organised and financed by the government and known as TTS, successors to ZOAM, who roamed around Antananarivo extorting money by threats, discouraging opposition and helping to suppress student demonstrations. As a defence against their depredations, students and other young men mainly of bourgeois families formed vigilante groups which practised the martial arts of Kung-Fu. Various clashes led the government to prohibit the practice of Kung-Fu in September 1984. But on December 4 a virtual pitched battle between TTS and Kung-Fu in Antananarivo left more than 50 dead. In a government reshuffle in February 1985 the Minister for Population and Social Affairs, believed to be responsible for financing TTS activities, was removed; and in the following month Colonel Raveloson-Mahasampo was removed from the command of the DGID (but in the following year he was appointed Minister of Defence). Meanwhile the Kung-Fu's vigilante role and defiance of the government's ban were seen as a serious threat to the régime's authority. On August 1 1985 the Kung-Fu headquarters in Antananarivo was attacked by police and army units supported by tanks and artillery. The building was destroyed with the death of 20 young men, while over 200 more were arrested.[7] This brutal assault marked a decisive point in the loss of the goodwill which Ratsiraka had initially enjoyed amongst many people in the capital. Increasingly obsessed with his own security he appeared rarely in public and then surrounded by bodyguards so that he became a remote figure isolated from the people. Advised by Communist security experts that his residence in the heart of Antananarivo was too open to attack, he had a new residence constructed by North Koreans at Iavoloha, some distance outside the capital, which was a veritable fortress, generally referred to as "the bunker".

The economic picture remained gloomy. Although Ratsiraka continued to proclaim the virtues of the revolution and socialism, his government earned the praise of the IMF and World Bank for its acceptance of structural adjustment policies and was held up as an example to other indebted third-world countries. Austerity measures reduced the budget deficit and the foreign exchange gap, and World Bank officials spoke of the economic decline "bottoming out". But implementation of the adjustment policies was often half-hearted, especially in relation to the size of the civil service and expenditure on the armed forces, and the international terms of trade remained unfavourable. Despite the repeated rescheduling of debt and massive injections of aid, the upturn of the "J-curve" (under which corrective measures cause the economy to decline further before it begins to improve) was stubbornly slow to appear. The external public debt more than trebled from 1982 to 1985 and then doubled in the following two years to reach over $2.6 billion, more than total GNP, with debt service exceeding export earnings. Successive devaluations reduced the Malagasy franc from 50 to the French franc in 1980 to 231 at the official rate, and 350-400 on the black market, in 1988. Annual inflation averaged between 15 and 20%, with prices of basic foods such as rice, sugar, cooking oil, beef and tinned milk rising two, three or four times faster than the minimum wage. During most of the eighties GNP stagnated or declined so that, with population increasing relentlessly by more than 3% per year, GNP per head fell by some 25% between 1980 and 1987.

Translating these statistics into daily life, living standards of all classes were sharply cut, and the effect on the poorer sections of the urban population was little short of catastrophic. In a country where food had always been plentiful and cheap, supplies of many basic items, even rice, became uncertain and often disappeared into a black market at prices beyond the means of many. The continuing drift to the towns increased the numbers of unemployed and homeless, especially in the capital. Child beggars, hitherto unknown, roamed the streets while pickpockets made visits to the famous Zoma market a hazardous operation. The more desperate homeless families occupied the rubbish dumps where children scrabbled among the refuse competing with dogs and pigs for scraps of food and seeking items of metal, glass or plastic which might fetch a few francs on the street market: bones were particularly sought as they could be sold to an animal food manufacturer. The inadequacy of salaries inevitably caused an increase in corruption and also armed robberies which made it unsafe to venture out at night. The churches and charitable organisations worked long hours to care for the thousands of homeless and orphans living in shanties or sleeping in the open, but starvation, insanitary conditions and exposure caused many deaths. Malaria spread from the coastal areas, where it had always been endemic, to the plateau where it was previously rare; and with anti-malarial drugs expensive or unobtainable it was often fatal. In the countryside there was usually enough to eat, except in the drought-ridden south and areas hit by cyclones which seemed to occur more frequently than usual in the eighties. But many peasant families suffered from the isolation caused by the worsening state of the roads and from the shortages and high prices of basic items they needed to buy, such as soap, oil and simple medicines.

Not everyone was impoverished. Those from various levels of society who operated the black market were able to amass substantial sums. Those with access to the levers of economic power in government, in the parastatals and in commerce were also able to exploit the situation to their personal advantage as corruption, rare in the early days of independence, became the normal pattern. One organisation singled out for particular criticism was PROCOPS (*Société de Promotion des Coopératives Socialistes*), which was set up in 1984 as a cooperative organisation attached to AREMA but became in effect a private company run by the President's sister-in-law Hortense Raveloson-Mahasampo. It soon became heavily involved in commercial and industrial activities and acquired a dominant position in the supply and marketing of rice, vegetables, poultry and other foodstuffs, which it was able to exploit to the great profit of the régime.

Another group who continued to do very well were the Indian and Pakistani shopkeepers, traders and industrialists, known to the Malagasy as the Karana (from the Koran, as most were Moslems). Resentment at their prosperity in the midst of poverty and hardship led to attacks on their shops and homes in various towns in the early part of 1987; a number were killed and many took refuge in the French consulates (most were French citizens) or fled to Réunion. In 1986 and 1987 famine in the arid south, causing many deaths from starvation, provoked further outbreaks of violence and a substantial migration to the north of the island. The port of Tamatave saw serious unrest in November 1986 because of food shortages and fears of job losses arising from plans to rationalise the port; several people were killed when mobs attacked warehouses where they believed PROCOPS was hoarding food. In the same month the government proposed to reduce student numbers at the overcrowded university by 20%, through measures such as prohibiting students from repeating academic years. After six months of protest, boycott and strikes by students and university staff, during which six students were killed in clashes with the security forces or in fighting between striking and non-striking students, the government was compelled to withdraw the proposed reforms.

Chapter 22

Return to democracy

Throughout this period of turbulence and economic decline, criticism of the government was muted by press censorship and the ban on political parties outside the FNDR. But a notable exception was the Catholic Church. Through its weekly newspaper *Lakroa* it drew attention to the growing poverty and misery throughout the country and regularly denounced examples of corruption, denial of human rights and abuses of power. Pastoral letters from the bishops also criticised the government with increasing severity, notably in a letter of 1985 entitled "The anatomy of a dictatorship". The FJKM Protestant churches, traditionally sympathetic to the left wing, gradually distanced themselves from the AKFM and the government; and in January 1980 they had joined with the Catholics, Lutherans and Anglicans in forming the Council of Christian Churches of Madagascar (FFKM).[1] This united church front was to become in the later eighties a political force which Ratsiraka could not ignore.

With no legal outlet in Madagascar, a political opposition in exile appeared in Paris and in October 1987 set up the *Union des opposants malgaches à l'extérieur* (UOME). Its leading figures included the former minister Alexis Bezaka and Lucile Ramanandraibe, a former diplomat and member of one of the wealthiest bourgeois families of Antananarivo, who published *Le livre vert de l'espérance malgache* setting out a liberal-democratic alternative to the revolutionary socialism of the Little Red Book. The UOME gave its support to Monja Jaona as the most trenchant critic of Ratsiraka within Madagascar and campaigned strongly for the release of Commandant Andriamaholison. It had some success in weakening support for Ratsiraka within the French government, but its effectiveness within Madagascar was inevitably somewhat limited. More worrying to Ratsiraka was the growth of opposition within FNDR. The Front began to fall apart in 1987, partly because of disagreement with the government's handling of the student strikes and other disturbances. AKFM remained loyal, despite growing reservations on the part of its leader Andriamanjato. But MFM and *Vonjy* began to cooperate openly with MONIMA in opposing government policies and, from May 1987, in calling for the resignation of the government and the holding of early elections.

By now Ratsiraka's policy could be summed up in one word - survival, based on keeping potential opposition divided while ensuring the support, or at least the benevolent neutrality, of the armed forces. To strengthen his authority over the forces he promoted himself to full Admiral, thus becoming the highest ranking officer in any of the services; and he was always careful to keep the military closely associated with his government. The CSR usually contained at least five senior officers; and in successive governments the posts of Minister of Defence and, with one brief exception, prime minister were always held by serving officers. The only civilian prime minister was Justin Rakotoniaina who was appointed in August 1976 after the first prime minister, Colonel Joël Rakotomalala, was killed in a helicopter accident. A year later he was replaced by Colonel (later Brigadier-General) Désiré Rakotoarijaona, who was to hold the post for eleven years. However in the mid-eighties there were indications that Rakotoarijaona was unhappy about various aspects of government policy and shared the concern of other senior officers regarding their dependence on the USSR and North Korea for military training and supplies. The Minister of Defence, Rear-Admiral Guy Sibon, and the Chief of Staff of the Armed Forces, General Lucien Rakotonirainy, were both believed to favour closer military cooperation with France rather than with the Communist powers. So when the former was killed, along with other senior officers, in an air crash in May 1986 and the latter collapsed and died while reviewing troops in June 1987, there was no shortage of rumours that the Soviet KGB was responsible for their elimination[2]. In February 1988 General Rakotoarijaona resigned (or was dismissed) as prime minister, allegedly for health reasons but more probably because of policy differences with the President. He was replaced by the Minister of Public Works, Colonel Victor Ramahatra, the grandson of Prince Ramahatra and therefore closely related to the old Merina royal family.

The approach of the presidential election due in November 1989 accelerated the disintegration of the FNDR, which had not in fact met formally since 1982. During 1988 the three parties opposed to Ratsiraka each nominated their leader as a presidential candidate. To pre-empt the possibility that they might agree to unite behind one candidate, Ratsiraka had the Constitution amended to bring the election forward to March 1989. The opposition vote was split between Manandafy Rakotonirina (MFM) 20%, Dr Razanabahiny (*Vonjy*) 15% and Monja Jaona (MONIMA) only 3%. Ratsiraka was accordingly re-elected with 62% of the vote. This was a very low figure by Malagasy standards for an incumbent head of state and, bearing in mind the usual heavy pro-government vote in the countryside, it amounted to a rejection by the educated and politically sophisticated voters in the capital and most other towns. The opposition candidates maintained that there had been serious irregularities and that the true vote for Ratsiraka was less than 50%. But this did not alter the fact that he had been re-elected for another seven years. And in the legislative elections in May, characterised by a high abstention rate, especially in the towns, AREMA actually increased its large majority, winning 120 out of 137 seats. Again there were complaints of electoral fraud, but the splitting of the non-AREMA vote among a number of parties certainly contributed to the result.

With a new mandate and a larger parliamentary majority, Ratsiraka's position seemed unassailable. But the ground swell of opposition to his policies and to him personally was strengthened by the collapse of socialism in the Soviet Union and by the movement towards multi-party democracy in many single-party states in Africa and elsewhere, partly because of pressure from aid donors to improve human rights. In successive negotiations with the IMF Ratsiraka had already had to reverse most of his socialist economic policies and embrace privatisation and economic liberalism. He now came under increasing pressure from the opposition, supported by the press (censorship had been lifted before the presidential election), to make corresponding changes in the areas of politics and human rights. His long-time ally Richard Andriamanjato, who in March had left AKFM to form a new party AKFM/F (*Fanavaozana* = renewal), could now be counted among the opposition which was demanding democratic reform. Ratsiraka promised changes and followed his usual tactic of dividing the opposition. Having earlier dismissed six members of the CSR, including Rakotonirina and Andriamanjato, for opposing his re-election, he reshuffled the CSR again in August 1989 to admit Monja Jaona (once more), the Vice-President of *Vonjy* and other opposition figures. At the same time he consulted privately with leaders of the churches and other opinion groups to seek their views on reforms. The churches, through FFKM, spoke for many when they publicly called for abolition of the requirement for political parties to belong to FNDR, as well as the elimination of references to socialism in the Constitution.

Ratsiraka yielded to pressure by accepting the first demand, but not the second. Amendments to the Constitution agreed by the National Assembly in December 1989 left the privileged status of socialism virtually untouched, but abolished FNDR's political monopoly and thus effectively abolished FNDR itself. The formal resumption of multi-party politics in March 1990 saw the appearance of many new parties. They included several Christian parties, a *Parti Socio-Démocrate* (PSD) led by André Resampa, former Secretary-General of the old PSD, and the *Union Nationale pour le Développement et la Démocratie* (UNDD), whose leader was Dr Albert Zafy, a medical professor from Diego Suarez who had been a minister in Ramanantsoa's government in 1975. Manandafy Rakotonirina, who had moved a long way from the militant left to embrace market economics and political liberalism, was soon to change the name of his party from "Militants for government by the people" to "Militants for Malagasy progress" while keeping the same Malagasy acronym MFM. Not all the new parties were opposed to the President. A number of them joined AREMA, the hard-line remnant of AKFM and elements of *Vonjy* and MONIMA, including Monja Jaona, to form a new pro-government group MMSM (*Mouvement militant pour le socialisme malagasy*).

Having lost the support of Moscow, Ratsiraka had no choice but to turn back to the West, and particularly France. The seal was set on improved relations when President Mitterrand made a state visit in June 1990, the first visit by a French head of state since independence. It was preceded by the cancellation of a large part of Madagascar's public debt to France. During the visit Ratsiraka promised fair compensation to the French companies nationalised under his government and stated that the French navy could once again make use of the naval base at Diego Suarez for staging and refuelling. And it was probably pressure from Mitterrand that led to the release soon afterwards of Commandant Andriamaholison and his fellow-detainee: their immediate departure for Paris may have been a condition of the release. A more surprising visitor in August was President de Klerk of South Africa. Ratsiraka had been quick to respond to the reforms introduced by de Klerk and in May he had announced his readiness to resume commercial relations with South Africa[3], although diplomatic relations would have to await the complete dismantling of apartheid. De Klerk's visit produced agreements on tourism and the resumption of an air link between the two countries. The first flight from Johannesburg brought a large South African trade delegation, arousing hopes of substantial investment from Madagascar's natural trading partner.

Thus by 1990 Ratsiraka had reversed virtually all his policies, foreign as well as domestic, and met most of the opposition's wishes regarding the abandonment of socialist economics and the resumption of multi-party politics. Moreover he could now at last point to a turn-around of the economy which World Bank officials, with some exaggeration, were terming an economic miracle. After a decade of overall decline, 1989 saw growth in GNP of 4.9%, followed by an estimated 3.5% in 1990. In the new climate of economic liberalism numerous small businesses were set up; and foreign investors, mainly from France, Mauritius and Hong Kong, were encouraged by a new investment code adopted in December 1989. Madagascar continued to receive favourable treatment from Western aid donors. In 1988 they agreed a programme of $700 million of quick-disbursing aid as well as a further re-scheduling of external debts, which now amounted to $3.6 billion. Concern for the preservation of Madagascar's unique plant and animal life, threatened by population growth and the destruction of the forest, led to the establishment of a special conservation aid programme coordinated by the World Bank.

However the economic reforms which the government had carried out under international pressure did not satisfy the opposition. They believed, with good reason, that Ratsiraka remained committed to socialism and they were unhappy with the prospect of his continuing to exercise the dictatorial powers of the President for another six years. They did not as yet demand the President's resignation, but they insisted that the Constitution should be revised to eliminate the references to socialism and reduce the powers of the President. The Council of Churches (FFKM) now moved to the centre of the political stage. They invited all parties to attend a convention under the name *Hery velona*, or *Forces vives* (FV) in French, in August 1990 to discuss a "national concertation" programme aimed at finding solutions to the country's political and economic problems. The President denounced the initiative and the pro-government MMSM parties boycotted the convention. The meeting accordingly became a forum for coordinating opposition proposals for constitutional reform and at a further convention in December a permanent *Comité des forces vives* was set up for this purpose under the leadership of Andriamanjato, Rakotonirina and Professor Zafy.

In December 1990 the National Assembly formally abolished press censorship, ended the state monopoly of radio and television and authorised the establishment of private broadcasting stations. In the following February the President announced that further constitutional changes, notably the replacement of the appointed CSR by an elected senate, would be submitted to the next session of the National Assembly in May. However, when the Assembly reconvened on 10 May, a crowd of 5,000 hurled abuse at ministers and deputies (including Monja Jaona, who had now aligned himself with Ratsiraka[4]) as they arrived. They then forced their way into the Assembly chamber to hand over the FV proposals for amending the constitution, which included the elimination of the references to socialism, a reduction in the President's powers and a limit on the number of terms he could serve. But in due course the Assembly debated only the President's amendments which, though numerous, left the President's authority virtually intact and retained most of the references to socialism. As the AREMA-dominated Assembly would obviously carry out the President's wishes, the FV demanded that a special constitutional conference be convened within a month. When Ratsiraka failed to respond, the FV embarked on an extraordinary and prolonged non-violent confrontation with the aim of forcing him to resign. They also demanded the resignation of the government and its replacement by a 'government of transition to democracy".

On June 10 the FV called a general strike which, with occasional interruptions while negotiations took place, was to last over six months to become the most prolonged general strike ever known. From the same date the FV organised almost daily peaceful anti-government demonstrations of 100,000 or more in Antananarivo. Demonstrations also took place in the provincial capitals and occasionally in other areas, but the heart of the opposition movement remained in Antananarivo. After a slow start the general strike became more and more widespread, affecting government offices, postal services, banks, major commercial firms and transport. Together with the massive demonstrations, it soon paralysed life in the capital and caused serious disruption elsewhere. The army and police remained generally passive and the demonstrations were widely reported in the press and on radio and television.

In July various negotiations between FV and MMSM, promoted by FFKM or the French Embassy, collapsed on FV's insistence on the President's resignation, based on the argument that Ratsiraka's re-election in 1989 had not been democratic since only parties affiliated to the FNDR were then allowed to operate. At one stage the MMSM agreed to a constitutional conference but rejected FV's demand for a new transitional government. The FV accordingly on July 17 announced the establishment of its own transitional government, with a retired general, Jean Rakotoharison, as head of state, Professor Zafy as prime minister and Andriamanjato as government spokesman. Some of the ministers of this alternative government began to occupy deserted government offices with the help of civil servants observing the strike. On July 23 Ramahatra, the prime minister of the legal government, announced a state of emergency in the capital with a curfew, the re-imposition of censorship and a ban on public meetings. But the security forces took no action to enforce the state of emergency while the press ignored the censorship; and further demonstrations were provoked by the abduction of Zafy and three of his "ministers"[4] by armed men dressed in denims and gas-masks. There were also murders of FV leaders in Tamatave and Diego Suarez.

The beleaguered Ratsiraka now announced on July 28 the dismissal of Ramahatra and his government and promised a referendum on a new constitution by the end of the year. But at a demonstration the next day the FV demanded the resignation of the President, the lifting of the state of emergency and the release of their four "ministers" (they were released unharmed on July 30). Then in a shrewd move on August 8 the President appointed the respected Mayor of Antananarivo, Guy Razanamasy, as prime minister. Razanamasy immediately invited the FV to join his government, with their choice of posts. The offer was rejected as Ratsiraka would remain as Head of State with the portfolios of defence and foreign affairs. But the manoeuvre succeeded in widening a split in the FV between the radicals led by Zafy who wanted the complete overthrow of the existing régime and a more moderate group led by Rakotonirina who were willing to compromise with Razanamasy in working for a peaceful transition to a more democratic constitution.

The dominant radical FV group organised on August 10 a large but peaceful protest march on the President's fortress-like residence at Iavoloha, a few miles outside the capital, to demand his resignation. The march was turned back by helicopters dropping tear gas and stun grenades, while the President's bodyguard threw thunderflashes and fired into the marchers, killing an estimated 100 and wounding a larger number. On the same day a demonstration in Majunga was repressed at a cost of 20 lives. This bloodshed seriously weakened Ratsiraka's support both internally and externally. The Catholic Archbishop of Antananarivo joined those calling for the President's resignation and the FFKM stated that it was abandoning its rôle as honest broker and would henceforth support the FV. The French government suspended its military aid (which had included training for the President's bodyguard) and made it known that it had advised Ratsiraka to resign and offered him asylum in France.

Ratsiraka still refused to resign, insisting that he was the legally elected President, that the opposition was significant only in the capital and that the bulk of the rest of the country supported him. He organised expressions of support from leaders of the other five provinces; and on August 19 and 20 the elected representatives (mostly AREMA) of these provinces declared each province a federal state and recognised Ratsiraka as federal president. On August 26 Razanamasy announced the composition of his government, which contained some defectors from FV including Resampa and some non-political figures such as Césaire Rabenoro, the President of the Malagasy Academy, who became foreign minister. The FV denounced the new government as Ratsiraka's puppets and stated that the strikes and civil disobedience would continue. Razanamasy lifted the censorship but retained the state of emergency and threatened to dismiss any civil servant who failed to report for work on September 4. But on that date the ministries remained closed and a large FV demonstration confirmed that the strikes would continue.

The stalemate continued through September and October with two alternative governments purporting to rule the country but neither in a position effectively to do so. The FV continued to prove their control of the capital with almost daily demonstrations or meetings in the *Place du 13 Mai* (formerly *Avenue de l'Indépendance*) and with strikes which were largely effective. They also ensured the closure of all ports except Tamatave. But whilst they had shown considerable strength in some provincial capitals they failed to win much support in the countryside. In the absence of an effective government most aid donors suspended their aid and made it clear that aid would not be resumed until the crisis was resolved, preferably by the formation of a coalition government of consensus. The army remained neutral, refusing to use force to repress the opposition but equally reluctant to intervene to depose the President, at least partly because of the strength of his bodyguard – 1500 of the best-trained and best-equipped men in the army, entrenched in the "fortress" of Iavoloha. Various attempts at mediation by the French Embassy and others to promote a consensus government foundered on the intransigence of both sides. Finally on October 30, General Ramakavelo, speaking on behalf of the senior officers of the army, announced that if the politicians failed to agree on a settlement the army would "take whatever measures need to be taken" to bring the crisis to an end "within the shortest possible period of time".

In the face of this ultimatum Razanamasy convened an urgent meeting of representatives of FV, MMSM and the churches (FFKM) which led to an agreement on October 31 on transitional arrangements which would provide "a legal framework for the realisation of the popular desire for change". Under this agreement Ratsiraka surrendered his executive powers, retaining a largely ceremonial role as President of the Republic and titular Head of the Armed Forces. The Supreme Council of the Revolution and the People's National Assembly were suspended and their powers and functions were allocated for a maximum transitional period of eighteen months among three institutions. Professor Zafy was named as President of the *Haute Autorité de l'Etat* (HAE) consisting of 31 members appointed by FV and MMSM and more or less filling the role of the CSR in supervising the government. Andriamanjato and Rakotonirina were made joint presidents of the *Comité pour le redressement économique et social* (CRES) with up to 130 members proposed by FV, MMSM and FFKM and representing social, cultural, economic and professional groups; its function was to carry out studies and make recommendations on economic and social policy. Razanamasy was confirmed as prime minister, with specific responsibility for security and defence and executive authority over the armed forces, and his government was to be expanded to include representatives of the FV. The churches, through FFKM, were given the task of organising regional forums to elect delegates to a National Forum which would draft a new constitution to be submitted to a national referendum.

Unfortunately Zafy had been in Paris when the agreement was signed and he refused to be bound by it on his return, objecting especially to the retention of Ratsiraka as Head of State and Head of the Armed Forces. He reinstated the general strike, which had been called off in his absence, while he renegotiated certain aspects of the agreement, including the allocation of posts in the coalition government. It was not until December 19 that the strike was ended when agreement was announced on the composition of the new government, now enlarged to include more FV members. The former PSD minister Alfred Ramangasoavina became a second deputy prime minister alongside Francisque Ravony, a son-in-law of Tsiranana. Among other ex-PSD ministers of Razanamasy's original government, Resampa was dropped but Rabenoro remained as foreign minister.

The immediate task of the new government was to revive the economy, which had suffered severely from the prolonged strike. The loss of salaries because of the strike caused much individual hardship and a consequent growth in crime. Tourism had been badly affected by reports of the disturbances and the increase in crime; and industrial production had been reduced by more than 80%. Strikes at sugar plantations had put a stop to sugar exports and made it necessary to import sugar for the first time for many years. Fortunately agriculture in general was less affected and exports of coffee and cloves had been maintained, though earnings were lower because of the stagnating world market. But strikes at the main vanilla port of Antalaha reduced vanilla exports to a quarter of normal. Rice production had held up well and food supplies to the towns were maintained throughout the crisis. However at the end of the year future rice production was threatened by the prolongation of the dry season followed by torrential rains which caused much damage. In the arid south, in an extension of the drought covering much of southern Africa, the rains failed completely, causing serious famine and a flow of refugees to other areas in search of food.

The return of the economy to normal at the beginning of 1992 was delayed by further strikes in different sectors, this time for more pay to cope with inflation which had increased to an estimated 30% during the previous year. Otherwise shops, businesses, offices and schools reopened and the post office began clearing the huge backlog of mail which had piled up over six months. An exception to the general rule was the university in the capital, which was a major casualty of the disturbances, coming after more than a decade of student unrest. The new school year had to be postponed repeatedly because all classrooms had been destroyed, looted of furniture or occupied by squatters, often members of the extended families of students.

The other main task of the government was to maintain peace and security during the transition to a more democratic system under a new constitution. Ratsiraka was far from reconciled to his exclusion from power and his supporters, including gangs of TTS youth in Antananarivo, sought to disrupt the process of consultation starting with the regional forums. A number of churches were attacked and destroyed in protest against the role of the churches in the opposition to Ratsiraka. There were also clashes with the security forces in February after the combined new authorities, seeking to destroy Ratsiraka's political base, decreed the suspension of the elected local authorities and their replacement by appointed Special Delegations. When the National Forum met in the capital at the end of March to draft the constitution, grenades were thrown at the meeting-place and Zafy narrowly escaped death when an attempt was made to crash a lorry laden with petrol into his house. The Forum was then moved to a military camp, where on March 31 Monja Jaona led a protest march of Ratsiraka supporters. When they refused to stop, soldiers fired on them killing 8, including a former minister, and wounding 44, one of them the octogenarian Monja Jaona.

Ratsiraka, who continued to insist on his right to stand for re-election as President, now called for a federalist draft constitution to be submitted to the referendum as an alternative to the unitary draft being considered by the Forum. After much debate a clause was included in the electoral code excluding the presidential candidature of anyone who had been elected twice under the Second Republic. But the constitution approved by the Forum was of a parliamentary type under which the President would have little more than ceremonial and representative functions. There would be a Senate, two-thirds indirectly elected and one-third appointed on the nomination of economic, social, cultural and religious organisations. The National Assembly would be elected by proportional representation and all real executive power would be in the hands of a prime minister elected by, and dismissable by, the National Assembly. The Forum envisaged a referendum on the constitution on June 21, followed two months later by the presidential elections and, after a further two months, the National Assembly elections. But the threat of disruption by Ratsiraka's supporters and continuing disagreement among the transitional authorities on the division of power between the president and the prime minister caused the referendum to be postponed until August 19.

In the week before the referendum, federalist crowds invaded provincial and town headquarters in Majunga, Tulear and several other towns to burn voting papers and electoral lists. On the day of the referendum itself, federalists in Diego Suarez staged a local *coup* and closed many polling stations; while in Tamatave fighting between federalists and FV supporters caused six deaths. Otherwise the referendum was carried out peacefully and to the satisfaction of international observers. The result was a decisive reverse for Ratsiraka: with some 65% of the electorate voting, the new constitution was approved by 72% to 28% of the valid vote.

The defeated supporters of Ratsiraka set up a "Committee of the No Votes" to challenge the referendum result, and in Diego Suarez, Tamatave and Tulear they declared the provinces to be autonomous federal states. They also agitated in support of Ratsiraka's right to stand for re-election. In early October in Diego Suarez they temporarily occupied the radio and TV stations and tried to block the airport runway to prevent flights from the capital landing, provoking troops to fire on them, killing 8 and wounding 15. Federalists also succeeded in halting rail traffic between Tamatave and the capital by blowing up the line in three places, causing temporary shortages of fuel and other supplies. The threat that these disturbances might escalate into civil war persuaded the authorities to alter the electoral code to permit Ratsiraka to stand in the presidential election. This had the desired effect, and the election took place in due course on November 25 in a calm atmosphere, helped by a "gentlemen's agreement" among the candidates that they would avoid personal abuse and that government resources would not be used to favour individual candidates. With the national television station remaining neutral and offering equal space to every candidate, this was the first truly democratic election held in Madagascar.

At one time no fewer than 18 candidates declared themselves, but the requirement of a deposit of 25 million francs (about $13,000), to be forfeited by any candidate receiving less than 10% of the vote, reduced the number to 8. Apart from Ratsiraka the main candidates were Professor Zafy and Manandafy Rakotonirina. The most interesting among the others was the veteran nationalist Jacques Rabemananjara, who at the age of 78 was persuaded by the prime minister Razanamasy to return from 20 years of voluntary exile in France and campaign on a platform of national unity and reconciliation. Although Ratsiraka had the advantage of greater resources, including two Russian helicopters and his own radio station, the campaign was run in a fair, democratic manner under supervision from the international community, which also supplied financial support and help with the organisation. A relatively high turnout of 74% of the electorate gave 45% to Zafy, 29% to Ratsiraka and just over 10% to Rakotonirina; the remainder lost their deposits. Zafy won large majorities in his home province of Diego Suarez and in Majunga but also substantial support in all the other provinces; whereas Ratsiraka failed to win 50% of the vote even in his home province of Tamatave.

However Zafy's support fell short of the 50% required by the Constitution, so a second round was held on February 10 between the two leading candidates. With most of the defeated candidates throwing their support behind him, Zafy emerged as the clear victor, winning 67% of the vote to 33% for Ratsiraka. The first peaceful and democratic transfer of power in the history of Madagascar duly took place when the new President was formally invested on March 27 at an open-air ceremony at the Mahamasina stadium in front of a large and enthusiastic crowd. The outgoing President failed to attend this ceremony and rejected advice from many quarters that he should retire with dignity to France. Instead, he indicated at a press conference that, like de Gaulle at Colombey-Les- Deux-Eglises he would await the call of his countrymen to resume the leadership.

Meanwhile the transitional authorities remained in place pending the election of the National Assembly which would choose a new prime minister. For the legislative elections, held on June 16 under a system of proportional representation, no fewer than 121 political parties registered and some 4,000 candidates competed for

138 seats. A number of the component parties of the FV coalition which had elected President Zafy broke away to compete separately, but a residual coalition known as the Cartel FV (or in its Malagasy version HVR – *Hery Velona Rasalama*) emerged as the most successful group with 47 seats. Manandafy Rakotonirina's MFM came second with 15 seats, while a new pro-Ratsiraka group FAMIMA won 11 seats. Another new party LEADER FANILO, composed of eminent "non-politicians" and led by Herizo Razafimahaleo, did well with 14 seats. 9 seats went to prime minister Razanamasy's party FIHAONANA and 8 to the PSD/RPSD (successor to the old PSD of the First Republic). President Zafy's former party UNDD and Andriamanjato's AKFM/F each won 5 seats.

There followed weeks of intensive discussion and manoeuvrings in an attempt to reach a consensus on the election of the prime minister. Two of the leading potential candidates, Razanamasy and Andriamanjato, in the event did not stand for the premiership; instead they competed against each other for the post of President of the National Assembly, with Andriamanjato emerging as the winner. The election of the prime minister, by a simple majority in a single secret ballot, took place on August 9. Rakotonirina received 32 votes and Roger Ralison, regarded as the flag-bearer of the Cartel, 45 votes. The winner, with 55 votes, was Francisque Ravony, the deputy prime minister of the transitional government, who was the favoured candidate of the business sector and of President Zafy. Ravony, a lawyer from a well-known political family from Vohipeno on the south east coast, had been a consistent opponent of the previous régime and had played a prominent role in the movement for change since 1990.

The new government formed by Ravony on August 27 marked an almost complete break with the past. Apart from himself, it contained only three members of the transitional government, and there were no survivors from any of the Ratsiraka governments. There were however some echoes from the First Republic. Ravony himself was not only a son-in-law of Tsiranana but also the son of Jules Ravony, who was President of the National Assembly and later President of the Senate in the early years of independence. His foreign minister was Jacques Sylla, a lawyer from Tamatave who had previously played little part in politics but was the son of Albert Sylla, foreign minister from 1960 until his death in an air crash in 1967.

The assumption of power by the new government completed the long process, started by the Council of Churches when they convened a national convention three years earlier, by which a virtual dictatorship dedicated to revolutionary socialism was transformed into a parliamentary democracy. The change was not without bloodshed, as supporters of the previous régime, mainly in the coastal areas, sought to block or disrupt the process. But by and large it was carried out peacefully, with no overt intervention by the military and with proper regard for constitutional processes – an achievement much to the credit of the Malagasy people and its leaders.

Sources

A complete bibliography of the history of Madagascar would fill a very sizeable volume. The list given below of works consulted in the preparation of this book cannot therefore claim to be exhaustive. In addition to the many works, mainly in French, published in the twentieth century, Madagascar has, unlike most African countries, a relatively well documented pre-colonial history, with many of the essential sources located in London. Apart from the very complete collection of published works and periodicals in the British Library, there are the unpublished archives of the British Museum Manuscripts Department, the Public Record Office and the London Missionary Society (now housed in the library of the School of Oriental and African Studies) which together constitute the most important collection of source material on pre-colonial Madagascar. Use has also been made of the Bibliothèque Nationale in Paris and the library of the Académie Malgache in Antananarivo.

The section on the twentieth century relies largely on published works, including a vast number of articles in learned journals appearing mainly in France and Madagascar. The author is particularly indebted to Alain Spacensky for his detailed study of the complex politics of the fifties and sixties in his *Madagascar, Cinquante ans de vie politique*. For the last twenty-five years much use has been made of newspapers and weekly journals as well as the author's own experiences and conversations with many of the leading figures on the political stage.

The sources have been listed in alphabetical order of authors under the part of the book to which they are most relevant. They have been given a letter and number to facilitate reference to them on the notes. To avoid cluttering up the text with references, the notes have in general been confined to the identification of the source of quotations together with a few points of clarification.

ABBREVIATIONS

Archives

BMM	British Museum Manuscripts Department
CSP	Calendar of State Papers
	CSP Dom. Domestic Series

Sources

	CSP Col.AWI Colonial Series, America and West Indies
LMS	London Missionary Society
	Mad.IL Madagascar, Inward Letters
	(B – Box, F – Folder, J – Jacket)
PRO	Public Record Office, London
	CO Colonial Office
	FO Foreign Office
SOAS	School of Oriental and African Studies, London University

Periodicals and series

AA	Antananarivo Annual
AUM	Annales de l'Université de Madagascar, Antananarivo
AVG	Annuaire des Voyages et de la Géographie, Paris
BAM	Bulletin de l'Académie Malgache, Tananarive
	n.s. nouvelle série
B.Mad.	Bulletin de Madagascar, Tananarive
CEA	Cahiers d'études africaines, Paris
CHJAM	Colloque des Historiens et Juristes, Académie Malgache(75th Anniversary) September 1977
COACM	Collection des ouvrages anciens concernant Madagascar (Grandidier, see B26)
EHR	English Historical Review, London
GA	Géopolitique Africaine, Paris
GM	Gentlemen's Magazine, London
HPNPM car	Histoire Physique, Naturelle et Politique de Madagascar (Grandidier, see G6)
JA	Journal Asiatique, Paris
JAH	Journal of African History, London
JRAI	Journal of the Royal Anthropological Insitute, London
MAM	Mémoires de l'Académie Malgache, Tananarive
MM	Mémoires du Muséum, Paris
OSA Université	Omaly sy Anio (Revue d'études historiques). de Madagascar, Antananarivo
RA	Revue anthropologique, Paris
RFEPA	Revue française d'études politiques africaines, Paris
RFHO	Revue française d'histoire d'outre-mer, Paris
RHC	Revue d'Histoire des Colonies, Paris
RM	Revue de Madagascar, Tananarive
TNR es	Tanganyika (later Tanzania) Notes and Records, Dar Salaam

Sources

GENERAL

G1 Pierre Boiteau. Contribution à l'histoire de la Nation Malgache. Paris 1958.
G2 A Dandouau and G-S Chapus. Histoire des Populations de Madagascar. Paris 1952.
G3 Raymond Decary. Moeurs et Coutumes des Malgaches. Paris 1951.
G4 Hubert Deschamps. Madagascar. Paris 1950.
G5 Hubert Deschamps. Histoire de Madagascar. 1960. and 4th (revised) edition 1972
G6 Alfred Grandidier. Histoire de la Géographie de Madagascar. Paris 1885. (Vol I of HPNPM).
G7 Alfred et Guillaume Grandidier. Ethnographie de Madagascar (4 tomes). Paris 1908–1928 (Vol IV of HPNPM).
G8 Nigel Heseltine. Madagascar. London 1971.
G9 Bruno Hübsch (ed.) Madagascar et le Christianisme – Histoire Oecumenique. Antananarivo and Paris 1993.
G10 F Labatut and R Raharinarivonirina. Madagascar – Etude Historique. Tananarive 1969.
G11 Philippe Oberlé. Tananarive et l'Imerina. Description historique et touristique. Tananarive 1976.
G12 Philippe Oberlé. Provinces malgaches Art–Histoire–Tourisme. Tananarive 1979.
G13 S Pasfield Oliver. Madagascar (2 vols). London 1886
G14 Edouard Ralaimihoatra. Histoire de Madagascar. Tananarive 1965.
G15 Régis Rajemisa-Raolison. Dictionnaire historique et géographique de Madagascar. Fianarantsoa 1966.
G16 H Rusillon. Un petit continent, Madagascar. Paris 1933.
G17 James Sibree. Madagascar and its people. London 1870.
G18 James Sibree. Madagascar before the conquest. London 1896.
G19 Solange Thierry. Madagascar. Paris 1961.
G20 Pierre Vérin. Madagascar. Paris 1990.

Part 1. The island and the people

A1 David Attenborough. Zoo Quest to Madagascar. London 1961.
A2 G Bastian. Madagascar, étude géographique et économique. Tananarive 1967.
A3 René Battistini. L'importance de l'action de l'homme dans les transformations protohistoriques du milieu natu-

ral à Madagascar. AUM special edition 1965 – Problèmes généraux de l'archéologie malgache.

A4 R Battistini and G Richard-Vindard (editors). Biogeography and Ecology in Madagascar. The Hague 1972.

A5 R Battistini and P Vérin. Irodo et la tradition vohémarienne. RM No 36 (1966) pp 17–32.

A6 Emil Birkeli. Les Vazimba de la Côte Ouest. MAM. Tananarive 1936.

A7 Emil Birkeli. Marques de boeufs et traditions de race: documents sur l'ethnographie de la côte occidentale de Madagascar. Oslo 1926.

A8 Maurice Bloch. Astrology and writing in Madagascar. Essay in "Literacy in Traditional Societies" ed. J R Goody. Cambridge 1968.

A9 Mervyn Brown. Historical Links between Tanzania and Madagascar. TNR Nos 79–80 (1976) pp 49–56.

A10 Marie-Claude Chamla. Recherches anthropologiques sur l'origine des malgaches. MM Paris 1958.

A11 Sally Crook. Distant Shores. By traditional canoe from Asia to Madagascar. London 1990.

A12 A T and G M Culwick. Indonesian Echoes in Central Tanganyika. TNR October 1936, pp 60–66.

A13 Otto Dahl. Malgache et Maanjan, une comparaison linguistique. Oslo 1951.

A14 Raymond Decary. La Légende du Rokh et de l'Aepyornis. BAM n.s.XX (1937) pp 107–13.

A15 Hubert Deschamps. Les Anteisaka. Tananarive 1936.

A16 Hubert Deschamps and Suzanne Vianès. Les malgaches du sud-est. Paris 1959.

A17 Hubert Deschamps. Les migrations intérieures à Madagascar. Paris 1959.

A18 Jacques Dez. La linguistique et les origines de la civilisation malgache. RM No 22 (1963) pp 33–40.

A19 Jacques Dez. Quelques hypothèses formulées par la linguistique comparée. AUM special edition 1965.

A20 Jacques Dez. De l'influence arabe à Madagascar à l'aide de faits de linguistique. RM special edition 1967 – Arabes et Islamés à Madagascar et dans l'océan indien.

A21 G Donque. Le contexte océanique des migrations malgaches. AUM special edition 1965

A22 Edvin Fagereng. Histoire des Maroserana du Menabe. BAM n.s.XXVIII (1947–8), pp 115–35.

A23 Edvin Fagereng. Une famille de dynasties malgaches.

Oslo 1971.
A24 Jacques Faublée. L'Ethnographie de Madagascar. Paris 1946.
A25 Gabriel Ferrand. L'origine africaine des malgaches. JA Vol 10 No XI (1908) pp 353-500
A26 Gabriel Ferrand. Les Musulmans à Madagascar et aux Iles Comores (3 volumes). Paris 1891-1902.
A27 Gabriel Ferrand. Les îles Ramny, Lamery, Waq-Waq, Komor des géographes arabes, et Madagascar. JA 1907, pp 433–500.
A28 Gabriel Ferrand. Les Kouen-Louen et les anciennes navigations interocéaniques dans les mers du sud. JA 1919, Vols XIII and XIV.
A29 G S P Freeman-Granville. The East African Coast. Select documents from the first to the earlier nineteenth century. Oxford 1962.
A30 Charles Guillan. Documents sur l'histoire, la géographie et le commerce de la partie occidentale de Madagascar. Paris 1845.
A31 J-C Hébert. La cosmographie ancienne malgache. AUM special edition 1965.
A32 J-C Hébert. Simples notes sur les Vazimba du Betsiriry. B.Mad. No 304 (September 1971) pp 721–33.
A33 James Hornell. The common origin of the outrigger canoes of Madagascar and Africa. Man, No 67 (September 1920).
A34 James Hornell. Indonesian influence on East African culture. JRAI Vol LXIV (1934) pp 305-32
A35 Yves Janvier. La géographie gréco-romaine a-t-elle connu Madagascar? OSA Nos 1–2 (1975) pp 11–42.
A36 G Julien. Institutions politiques et sociales de Madagascar (2 vols) Paris 1908.
A37 Raymond K Kent. Madagascar and Africa:
The Problem of the Bara. JAH IX,3 (1968)
The Sakalava. JAH IX,4 (1968)
The Anteimoro. JAH X,1 (1969)
A38 Raymond K Kent. Early Kingdoms in Madagascar 1500–1700. New York 1970.
A39 John Mack. Madagascar, Island of the Ancestors. London 1986.
A40 J Mahé. Les subfossiles malgaches. RM No 29 (1965) pp 51–8.
A41 Marco Polo. The travels of Marco Polo (Penguin edition). London 1958.

Sources

A42 Louis Molet. Les Mikea de Madagascar. RM No 36 (1966)
A43 G P Murdock. Africa, its people and their culture history. New York 1959.
A44 Roland Oliver and J D Fage. A Short History of Africa. (Penguin) Harmondsworth 1962.
A45 Roland Oliver and Gervase Mathew (ed.) A history of East Africa (Vol I). Oxford 1963.
A46 S Pasfield Oliver. Has there been a race of pygmies in Madagascar? AA 1891, pp 257–72.
A47 Jean Poirier. Données écologiques et démographiques de la mise en place des Proto-malgaches. AUM special edition 1965.
A48 Jean Poirier. Madagascar avant l'histoire. B.Mad.No 247 (December 1966) pp 1171–85 and No 249 (February 1967) pp 171–92.
A49 Jean Poirier and Jacques Dez. Les groupes ethniques à Madagascar. Tananarive 1963.
A50 Françoise Raison-Jourde (ed.) Les souverains de Madagascar. Paris 1983.
A51 Albert Rakoto-Ratsimamanga. Tache pigmentaire congénitale et origine des malgaches. RA 1940, pp 6–150.
A52 Edouard Ralaimihoatra. Une identification géographique de Madagascar. Paper presented to CHJAM 1977.
A53 F Ramiandrasoa. L'oiseau "Rock" et le "Madeigascar" dans le livre de Marco Polo. RM No 37 (1967) pp 56–8.
A54 Elisoa Ranaivoarivo – La faune protégée de Madagascar. RM Nos 47 and 48 (1969).
A55 G Razafintsalama. La langue malgache et les origines malgaches. Tananarive 1928–29.
A56 C Robequain. Madagascar et les bases dispersées de l'Union Française. Paris 1958.
A57 Curt Sachs. Les instruments de musique de Madagascar. Paris 1938.
A58 Andrew Sharp. Ancient voyagers in the Pacific. (Pelican) Harmondsworth 1957.
A59 Andrew Sharp. Ancient voyagers in Polynesia. London 1964.
A60 James Sibree. The great African island. London 1880.
A61 James Sibree. A naturalist in Madagascar. London 1915.
A62 W Solheim. Indonesian culture and Malagasy origins. AUM special edition 1965.
A63 Université de Madagascar. Civilisation du Sud-Ouest – archéologie, anthropologie sociale et art de Madagascar. Tananarive 1971.

A64 Université de Madagascar. Civilisation de l'Est et du Sud-Est – archéologie, anthropologie sociale et art de Madagascar. Tananarive 1974.

A65 Jean Valette. De l'origine des malgaches. AUM special edition 1965.

A66 Pierre Vérin. Retrospective et problèmes de l'archéologie à Madagascar. B.Mad. No 212 (January 1964) pp 37–59.

A67 Pierre Vérin. L'origine indonésienne des malgaches. B.Mad. No 259 (December 1967) pp 947–76.

A68 A R Wallace. The Geographical Distribution of Animals. London 1876.

A69 P J Wilson. Freedom by a hair's breadth – Tsimihety in Madagascar. Ann Arbor 1992.

Part 2. Early European contacts

B1 Edward A Alpers. Madagascar and Mozambique in the nineteenth century: the era of the Sakalava raids (1800–1820). OSA Nos 5–6 (1977) pp37-53.

B2 John Benbow's Journal. GM xxxix (1769) p 172

B3 Count Benyowsky. Memoirs and Travels (translated by W Nicholson). London 1790.

B4 Richard Boothby. A brief discovery or description of the most famous island of Madagascar. London 1646.

B5 Maurice Bloch. Placing the Dead. Tombs, ancestral villages and kinship organisation in Madagascar. London & New York 1971.

B6 George Buchan. A narrative of the loss of the Winterton, East Indiaman, wrecked on the coast of Madagascar in 1792. Edinburgh 1820.

B7 G S Chapus and E Ratsimba. Histoire des Rois (translation of Révérend Père Callet – Tantaran'ny Andriana eto Madagasikara). 4 vols. Tananarive 1953–60.

B8 Georges Condominas. Fokon'olona et collectivités rurales en Imerina. Paris 1960.

B9 P Cultru. Un empéreur de Madagascar au XVIIIe siècle. Paris 1906.

B10 John Davis. The voyages and works of John Davis the Navigator, ed. A H Markham. Hakluyt Society First Series No LIX. London 1880.

B11 Raymond Decary. La piraterie à Madagascar au XVIIe et XVIIIe siècles. BAM n.s. XVIII (1935)

B12 Raymond Decary. Coutumes guerrières et organisation militaire chez les anciens malgaches. Vol.I: Les anciennes pratiques de guerre. Paris 1966.

Sources

B13 Daniel Defoe (Captain Charles Johnson). A general history of the Pyrates, ed. Manual Schonhorn. London 1972. (See also B41.)
B14 Alain Délivré. Histoire des Rois de l'Imerina (Interprétation d'une tradition orale). Paris 1974.
B15 Hubert Deschamps. Les pirates à Madagascar. Paris 1949.
B16 Clement Downing. A compendious history of the Indian wars. London 1737.
B17 Robert Drury. Madagascar, or Robert Drury's Journal during Fifteen Years Captivity on that Island. London 1729.
B18 Robert Drury. Madagascar, etc., ed. by S P Oliver. London 1890. (Also French translation ed. Grandidier in COACM Tome IV – see B26.)
B19 East India Company. A Calendar of the Court Minutes of the East India Company, ed. Ethel B. Sainsbury 1635–39 (1907), 1640–43 (1909), 1644–49 (1912), 1650–54 (1913). Oxford.
B20 Robert Everard. Relation of Three Years Sufferings upon the Coast of Assada near Madagascar. 1693. Churchill's Voyages, Vol 6 pp 257–82.
B21 J-M Filliot. La traite des esclaves vers les Mascareignes au XVIIIe siècle. Mémoires ORSTOM No 72. Paris 1974.
B22 E Flacourt. Histoire de la Grande Ile de Madagascar. Paris 1658. (Also in Grandidier COACM, Tome VIII – see B26.)
B23 E Flacourt. Relation de la Grande Ile de Madagascar. Paris 1658. (Also in Grandidier COACM, Tome IX – see B26.)
B24 Eugène de Froberville. Histoire des invasions madécasses aux Iles Comores et à la Côte Orientale de l'Afrique. AVG 1845, pp 194–268.
B25 Sir Wm Foster. An English settlement in Madagascar in 1645–6. EHR April 1912.
B26 Alfred et Guillaume Grandidier. Collection des ouvrages anciens concernant Madagascar. Paris 1903–20. Tome I 1500–1613; Tome II 1613–40; Tome III 1640–1716; Tome IV (Drury – B18); Tomes V and VI 1718–1800; Tome VII 1604–1658; Tome VIII (Flacourt – B22); Tome IX (Flacourt – B23 and Martin – B48).
B27 Guillaume Grandidier. Histoire politique et coloniale (Vol V of HPNPM) Tome I Histoire des Merina avant 1861. Tome III (with R Decary) Histoire des peuples non Merina. Paris 1958.
B28 Charles Grey. Pirates of the Eastern Seas (1618–1723). London 1932.

Sources

B29 Walter Hamond. Madagascar, the richest and most fruitful island in the World. London 1643.
B30 Captain Alexander Hamilton. A new account of the East Indies. Edinburgh 1727.
B31 J-C Hébert. Les "sagaies volantes" d'Andriamanelo et les "sagaies à pointe d'argile" des Vazimba. Paper presented to CHJAM 1977.
B32 Sir Thomas Herbert. Some Yeares Travels into Africa and Asia. London 1638.
B33 S Charles Hill. Episodes of Piracy in the Eastern Seas. Bombay 1920.
B34 S Charles Hill. Notes on Piracy in Eastern Waters. Bombay 1923.
B35 Sonia E Howe. The Drama of Madagascar. London 1938. Part I: An Island of Disappointed Hopes.
B36 Sonia E Howe. In Quest of Spices. London 1946.
B37 Barthélemy Hugon. Aperçu de mon dernier voyage à Ancova de l'an 1808. BMM, Add. Mss. 18137.
B38 Lt-Colonel Robert Hunt. The island of Assada. London 1650.
B39 Dr Edward Ives. A Voyage from England to India in the year 1754. London 1773.
B40 John Franklin Jameson. Privateering and Piracy in the Colonial Period. New York 1923.
B41 Captain Charles Johnson (Daniel Defoe). A general History of the Robberies and Murders of the most notorious Pyrates. London Vol I, 1724. Vol II, 1726. (See also B13.)
B42 Albert Kammerer. La découverte de Madagascar par les Portuguais et la cartographie de l'Ile. Lisbon 1950.
B43 Raymond K Kent. Madagascar, the Comoro and Mascarene Islands between 1500 and 1800. Chapter XXVII of UNESCO General History of Africa.
B44 Sir James Lancaster. The Voyages of Sir James Lancaster to Brazil and the East Indies 1591–1603, ed. Sir Wm. Foster. Hakluyt Society Second Series No LXXXV. London 1940.
B45 H C V Leibbrandt. Précis of the Archives of the Cape of Good Hope: Letters dispatched 1696–1708, pp 310–312.
B46 G Lejamble. Les fondaments du pouvoir royal en Imerina. B.Mad. No 311 (April 1972) pp 349–67.
B47 Révérend Père Malzac. Histoire du Royaume Hova. Tananarive 1912.
B48 François Martin. Mémoires 1665–1668. Grandidier COACM Tome IX (see B26).

B49	Alexandre Mavrocordato. L'étrange journal de Robert Drury. B.Mad. No 238 (March 1966) pp 191–214.
B50	Nicolas Mayeur. Histoire de Ratsimilahoe, roi de Foulpointe et des Betsimiçaracs. BMM Add. Mss. 18129, Folio 82–143.
B51	Nicolas Mayeur. Voyage au Pays d'Ancove, autrement dit des Hovas ou Amboilambes. Dans l'intérieur des terres, Isle de Madagascar. Janvier 1777–Novembre 1777. BMM Add. Mss. 18128. Folio 75–98.
B52	Nicolas Mayeur. Voyage au Pays d'Ancove, par le Pays d'Ancaye, autrement dit des Baizangouzangoux. Juillet 1785. BMM Add. Mss. 18128. Folio 99–120.
B53	Anne Molet-Sauvaget. Le Journal de Robert Drury par Daniel Defoe. B.Mad. No 286 (March 1970) pp 259–65.
B54	Sir William Monson. How to plant the island of St Lawrence. London 1640.
B55	Peter Mundy. The Travels of Peter Mundy. Vol III, Part II. Hakluyt Society Second Series No XLVI. Cambridge.
B56	Maximilian E Novak. Introduction to: Daniel Defoe – Of Captain Mission. Augustan Reprint Society, Pub. No 87. Los Angeles 1961.
B57	John Ovington. A voyage to Suratt in the year 1689. London 1696.
B58	J H Parry. The Age of Reconnaissance. London 1963.
B59	H Pouget de St. André. La colonisation de Madagascar sous Louis XV, d'après la correspondence inédite du Comte de Maudave. Paris 1886.
B60	Edouard Ralaimihoatra. Vazimba et Hova à Madagascar. RM No 3 (1948)
B61	Gilberte Ralaimihoatra. Les premiers rois merina et la tradition Vazimba. BAM n.s. tome 50/2 (1972)
B62	Gilberte Ralaimihoatra. Généalogie des anciens rois vazimba et merina. BAM n.s. tome 51/1 (1973)
B63	Clovis Ralaivola. Etymologie du mot Hova. B.Mad. No 258 (Nov 1967) pp 897–900.
B64	G M Razi. Le récit de captivité à Madagascar de Robert Everard. BAM n.s. tome 53/1–2 (1975).
B65	Abbé Rochon. Voyage à Madagascar et aux Indes orientales. Paris 1791.
B66	C Savaron. Contribution à l'Histoire de l'Imerina. BAM n.s. Vol XI (1928) pp 61–81.
B67	Arthur W Secord. Robert Drury's Journal and other studies. University of Illinois 1961.
B68	Captain John Smart. Letters. BMM Add. Mss. 14037, folio 1–48.

B69   Sir Richard Temple. The Mysterious Tragedy of the "Worcester" 1704–5. London 1930.

B70   Jean Valette. Quelques textes rélatifs aux expéditions malgaches aux Comores. B.Mad. No 394 (Sept 1971) pp 761–4.

B71   Jean Valette. Le commerce de Madagascar vers les Mascareignes au XVIIIe siècle. RM No 33 (1966) pp 35–52.

B72   Jean Valette. Histoire du Boina de 1700 à 1840. B.Mad. No 149 (Oct 1958) pp 851–8.

B73   Jean Valette and Geneviève Beauchesne. La Mort de Gosse (1750). B.Mad. No 298 (March 1971) pp 265–70.

B74   Powle Waldegrave. An answer to Mr Boothby's book. London 1649.

Part 3. Towards a new civilisation

C1   Simon Ayache. L'accession au trône de Ranavalona I, à travers le temoignage de Raombana. B.Mad. No 205 (June 1963) pp 485–505 and No 206 (July 1963) pp 609–26.

C2   Simon Ayache. La destinée du Prince Ratefy vue par Raombana. B.Mad. No 258 (nov 1967) pp 874–81.

C3   Simon Ayache. Esquisse pour le portrait d'une reine: Ranavalona Ière. OSA Nos 1–2 (1975) pp 251–70.

C4   Simon Ayache. Raombana l'historien (1809–1885). Introduction à l'édition critique de son oeuvre. Fianarantsoa 1976. (See also C49.)

C5   R P Adrien Boudou. Le complot de 1857. Académie Malgache. Collection de documents concernant Madagascar et les pays voisins. Tome 3. Tananarive 1943.

C6   R P Adrien Boudou. Le meurtre de Radama II. MAM Fascicule XXVI. Tananarive 1938.

C7   Mervyn Brown. Ranavalona I and the missionaries. OSA Nos 5–6 (1977) pp 107–38.

C8   James Cameron. Recollections of mission life in Madagascar during the early days. Antananarivo 1867.

C9   Gwyn Campbell. Madagascar and the Slave Trade. JAH XXII (1981) pp 203–27.

C10   Gwyn Campbell. Problèmes de main d'oeuvre et de transport à Madagascar au XIXe siècle (1810–1895). OSA No 16 (1982) pp 21–39.

C11   L Carayon. Histoire de l'établissement français de Madagascar pendant la Restauration. Paris 1845.

C12   C S Chapus. Quatre-vingt années d'influences européennes en Imerina. BAM n.s. vol VII (1925).

C13   J Chauvin. Jean Laborde. MAM Fascicule XXIX. Tananarive 1939.
C14   W G Clarence-Smith (ed.). The Economics of the Indian Ocean Slave Trade in the Nineteenth Century. London 1989.
C15   Samuel Copland. A History of the Island of Madagascar. London 1822.
C16   André Coppalle. Le Journal de Coppalle. BAM Vol VII (1909) pp 7–46 and Vol VIII (1910) pp 25–64.
C17   Dr Andrew Davidson. Choreomania: an historical sketch, with some account of an epidemic observed in Madagascar. Edinburgh Medical Journal, August 1867.
C18   Eugène David-Bernard. Ramose – La vie aventureuse de Jean Laborde. Paris 1946.
C19   Raymond Decary. Coutumes guerrières et organisation militaire chez les anciens malgaches. Vol II: L'histoire militaire des Merina. Paris 1966.
C20   Raymond Delval. Radama II, Prince de la Renaissance malgache 1861–63. Paris 1972.
C21   Bakoly Domenichini-Ramiaramanana. Hainteny d'autrefois. Poèmes traditionnels malgaches recueillis au début du règne de Ranavalona I, 1828–1861. Tananarive 1968
C22   Bakoly Domenichini-Ramiaramanana et Jean-Pierre Domenichini. Aspects de l'esclavage sous la monarchie merina. OSA No 15 (1982) pp 53–98.
C23   Capitaine J Dupré. Trois mois de séjour à Madagascar. Paris 1863.
C24   Yvon Durand. Protestants et Catholiques en Imerina des origines à la mort de Radama II. Typescript in SOAS library, May 1964.
C25   John E Ellis. Life of William Ellis, Missionary to the South Seas and to Madagascar. London 1873.
C26   William Ellis. History of Madagascar (2 vols). London 1838.
C27   William Ellis. Three visits to Madagascar. London 1858.
C28   William Ellis. Madagascar Revisited. London 1867.
C29   William Ellis. The Martyr Church. London 1870.
C30   J J Freeman and D Johns. The Persecution of the Christians in Madagascar. London 1840.
C31   G S Graham. Great Britain in the Indian Ocean, 1810–1850. Oxford 1967.
C32   David Griffiths. A history of the Malagasy Christians. London 1841.

C33	James Hastie. Journal. French translation of extracts in BAM Vol II (1903), Vol III (1904), Vol IV n.s. (1919).
C34	Sonia E Howe. The Drama of Madagascar. London 1938. Part II – Madagascar in Anglo-French diplomacy.
C35	Keturah Jeffreys. The Widowed Missionary's Journal. Southampton 1827.
C36	G D Laverdant. Colonisation de Madagascar. Paris 1844.
C37	B-F Leguével de Lacombe. Voyage à Madagascar et aux Iles Comores (1823 à 1830). Paris 1840.
C38	Rev. R Lovett. History of the London Missionary Society (1795–1895). Oxford 1899. (Madagascar – Vol I, pp 673–792).
C39	Robert Lyall. Le journal de Robert Lyall (translated and edited by G-S Chapus and G Mondain). Tananarive (Académie Malgache) 1954.
C40	G Mondain. Une ambassade envoyée par Ranavalomanjaka I en Angleterre et en France. MAM Tananarive 1928.
C41	G Mondain. Un siècle de mission à Madagascar. Paris 1948.
C42	Liliana Mosca. Il Madagascar nella vita de Raombana, primo storico malgascio (1809–1855). Napoli 1980.
C43	L Munthe, C Ravoajanahary and S Ayache. Radama Ier et les anglais: les négotiations de 1817 d'après les sources malgaches. OSA Nos 3–4 (1976) pp 9-104.
C44	S Pasfield Oliver. Madagascar and the Malagasy. London 1866.
C45	Ida Pfeiffer. The last travels of Ida Pfeiffer, inclusive of a visit to Madagascar. London 1861.
C46	Michel Prou. Malagasy – "Un pas de plus" ... vers l'Histoire du "Royaume de Madagascar" au XIXe siècle. Tome I: 1793–1894. Paris 1987.
C47	Berthe Raharijaona. Le procès Rasalama. RM No 21 (1963) pp 45–48.
C48	Raombana. History, Annals and Journal. (Original manuscripts mainly in archives of Académie Malgache and Archives Nationales in Antananarivo.)
C49	Raombana. Histoires, edited with French translation by Simon Ayache. Vol I (des origines à 1810) Fianarantsoa 1980; Vol II (1810–1828) Antananarivo 1994.
C50	Ary Robin. Centenaire du Meurtre de Radama II. RM No 22 (1963) pp 13–16.
C51	Rev D Tyerman and G Bennet. Journal of Voyages and Travels, Vol II. London 1831.

C52	R P de la Vaissière. Histoire de Madagascar, ses habitants et ses missionaires (2 vols). Paris 1884.
C53	Jean Valette. Etudes sur le règne de Radama Ier. Tananarive 1962.
C54	Jean Valette. Documents pour servir à l'histoire des relations entre la Grande Bretagne et Madagascar sous Radama I. RM Nos 22, 23, 24, 25, 26 and 29 (1963–1965).
C55	Jean Valette. La Mission de Chardenoux auprès de Radama I (1816). B. Mad. No 207 (August 1963) pp 657–702.
C56	Jean Valette. La Mission de Le Sage auprès de Radama I (1816–1817). B.Mad. No 275 (April 1969) pp 315–88; Nos 277–8 (June–July 1969) pp 505–39; and No 279 (August 1969) pp 693–6.
C57	Jean Valette. Etude sur les journaux de James Hastie. B.Mad. No 259 (Dec 1967) pp 977–86.
C58	Jean Valette. L'accession au trône de Ranavalona I. RM No 3 (1965) pp 51–59.
C59	Jean Valette. Etude sur la mort du Prince Ratefy (1828). B.Mad. No 257 (Feb 1971) pp 107–37.
C60	Dr Auguste Vinson. Voyage à Madagascar au coronnement de Radama II. Paris 1865.

Part 4. *The kingdom in danger*

D1	Simon Ayache. Introduction à l'oeuvre de Rainandriamampandry. AUM 10.
D2	Jean Bianquais. L'oeuvre des missions protestantes à Madagascar. Paris 1907.
D3	R P Adrien Boudou. Les Jésuites à Madagascar au XIXe siècle (2 vols). Paris 1940.
D4	Bennet Burleigh. Two Campaigns – Madagascar and Ashantee. London 1896.
D5	Gwyn Campbell. Missionaries, Fanampoana and the Menalamba Revolt in late nineteeth century Madagascar. Journal of Southern African Studies XV.1, pp 54–73.
D6	Jean Carol. Chez les Hova. Paris 1898.
D7	Dr Louis Catat. Voyage à Madagascar (1889–90). Paris 1895.
D8	G-S Chapus. Une éclatante querelle à Tananarive. BAM n.s. XVIII (1935) pp 85–95.
D9	G-S Chapus and G Mondain. Rainilaiarivony, Une Homme d'Etat Malgache. Paris 1953.
D10	G-S Chapus and G Mondain. Quelques rapports du

gouvernement malgache avec les étrangers. MAM Fascicule XXXI. Tananarive 1940.
— Historique de l'ambassade malgache en Europe et en Amérique.
— Abraham Kingdon et ses entreprises à Madagascar.
— L'affaire Willoughby.

D11 Jacqueline Chastanier-Atger. Le *Madagascar Times* d'Anthony Tacchi 1882–1890. University of Paris 1977.

D12 Médecin-Colonel G Chauliac. Contribution à l'étude médico-militaire de l'expédition de Madagascar en 1895. B.Mad. Nos 140–3 (May–August 1966).

D13 J Chauvin. Le prince Ramahatra. RHC No 118 (1939).

D14 A D'Anthouard and A Ranchot. L'expédition de Madagascar en 1895 – Journaux de route. Paris 1930.

D15 Jean Darcy. France et Angleterre – Cent Années de Rivalité Coloniale – L'affaire de Madagascar. Paris 1908.

D16 Raymond Decary. Contribution à l'histoire du Sud-Est. RM No 30 (1965) pp 36–50.

D17 Général Duchesne. L'expédition de Madagascar. Paris 1896.

D18 Stephen Ellis. The Rising of the Red Shawls: a Revolt in Madagascar. Cambridge 1985.

D19 Stephen Ellis. Un complot colonial à Madagascar. L'affaire Rainandriamampandry. Paris 1990.

D20 Faranirina V Esoavelomandroso. L'attitude malgache face au traité de 1885. Université de Madagascar, Etudes Historiques III. Antananarivo 1977.

D21 Manassé Esoavelomandroso. La province maritime orientale du "Royaume de Madagascar" à la fin du XIXe Siècle (1882–1895). Antananarivo 1979.

D22 Manassé Esoavelomandroso. Le Mythe d'Andriba. OSA Nos. 1–2 (1975) pp 43–65.

D23 French Governement *livres jaunes*, Affaires Etrangères. Documents diplomatiques. Affaires de Madagascar 1881–1883, 1882–1886 and 1885–1895.

D24 Friends Service Council. Friends in Madagascar, 1867–1967. London 1967.

D25 Général Gallieni. Neuf ans à Madagascar. Paris 1908.

D26 Général Gallieni. Lettres de Madagascar 1896–1905. Paris 1928.

D27 Maurice Gontard. La situation réligieuse en Madagascar en 1897. B.Mad. No 300 (May 1971) pp 405–17.

D28 Guillaume Grandidier. Histoire politique et coloniale. Tome II, Histoire des Merina 1861–1897.

D29 Dr E Hocquard. L'expédition de Madagascar. Journal de campagne. Paris 1897.
D30 E F Knight. Madagascar in War Time. London 1896.
D31 Hippolyte Laroche. Les rapports de quinzaine d'Hippolyte Laroche Résident-Général de France à Madagascar 1896. Ed. R Pascal. B.Mad. Nos 246–9 (Oct 1966–Feb 1967).
D32 Pierre Lupo. Gallieni et la laïcisation de l'école à Madagascar (1896–1904). OSA No 16 (1982) pp 69–99.
D33 London Missionary Society. Ten Years Review of Mission Work in Madagascar, 1870–1880. Antananarivo 1880.
D34 Malagasy Government *Red Books*. No 1 Correspondance diverse et Rapports de conférences entre les Plénipotentiaires etc (July 24, 1882–June 10, 1884), Antananarivo 1884; No 2 Rapport des Négociations qui eurent lieu entre le Gouvernement de Madagascar et les Plénipotentiaires Français, à Tamatave ... (June 13–August 17, 1885). Antananarivo 1885.
D35 T T Matthews. Thirty Years in Madagascar. London 1904.
D36 Colonel F C Maude. Five years in Madagascar. London 1895.
D37 Joseph Mullens. Twelve Months in Madagascar. London 1875.
D38 Phares M Mutibwa. The Malagasy and the Europeans (1861–1895). London 1974.
D39 S Pasfield Oliver. The true story of the French dispute in Madagascar. London 1885.
D40 S Pasfield Oliver. Madagascar (London 1886) Vol II. Chapter XVI (The Franco-Malagasy War) and Appendices pp 271–562.
D41 Césaire Rabenoro. Rainijaonary, grand chef militaire malgache. BAM n.s. tome 51/1, 1973.
D42 Rajestera. Journal de campagne. (Ed. G Mondain under title "Des soldats français chez Ranavalona III"). Documents historiques malgaches. MAM Tananarive 1928.
D43 Pierre Randrianarisoa. La diplomatie malgache face à la politique des grandes puissances. 1882–1895. Paris 1968.
D44 Reuben Saillens. Nos droits sur Madagascar et nos griefs contre les Hovas examinés impartialement. Paris 1885.
D45 Dan Avni Segre. Madagascar – An example of indigenous modernisation of a traditional society in the nineteenth century. St Anthony's Papers No 21, African Affairs No 3. Oxford 1969.
D46 George A Shaw. Madagascar and France. London 1885.

D47 James Sibree (collected). A Madagascar Miscellany (articles and press cuttings), 19 vols in SOAS library. For partial list of contents see Mutibwa (D39) pp 382–6.
D48 James Sibree. Fifty Years in Madagascar. London 1924.
D49 Jean Valette. Les relations américano-malgaches aux XVIIe et XIXe siècles. B.Mad. No 195 (Dec 1970) pp 965–83.

Part 5. Madagascar in the modern world

E1 Gérard Althabe. Les luttes sociales à Tananarive en 1972. Cahiers d'études africaines, 1981, pp 407–447.
E2 Richard Andriamanjato. L'Anthropocratie ou le Devenir de l'humanité. Chapter III – Le cas de Madagascar. Seen in typescript April 1993.
E3 Armand Annet. Aux heures troublées de l'Afrique française (1939–43). Paris 1952.
E4 Anonymous. L'enseignement à Madagascar. RFEPA April 1970, pp 57–73.
E5 Anonymous. Le film des récents évènements à Madagascar. RFEPA August 1971, pp 92–98.
E6 Ramanisa Andriantsoa. La politique extérieure de la République Démocratique de Madagascar. Paris 1981.
E7 Robert Archer. Madagascar depuis 1972, la marche d'une révolution. Paris 1976.
E8 Victor Augagneur. Erreurs et brutalités coloniales. Paris 1927.
E9 Antoine Bouillon. Le MFM malgache. RFEPA November 1973, pp 46–71.
E10 Charles Cadoux. La République Malgache. Paris 1969.
E11 Pascal Chaigneau. Rivalités politiques et socialisme à Madagascar. Paris 1985.
E12 Olive Murray Chapman. Across Madagascar. London 1942.
E13 Winston S Churchill. The Second World War. Vol.IV: The Hinge of Fate. Chapter XIII Madagascar. London 1951.
E14 Maureen Covell. Madagascar. Politics, Economics and Society. London 1987.
E15 Rupert Croft-Cooke. The Blood-Red Island. London 1953.
E16 Pierre Dabeziès. Le développement des partis politiques malgaches. Paris 1959.
E17 J Bois De Gaudusson. L'administration malgache. Paris 1976.
E18 Ferdinand Déléris. Ratsiraka, socialisme et misère à

Madagascar. Paris 1986.
- E19 Ferdinand Déléris. De la Charte de la révolution malgache aux assises de la francophonie. Géopolitique Africaine June 1986 pp 63–86.
- E20 Hubert Deschamps. Roi de la brousse. Paris 1975.
- E21 Alain Escaro. La politique extérieure du gouvernement Ramanantsoa vue par "Lumière". OSA No, 10 (1979) pp 7–92.
- E22 Faranirina V Esoavelomandroso. Langue, culture et colonisation à Madagascar: malgache et français dans l'enseignement officiel (1916–40). OSA Nos. 3–4 (1976) pp 105–163.
- E23 Yves Feugeas. Le marché du riz pendant la période coloniale à Madagascar (1905–1940). Université de Madagascar, Etudes Historiques IV. Antananarivo 1979.
- E24 Jean Fremigacci. L'administration coloniale: les aspects oppressifs. OAS Nos. 7 & 8 (1978) pp 209–237.
- E25 Jean Fremigacci. Origines et limites d'un parlement colonial: les premiers Délégations Economiques et Financières (1921–1924). Paper presented to Colloque international d'histoire malagasy at Antananarivo, August 1989.
- E26 K C Gandar Dower. Into Madagascar. London 1943.
- E27 Lawrence Grafftey-Smith. Hands to Play (Chapter 2). London 1975.
- E28 Philippe Hugon. Economie et enseignement à Madagascar. Paris 1976.
- E29 Philippe Hugon. L'évolution économique de Madagascar de la 1ère à la seconde république. RFEPA November 1977 pp 26–57.
- E30 Raymond K Kent. From Madagascar to the Malagasy Republic. London 1962.
- E31 Francis Koerner. Le Front Populaire et la question coloniale à Madagascar. Revue française d'histoire d'outre-mer. Vol. 62 (1974) pp 436–457.
- E32 Jacques Lefèvre. Le parti social-démocrate de Madagascar. RFEPA April 1969, pp 67–84.
- E33 Philippe Leymarie. Le fokonolona: la voie malgache vers le socialisme? RFEPA April 1975, pp 42–67.
- E34 Philippe Leymarie. Le parti du congrès pour l'indépendance de Madagascar (AKFM). RFEPA April 1979, pp 44–59.
- E35 Raymonde Litalien. Madagascar 1956–60. Etude d'opinion à travers la presse malgache francophone. Une étape vers la décolonisation. Paris 1975.

E36 London Missionary Society. Ten years' review of mission work in Madagascar, 1921–1930. Tananarive 1931.
E37 Pierre Lupo. Eglise et décolonisation à Madagascar. Fianarantsoa 1974.
E38 Monique Lupo-Raveloarimanana. Soldats et travailleurs malgaches en France pendant la deuxième guerre mondiale. Paper presented at Colloque international d'histoire malagasy at Antananarivo, August 1989.
E39 O Mannoni. Psychologie de la Colonisation. Paris 1950. (English translation entitled "Prospero and Caliban" published in New York 1956).
E40 Walter D Marcuse. Through Western Madagascar. London 1914.
E41 M Massiot. L'organisation politique, administrative, financière et judiciaire de la République Malgache. Antananarivo 1970.
E42 Marcel Olivier. Six ans de politique sociale à Madagascar. Paris 1931.
E43 Yvan-Georges Paillard. The First and Second Malagasy Republics: The Difficult Road of Independence. Essay in *Madagascar in History* ed. R K Kent. Albany, California 1979.
E44 Roger Pascal. La République Malgache. Paris 1965.
E45 André Prunières. Madagascar et la crise. Paris 1934.
E46 Lucile Rabearimanana. La presse d'opinion à Madagascar de 1947 à 1956. Antananarivo 1980.
E47 Lucile Rabearimanana. L'est d'Antananarivo pendant la seconde guerre mondiale: Désorganisation de l'économie et restructuration sociale. Paper presented to Colloque international d'histoire malagasy at Antananarivo, August 1989.
E48 Jacques Rabemananjara. Nationalisme et problèmes malgaches. Paris 1958.
E49 Raymond W Rabemananjara. Histoire de la nation malgache. Paris 1952.
E50 Raymond W Rabemananjara. Madagascar sous la Rénovation Malgache. Tananarive 1953.
E51 Césaire Rabenoro. Les rélations extérieures de Madagascar de 1960 à 1972. Paris 1986.
E52 Patrick Rajoelina. Quarante années de la vie politique de Madagascar 1947–1987. Paris 1988.
E53 Patrick Rajoelina and Alain Ramelet. Madagascar, la Grande Ile. Paris 1989.
E54 Julien Rakoto. La crise de l'enseignement supérieur à

Madagascar. RFEPA November 1971, pp 53–79.
E55 Lucile Rasoamanalina Ramanandraibe. Le livre vert de l'espérance malgache. Paris 1987.
E56 Solofo Randrianja. Le parti communiste de la région de Madagascar 1930–1939. Antananarivo 1989.
E57 Solofo Randrianja. La formation de l'idéologie des "élites" durant l'entre-deux-guerres. Paper presented to Colloque international d'histoire malagasy at Antananarivo August 1989.
E58 Didier Ratsiraka. Charte de la révolution socialiste malagasy tous azimuts. Tananarive 1975.
E59 Service Général de l'Information de Madagascar. Madagascar à travers ses provinces – Aspect géographique, historique, touristique, économique et administratif du territoire. Paris 1954.
E60 Alain Spacensky. Madagascar, cinquante ans de vie politique de Ralaimongo à Tsiranana. Paris 1970.
E61 Virginia Thompson and Richard Adloff. The Malagasy Republic. Stamford 1965.
E62 Robin Thorne. Memoirs (unpublished). Chapters 18 to 20 covering service as a staff officer with the East African Brigade in Madagascar 1942–43.
E63 Jacques Tronchon. L'insurrection malgache de 1947. Paris 1974.
E64 Philibert Tsiranana. Le cahier bleu, pensées, souvenirs. Tananarive 1971.

Periodicals: *Le Monde, Courrier de Madagascar, Madagascar Matin, Lumière, Lakroa, Lettre de l'Océan Indien.*

See also relevant chapters of G1, G5 and G13.

Notes

Chapter 1. A world apart
1. Marco Polo. A41, pp 274–5.

Chapter 2. The first Malagasy
1. Sibree, G17, p 349.
2. See especially Vérin, A67, for Indonesian cultural links. Kent, A38 (esp. Chapter II), emphasises the African links and the fact that many cultural elements are common to both East Africa and Indonesia.
3. The author spent a month among the Kha, the aboriginal people of southern Laos, in 1962.
4. See Donque, A21.
5. In 1985 a KonTiki-like journey by traditional canoe from Indonesia to Madagascar (Crook, A11) proved that the direct route was possible, although it seems likely that, without foreknowledge of the destination and constant steering to the south, winds and currents would have carried the canoe well to the north of Madagascar.
6. An anonymous Greek document, the Periplus of the Erythrean Sea (English translation in Freeman-Granville, A29, Document No 1) dating from approximately AD 100. It mentions the existence on the coast of East Africa (Azania) of a trade in coconut oil, two types of boats known to have been used by the Indonesians, and sea-turtle fishing, practised in Indonesia but not elsewhere in Africa.
7. For example Birkeli, A6 and Hébert, A32.
8. Battistini and Vérin. *Témoignages archéologiques sur la côte vézo*. Article in A63. In 1992, carbon-dating of some dwarf hippopotamus bones found on a west coast beach and clearly butchered by human beings suggested a date of between 100 BC and 100 AD. However one should perhaps await further evidence before concluding that the animals were killed by early Malagasy settlers rather than by some passing sailors, whether proto-Malagasy or others, on some hitherto unknown exploratory voyage.

9. Poirier, A47.
10. Battistini, A3.
11. For a full discussion of the timing of the first migration, see Poirier, A48.
12. Dahl, A13.

Chapter 3. The occupation of the island

1. Oliver and Fage. A44, p 32.
2. The modern ethnic groups, usually called "tribes" until relatively recently, emerged and acquired their individual characteristics and customs with the development of regional kingdoms beginning in the sixteenth century.
3. Sibree. A60, p 108.
4. Battistini and Vérin. A5.
5. Kent. A38, p 111–12.
6. See Kent, A38, pp 69–74.
7. Kent. A38, p 140.
8. Kent. A38, especially pp 190–6.
9. For example Drury's description of Ratsimonongarivo, B18, p 69 and Buchan's description of King Baba, B6, p 115. See also Chapter 9 note 5.
10. Mathew, A45, p 110.
11. Put forward by Kent, A38, Chapter 6.

Chapter 4. The arrival of the Europeans

1. For example Janvier, A35.
2. Grandidier B26 COACM Tome I, pp 77–80.
3. He is sometimes confused with another John Davis, of Limehouse, who travelled on this expedition and later made five more journeys to the East for the East India Company as pilot or master, during which he called several times at Madagascar. John Davis of Sandridge made one more journey to the East but was killed by Japanese pirates near Singapore in December 1605.
4. Lancaster appears to have been the first to discover the efficacy of lemon or lime juice against scurvy.
5. B44, p 85.
6. B55, pp 366–7.
7. B32, p 22.
8. B4, pp 4–5.

Chapter 5. The dream of Madagascar

1. Sir Thomas Roe to Queen Elizabeth of Bohemia, May 8 1637. CSP Dom. 1637, p82
2. Smart, letter of August 18, 1645. B68 folio 12v-14v.
3. The Malagasy word for chief or prince, *andriana*, was variously transcribed as Dian, Dean or Deaan by early English writers.
4. Smart, letters of May 15 and 20, 1646. B68, folios 21v-25v.
5. Waldegrave. B74, p28
6. Hunt. B38 p6.

Chapter 6. The shipwrecked sailor

1. By Secord, B67.
2. e.g. Dr Lotte Schomerus-Gernböck, the ethnologist who lived for a number of years in the Mahafaly country, and who discussed the problem with the author at Ampanihy in 1970.
3. One of the very few survivors of the *Degrave* to return to England, Benbow gave his Dutch rescuers an account of what happened which closely corroborates Drury's version (Leibbrandt, B45). See also B2.
4. Various second-hand accounts, including one reported by Drury, suggest that Samuel may have been a West Indian mulatto "recognised" by the queen of Anosy as her long-lost son who had been taken away by the father, an English sea-captain.
5. Carravances, also mentioned by Boothby, were not, as some writers have suggested, *pois du Cap* or butter beans, but almost certainly chick peas, the name deriving from the Spanish *garbanzo*. Butter beans were introduced to Madagascar (from the USA) only in 1864. See E40, pp 237–9.
6. This custom, known as *sombili*, is of Zafi-Raminia origin. (Kent, B43.)
7. Drury's Journal. B18, p 182.
8. Ibid., pp 171–2.
9. Ibid., p 262.
10. It was the custom of the Sakalava, and to a lesser extent of other peoples of the southwest, to bestow a prestigious new name on a chief when he died, after which it was taboo (*fady*) to refer to him by his previous name.
11. Drury's Journal. B18, p 294.

Notes

Chapter 7. The pirates of Madagascar

1. Letter of September 7, 1699. CSP Col. AWI 1699, para 769 XVIII (p 431).
2. Novak, B56.
3. Macaulay's History of England (London 1861) Vol V, p 249.
4. The Earl of Bellamont to the Council of Trade and Plantations, July 22, 1699. CSP Col. AWI 1699, para 675 (p 361).
5. Colonial Office Records 5. 1942, No 30, ii. Quoted in Hill, B33, pp 35–9.
6. Defoe records (B13, p 462) that at one stage Captain Bowen's company consisted of "164 fighting men, 43 only were English, the greater number French, the rest Danes, Swedes and Dutch; they took aboard 70 Indians to do the drudgery of the ship."
7. Defoe. B13, pp 484–5.
8. From the latitude given, this must be the modern Foulpointe. It seems likely that Hopeful Point, perhaps mispronounced by a Frenchman, is the origin of the modern name.
9. Defoe. B13, p 467.
10. Ibid., p 494.
11. Ibid., p 121.
12. Ibid., p 134.
13. The reference is to the South Sea Company, whose proposal to take over the National Debt in return for shares in the Company unleashed the disastrous fever of speculation known as the South Sea Bubble.

Chapter 8. The sons of pirates

1. Downing. B16, pp 62–4.
2. Presumably Rantabe which means "large beach". There is a modern village of this name, some 80 miles /130 km to the north in the Bay of Antongil.
3. CSP Col. AWI 1675–76, p 349.
4. Present-day production of rice in the Carolinas has its origin in rice brought from Madagascar in 1696. AA Vol VIII (1884) p 123.
5. CSP Col. AWI 1675–76, p 465.
6. Defoe. B13, pp 485–6.
7. A study by Commandant Ratsivalaka, based on the writings of Mayeur, maintains that Betia did not legally inherit Sainte Marie and hence that the subsequent cession to France was illegal (information from Professor Ayache in 1978).

8. Valette and Beauchesne. B73.
9. Valette. B71, pp 35–9.
10. This is the explanation given in Froberville's account, B24.
11. See Alpers, B1, which is based on Portuguese documents. These refer to the Malagasy pirates as Sakalava. But an English contemporary traveller Henry Salt (quoted in Hill, B34, p 191) says that although they were known to the Portuguese as Sekelaves, their real name was Marati (obviously Malata).

Chapter 9. The rise of the Merina

1. Ives, B39, p 6.
2. Ibid., p 13.
3. Ibid., p 9.
4. Buchan. B6, pp 135–42.
5. A drawing of the king made about this time appears in GM (March 1793) opposite p 201. The accompanying text states that "his form seems well proportioned and his features partake more of the European than the African".
6. Buchan, B6, pp 144–6.
7. Report from Fort William, October 8, 1793. GM (April 1794) p 378.
8. Grandidier. G6, Plates 22–3.
9. Translated into French by Chapus and Ratsimba, B7.
10. Both Rafohy and Rangita ruled in succession at Imerimanjaka; according to different traditions they were either sisters, or mother and daughter, or daughter and mother.
11. Hébert (B31) convincingly demolishes the established interpretation of the *Tantara* under which the Vazimba did not know iron and had only clay-tipped spears against Andriamanelo's new iron-tipped spears. He suggests more plausibly that the Vazimba already had iron-tipped spears and that Andriamanelo's "flying iron" was a projectile such as the bolt launched by a crossbow.
12. Hébert, B31.
13. *Kelimalaza* came to be regarded as the most powerful of the royal idols. It was destroyed with the other idols in 1869 (see p 190); and its absence was regarded by some traditionalist Malagasy as the cause of the defeat by the French in 1895.
14. The Malagasy word *vohitra*, which is incorporated in so many village names beginning with *ambohi-*, can mean either "hill" or "village".
15. It is not certain whether Andrianampoinimerina ever had

precisely twelve wives. But the number twelve had special ritual significance in Imerina, eg the twelve "sacred villages".
16. Hugon. B37, folio 17v.
17. Deschamps. G5, p 127.

Chapter 10. The king, the governor and the sergeant

1. Leguével de Lacombe. C37, p 125 (English translation by the author).
2. Bourbon was renamed Réunion in 1793, and later Ile Bonaparte. The name Bourbon was restored in 1815, but it finally became Réunion again in 1848.
3. The correspondence is quoted in Graham C31, pp 59–60.
4. Letter of April 2, 1811, quoted in Howe C34, p 122.
5. The ambiguity was due to loose drafting or poor translation. The word "nommément" in the French text can sometimes mean "especially", but in this context was almost certainly meant to convey the sense of "specifically" or "namely".
6. By the Treaty of Paris the French agreed to abolish the slave trade but only after a period of five years to permit the restocking of her colonies.
7. Now in the British Museum Manuscripts Dept as the Farquhar Collection (Add. Mss. 18118–18135).
8. Quoted in Howe C34, p 125.
9. Sir R Farquhar to Pye at Tamatave June 28, 1817. PRO, CO167/34, folio 76.
10. Ibid., folio 75.
11. In common with most Europeans in the nineteenth century, Hastie refers to the Merina as the Hova.
12. Quotations from the original of Hastie's journal in PRO CO167/34, folio 133 and 134.
13. Ibid., folio 151r.
14. Ibid., folio 154v.
15. Ibid., folio 151v.
16. Letter from Hastie to D Griffiths, Feb. 18, 1821. See B.Mad. Nos 293–4 (Oct–Nov 1970), p 879.
17. Especially S Pasfield Oliver in *General Hall and the Export Slave Trade from Madagascar* AA 1888, and *Sir R Farquhar and the Malagasy Slave Trade* AA 1891.
18. Manuscript *Journal to Madagascar in 1820*, entry for October 3, 1820, LMS Journals Madagasacar/Mauritius, B1, F1, JA.
19. This system was gradually expanded later in the century to provide equivalents to all ranks in the British army, culminating in 16 honours for a field-marshal, with equivalent honours for civilian officials.

20. Leguével de Lascombe. C37, pp 129–30 (translated by the author)
21. Coppalle, C16 BAM Vol VIII, p 49.
22. Ellis, C26, Vol II, p 374.
23. Ellis, C26, Vol II, pp 381–2.
24. Apparently a common-law wife. Hastie's will, made in 1822, refers to "one Mary Gates now living with me as my wife" (letter from T S Kelsey, October 27, 1827. LMS Mad. IL, B2, F4, JC). The missionaries accepted her as Mrs Hastie to avoid a scandal. But she later caused them much embarrassment by marrying and then subsequently divorcing a Malagasy student of the missionaries, much younger than herself.

Chapter 11. The missionaries

1. The French habitually, but incorrectly, referred to the LMS missionaries as "Methodists".
2. Jones to Mrs Telfair, Oct 16, 1820. LMS Mad. IL, B1, F2, JA.
3. Radama to Directors of LMS, Nov 2, 1820. LMS Mad. IL, B1, F2, JB.
4. Cameron, C8, p 5.
5. Jones to LMS, May 3, 1821. LMS Mad IL, B1, F2, JC.
6. Copland. C15, p 360.
7. Various vocabularies had been compiled by early sailors, by Flacourt, by Drury and by Froberville in Mauritius, but these related to coastal dialects and none of them amounted to a comprehensive study of the language.
8. Jones to LMS, May 3, 1821 (already quoted in Note 5).
9. Laverdant, C36, pp 84–5.
10. Coppalle. C16, BAM Vol VIII, p 44.
11. Griffiths to LMS, November 4, 1824. LMS Mad. IL, B2, F1, JC.
12. Griffiths to LMS, December 20, 1825. LMS Mad. IL, B2, F1, JD.
13. Jones to LMS, April 21, 1824. LMS Mad. IL, B2, F1, JA.
14. Raombana C48. History, A1 No 3, pp 1105–10 and 1121.
15. The *Tantara* (p 1056) record that Andrianampoinimerina on his deathbed named Ramovo to succeed Radama, but this was almost certainly an apocryphal addition designed to justify the usurpation.
16. Coroller, cousin of Jean René, became one of Radama's closest advisers. His views on Radama's character are given at length in Ellis C26, Vol II, pp 400–3.

Notes

Chapter 12. The queen and the martyrs

1. From the journal of Raombana, one of her private secretaries (C48).
2. Valette. C59.
3. Lyall's Journal. C39, p 118.
4. The question is examined in detail in Brown, C7.
5. Freeman to LMS, October 12, 1831. LMS Mad. IL, B4, F2, JC.
6. The prefix "Raini" means "father of". In accordance with a custom fairly widespread among the Hova, they had changed their names on the birth of their first sons.
7. Freeman to LMS, April 6, 1832. LMS Mad. IL, B4, F2, JB.
8. Baker to LMS, March 17, 1835. LMS Mad. IL, B5, F2, JA.
9. Translation of message, dated February 21, 1835, is in LMS Mad. IL, B5, F2, JA.
10. Jones to LMS, July 20, 1840. LMS Mad. IL, B5, F3, JC.
11. See Domenichini-Ramiaramanana C21.
12. In 1978 Professor Ayache was undertaking the publication of a critical edition of all Raombana's surviving writings, and he kindly permitted the author to consult pre-publication typescripts of the texts. So far (1995) two volumes of the *History* (see C49) have been published.
13. The prince had addressed a similar appeal to the emperor in 1854, and had previously, in 1848 and 1852, corresponded with various French authorities through Laborde, about the possibility of French military intervention and a protectorate. See Delval C20, pp 140–6.
14. Pfeiffer. C45, p 208.
15. Chapus and Mondain. D9, p 22.
16. In the absence of an Englishman on the spot to blame, contemporary French Jesuit historians attributed responsibility for the plot, and its betrayal, to the Malagasy (Protestant) Christians. But Chapus and Mondain (D9, pp 20–1) have convincingly demolished this version.
17. Pfeiffer. C45, p 294.
18. Ibid., p 308.
19. See Segre, D45.

Chapter 13. The tragedy of the prince and the playboys

1. Ellis. C28, pp 43–4.
2. De La Vaissière. C52, p 363.
3. At one banquet, Radama proposed a toast to the prosperity and union of France, England and Madagascar, and to rein-

force this concept, ordered three bands to play simultaneously the national anthems of the three countries, producing an indescribable cacophony. Vinson C60, pp 412–3.
4. Delval. C20, pp 644–5.
5. Pakenham to Lord John Russell, April 14, 1863. PRO FO 48/10, folio 65.
6. When the French delegate to the coronation, Captain Dupré, had a private audience with the king, they both spoke (badly) in English, which Dupré said was their only common language. Dupré C23, pp 210–11.
7. In a secret treaty signed on October 3, 1862, Radama recognised particular French rights over territories acquired by previous treaties, in return for explicit French recognition as king of Madagascar and withdrawal of French claims to sovereignty over the whole island. However the French foreign minister decided to ignore this secret treaty. Delval C20, p 403.
8. Ellis. C28, p 173.
9. Quoted by John E Ellis, C25, p 271.
10. Davidson. C17.
11. Pakenham to Lord John Russell, April 14, 1863. PRO FO 48/10, folio 60–1.
12. Ellis. C28, pp 268–71.
13. Ibid., p 277.
14. Ibid., p 300.
15. Boudou, C6.
16. Delval (C20, pp 757–918) quotes impressive evidence of the king's survival from contemporary sources and from his own investigations in the remote area where Radama is alleged to have lived out his exile.

Chapter 14. The prime minister and the Christian monarchy

1. By the end of 1870 there were 25 Malagasy ordained pastors and nearly 2,000 native preachers (Report of the LMS for the year ending May 1, 1871).
2. Chapus and Mondain, D9 Chapter X, especially p 309.
3. Letter from Rev W E Cousins, September 24, 1869. Quoted in Lovett, C38, p 734.
4. In fact a son born to his wife before their marriage and adopted by Rainilaiarivony after he married her. D9, p 293.
5. Lovett. C38, p 738–9.
6. Resolution of the Imerina District Committee to the Directors of the LMS, Jan 16, 1895.
7. The piastre, equivalent to a US dollar, was the currency in

use before the French occupation.
8. Quoted by Ellis, C28, p 222. In a postscript Dr Livingstone asked "Can you get any of those famous big eggs? (Dinornis). I got a small bit." The first aepyornis egg had been discovered in 1850.

Chapter 15. War and diplomacy

1. Meyer's letter of Sept 18, 1881, quoted by Boiteau, G1, pp 173–4.
2. PRO FO 48/34.
3. See Paul Rosenblum, Le séjour aux Etats-Unis de l'ambassade malgache. B.Mad. No 263 (April 1968) p 363.
4. Quoted by Mutibwa, D38, p 229.
5. Letter from Procter to Rainilaiarivony, Nov 9, 1882, quoted by Mutibwa, D38, p 231.
6. Ramaniraka to Rainilaiarivony, June 4 1883, quoted by Mutibwa, D38, p 240.
7. Quoted by Mutibwa, D38, p 253.
8. French foreign minister to French ambassador in London Oct 18, 1883. See Oliver, D39, p 144.
9. Rev J Richardson, *The Coronation of Ranavalona III*. AA Vol VII (1883) pp 102–10.
10. Red Book No 1 (1884) was followed by Red Book No 2 (1885) describing attempts at mediation by the Italian consul (D34).
11. The heading of Chapter VI of Saillens, D44.
12. Quoted by Mutibwa, D38, p 285.
13. Nor was the letter published along with the other diplomatic documents in the relevant "Yellow Book".
14. Campbell was replaced in 1891 by John Waller, one of the earliest black American diplomats. Waller upset the French by his strong support for Malagasy independence and after French complaints to Washington he was replaced at the end of 1893. But he stayed on in Madagascar to pursue business interests. In March 1895 he was arrested by French troops in Tamatave and sentenced to 20 years in a French prison on a charge of giving information to the enemy. An outcry by the "black lobby" in Washington led to his release in February 1896. See pp 11–12 of *Black and Blue – the Life and Lyrics of Andy Razaf* by Barry Singer, New York 1992. Razaf (full name Andriamantena Paul Razafinkeriefo), who wrote the lyrics for many of "Fats" Waller's songs, was Consul Waller's grandson by his daughter, who married a nephew of Queen Ranavalona III.

Chapter 16. The French conquest

1. Knight. D30, p 128.
2. Ibid., p 146.
3. Maude. D36, pp 158–9.
4. e.g. Savaron, quoted in Chapus and Mondain, D9, pp 355–6.
5. Dr Rajaonah, the son of Rainandriamampandry, had married a daughter of the prime minister. He had been the first Malagasy to qualify as a doctor.
6. Text of the will in Annex 3 of Chapus and Mondain D9. Much of the property was seized by the French colonial government. But descendants of Ratelifera continued to live in the prime minister's country house just outside Antananarivo where a century later the Victorian hangings and furniture are left in their original state.
7. G Grandidier (D28, pp 212–14) lists ten Frenchmen murdered between 1887 and 1895.
8. By Mutibwa, D38, especially pp 347–52.
9. Letter from Rainilaiarivony to Le Myre de Vilers, Oct 22, 1894. Text in Annex IV of Boiteau G1, pp 410–15.
10. Letter of Nov 3, 1894, quoted in Randrianarisoa, D43, pp 195–6.
11. Letter of Nov 7, 1894, quoted in Randrianarisoa, D43, pp 196–7 (translations by the author).
12. Mr Jarvis to Lord Rosebery, Feb 22, 1895. PRO FO 48/77 (quoted by Mutibwa, D38, pp 353–4).
13. Sibree, D48, p 269.
14. Decary, C19, p 75.
15. They had available maps supplied by the explorer and geographer Alfred Grandidier. G Grandidier, D28, p 222, footnote 3.
16. Knight, D30, p 269.
17. Rajestera. D42, p 62.
18. Ibid., p 63–5.
19. He was a rich banker and it has been suggested that one consideration in making his appointment was that, if he failed, his wealth could be appropriated on grounds of treason. Hocquard, D29, p 75.
20. Knight, D30, p 269.
21. Ibid., pp 270–2.
22. It is not clear whether their *lamba* were in fact red in colour. Sibree, a contemporary witness (D48, p 277) states that the rebels wore the traditional white *lamba* which, rarely washed in the bush, became stained by the red laterite soil.

Notes

For a full study of the rebellion, see Stephen Ellis, D18.
23. Letter from Gallieni to Alfred Grandidier, quoted in G Grandidier D28, p 281.
24. See Stephen Ellis' detailed study of the 'colonial plot', D19. It became known at the time that the text of the official Gazette, announcing the death sentence and the rejection of the appeals, was sent to the printers before the trial started (Carol, D6 p 274).
25. Rasanjy, who probably had more contacts with the *menalamba* than most people in Antananarivo, and Prince Ramahatra, whom many of the rebels wanted to be their leader, were both involved in providing 'evidence' against Rainandriamampandry and Prince Ratsimamanga at their trial.
26. Two years later the queen was removed to Algiers where she lived in tolerable comfort until her death in 1917. Her remains were repatriated to the royal tomb in Antananarivo in 1938.
27. However some years later (1902) Rainibetsimisaraka was convicted of armed robbery and executed. Rabezavana died in 1900 in mysterious circumstances, apparently killed by a French officer against whom he had lodged a complaint (S Ellis, D18 p 73 and caption to photograph no 10).
28. S Ellis, D18, Chapter 4.
29. Knight, D30, p 308.
30. After independence the building housed the Ministry of Justice.
31. The Paris Society found the burden too heavy, and the LMS resumed control of its elementary schools in 1900 (Sibree D48, p 285 footnote).
32. Ambohipotsy church was used as a military barracks for some time, but was later restored to the LMS.
33. Boiteau G1, pp 209–12, quotes an eyewitness account. It is fair to say that this was an isolated and untypical incident, and countrary to Gallieni's instructions.
34. Boiteau G1, p 216, quotes several estimates, of which the lowest is Savaron's figure of 100,000, but even this seems exaggerated. Previous efforts at unification under Radama I and Ranavalona I were certainly more expensive in human life.
35. However on his return to France he was promoted General of Division; and five years after his death in 1916 he was posthumously created Marshal of France.

Notes

Chapter 17. *Colonial rule and nationalism*

1. Boiteau (G1, p 291) quotes a figure of 159,000 primary school pupils in 1930. Attendance at church schools in 1894 was 164,000.
2. One way of asserting his dignity was to *tutoyer* in return whenever French men and women addressed him with the familiar, condescending "tu" as used with children. Boiteau G1, p 311.
3. Malagasy troops were used in the unpopular "colonial wars" in Syria and Morocco and there were hostile demonstrations in Marseilles harbour when they embarked for these campaigns. Ibid. pp 318–9.
4. Planque and Vittori were later deported back to France. Vittori played a prominent part in the resistance movement in his native Corsica, and survived the war. Planque, who also joined the Resistance, was arrested by the Vichy police in 1941 and handed over to the Germans. He died in Dachau a few weeks before the camp was liberated. Ibid. 324, footnotes.
5. See articles by Dussac in *l'Aurore malgache* of June 16 1933 and by Ravoahangy in *l'Opinion* in July 1934, quoted by Boiteau in G1 pp 332–3.
6. An exception was a final episode of tribal warfare in the south in 1932 – an attack by an Antandroy clan on a neighbouring village, in which all the inhabitants of the village were massacred. Hubert Deschamps, as local magistrate, sentenced the leaders of the attack to seven years' hard labour. Deschamps E20 pp 142–3.
7. A notable case was Léon Réallon who married a Malagasy lady connected with the family of Rainilaiarivony. He served in the administration in Madagascar for nearly twenty years, finishing as a popular secretary-general (occasionally acting as governor-general) from 1936–1941. It is difficult to imagine an equally senior, or even a more junior, British colonial official of the time marrying an African or Asian and remaining in his post.
8. See, for example, Deschamps E20 pp 215–225. Deschamps, at the time governor of French Somaliland, was like de Coppet a socialist and anti-fascist but, having served in the French navy, was even more outraged by the bombardment at Mers-el-Kebir.
9. See LMS Review E36.
10. Marcuse, E40, gives a vivid picture of the pioneering hardships in this inhospitable region.

Notes

11. Churchill E13, p 200 and Annet, E3, p 131. For Vichy willingness to collaborate with the Japanese, see Boiteau G1 pp 341–2.
12. Thanks at least partly to a group of anti-Vichy Frenchmen who, forewarned of the date of the landing, arrested the local administrator and chief of police the night before. Private letter to author from Pierre Boiteau.
13. The Malagasy invariably referred to British African troops as Zulus; whilst French west African troops were always "Sénégalais", though only a small proportion of them came from Senegal.
14. Thorne E62. Annet was flown out to internment in South Africa, followed by imprisonment in north Africa and France until 1947 when he was sentenced by a French court to "national degradation". Grafftey-Smith E27, p 55.
15. Of the first 120 French prisoners interrogated, only four declared themselves for de Gaulle. Grafftey-Smith E27, p 67.
16. Lawrence Grafftey-Smith, a Foreign Office counsellor who had served as political officer with the military administration, now became consul-general.
17. Author of G1 and later a respected member of the Académie Malgache.
18. Dr Rakoto-Ratsimamanga (author of A51) was the grandson of Prince Ratsimamanga who was shot in 1896. He was to be Madagascar's ambassador in Paris for over a decade after independence.
19. Wilson, A69, pp 21–2, records vivid memories of Merina oppression and cruelty among the Tsimihety as late as 1963.
20. Tronchon E63, pp 70–4.
21. One of the defence lawyers was Réallon (see Note 7 above) who, after retirement with the honorary rank of governor-general, set up a legal practice in Antananarivo and had many Malagasy as clients.

Chapter 18. The road to independence

1. As early as 1947 Governor Raveloson-Mahasampo, objecting to PADESM setting up its headquarters in Antananarivo, broke away to set up a purely coastal party, the Union Démocratique Côtière, covering the west and south of the country. In 1948 PADESM agreed to a division of responsibility under which UDC would operate in the west and south, leaving the rest of the country to PADESM.
2. See E59 pp 53–61.
3. In 1964 the population of Madagascar (excluding foreigners)

was just under 6 million. Of these, just over a quarter (1,569,649) were Merina. The size of the other main ethnic groups was as follows:

Betsimisaraka	929,016	Bara	227,864
Betsileo	735,791	Antemoro	221,365
Tsimihety	428,511	Antanosy	148,880
Sakalava	360,379	Sihanaka	135,001
Antandroy	326,616	Mahafaly	90,573
Antesaka	324,987	Others	288,316
Tanala	236,769		

4. A leading Merina whose personal ambitions contributed to Merina disunity was Razafy-Andriamihaingo who founded a conservative Catholic party UDIM but then joined the extreme left-wing coalition of CEAP as its president, hoping to become CEAP's candidate for mayor in 1956. When this seemed unlikely, he took UDIM out of CEAP and subsequently formed two other parties before joining with the conservative UDSM for the 1959 municipal elections, with equal lack of success. In 1960 he was appointed the first Malagasy ambassador to London.
5. For a time the RPM incorporated the Union des Travailleurs et Paysans set up by Raymond Rabemananjara on his return from France as a vehicle for his own ambitions. But despite his prestige as one of the founders of MDRM, his long absence from Madagascar ruled out any hopes of assuming the leadership of the nationalists.
6. The nationalists referred to the new law as the *loi gadra* ("*gadra*" being the Malagasy word for "chains").
7. An Antandroy peasant by origin, Monja Jaona was the founder of the secret society *Jina* in 1943, but being imprisoned between 1946 and 1950 he took no part in the 1947 insurrection.
8. PSD absorbed the Malagasy branch of SFIO and remained for a long time affiliated to the French SFIO. The party's original name was Parti Socialiste Malgache et Comorien; at the time the Comoros were administered as part of Madagascar, and most Malagasy expected that they would be incorporated in Madagascar when it became independent.
9. Another minister, Gervaise Randrianasolo, elected on a Christian list in Fianarantsoa, joined UDSM in the following year.
10. The former senator, Paul Longuet, was appointed Minister

of the Economy, although he had failed to be elected to the Tamatave Provincial Assembly.
11. The threat was no idle one. When Guinea voted "no" all French official personnel were pulled out along with all mobile equipment including, it was said, even the telephones.
12. Père de Puybaudet went so far as to call for a "holy war" against the PSD.
13. His son Francisque was to play a leading part in the events of 1991–93, emerging as prime minister under the new parliamentary constitution.
14. Spacensky E60 p 357.
15. He was offered immediate promotion to brigadier-general but refused to accept it until he had qualified for promotion, and been designated brigadier-general, in the French army.
16. See Guy Jacob's review of Manassé Esoavelomandroso's book (D21) in OSA Nos 3–4 (1976) p 339: "La colonisation française ... ne doit constituer finalement qu'un accident dans l'évolution de Madagascar. En revanche la domination merina ... s'inscrit au coeur de l'histoire malgache."

Chapter 19. Independence and neocolonialism

1. Even relatively stable countries such as Senegal, Ivory Coast and Niger suffered unrest and attempted *coups* in the early sixties.
2. Tsiranana magnanimously appointed his old rival to the important post of director-general in the ministry of foreign affairs.
3. Quoted by Spacensky, E60 p 370.
4. Louis Rakotomalala, who had been appointed foreign minister at independence, was now sent as ambassador to Washington and to the United Nations in New York.
5. After passage of a law in July 1963 limiting the right of French citizens to vote and stand for election only in municipal elections, Longuet resigned his ministerial post; but Lechat, who had taken Malagasy citizenship and a Malagasy wife, remained in government until 1972.
6. Partly perhaps because the great majority of qualified professional women were Merina.
7. Spacensky, E60 p 385.
8. SOMASAK was one of the few projects singled out for praise by René Dumont in *L'Afrique Noire est Mal Partie* (Paris 1962) Appendix II.
9. In a concession to French feeling, no publicity was given

inside Madagascar to the presence of the RAF detachment.
10. Rabenoro, E51 p 127.
11. A constitutional amendment of May 1962 provided for direct election of the president by universal suffrage instead of by electoral college.
12. This huge vote inevitably raises the question of whether the voting was rigged. Déléris (E18, p 36), generally an apologist for the PSD régime, admits that it was, at least in the countryside, where in any case confusion between party and government and pressure to conform would lead to a high vote for the sitting president. But in 1965 Tsiranana was genuinely popular and there was no serious alternative.
13. His fellow VVS veteran, Ravoahangy, remained in the government, latterly as minister of state in the president's office, until his death in 1970.
14. Author of E51. Later ambassador to London and holder of two ministerial posts under Tsiranana before becoming president of the Académie Malgache and later foreign minister in the transitional government from 1991 to 1993.
15. Statistics have been taken mainly from Heseltine G8, Rabenoro E51 and Déléris E18.
16. In fact substantial quantities of rice from Indo-China were imported in the mid-thirties, not because there was any shortage in Madagascar but because, owing to the vagaries of exchange rates, the Indo-Chinese rice was cheaper. Feugeas, E23.
17. Notably in Archer E7 p 86, taken up by Covell E14 p 35 among others.
18. For what it is worth, the author's own observations support Déléris's refutation of Archer's allegations (E18 p 35). It needs to be borne in mind that ministers were relatively well paid, enjoyed benefits such as official cars and sometimes houses and were permitted to take directorships in state-owned companies or commercial companies; so that anyone in office for a number of years could become rich by Malagasy standards without resorting to corruption.
19. The French justification was that Madagascar, uniquely, had been a modern-type state, maintaining relations with European powers, before colonial rule. Whereas other colonial "residences" were built during colonial rule out of the colony's revenues, the Madagascar residence had been built before 1895, as the residence of Le Myre de Vilers, with French government money, on land bought from the prime minister Rainilaiarivony. But whatever the historico-legal

position, it was politically and psychologically obtuse for the French to continue to occupy what had been the central seat of power under colonial rule.

Chapter 20. The fall of the First Republic

1. At official entertainments for South African delegations the guests invariably included Lechat with his Malagasy wife and Rabemananjara with his French wife.
2. The FRS to some extent duplicated the rôle of the gendarmerie which Tsiranana had built up and placed directly under the control of the presidency as a counter to the army which was officered predominantly by Merina. The existence of three separate armed forces was no doubt intended to reduce the possibility of a military coup.
3. Resampa was arrested in the early hours of the morning on leaving an important function at the French embassy where he had been representing the president. According to an excellent source the French were taken completely by surprise by the arrest.
4. The Faculty of Medicine at the university provided only the first three years of French medical training, with successful students completing their studies in France.
5. Botokeky, a *côtier* from Morondava, had held the education portfolio throughout Tsiranana's government. At a meeting of francophone African education ministers in 1969 the majority had favoured separate national curricula while retaining *équivalence* with French qualifications; Botokeky had opposed, insisting on retaining not only "equivalence" but also "identity" with the French system. Rakoto E54 p 58.
6. ZOAM – *Zatovy Orin'asa Anivon'ny Madagasikara*, ie unemployed youth of central Madagascar, mainly partly-educated dropouts from the system, who generally acted as storm troops of the movement.
7. On the same day eight striking students in Majunga were killed by the FRS.
8. The City Hall was associated with AKFM because its leader Andriamanjato was both mayor and president of the Municipal Council of Antananarivo.
9. He owed his appointment as foreign minister to the recommendation of his predecessor Jacques Rabemananjara, who had come across him in Paris and, as a fellow Betsimisaraka, knew his family.
10. The Chinese advanced a loan to enable the Malagasy to compensate the South African companies affected by the

cancellation of the commercial agreements.
11. Around the same time the RAF detachment operating from the civil airport at Majunga (see p 302) was asked to leave.
12. They were all released four months later after a trial during which Rakotonirina went on hunger strike.
13. In June 1973 Bezaka's PDCM had merged with USM.
14. One theory current in gossip at the time was that Ratsimandrava had been shot accidentally by his own bodyguard returning fire from the ambushers.

Chapter 21. Revolutionary socialism

1. But not including General Andriamahazo who was given the relatively powerless post of head of the CMD (Conseil Militaire pour le Développement).
2. Appointed in December 1975 after the referendum. Killed in a helicopter accident on 30 July 1976 along with the army chief of staff and the minister of rural development.
3. One of his first acts was to transfer to his new office from the Queen's Palace Museum a fine painting of the first Malagasy embassy to Britain in 1837 being received by Queen Adelaide (see p 155).
4. Between 1975 and 1984 Madagascar slipped from 109th to 139th in the world ranking of countries by GDP per head. Whereas GDP per head had risen steadily from 1960 to 1973, in the following eleven years it declined at an average rate of 2.5 per cent per year, a rate exceeded only by Cambodia and Bangladesh. See Chaigneau E11 pp 189–98.
5. See Chaigneau E11 p 179.
6. Son of the arch-conservative founder-member of PADESM, later president of UDCM. Colonel Raveloson-Mahasampo and President Ratsiraka had married two sisters, daughters of another leading PADESM conservative, Pascal Velonjara.
7. Most were subsequently released pending trial, which did not take place until March 1988. Of 245 accused, 217 were acquitted; the remainder were given two-year prison sentences but immediately released as they had already been in prison for two and a half years awaiting trial. This result was seen as a setback to the president but also as a vindication of the Malagasy legal system, which had escaped being "revolutionised".

Chapter 22. Return to democracy

1. The long-established churches which joined to form FFKM represented the great majority of Christians. But over the previous century at least a dozen other "independent" churches had grown up, some imported from abroad such as the Seventh Day Adventists and the Baptists, but the majority founded by Malagasy as breakaway groups from one or other of the main churches. Together they account for some 400,000 Christians. See G9, pp 420–2.
2. See, for example, *La Lettre de l'Océan Indien*, No. 289, 4 July 1987.
3. In fact some clandestine trade with South Africa, at times involving the national shipping company, had continued despite the official boycott.
4. The most likely explanation of this surprising reversal is that Monja Jaona saw the FV opposition as an essentially plateau movement, threatening a return to Merina domination. But it is generally believed that there were also financial considerations.
5. They included Madame Andriamanjato who, as a qualified engineer, had been appointed minister of public works.

Index

ACFOM (Association of French Citizens of Malagasy Origin), 269
AEMEP (Befalatanana medical students' union), 316
AEOM (Association of Students of Malagasy Origin), 270, 276-7, 281, 283-4, 313
AKFM (Malagasy Congress Party), 285-6, 288-90, 292, 295-300, 303-4, 310, 312, 314, 316, 320, 322, 333, 342, 345
AKFM/F (Renewed Malagasy Congress Party), 344, 354
APAEM (Association of Parents and Friends of Malagasy Students), 269
AREMA (Avant-garde of the Malagasy Revolution), 333-4, 338-9, 341, 344-5, 347
AVM (Betsileo political party) 288, 298
Académie Malgache, 236, 251
Action Madécasse, 274
administration, colonial, 237-8, 245, 262, 270, 274, 293
administrative reform, 109, 196-7, 248, 271, 299, 320
aepyornis maximus, 4-5, 14, 19
African racial and cultural influences, 10-15, 17-18, 25, 26
agriculture, 110, 246, 270-2, 301-2, 305-6, 332-3, 336, 350
aid, foreign, 302, 305, 322, 336, 346, 349
air services, 253, 272, 311, 324, 326, 345
Aláotra, Lake, 97, 118, 129, 192, 247, 270, 302
Alasóra, 100, 103
Ambatománga, 106, 110, 112, 118
Ambátonakánga, 150, 151, 186
Ambiki massacre, 237
Ambóhidrabíby, 101, 103
Ambóhidratrímo, 103, 106, 230
Ambohimánga, 101, 103, 104, 110, 168, 177, 217, 230
Ambohipótsy, 155, 157, 186
American Embassy, 314-5

amnesty, for VVS, 246; for MDRM leaders, 270, 273-4, 276, 281, 283-4, 289-90
Ampamarínana, 163, 186
Analamánga (see also Antananarivo), 101-2
ancestors, cult of, 10-11, 293
Andáfiaváratra family, 152, 170, 181
andévo (slave class), 28, 109
Andevoránto, 28, 109
Andohálo, 138, 151
Andrantsáy, 97, 107
Andriamaházo, General Gilles, 326, 328, 394 (note 1)
Andriamahólisón, Commandant, 333, 342, 345
Andriamampándry, adviser to Andriamasinavalona, 103
Andriamanálina, Betsileo king, 107-8
Andriamánanjáka, Antandroy prince, 52, 54-6
Andriamandísoarívo, Sakalava king, 59
Andriamandrésy, founder of Antesaka, 43
Andriamanélo, Merina king, 100-1
Andriamanétriarívo (see Ratsimonongarivo)
Andriamanjáto, Rev. Richard, 276, 283-5, 288, 292, 298, 304, 333, 343-4, 346-7, 350, 354, 393 (note 8)
Andriamanjáto, Madame, 299, 395 (note 5)
Andriamásinaválona, Merina king, 102-3
andriambaventy, local justices, 196
Andriambélo, Pastor, 189
Andriambélomásina, Merina king, 104
Andriamihája, Queen's guardian, 148
Andriamisára, Sakalava king, 43
Andriamitránga, Fiherenana chief, 56, 58
Andriamivárotra, Antandroy prince, 53-6, 58
Andriampiróky, Antandroy prince, 54
andríana (noble class), 28-9, 101, 109,

[396]

Index

147, 261
Andrianafárana, Antandroy prince, 56
Andrianambóatsimarófy, Merina king, 97, 103-4, 106
Andrianampóinimérina, Merina king, 25, 104-110, 112, 147, 179, 188
Andriandáhifótsy, Sakalava king, 43-4
Andriandrámaka, Antanosy chief, 45-6
Andrianály, Dr., 195
Andrianjáfy, Merina king, 104
Andrianjáka, Merina king, 102
Andriankiríndra, Antandroy king, 52-8, 91
Andriankósintány, Mahafaly king, 54-6, 58, 91
Andriantávy, Merina commander, 227
Andriantóakáfo ("King Dick"), 62, 76, 92
Andriantsámbo, Antandroy prince, 54-5
Andriantsimitóviaminandríandéhibé, Merina king, 102
Andriantsóly, Sakalava king, 130, 158
Andríba, battle, 228-9
Andróy, region, 77, 130
Anglican Church, 187, 256, 300
Anglo-French Treaty 1890, 216, 221
Anglo-German Convention 1862, 215
Anglo-Merina Treaty 1817, 123
Anglo-Merina Treaty 1820, 126
Animation rurale, 301, 306
Annet, Armand, Governor-General, 256, 258-9, 389 (note 14)
Anósy, region, 23, 27
Anósy, Lake, 150
Antaláotra, 20-22, 25
Antambahóaka, 19, 23, 78
Antanánarívo, passim, 28, 100, 102 et seq., 118 et seq., 217, 228-31, 232, 252, 265, 278, 281, 296, 298-300, 339, 347
Antananarivo Annual, 194
Antandróy, 11, 19, 23, 51-8, 91, 92, 237, 252, 313
Antankárana, 92, 129
Antanósy, 19, 23, 25, 45-9, 78, 91
Antatsímo, 78, 82
Antaváratra, 78, 80, 81
Antemóro, 19, 22-6, 29, 78, 107, 129
Antesáka, 43, 158
anti-Communism, of Catholic church, 274, 281, 283; of Tsiranana, 302, 314
Antongil, Bay of, 28, 34-5, 39, 68, 76, 78, 81, 84, 115, 128
Antsirabé, 97, 107, 243, 246

Antsiránana, see Diego Suarez,
Arabs, calendar, 29, 101; cultural influences, 19-21; linguistic, 23-24; merchants, 17, 21-22
arms, supply to Merina, 110, 123; manufacture of, 160, 200, 210, 225; importation of, 200, 210, 222, 225
army, Merina, training of 122, 126, 128, 170, 211, 215, 225, organisation of, 199-201,
army, Malagasy, 291, 295, 308, 317, 343, 347, 349
Asian traders, 302, 304, 323-4, 341
Assada, see Nosy Be,
assimilation, 242, 250-1, 254, 261, 263
Atkinson, Theophilus, missionary, 250-1
Augagneur, Victor, Governor General, 242-3
L'aurore malgache, 250-1
autonomy, proposals for, 273, 277, 281-2, 284, granted 1958, 285-6
Avery, Capt. Henry, pirate, 66-7
Baba, King of, 93-97
Baker, LMS printer, 152, 154
Baldridge, Adam, pirates' supplier, 69-70
bandits (fahavalo, dahalo), 219, 221, 229, 232, 336
Bantu language, 10, 17
Bara, 11, 19, 26, 91-2, 158, 200, 237
Bargues, Robert, High Commissioner, 272
Baron, Rev. Richard, 194, 236
Baudais, Commissaire, 204-5, 208, 211
Béfalatánana, medical school, 315-6
Bellamont, Lord, 64, 67, 69
Benbow, John, 51, 53
Bennet, LMS inspector, 144, 148
Benyowski, Baron, 84-6, 97
Bétaniména, 81
Betsiléo, 13, 18-19, 24, 92, 100, 107-110, 112, 188, 192, 236
Bétsimisáraka, 78, 82-7, 192
Betía, princess, 129
Bevan, Thomas, missionary, 134
Bezáka, Alexis, 280, 282-6, 289-90, 297, 303, 342
Bézanozáno, 61, 106, 110, 112
Bezára, Justin, 280, 282, 284-5, 298
Bible, translation into Malagasy, 139-40, 150, 154, 176, 194
Bien-Aimé, Admiral, 226
"Bigorne", see Filet,
black market, 260, 340-1

Index

Blum, Léon, 253-4
Boina kingdom, 59, 62, 76, 78, 82, 92, 102, 108, 110, 129-31, 158
Boiteau, Pierre, 261, 269
Bompard, Resident-General, 215
Booth, Capt. George, pirate, 70-1,
Boothby, Richard, 37, 39, 41
Botokéky, Minister of Education, 288, 316, 321
Boué, R.P., 274, 281
Bourbon island (see also Réunion) 45, 48-9, 73, 83, 86, 110, 113-5
Bowen, Captain John, pirate, 70-2
Brady, Sergeant (later General), 120, 122, 125-6, 131, 142, 149
Brazzaville Conference, 261
British Navy, 73, 75, 113-4, 126, 129-30, 198, 257
British Foreign Office, 202, 207, 215-6
British mercenary officers, 210, 225
British troops in Madagascar, 257-60
Brossard de Corbigny, Baron, 171
Buchan, George, 75-6
butter beans (pois du Cap), 252, 256, 271, 378 (note 5)
CAPSIM (Committee for social and political action for the independence of Madagascar),283, 286
CAR (collectivités autochtones rurales), 271
CCSM (Christian confederation of Malagasy trade unions), 276
CEAP (Committee of understanding and political action), 279-283
CFTCM (Malagasy section of French confederation of Christian workers), 276
CGT (General Confederation of Labour), 249, 253, 270, 275-6
CMD (Military Development Committee), 330, 394 (note 1)
CNAC (National Amnesty Committee), 275
CNM (Malagasy National Council), 276
CNPD (People's National Council for Development), 320, 324, 326
COSOMA (Madagascar Solidarity Committee), 270, 275, 283
CRAM (Collectivités rurales autochtones modernisées), 271
CRES (Committee for Economic and Social Recovery), 350
CSR (Supreme Council of the Revolution), 329-30, 337, 343, 346, 350
CTM (Confederation of Malagasy Workers), 299
CTMC (Confederation of Workers of Madagascar and the Comoros), 276
Caldwell, trader, 175, 179-80
Callet, R.P, 98, 187
Cameron, James, 140-1, 150, 154, 160, 163-4, 185-6, 194-5, 203
Campbell, John P, American Consul, 214
Canham, tanner, 140
Capitation tax, 239, 313
Cassas, Eugène, commissaire, 203
Castellani, Jules, senator, 273-4
Catholic Church in Madagascar, 192-3, 232-3, 236, 274, 284, 315, 342, 348
cattle herding, 10, 12, 18, 40-41, 61, 252, 271, 313
cattle stealing, 92, 336
Cayla, Léon, Governor General, 250-3, 255
Chambers of Commerce, 246-7
Champmargou, governor of Fort-Dauphin, 47-8
Chardenoux, Jacques, slave trader, 117-9
Charles I, King of England and Scotland, 38
Charter of the Socialist Revolution ("Little Red Book"), 329-31, 333-5
Chevigné, Pierre de, High Commissioner, 266, 270, 272
Chick, blacksmith, 140, 150
China, 19, 20, 302, 304, 322, 332
Christian political parties, 283-4, 286, 333, 345
chromite, 3, 305, 332
Churchill, Winston, 257-8
citizenship, access to French, 242, 250-1, 254, 263
Clarendon, Lord, 164
class hierarchy of Merina, 101, 109
cloves, 31, 240, 252, 271, 295, 336, 350
'Club of 48', 323, 327-8
coal, 3, 205, 270
cochineal beetle, plague of, 252
coffee, 240, 252, 270-1, 305, 334-6, 350
communists, French, 250, 253, 261, 267, 269
communists, Malagasy, 254-5, 270, 273-6, 278-80, 283, 285, 292, 298
Comorians, 264,
Comoros, 15, 20, 21, 23, 35, 41, 65, 73, 130, 148, 202, 336
  pirate expeditions to, 86-90, 123
Compagnie de Madagascar, 175, 180

Index

Compagnie des Indes Orientales, 47-8, 83
Comptoir d'Escompte de Paris, 213, 221
Congregational Union, 191
Congregationalists, see London Missionary Society
Conseil Supérieur de la République, 287
Conseil Supérieur des Colonies, 247, 255
conservation, 346
Constitutions, French (1946) 263; (1959) 284; Malagasy (1959) 287, 296; (1972) 320; (1975) 330-1, 333, 337, 343-7; (1992) 351-2
Constituent Assembly, Paris, 261, 263; Antananarivo, 285, 288
Cooperation Agreements, 291-2, 303, 308, 316, 318-9, 321-2
cooperatives, 254, 302, 307, 332, 336
Coppalle, French painter, 111, 132
Coppet, Marcel de, Governor General/High Commissioner, 255, 262, 264-6
Coroller, prince, 86, 145
corruption, 196, 219, 225, 302, 306-7, 313, 324-7, 336, 340-1
côtiers (coastal people), 262, 269, 272, 276-7, 279, 283, 304, 308, 311, 318, 321, 325-6, 328
cotton, 140, 271
Council of Christian Churches (see FFKM),
Council of Government, 279-80, 282, 285
Council of the French Union, 263-4
Courrier de Madagascar, 299, 308, 318
Courteen's Association, 38-9
Cousins, Rev. W.E., 176
crime, 219-221, 337, 340, 350
culture, passim, 12, 245, 251, 316
Cummins, spinner, 140-1
DGID (General Directorate of Investigation and Documentation), 339
dahálo (see bandits),
Daladier, Edouard, 254
Davidson, Dr Andrew, 176, 191-2, 195
Davis, John, of Sandridge, 34
Deaan Afferrer, see Andrianafarana,
Deaan Crindo, see Andriankirindra,
Deaan Frukey, see Andriampiroky,
Deaan Mevarrow, see Andriamivarotra,
Deaan Murnanzack, see Andriamananjaka,
Deaan Sambo, see Andriantsambo,

Deaan Toakoffu, see Andriantoakofo,
Deaan Trongha, see Andriamitranga,
Deaan Woozington, see Andriankosintany,
debt, external, 305, 334-5, 340, 345-6
defence, in Cooperation Agreements, 291
Defferre, Gaston, 279
Defoe, Daniel, 50, 65-6, 71, 73
Delval, Raymond, 181
Deschamps, Hubert, 110, 388 (notes 6 and 8)
devaluation, 336, 340
Development Plans, 246, 270, 324, 333
Dian Ramaka, see Andriandramaka,
Dias, Diogo, 31
dictionaries of Malagasy, 140, 154, 187, 190
Diego Suarez (Antsiranana), port, 2, 32, 66, 222, 224, 248-50, 252, 265, 291, 307, 321,332, 345, 352; province, 279-80; French occupation, 210-2, 214; British attack, 257-9
Downing, Clement, midshipman, 75-6
Drummond, Capt, 52-3
Drury, Robert, 50-63
Duchesne, General, 224, 227-8, 231-2
Dupré, Capt, 175, 180, 384 (note 6, Ch.13)
Dussac, Paul, 249-51, 253-5
Dutch sailors and traders, 33-35, 39, 44
Duveau, Roger, Deputy, 269, 273, 278
East African troops in Madagascar, 258-9
East India Company, 34, 37-8, 67, 97, 113
Ecole Le Myre de Vilers, 238, 243, 245, 277
Economic and Financial Delegations, 247
economy, passim, under colonial rule, 238, 244, 246, 248, 252, 256, 260, 270-2, 291-3 post-independence, 293, 301-2, 304-6, 320, 323-4, 332-7, 339-41, 346, 350-1
education, in mission schools, 135-9, 150, 159, 193-4, 218, 236, 242-3
under colonial rule, 238, 263, 272-3; post-independence, 291, 293, 306-7, 316, 319-21, 337
elections, French, 255, 263, 272-3, 278-80, 312
elections, Malagasy, 263; under loi cadre, 279-82; post-independence, 296-7, 303, 315, 324, 330, 334, 338-9,

Index

343-4, 352-4
Ellis, Rev. William, 164, 171-80, 186-8, 198
England, Capt Edward, pirate, 72-3
English expeditions to Madagascar, 35-7
  settlement (St Augustine's Bay) 39-41
  "equivalent" paid to Radama I, 123, 126, 149, 160
exequaturs, 214, 222
FAEM (Federation of Students' Associations of Madagascar) 300, 313-4, 316
FAMIMA (pro-Ratsiraka party), 354
FFKM (Council of Christian Churches of Madagascar) 342, 344, 346-50, 354
FISEMA, communist trade union, 276, 280, 283
FJKM (Malagasy Church of Jesus Christ), 300, 342
FNDR (National Front for the Defence of the Revolution), 330, 333-4, 337, 342-5
FNM (Malagasy National Front), 279-81, 283, 285, 288, 290, 298
FRS (Republican Security Forces), 311-2, 317-8, 325
famadíhana,"turning of the dead", 11, 293
Fanásina, Protestant newspaper, 300
fanampóana (compulsory labour), 137, 170, 177, 200, 219
Farquhar, Sir Robert, Governor of Mauritius, 90, 111-121, 123-6, 129, 132, 146, 202
federalism, 349, 351-2
Fénérive, 78, 80-2, 87, 97
Fiánarantsóa, 243, 249, 252, 265
Fiherénana, river, 43; people, 56, 58-9; king of, 55
Filet, Jean Onésime, ("La Bigorne"), 83-4
finance, 291, 305, 338
Finaz, R.P, 164, 168
Finkelmeier, Major John P, 185
Físatra (Fiche or Fish), Betsimisaraka chief, 86, 119, 121, 134
Flacourt, Etienne de, 46-7, 49-50
fokonólona, village organisation, 109, 237, 271, 320, 323, 325-6, 328, 330
forced labour (see fanampoana, prestations, SMOTIG)
Forces Vives (FV) 346-50, 354
foreign policy, 291, 302-3, 322, 331-2, 345
Fort Dauphin (Taolañaro), 23, 25, 31, 68, 91, 129, 163-4, 188, 249
French settlement, 44-9, 84
Foulpointe, 71, 78, 80-1, 84-5, 87, 97, 129, 151, 379 (note 8, Ch.7)
Fox, Dr Tregelles, 195
Franc Zone, 292-3, 305, 307, 322
France, Ile de (see Mauritius),
francophonie, 329
Free French, 257, 259-61
Freeman, Rev Joseph, 140, 149-51, 155
French advisers (conseillers techniques), 306-8, 320, 322
French Community, 281-2, 284, 291
French Embassy, 308-9, 312, 315, 319, 322, 347, 349
French language, 231, 321, 330, 337
French navy, 161, 207-210, 224, 226
French settlers (colons), 204, 239, 242-7, 250, 267, 274, 301
French teachers, 291, 307, 322, 337
French trading companies (see also Lyonnaise, Marseillaise and Rochefortaise), 274, 307,323-4, 332
Friends, Society of, 188, 192, 195, 256, 300
Froberville, Barthélémy de, 115-6
funeral rites, 11-12
GEC (Communist Study Group), 270
GMP (Mobile Police Group), 325-7
Galiber, Admiral, 210
Gallieni, General Joseph, 233-242
Garbit, Hubert, Governor-General, 243-4, 246-7
Garnier, commissaire, 185, 203
Gaulle, Charles de, General, 255, 259, 284, 290, 292, 302-3
gendarmerie, 308, 313-4, 317, 322-3, 325-6, 328, 393 (note 2)
Giles, Major, 225-6
gold, 7, 219
Gore Jones, Admiral, 205,
Gosse, Guillaume, 83-4
Grands Moulins de Dakar, 310
Granville, Lord, 207
graphite, 244, 252, 256-7, 305
Graves, Major (Colonel), 225-6, 228
Griffiths, Rev David, 136, 138-40, 142, 146, 149, 152, 154, 156-7, 173, 182
Gros, Louis, architect, 141,
groundnuts, 271
HAE (Haute Autorité de l'Etat), 350
HVR (Héry Vélona Rasaláma) see Forces Vives
Haggard, Capt, British Consul, 214
Hall, Major-General John, 124-5, 134

[400]

Index

Halsey, Capt, pirate, 71-2
Hamond, Walter, 37, 39, 114
Hastie, Sergeant James, 120-32, 135, 138, 146, 182, 203
Haye, Admiral de la, 48
honours system, 126
Houtman,Cornelius van, 33-4
Hova, 28-9, 98, 100, 109, 147, 261
Howard, Capt Thomas, pirate, 70, 72
Hugon, Barthélémy, slave trader, 110, 116
Hunt, Colonel Robert, 42
IMF (International Monetary Fund), 334-6, 339
Iavolóza, presidential palace, 339, 348-9
Iávy, Betsimisaraka chief, 84-5
Ihárana, 22-3, 29
Iláfy, 104, 160, 178
imanénjana (dancing mania), 177-8
Imérina, 28-9, 101, 246
independence, demands for, 251, 253-5, 261-3, 273, 276, 281-3, 285-6, 289 negotiations, 290-1; proclamation of, 292
Independence Congress at Tamatave, 284-5
India, 19-20, 304
Indian Ocean, haunt of pirates, 64 et seq.; demilitarisation of, 332
Indian traders, see Asian traders
indigénat, 245, 261, 263
Indo-China, 264, 273
Indonesia, linguistic influences, 10, 12, 14, 18; racial and cultural influences, 11-15, 18
industry, 110, 141, 159-61, 168-9, 301, 305, 332, 334, 336, 350
inflation, 306, 324, 334, 340, 350
Insurrection of 1947, 264-6
investment, 239, 334-5, 345-6
iron, 14, 29, 100-1, 110, 130
Islamic influences, 20-1, 24, 30
Israel, 302-3, 310, 322
Itoéra, Sakalava prince, 200-1
Iváto airport, 291, 307
Ives, Edward, ship's surgeon, 93-4
JSD (Social Democratic Youth) 299-300
Japanese threat, Indian Ocean, 257-8
Java, 12, 28
Jean Harre, see Zanahary
Jeffreys, Rev John, 137 ,140
Jesuits, 172, 174, 176, 187, 191, 195, 232, 236, 274, 278, 282-4, 286, 300, 312

Jina (nationalist secret society), 264, 266-7, 390 (note 7)
Johasy, Minister of Interior, 313, 317
Johns, Rev David, 140, 154, 156-7
Johnson, William, Quaker missionary, 232
Jones, Rev David, 125, 134-40, 142, 146, 149, 152, 157, 173
Jouen, R.P, 171
justice, 196-7, 238, 245, 394 (note 7)
KIM (Joint Committee for the Struggle) 319-21,
Kalahéka, Betsimisaraka chief, 82
Karána, see Asian traders
Kélimaláza, 101, 149, 190
Kelly, Capt, 161, 202
Kidd, Capt William, pirate, 66-8
"King Dick", see Andriantoakofo
Kingdon, Abraham, 213, 229, 235
Knight, E F, Times correspondent, 219, 229, 235
Kung-Fu, 339
LDDP (Liste de Défense des Droits du Peuple), 281-2
LEADER FANILO ("non-political" political party), 354
La Bretèche, Major, 48
La Case, 47, 97
Laborde, Clément, 177, 203
Laborde, Edward, 203
Laborde, Jean, 160-2, 164, 166, 168, 171-4, 176, 180-1, 184, 185, 199, 203-4, 208
Labour Offices, 242, 253
Lahifótsy, see Andriandahifotsy,
Lakroa (Catholic newspaper), 342
Lambert, 164-8, 171, 173-4
Lambert Charter, 164, 171, 173, 175, 177, 179-80, 184
Lancaster, Sir James, 33-4
land, 175, 177, 184, 203, 206, 212, 246, 248, 301, 332
Laroche, Resident General, 232, 235
Lastelle, Napoléon de, 159, 160, 162
laws, see Legal Codes and justice,
Lazarist missionaries, 46-7
Le Brun, Rev, missionary, 133; son John, 171
Lechat, Eugène, 281, 288, 298
Legal Code of 1868, 196; of 1881, 197, 203-4, 238
Legentilhomme, General, 260
Le Libéré, newspaper, 248
Lemurs, 5-7
Le Myre de Vilers, Resident General,

Index

212-5, 223-4
Le Sage, Capt, 115, 119-20
Libertalia, 66
"Little Red Book", see Charter of the Socialist Revolution,
Liverpool, Lord, 114
Livingstone, Dr David, 198
loi cadre, 279
London Missionary Society, passim, 126, 131, 133-157, 171-2, 176, 185-198, 216, 235-6
Longuet, Paul, 273, 288, 298, 390 (note 10)
Louis XIV of France, 44, 47-8
Louis Philippe, Government of, 151
Louvières, Count de, French negotiator, 184
Lumière, Catholic weekly, 297
Lutheran missionaries, 187-8, 192-3, 195, 256, 300
Lyall, Dr Robert, British Agent, 148-9
Lyautey, Colonel, 237
Lyonnaise, French trading company, 307
MAPAI (Israeli Labour Party), 301
MDRM (Democratic Movement for Malagasy Renewal) 254, 261-4, 266-9 272, 276, 279-80, 283, 286, 291
MFM (Militants for Government by the People - later Militants for Malagasy Progress),321-2, 343-5, 354
MM (Miara Mirindra), Betsimisaraka party, 297-8
MMSM (Militant Movement for Malagasy Socialism), 345-7, 349-50
MONIMA (National Movement for the Independence of Madagascar), 284, 289-90, 297,299, 303, 313-4, 318, 320, 322, 326, 333-4, 337, 343-5
MSM (Malagasy Social Movement), 262, 269
Madagascar Committee, 206
Madagascar Matin, 325
Madagascar Missionary School Society, 138
Madagascar News, 194, 217, 229
Madagascar Times, 194, 206
Mahábo, Sakalava capital, 58, 61, 108
Mahafály, region and people, 11, 19, 26, 53-4, 56, 58, 77, 91, 92, 130, 158, 237, 313
Mahamásina, 175, 252, 284, 292, 353
Mahítsy, battle, 259
Mahy, François de, 207
Majunga (Mahajánga), 92, 130-1, 192, 348, 352; French occupy, 208-9, 226; British capture, 258; British aircraft at, 302
Malagasy language, 10, 12, 23, 139; in official use, 218, 319
Malagasy Medical Mission, 196
Malagasy soldiers in French army, 244, 247, 249, 255, 258, 261, 264-5, 291
Malata, see Zana Malata,
Malgachisation, 320-1, 337
Malzac, R.P, 187
Manakára, 249, 252, 265
Mananjáry, 22-3
Manífatra, R.P.Venance, 245
Manisótra, warriors, 106
Mantasóa, centre of industry, 160-1, 168
manufacture, see industry
Marco Polo, 4, 30-1
Mariano, Father Luis, 22, 25, 32, 36
Mariavélo, see Rainiharovony,
Marks, William, American trader, 162; becomes Foreign Minister, 177
Maroserána dynasty, 26-7, 43, 59, 91
Marovoáy, Boina capital, 92; battle, 227
Marseillaise, French trading company, 307, 324-5
Martin, François, 97
Martyr Memorial Churches, 172, 185-7, 236
martyrs, Christian, 154-7, 162-3, 167, 173
Marxism, 275, 331-3, 338 (see also communists)
Masikóro, 26, 92, 158
Matitanana, see Vohipeno
Mathews, Commodore Thomas, 75-6
Maudave, Count, 84
Mauritius, 12, 35, 44, 49, 83, 86, 110-11, 119, 123-4, 126, 135, 156, 158-9, 302; British annexation, 113-4
Mayeur, Nicolas, 80-1, 97-8, 103, 109, 116
Medical Missionary Academy, 195
medical services, 195, 218, 238; training of personnel, 195, 238
Meilleraye, Duc de la, 46-7
Menabé kingdom, 43, 59, 61-2, 92, 102, 108, 112, 130-1, 200, 237
menalámba, resistance movement, 232-5, 264
menamáso, Radama II's companions, 176, 179
Mendès-France, Pierre, 273
Mérina, passim, people, 13, 18-19, 25,

[402]

Index

28-9; kingdom, 61, 98, 100 et seq., 217, 220;under colonial rule, 237-8, 244, 261; and côtiers, 262, 269, 272, 278-9, 281-3, 289, 304, 308, 321, 323, 325-6
Mers-el-Kebir, 255, 259
Metzinger, General, 226
Meyer, Commissaire, 203-4
Miádana, Victor, 282, 313
mica, 252, 257, 305
Military Directorate, 326-9
minerals and mining, 3, 215, 219, 270, 305, 311
Miot, Admiral, 210-11
Misson, Capt, pirate, 66
Missionaries, passim, 32, 47, 133-157, 171, 185-96, 205, 229-31, 256, 280
Missionary Societies, see London Missionary Society, Jesuits, Paris Missionary Society,Society of Friends, SPG, Lutherans
Mitterrand, President, 345
Mollet, Guy, 279
Mónja Jáona, 280, 282, 284, 303, 313-4, 320, 333-4, 337-9, 342, 344-5, 347, 351
Moslems, 20, 22, 341,
Mozambique, 25-6, 86, 89, 109, 198, 331 Channel, 93, 258,
Mpanólo-Tsáina, periodical, 194
mpsikídy (diviners), 22, 24, 29, 101, 151, 182
mpitáiza andríana, Queen's guardian, 148
Nampoina, see Andrianampoinimerina
Napoleon III, Emperor, 164, 171, 180, 184
National Forum, 350-2
National Assembly, French, 223-4, 263, 272-3, 279, 284; Malagasy, 287-8, 296, 303, 310, 312, 330, 338, 343, 346-7, 350, 352-4
nationalisations, 292, 301, 329, 332,
nationalism and nationalists, 244-6, 255, 260-4, 269-70, 273-9, 281, 283, 329
La Nation Malgache, 253-4
neo-colonialism, 308, 316, 319, 329-30
non-alignment, 303, 322, 328-9, 331
North, Capt Nathaniel, pirate, 70-2
North Korea, 332, 339, 343
Nosy Be (Nossi Be, Assada), 39, 68, 87, 89, 92; British settlement, 42-3; annexed by France, 157-8, 202, 204; South African investment, 311

Nosy Láva, 267, 317
Nourse, Commodore, 130
Ny Gazety Malagasy, 194
OAU (Organisation of African Unity), 303, 311, 322, 332
OCAM (African and Malagasy Community), 303, 311-2, 322
Oantítsy, Queen of Boina, 130
oil exploration, 270
oil prices, 324, 335-6
Olivier, Marcel, Governor-General, 248-50
ombiásy (priest-doctors), 22-3, 25, 149, 338
Onjatsy, 22
L'Opinion, 250
ordeal, trial by, see tangena
outrigger canoe, 13-15, 22
PADESM (Party of the Disinherited of Madagascar), 262-4, 267, 269, 272-3, 277, 280
PANAMA (Malagasy Nationalist Party), 264, 266-7
PCF (French Communist Party), 253-4, 270, 275-6
PCRM (Communist Party of the Region of Madagacar), 254
PDM (Malagasy Democratic Party), 262, 269
PROCOPS (Society for the Promotion of Socialist Cooperatives), 341
PSD (Social Democratic Party), 281-3, 286-90, 295-301, 304-7, 310-4, 318, 321-4; (new party), 345; PSD/RPSD, 354
PSM (Malagasy Socialist Party), 269; (new party) 324, 327
Pakenham, Thomas, British Consul, 173-5, 177, 179, 198, 209
Pakistani traders, see Asian traders,
Palace church, 191
Palmerston, Lord, 155, 180
Paris Missionary Society, 236, 256, 300
Paris, Treaty of (1814), 114-5
Parmentier, Jean, 32
Parrett, printer, 176, 194, 205, 211
Patrimonio, French negotiator, 211-2
Peake, Rev P G, 190, 195
Pfeiffer, Frau Ida, 165-8
Phillips, Frederick, New York merchant, 69-70
Pickersgill, William C, missionary and vice-consul, 190, 205
Picquié, Governor-General, 243
Pierre, Admiral, 207-8, 210

[403]

Index

Planque, Edouard, 250
Plantain, James, 75-6, 82
"politique des races", 237, 243, 262
Pool, William, builder, 185-6
Popular Front in France, 252-4
population growth, 340
Portugal, links with Madagascar, 21-2, 30-32
postal services, 239
Présence Française, 273-4
press, 194, 250, 253, 255-6, 275-6, 299-300, 346, 348
printing, 141, 149-50, 154, 194, 196
prestations (compulsory labour), 239, 242, 253, 260, 263
privatisation, 336, 344
Procter, Samuel, 207, 211
Le Prolétariat Malgache, 254
Pronis, Sieur, 44-7, 49
Protestant churches in Madagascar, 191-3, 232-3, 274-5, 284, 300, 342
proto-Malagasy, 13-15, 17, 21
provincial assemblies, 263, 280, 288
Provincial Councils, 288-9, 349
Provisional Government (1958), 285
Puybaudet, R.P. de, 296
Pye, Thomas, British Agent, 120-1, 123
Quakers, see Friends, Society of
Queen's Palace, 160, 185,
RAF (Royal Air Force), at Majunga, 302-3, 394 (note 11)
RCM (Rassemblement Chrétien Malgache), 286, 289-90, 297-8
RNM (Rassemblement National Malgache), 286, 289-90, 297, 303
RPM (Rassemblement du Peuple Malgache), 279
Rabáry, pastor, 245
Rabéarivélo, Jean-Joseph, poet, 251
Rabémananjára, Jacques, poet, nationalist and minister, 251, 261-3, 166-7, 290-2, 296-8, 310-13, 315, 353
Rabémananjára, Raymond W, co-founder of MDRM, 261, 276, 280, 390 (note 5)
Rabenóro, Dr Césaire, 304, 349-50
Rabesahála, Gisèle, 275-6, 288, 333
Rabetáfika, Colonel Roland, 322-8
Rabezavána, menalamba leader, 232, 234, 387 (note 27)
Rabíby, Merina king, 101
Rabódo, Queen, 172, 174, 179 (see also Rasoherina)
Rabózaka, menalamba leader, 232, 234
Radáma I, 110-12, 116-33; and the missionaries, 135-43; funeral, 144; character, 145-6
Radáma II (see also Prince Rakoto), 170-181, 183, 198-9
Radáorosón, Michel, insurrection leader, 265
Radiliféra, see Rainilaiarivony,
Rafaraláhy, martyr, 156
Rafaravávy, Marie, 151, 154-6
Rafóhy, Vazimba queen, 100
Rahaníraka, Queen's secretary, later Foreign Minister, 159, 162-3, 172, 182
Raháro (Rainivóninahítrinióny), chief minister, 158, 163, 166, 170, 178-81, 183, 186, 188
Rahóvy, Merina prince, 118, 120
railways, 239, 243, 247, 249, 272, 293
Ráinandríamampándry, Governor of Tamatave, 159, 208, 210, 226; Minister of Interior,231, 233-5
Ráiniánjaláhy, army commander, 227-8
Ráinibétsimisaráka, menalamba leader, 232, 234, 387 (note 27)
Ráiniharovóny (Mariavelo), 215, 219
Rainiháro, chief minister, 151, 158-9, 163, 182
Ráinijoháry, chief minister, 152, 163, 165-7, 170, 189
Ráiniláiarivóny, Prime Minister, passim, 163, 166, 170, 178, 181-5, 188-93, 196-202,204-16, 218-23, 225-6, 229, 231
Rainimahárávo, Foreign Secretary, 188-9, 200-1
Rainitsímbazáfy, Prime Minister, 231, 234
Ráinivóninahítriniarívo, Foreign Secretary, 206, 220
Ráinivóninahítrinióny, see Raharo
Rajáonah, Dr, 195, 219
Rajáonarisón, Colonel Bréchard, 325
Rajestéra, army officer, 227
Rajoélina, prime minister's son, 220
Rakétaka, daughter of Radama I, 144
Rakóto (Rakótond'Radáma), prince (see also Radama II), 148, 162, 164-8
Rakótoarijáona, General Désiré; prime minister 1977-88, 343
Rakotobé, prince, 144, 148
Rakotobé, Rémi, nationalist, 275-6
Rakótoharisón, General Jean, 347
Rakótomalála, Cardinal Jérome, 300
Rakótomalála, Colonel Joël, prime minister 1976, 329, 343
Rakótomalála, Louis, nationalist, 269,

[404]

Index

278, 281, 285, 287-8, 391 (note 4)
Rakótondrabé, Samuel, insurrection leader, 267
Rakótoniáina, Justin, prime minister 1976-7, 343
Rakótoniráiny, General Lucien, 343
Rakótonirína, Manandafy, founder of MFM, 318, 321-2, 344-6, 348, 350, 353-4
Rakótonirína, Stanislas, Merina nationalist, 272, 278, 280-3, 285-6
Rakóto-Ratsimamánga, Dr, co-founder of MDRM, 261, 276, 391 (note 16)
Rakotováo-Razakabóana, Minister of Finance, 338
Rakotovélo, Deputy, 278
Raláiarivóny, eldest son of PM, 219
Raláimihóatra, Edouard, historian, 262
Ralaimóngo, Jean, nationalist, 247, 249-50, 253-5, 263
Ralámbo, Merina king, 101, 109
Ralarósy, Dr, 195-6
Ralisón, Roger, Deputy, 354
Ramáhatra, Colonel Victor, prime minister 1988-91, 343, 347-8
Ramáhatra, prince, 215, 226, 246, 387 (note 25)
Ramakavélo, General, 349
Ramanáno, Betsimisaraka chief, 78, 81-2
Ramánandraibé, Lucile, external opposition leader, 342
Ramánantsóa, General Gabriel, 259, 291, 295, 318-22, 324-6
Ramanétaka, Governor of Majunga, 148
Ramangasoávina, Alfred, nationalist and minister, 276, 281-2, 284-5, 288, 304, 350
Ramáromanómpo, see Ratsimilaho,
Ramárosáona, Emile, nationalist and minister, 279, 282, 301-2, 304
Ramárosáona, ZaÜveline, women's leader, 299
Ramásombazáha, Governor of Majunga, 227
Ramávo, see Ranavalona I,
Rambo, Antemoro chief, 24
Ramboasaláma (Andrianampoinimerina), 104
Ramboasaláma, nephew of Queen Ranavalona I, 163, 168, 170
Ramitény, Sakalava king, 93
Ramitráho, Sakalava king, 112, 128, 131, 201

Ramóma, Sakalava king, 61-2, 92
Ramóma, princess, see Ranavalona II,
Ramónja, prince, 162, 189
Ranáivo, Flavien, poet, 251
Ranáivo, Jonah, Deputy, 272,
Ranáivo Jules, nationalist, 250, 254-5, 267, 275
Ranáivo, Paul, nationalist, 254
Ranáona, Fiherenana chief, 55-6
Ranaválona I, Queen, 144, 147-54, 158-9, 165-9, 182; persecution of Christians, 154-7, 162-3, 167
Ranaválona II, Queen, 179, 188-91, 205, 208-9, 220,
Ranaválona III, Queen, 209, 217, 229, 231, 234, 255
Randría, Dr Michel, 280, 286
Randríanasólo, minister, 288, 390 (note 9)
Rangíta, Vazimba queen, 100
Raombána, Queen's secretary and historian, 159, 162-3, 182
Raóndry, Philibert, minister, 282, 288
Rasaláma, martyr, 155-6, 186,
Rasalímo, wife of Radama I, 128, 142
Rasánjy, prime minister under Gallieni, 234
Raséta, Dr Joseph, nationalist, 245, 254-5, 260-1, 263, 266-7, 277, 290, 292, 296, 298,303-4
Rasóamampiónona, Elise, women's leader and Deputy
Rasoanálina, wife of Rainilaiarivony, 189
Rasoamiéja, Mary, mistress of Radama II, 174, 178
Rasohérina, Queen (see also Queen Rabodo), 174, 179, 185, 188
Ratéfy, prince, 129, 137, 148
Rateliféra, prime minister's grandson, 220
Ratoakéfo, Sakalava king, 93
Ratrimoláhy, Sakalava king, 93
Ratsimamánga, Prince, 233, 235
Ratsimandráva, Colonel Richard, 322-8, 330
Ratsimiláho (Ramaromanompo), founder of Betsimisaraka, 80-4
Ratsimónongarívo, Sakalava king, 58-9, 92, 102
Ratsíraka, Admiral Didier, President, 321-2, 325-9, 331-9, 342-354
Ravahíny, Sakalava queen, 92, 108, 110, 130
Ravélojáona, Pasteur, 243, 245, 255,

[405]

Index

261-2, 269, 273, 275
Ravéloson-Mahasámpo, governor, 262, 272, 278, 280-2
Ravéloson-Mahasámpo, Colonel Christophe, 339
Ravéloson-Mahasámpo, Madame Hortense, 341
Ravoahángy-Andrianaválona, Dr Joseph, nationalist, 245-6, 249-50, 253-5, 260-1, 263, 266-7, 270, 277, 290, 292, 296-8, 304, 392 (note 13)
Ravóninahítriniarívo, Foreign Minister, 201, 206, 219
Ravóny, Francisque, prime minister, 350, 354
Ravóny, Jules, President of National Assembly, 288, 354
Ravóvy, Sakalava prince, 58, 61
Razáfimahaléo, Herizo, founder of LEADER-FANILO party, 354
Razafindrabé, Victor, insurrection leader, 265
Razáfindrahéty, princess, see Ranavalona III
Razáfindrakóto, Emmanuel, trade union leader, 250, 253-4
Razáfintsaláma, Gabriel, journalist and politician, 269, 281, 285
Razáfy-Andriamiháingo, ambassador, 390 (note 4)
Razanakómbana, minister of justice, 159
Razanamásy, Guy, mayor and prime minister, 348-50, 353-4
Razánatsehéno, Henry, nationalist, 279
Réallon, Léon, Governor, 388 (note 7), 389 (note 21)
rebellion of 1947, see insurrection,
referendum (1958), 284-5; (1972), 320; (1975), 330-1; (1992), 350, 352
René, Jean, chief of Tamatave, 86, 119, 121, 124, 129, 134
Lord Rennell, head of British Military Administration, 259
Representative Council, 261
Representative Assembly, 263-4, 277, 280, 282-5
Rer Moume, see Ramoma
Rer Trimmonongarevo, see Ratsimonongarivo
Rer Vove, see Ravovy,
Resámpa, André, PSD secretary-general and minister, 281-2, 288-90, 297-8, 311-5,320-1, 324, 326-7, 345, 349-50
Réunion (see also Bourbon), 12, 158-9,

204, 239
rice cultivation, 10, 12, 18, 102, 109, 270-1, 305, 335, 351;trade, 25, 161, 244, 252, 260, 305, 335
Richardson, James, missionary, 190, 193
road building, 123, 239, 243, 249, 253, 272, 293, 332
Robin, Sergeant, 124-6, 128, 131, 149
Robin, Malagasy intellectual, 245-6
Robinson, Colonel William, American consul, 206
Rochefortaise, French trading company, 307
Romain-Desfossés, Commander, 161
Rontaunay of Réunion, trading company, 159
Roux, Sylvain, French agent at Tamatave, 86, 114, 124, 128
Rowlands, weaver, 140-1
Rowles, Capt Richard, 35-6
royal bath festival (fandróana), 101, 106, 122
Russell, Lord John (later Earl), 172, 180
Ry-Nanno, see Ranaona,
SDP (German Social Democrat Party), 301
SFIO (French Socialist Party), 277, 301, 390 (note 8)
SINPA (Society for the Marketing of Agricultural Products), 323-4, 332
SMOTIG (national labour service), 249, 253, 301
SOMALAC (Society for the development of Lac Alaotra), 302, 306
SOMASAK (Society for the development of the Sakay region), 302
SONACO (National Society for Foreign Trade), 323-4, 332
SPG (Society for the Propagation of the Gospel), 187, 192-3, 256
Saillens, Reuben, 211
St Augustine's Bay, 13, 33-5, 37, 68, 93, 154, 158; English settlement, 39-41;
Saint-Mart, Pierre de, Governor-General, 260-1
St Mary's Island, 20, 34; pirate haven, 68-71, 73, 78; annexed by France, 83, 85, 128-9, 202
Ste Marie, Ile, see St Mary's Island
sakáizam-bóhitra, local justices, 196
Sakaláva, passim, 12, 19, 22, 26-7, 43, 51, 58-62, 87, 92-4, 102-4, 108, 112, 128-30, 157, 171, 192, 200-1, 204-5, 210, 212, 219, 224, 236-7

[406]

Index

Salisbury, Lord, 214-5, 224
Samuel, Antanosy king, 52-3
Schrameck, Abraham, Governor-General, 246
Senate, French, 263-4, 273; Malagasy, 287, 297, 303, 346, 352
Senegalese troops in Madagascar, 258, 266
Service Civique (national service), 301, 337
Sewell, Joseph, Quaker missionary, 188
Shaw, George, missionary, 209-10
Shervinton, Colonel, 225-6
Sibon, Rear-Admiral Guy, 343
Sibree, James, missionary, 185-6, 190, 192-4, 225, 236
Sihánaka, 61, 97, 129, 192
sisal, 271
slavery and slave trade, 21, 25-6, 62, 77, 83-4, 86, 109-10, 113-6, 118, 120, 122, 124,129, 158-9, 161, 218, 222, 225; export of slaves prohibited, 123, 149, 197;African slaves freed, 197-99; domestic slavery abolished, 233
Smart, John, leader of English settlement, 39-41
Smuts, Field-Marshal, 258
socialists and socialism, passim, 253, 267, 281, 301, 329-32, 338-40,344-7
Société Française de l'Orient, 44
Sorabé, Antemoro manuscripts, 23, 25
Soucadaux, André, High Commissioner, 273, 285-6, 289, 391 (note 16)
South Africa, 303, 310-11, 315, 322, 338, 345
spice trade, 30-1, 33
Stanfell, Capt, RN, 123
Steward, Capt, 52-3
strikes, 283, 313, 315-9, 333, 337-8, 341, 347, 349-51
students, 270, 276, 283, 299-300, 306, 311, 313-19, 321, 337, 341, 351
Sturges, Major-General, 257
Suez Canal, 202, 257, closure of, 310
sugar, 271, 332, 350
Syfret, Admiral, 257
Sylla, Albert, foreign minister, 286, 288, 297-8, 310, 354
Sylla, Jacques, foreign minister, 354
syndicats de commune, 301, 307
TTS, unemployed youth, 339, 351
Tacchi, Anthony, editor, 206
Taiwan, 302, 322
Tamatave (Toamasina), 76, 78, 80-1, 85, 151, 172, 184, 192, 208, 215, 249, 252, 321,341, 352; British in, 114-5, 117, 123, 125, 128, 134, 258; French occupation, 208-9,212-3, 226
Tanála, 19, 24, 158, 265
Tangéna shrub, 122; ordeal by, 122, 131, 150, 153-4, 157, 161, 167, 170, 184
Tantáran'ny Andríana (History of the Kings), 98, 100, 103, 186
taxation, 171, 177, 179, 219, 221, 223; under colonial rule, 239, 260; post-independence, 301, 313, 320
Taylor, pirate captain, 72-3
technical assistance, 302, 308
telegraphic services, 239
Tény Sóa, periodical, 194
Tew, Captain Thomas, pirate, 66, 80
textiles, 238, 305, 332
"Third Force", 269, 274, 298, 300, 303
Toamásina, see Tamatave
tobacco, 247, 271
Toliára, see Tulear,
tombs, importance of, 11, 12, 317; violation, 80; royal tombs, 7, 120, 130, 165, 255
Toualé incident, 203-4
trade, passim, Indonesian, 15, 17; Arab, 17, 21-2, 25, 27, 31, 93; Graeco-Roman, 30; English, 33-7, 39-41; French, 32, 45-9, 204; Sakalava, 92, 102; New York and pirates, 69-70; Mauritius and Réunion, 83, 85, 87, 91, 159, 161, 163, 171; United States, 162, 238, 256; Britain, 217-8, 238, 256; under colonial rule, 252, 256, 270; post-independence, 305, 307, 310, 332, 334-6; South Africa, 310-11, 345, 395 (note 3)
trade unions, 235, 255, 260, 269-70, 275-6, 280, 299, 318
transitional government (1991-3), 347-353
Treaties: Anglo-Merina 1817, 123; 1820, 126, 149; Anglo-Malagasy 1865, 184, 198, 207; Franco-Malagasy 1868, 185, 198, 203-4; 1885, 212, 214, 223; 1895, 231; American-Malagasy 1867, 185; 1881, 207; German-Malagasy 1883, 207; Italo-Malagasy 1883, 207
Tristan da Cunha, 25, 31
Tsarasáotra, battle, 228
Tsiébo, Calvin, Vice-President, 281, 298, 311-4
Tsikóa alliance, 80-1
Tsimihéty, 19, 59, 129, 389 (note 19)

Index

Tsiránana, Philibert, President, 262, 277-9, 281-3, 285-292, 294-308, 310-15, 317-21,324, 326-7
Tsitávana, Sakalava king, 92
Tsisípy, Betsimisaraka chief, 115
Tulear (Toliara), 95-6, 215, 249, 252
UDECMA (Union of Christian Democrats of Madagascar), 333
UDSM (Union of Social Democrats of Madagascar), 280-2, 286-90, 297-8
UESM (Union of Malagasy Socialist Students), 299-300, 313
UIT (Union of Tananarive Independents), 280-2, 284-6, 289-90
UN (United Nations), Madagascar in, 286, 332
UNDD (National Union for Development and Democracy), 345, 354
UNIUM (Union of Malagasy intellectuals and university graduates), 282-4, 290
UOME (Union of the Malagasy Opposition Abroad), 342
UPM (Union of the Malagasy People), 278-80, 283, 285, 288
USA (United States of America), 265, 302
USM (Malagasy Socialist Union), 321, 324
USSR (Soviet Union), 302-3, 322, 331-2, 343-4
unemployment, 306, 317, 321, 337, 339-40
University of Antananarivo/Madagascar, 291, 300, 307, 313, 316-7, 319-20, 333, 337,341, 351
VITM, see Vonjy
VSM/MONIMA (splinter group of MONIMA), 334
VVS (nationalist movement), 245-6, 248, 264
vádin-tány, royal agents, 109
vanilla, 240, 252, 256, 271, 305, 336, 351
Vaováo, newspaper, 299
Vazímba, 13, 18, 28-9, 59, 61, 98, 100-102
Velonjára, Pascal, PADESM leader, 262-3, 272, 278, 322, 394 (note 6)
Vichy régime, 255, 257-260
Victoire, Madame, 191
Victoria, Queen of Great Britain, 172, 180, 207, 216
Vittori, François, 250
vódi-héna, tax, 109

Vohipéno, 20, 23, 129
Volaména, see Maroserana dynasty,
Vonjy (VITM - Support for National Unity), 321, 324, 326, 333, 343-5
Waldegrave, Powle,41
Waller, John, US Consul, 385 (note 14)
Watson, Admiral, 93-4
Webber, R.P, 164, 167, 171
White, Capt Thomas, pirate, 70-2, 80-1
Willoughby, Colonel Digby, 210-3
Winterton, ship, 94, 96
World Bank, 338-40, 346
World War I, 243-4
World War II, 255-61
YMCA (Young Men's Christian Association), 243
Yong-Owl, see Morondava
Younge, Nicholas, 51, 53
Youth organisations, 299-300
ZOAM (Unemployed Youth of Central Madagascar), 317, 319-20, 339
Zafimahóva, Norbert, leader of PADESM and UDSM, 262, 273, 281-2, 286-9, 297
Zafimanély dynasty, see Maroserana
Zafindravóla, 26
Zafi-Rámbo, 24
Zafi-Raminía, 22-3, 27, 29, 101
Zafy, Albert, President, 345-8, 350-1, 353-4
Zafy-Ibrahim, 20
Zakavóla, Betsimisaraka chief, 85-6
Zana-Maláta, descendants of pirates, 78-81, 83, 86-90
Zanaháry, Betsimisaraka chief, 82-4
Zanzibar, 90, 215-6, 224
Zimbabwe empire, 26-8

www.ingramcontent.com/pod-product-compliance
Lightning Source LLC
Chambersburg PA
CBHW030125240426
43672CB00005B/23